MEDICINE *for* MOUNTAINEERING

MEDICINE *for* MOUNTAINEERING

Second Edition

Edited By

JAMES A. WILKERSON, M.D.

Associate Professor of Pathology
University of Alabama Medical School
Birmingham, Alabama

THE MOUNTAINEERS
Seattle, Washington

The Mountaineers: Organized 1906 ".. . to explore, study, preserve and enjoy the natural beauty of the Northwest . . ."

Published by The Mountaineers
715 Pike Street, Seattle, Washington 98101

Published simultaneously in Canada by Douglas & McIntyre Ltd.
1615 Venables Street, Vancouver, B.C. V5L 2H1

Manufactured in the United States of America

First edition 1967
Second edition 1975; second printing 1978;
third printing 1979; fourth printing 1982

The Library of Congress catalogued the first
issue of this title as follows:
Medicine for mountaineering/edited by James A. Wilkerson. —
    2d ed. — Seattle: The Mountaineers, 1975.
        368 p. : ill. ; 20 cm.
        Includes bibliographical references and index.
    1. Sports medicine.   2. Mountaineering — Accidents and injuries.   I. Wilk-
erson, James A., 1934-
RC1220.M6M4   1975   617′.1027   75-31059
ISBN 0-916890-06-6   MARC

Contributors

EARL E. CAMMOCK, M.D., General and Thoracic Surgeon, Mount Vernon, Washington, Clinical Instructor in Surgery, University of Washington School of Medicine, Seattle, Washington. Chapter 7.

FRED T. DARVILL, M.D., Clinical Assistant Professor of Medicine, University of Washington School of Medicine, Seattle, Washington. Chapter 20.

BEN EISEMAN, M.D., Professor of Surgery, University of Colorado School of Medicine; Director, Department of Surgery, Denver General Hospital, Denver, Colorado. Chapters 10, 11, 21.

THOMAS F. HORNBEIN, M.D. Professor of Anesthesiology, University of Washington School of Medicine, Seattle, Washington. Chapter 4.

CHARLES S. HOUSTON, M.D., Professor of Medicine, The University of Vermont College of Medicine, Burlington, Vermont. Chapters 12, 18.

HERBERT N. HULTGREN, M.D., Professor of Medicine, Stanford University Medical School; Chief, Cardiology Division, Palo Alto Veterans Administration Hospital, Palo Alto, California. Chapters 12, 13, 19, 25.

THOMAS O. NEVISON, M.D., Aerospace Medicine and Bioinstrumentation, Arlington Virginia. Chapters 14, 15, 16.

JAMES A. WILKERSON. Chapters 1, 2, 3, 5, 6, 8, 9, 17, 22, 23, 24, 26.

NOTE: The chapter numbers indicate the author who was primarily responsible for each chapter and made the greatest contribution as it was written. However, as in the first edition, the text has been extensively rewritten to provide the uniform approach and consistent style which were considered necessary to reduce misunderstanding to a minimum for the nonprofessional audience for whom this book is intended. As a result, no single person is responsible for all of the material in any chapter. The contributors have been most understanding in consenting to such changes in the manuscripts they have submitted. —Ed.

Table of Contents

Section 1: General Principles

Section 2: Traumatic Injuries

Section 3: Environmental Injuries

Section 4: Nontraumatic Diseases

Section 5: Appendix

Foreword

NOT very many years past, so the story goes, a physician at an emergency receiving hospital in Seattle examined a badly mangled member of The Mountaineers and said, "It's lucky the truck hit him right here in the neighborhood — he couldn't have survived a long ambulance ride."

What the physician did not know was that the accident had nothing to do with a truck, nor the evacuation with an ambulance. The victim had fallen from a cliff high in the Cascades; had been held by a belay but left dangling in space; had been lowered to the talus below, carried several miles through brush and over trail to the highway, and driven 80 miles in a private automobile to the nearest medical aid available (in those days).

The climbers involved, both casualty and rescuers, were leading doers and teachers of wilderness mountaineering in the Northwest. That their efforts had prevented a tragedy strengthened their faith in the value of the first aid instruction included in the Climbing Course of the day, but raised many questions in their minds — such as, "what if the accident had happened in a more remote area?" and "what if the injuries had been beyond our training?" and "what if the rescuers on hand had been less experienced?" Furthermore, during the rescue they had employed medications and treatments — lifesaving, as it proved — that were then and still are traditionally forbidden to laymen as being too dangerous in any hands except those of licensed medical doctors. And so they asked themselves, while mulling over the emergency and its resolution, "what if we had gone strictly by the book?"

Thus it was — a generation ago now — that The Mountaineers began to teach a somewhat different variety of first aid in their Climbing Course (presented annually since 1935) than that designed for emergencies on the street, beach, and in the home; "first plus *second* aid" would be a more accurate description. The teachers enlisted were climber-doctors who recognized that a little knowledge can be a dangerous thing, but also that in some circumstances *no* knowledge can be worst of all. Dr. Howard Snively is remembered as the first of his profession to entrust "dangerous" but essential knowledge to his fellow Mountaineer students of a potentially dangerous sport.

Succeeding Dr. Snively, and building on his foundations, was Dr. Warren J. Spickard, Jr. Starting in the 1950s Spick lectured to the Climbing Course (and as a teaching aid produced a movie that is still used), offered classes in Mountaineering First Aid, wrote the "First Aid" chapter in *Mountaineering: The Freedom of the Hills*, and in 1961 made revisions to that chapter just several weeks before falling to his death on a North Cascades peak close by another mountain that has since been officially named Mount Spickard. Had Spick lived, he would have contributed a chapter or two here, having agreed to do so shortly before his last climb.

This book, then, springs from a need that has long and deeply been felt by climbers. Together with his contributors, Dr. James A. Wilkerson has maintained the Snively-Spickard tradition, and extended it beyond first aid (and second) into *Medicine for Mountaineering*, the first book of its kind in America, and one which we believe will prove of inestimable value to mountaineers everywhere.

HARVEY MANNING

Preface

"ANYONE who climbs very often for very long must expect sooner or later to be involved in misfortune, if not his own, then someone else's."[1] The outcome of such misfortune frequently depends on the injuries incurred and the medical care the victims receive. For mountaineering accidents, which frequently occur at a considerable distance from a physician or hospital, ordinary first aid sometimes does not provide the kind of treatment necessary for accident victims to recover with minimal permanent disability.

Most first aid texts are written for a general population in ordinary urban or rural surroundings, and are primarily intended to prevent aggravation of existing injuries by well-meaning but uninformed individuals. The usual approach is "what to do until the doctor comes." Such instructions are not sufficient for a wilderness situation in which the doctor is not coming and the victim must be evacuated, particularly when evacuation requires more than one or two days.

Members of mountaineering expeditions occasionally are victims of medical disorders other than those resulting from accidents. A member of the 1963 American Mount Everest Expedition contracted infectious hepatitis; another developed thrombophlebitis; several were found to have amoebic dysentery. One member of the 1957 British Machapuchare Expedition came down with poliomyelitis. A member of the 1955 French Makalu Expedition developed appendicitis. Few first aid books devote any attention to these diseases.

Climbers who are the victims of accident or disease require special care for the problems created by high altitude or a hostile environment. The environment can also cause diseases not encountered in more temperate surroundings, high altitude pulmonary edema being the prime example.

The unparalleled experience with traumatic wounds obtained in World War II and the Korean Conflict, which has been further amplified in Viet Nam and elsewhere during the intervening years, has led to a number of improvements in the medical management of such injuries. Many first aid texts have been slow to include this information and have not given it the prominence it deserves. The importance of *not* closing the skin over wounds of the soft tissues,

11

and the necessity for controlling hemorrhage by direct pressure, *not* with tourniquets, are two examples of the information which needs to be brought to the attention of climbers.

Misinformation abounds. Authoritative publications still recommend cold therapy of poisonous snake bites even though the assumptions upon which such therapy was based are erroneous, and subsequent studies have demonstrated that the cold therapy often does more harm than the snake venom.

In the past, large expeditions have generally included physicians among their members. However, more and more small parties are traveling to the Andes, Himalayas, and other remote areas. Furthermore, even though one of the climbers is a physician, he is subject to accidental injury or illness just like the other members of the party.

MEDICINE FOR MOUNTAINEERING has been compiled by physicians who are also climbers, in order to provide the information necessary for climbers who are not physicians to prepare for and cope with the medical problems which may be encountered in mountaineering. This is a handbook of medicine — not first aid. The treatment described for some conditions includes potent drugs or difficult procedures. Such remedies are necessary for optimal care for many disorders, but can lead to disaster if used in an incorrect manner. Some of the material presented is of such complexity or is potentially so dangerous that it generally has not been considered appropriate for presentation to individuals without a physician's training. However, extensive experience with physician's assistants has clearly demonstrated that such persons are capable of using such information safely and effectively. The writers are convinced that most climbers have the capacity to assimilate and understand the material presented here, and to use it in a beneficial way. The hazards of some techniques are not repeatedly emphasized to discourage their use, but to ensure that necessary diligence is observed. Thorough preparation and meticulous attention to detail are essential.

To increase its usefulness and reduce the hazard associated with some of the therapeutic programs, this book has been designed as a text for a course in medicine for mountaineering taught by a physician. Preferably a course of this type should be completed before the information presented is put into practice. Most mountaineering organizations have little difficulty organizing such programs during the months when weather limits climbing activities.

A second use for this book is as a reference during the actual treatment of medical disorders. By referring to the text, the exact details of therapy can be ascertained. Memory is not dependable and should not be relied upon when other sources of information are available. The book has been designed to slip into a small climbing pack without adding more than a few ounces of weight.

To reduce complications from the use of potent medications, the dosage for most drugs is not given in the text where such agents are recommended. This information can only be obtained by consulting the appendix, where the contra-indications and side-effects for the drug have also been listed. By this expedient the individual caring for the victim of an accident or illness is warned of the precautions which must be observed whenever a specific drug is used. (Most of the medications can only be obtained with a prescription from a physician, who should make certain the person obtaining the drugs understands their proper use.)

Because no alternate methods exist for treating some disorders, a few procedures have been included which are impractical in many mountaineering circumstances. Intravenous fluid therapy, which is necessary in the treatment of many disorders, is an obvious example. The solutions and equipment for administering fluids intravenously probably never would be carried by a small climbing party. Even a large group of climbers would have difficulty keeping such materials in locations where they always could be obtained quickly. However, intravenous fluid therapy is the only means of keeping the patient alive in those circumstances in which it is required.

No effort has been made to separate the disorders likely to be encountered on short outings from those usually occurring only on prolonged expeditions to remote areas. In most instances the distinction is obvious. When necessary, the optimum means of treatment under both circumstances and the situations in which either method is preferable have been described.

Various disorders likely to occur in specific geographic areas have not been segregated because the diseases are not so precisely localized and too much overlap between the various areas exists.

In this second edition a number of changes or additions have been made. Some of these are: updating the description of cardiopulmonary resuscitation; addition of a description of a technique for tracheostomy; addition of more recent information on high altitude problems; addition of more information on hypothermia; addition of brief discussions of gynecological disorders and venereal disease; and extensive revision and updating of antibiotic therapy recommendations. Many of these changes have resulted directly from letters received from a number of readers. The writers invite all readers with criticisms, suggestions, differing opinions, or experience using the information presented to pass them along. Anyone who takes the trouble to write can be assured their efforts will be welcomed and greatly appreciated.

The writers have been gratified to learn that the outlook for the victims of some mountaineering misfortunes has been improved by application of the principles of medical care presented by this book, and hope that it can continue to provide such service and assistance.

REFERENCE

1. Ferber, P., Editor: *Mountaineering: The Freedom of the Hills*, 3rd Edition, Seattle, The Mountaineers, 1974. (Quoted by permission of the Publishers.)

Acknowledgments

FOR THE SECOND EDITION

STARTING to work on the second edition of *Medicine for Mountaineering* has been much like trying to rekindle an old love affair. Recognition of new material to be added or inadequacies to correct has been rather easy, but developing the enthusiasm to attack the task and carry it through to completion has been surprisingly difficult. Contributors Herb Hultgren, Charles Houston, and Ben Eiseman have been principally responsible for initiating the second edition. John Pollock, of The Mountaineers, deserves credit for getting it finished. Without his encouragement and continuous gentle prodding the manuscript would still be half done.

Herb Hultgren; Dr. Burt Janis of the Division of Infectious Diseases, University of Utah College of Medicine; Dr. Warren Bowman of the Billings Clinic, Billings, Montana; Dr. Alen Barbour of the Stanford University Medical School; and Dr. Catherine MacInnes of Glenelg By Kyle, Highlands, Scotland have expended a considerable amount of time and effort to carefully go over the first edition and make many thoughtful suggestions and criticisms. Their interest and efforts have led to significant changes and improvements in the second edition and are acknowledged with gratitude. Dr. Paul Corbett of Merced has helped generously with ENT injuries and disesases. Herb Hultgren has invited the members of the Medical Committee of the American Alpine Club to review the first edition. Helpful comments have been received from Dr. Bruce Meyer, John Montgomery, Dr. Gil Roberts, Dr. Ben Ferris, and Dr. Harry McDade. Additional suggestions have been received from many other individuals, essentially all of which have contributed to the second edition and are certainly appreciated. My brother, Forrest C. Wilkerson, and his colleague Angela Roddey Holder have critically reviewed the appendix section "Legal Considerations."

Gerry Robertson, Medical Illustrator, Pacific Palisades, California, has produced the new or revised illustrations for the second edition with interest, understanding, and skill which have resulted in significant additions to the text.

15

Peggy Ferber has contributed her considerable knowledge and ability to smoothing the rough edges of the manuscript, preparing it for the printer, and shepherding it through the processes of printing, proofreading and publication. To Barbara McBurney and Joan Boland must go a word of thanks for their assistance in typing the manuscript and the considerable correspondence which has been associated with this undertaking.

"The Journal of the American Medical Association" and Drs. Lawrence Corey and Michael A. W. Hattwick have granted permission to reproduce the algorithm for postexposure rabies prophylaxis from the article "Treatment of Persons Exposed to Rabies," J.A.M.A. *232*:272, 1975, which is acknowledged with pleasure and appreciation.

My wife has accepted my preoccupation with this second edition and the accompanying clutter and confusion without complaint. My children have given up their river trip and mountaineering outings for an entire summer so the work could progress without greater delay. To them I must express my gratitude and deepest affection.

JIM WILKERSON
Merced, Calif.
October 26, 1975

Acknowledgments

FOR THE FIRST EDITION

ONE of the major difficulties encountered in preparing this book has been the problem of describing diseases and their diagnosis and treatment in terms which could be readily understood by individuals who are not familiar with the vocabulary or basic principles of medicine. Although each of the contributors solved this problem in his own way, their chapters varied widely in approach, terminology, and the style of writing. These variations, which are to be expected in works by multiple authors, would not have seriously detracted from a book directed to a professional audience. However, this material is intended for individuals with a limited knowledge of the subject. Therefore, to provide the uniform approach and consistent style which were considered necessary to reduce confusion and misunderstanding to a minimum, the text has been extensively rewritten. The contributors have realized the need for such alterations and have consented to them in a manner which the editor is pleased to acknowledge and for which he is deeply appreciative.

Special recognition must also go to Harvey Manning, writer, outdoorsman, conservationist, and highly valued member of The Mountaineers. Without his conviction of the need for a book of its kind, this work would never have begun. Without his continued encouragement, stimulation, and support it would not have been completed. Without his editorial assistance and judgment it would never have acquired what literary merit it may have.

John Rossiter, Medical Illustrator for the University of Virginia Medical School, who made the earlier drawings, and Alan Cole, Medical Illustrator, Altadena, California, who completed this work after John's untimely and tragic death, have combined their considerable talents with an interest and understanding of the purpose of this book to produce illustrations which are both fitting and highly informative. To Marlene Kuffel, Helen Hunterman, and Joyce Braine must go a word of thanks for their generous assistance in typing the manuscript during its various stages of development.

Further appreciation is gratefully expressed to Dr. F. Dennette Adams and the William & Wilkins Company of Baltimore for permission to quote from

Cabot and Adams Physical Diagnosis, 14th Ed.; to Dr. N. Howard-Jones, Director, Division of Editorial and Reference Services of the World Health Organization for permission to use the table of the treatment for rabies following varying types of exposure published by that organization; to the American College of Surgeons for permission to quote from *Early Care of Acute Soft Tissue Injuries*; to Harvey Manning and The Mountaineers for permission to quote from *Mountaineering: The Freedom of the Hills*; to H. V. J. Kilness, Editor, and "Summit" for permission to use illustrations from the article "Head Injuries" which appeared in Vol. 7, No. 5: 2-7, May 1961; to Dr. Julian Johnson and Year Book Medical Publishers, Inc., for permission to adapt for this book illustrations from *Surgery of the Chest, 3rd Ed.*; and to Walter L. Griffith, Director, Product Advertising and Promotion, and Parke, Davis & Company for providing photographs of their plastic inflatable splint, ReadiSplint, for use in preparing drawings of such splints.

Finally, to my wife and children, who have generously forgiven my frequent derelictions from the duties of a husband and father during the production of this book, I wish to express my heartfelt thanks and deepest affection.

J.W.

Introduction

THE ability to rationally analyze a problem or situation and then select and pursue a direct, logical course to a solution is a rare talent sometimes known as "common sense." No ability is more important in caring for the victims of medical disorders in mountaineering circumstances.

The functions of the body and the intricacies of its varied diseases are so complex and now so well known that no one could provide optimal medical care without prior instruction in the principles of diagnosis and therapy. The members of a mountaineering outing must be familiar with the basic principles of medical care and must be prepared to administer any treatment which is needed. The thoroughness of prior training and planning can well be the difference between life and death.

The knowledge and equipment required depends upon the location and duration of the outing. Traumatic disorders — the injuries produced by physical forces such as falls, falling objects, cuts, or burns — are the most common medical disorders encountered in mountaineering, particularly on short outings of three to four days. Nontraumatic disorders, such as infections or diseases of the heart or lungs, usually have a gradual onset over a period of several days and therefore usually do not become apparent during brief outings. In addition, the gradual onset usually permits the victim to be evacuated under his own power before he is fully incapacitated. Climbers as a group are younger and healthier than the population as a whole and thus are less susceptible to such nontraumatic disorders.

Members of an outing of any duration should — as a minimum — be capable of the following:

1. Caring for soft tissue injuries;
2. Recognizing and treating shock;
3. Recognizing and caring for fractures;
4. Diagnosing and treating head injuries;
5. Caring for an unconscious individual;
6. Diagnosing and treating major thoracic and abdominal injuries;

7. Recognizing and treating injuries due to heat or cold;
8. Recognizing and treating high altitude pulmonary edema;
9. Carrying out cardiopulmonary resuscitation.

In addition, members of extended expeditions should develop:

1. The ability to take a simple medical history and perform a physical examination;
2. A familiarity with the techniques of patient care;
3. A knowledge of the diseases which are likely to be encountered on that particular expedition.

Every climber should have a complete examination by a physician before beginning the climbing season. Climbing organizations should probably require documentation of such examination before permitting anyone to participate in an outing. (Medical disorders which would be recognized and treated during.a physician's examination are not included in this handbook.) On prolonged expeditions into isolated areas a prior examination by a physician is essential. Individuals with a peptic ulcer, gallstones, hernia, history of intestinal obstruction following an abdominal operation, or chronic malaria with a large spleen should be advised of the risk in prolonged isolation where surgical help is not available.

MEDICINE *for* MOUNTAINEERING

CHAPTER 1

General Principles of Diagnosis

"DISEASE manifests itself by abnormal sensations and events (symptoms), and by changes in structure or function (signs). Symptoms, being subjective, must be described by the patient. Signs are objective and these the physician discovers by means of physical examination, laboratory studies, and special methods of investigation."[1]

This paragraph succinctly describes the means by which medical disorders are recognized. The description of symptoms by the patient (the history) is the most important method for identifying nontraumatic diseases. In contrast, traumatic injuries are diagnosed primarily by physical examination, although the history is still necessary to ensure no underlying disease process is overlooked. The lack of facilities for laboratory studies and other methods of investigation should not prevent the diagnosis of illnesses occurring in mountaineering conditions. Most diseases — almost all of the common ones — were being accurately diagnosed by history and physical examination alone long before most of the special investigations currently in use were available.

The diagnosis is usually the most difficult aspect of the care of a patient with a nontraumatic disorder. Physicians expend more effort in diagnosing many diseases than in actual treatment. An attendant who is not a physician must appreciate the difficulties involved. At the end of his examination he must assemble his findings and *systematically* compare them with his knowledge of disease and the information that he is able to obtain from other sources.

Outlines are provided below which should enable anyone caring for a disease victim to recognize the site of the disorder. By consulting the section of this book concerning the appropriate organ systems — in which the pertinent signs and symptoms are more thoroughly discussed — a reasonably accurate diagnosis should be made. The examiner must repeatedly refer to these guides to ensure that no omissions occur. "Mistakes are just as often caused by lack of thoroughness as by lack of knowledge."[1]

HISTORY

The patient should be encouraged to describe in his own words his symptoms, the circumstances under which they appeared, and their chronological sequence. Leading questions should be avoided as much as possible, but *a patient's failure to mention a symptom is by no means evidence that it has not occurred.* The exact location of symptoms, intensity, quality, time of onset, and whether gradual or sudden in onset must be ascertained. Whether symptoms are continuous or intermittent, how they are aggravated or relieved, how they are related to each other, and how they are affected by such factors as position, eating, defecation, exertion, and sleep must also be determined.

A description of any past illnesses must be obtained in all cases, even though in mountaineering circumstances the present illness is usually the most significant part of the history. Any pre-existing diseases − such as diabetes or epilepsy − must be brought to light so that any necessary treatment can be continued. Furthermore, if the current ailment is a recurrence or manifestation of a previous disease, such knowledge may provide the key to a proper understanding of the disorder.

MEDICAL HISTORY

PAST HISTORY

Previous Illnesses:	Bronchitis, asthma, pneumonia, pleurisy, tuberculosis, rheumatic fever, any other heart or lung disease, malaria, diabetes, epilepsy, anemia, any other severe illnesses.
Operations:	Date, nature of the operation, complications.
Injuries:	Date, nature of injury, any residual disability; history of mountaineering-related injuries including cold injury, snow blindness, or altitude illness, including pulmonary edema.
Family History	Diseases which tend to run in the family, particularly heart, lung, kidney, or neurological disorders.
Exposure:	Recent exposure to any infectious disease; recent residence in an area which was the site of an epidemic.
Immunizations:	Initial immunizations, boosters.
Allergies:	Allergy to food, insect stings, or other substances, particularly intolerance to drugs including penicillin and sulfa drugs.

REVIEW OF SYSTEMS (Including both present and past illnesses)

Head:	Headache, dizziness, hallucinations, confusion, or fainting.
Eyes:	Inflammation, pain, double vision, loss of vision.

Nose: Colds, sinus trouble, post-nasal drip, bleeding, obstruction.

Teeth: General condition, abscesses, dentures.

Mouth: Pain, bleeding, sores, dryness.

Throat: Sore throat, tonsillitis, hoarseness, difficulty in swallowing or talking.

Ears: Pain, discharge, ringing or buzzing, hearing loss.

Neck: Stiffness, pain, swelling, or masses.

Heart and Lungs: Chest pain, palpitations, shortness of breath (except after strenuous exercise); cough, amount and character of material which is coughed up, coughing up blood.

Gastrointestinal: Loss of appetite, nausea, vomiting; vomiting blood or coffee ground material, indigestion, gas, pain; colic, use of laxatives, constipation, diarrhea, bloody, tarry-black or clay-colored stools, hemorrhoids; jaundice.

Genitourinary: Increase or decrease in frequency of voiding, back pain, pain with voiding; passage of blood, gravel, or stones; sores, purulent discharge, venereal disease or contact; menstrual abnormalities (including irregular periods, increased bleeding with periods, or cramps).

Neuromuscular: Fainting, unconsciousness from other causes, twitching, convulsions; muscle cramps, shooting pains, muscular or joint pains; anesthesia, tingling sensations, weakness, incoordination, or paralysis.

Skin: Rashes, abscesses or boils.

General: Fever, chills, unexplained weight loss.

PHYSICAL EXAMINATION

In order to perform a useful physical examination, the examiner should have some previous experience, particularly with the examination of the chest and abdomen. The examiner may be helped if he can compare any suspicious findings on the patient with a normal individual, but there is no substitute for prior tutelage by a physician.

A *complete* physical examination is essential in evaluating any medical disorder. For the victim of trauma it is imperative that no injury be overlooked, particularly in the presence of an obvious wound. In nontraumatic diseases the physical examination frequently provides vital diagnostic information. To make certain the examination is complete, a definite routine should be followed in every case. The outline provided below is easy to follow, relatively complete, and adequate for both traumatic and nontraumatic disorders. The examination of certain areas, particularly the chest and abdomen, is described in more detail in the chapters dealing with those areas.

PHYSICAL EXAMINATION

General:	Pulse rate, respiratory rate, temperature, blood pressure, general appearance.
Skin:	Color, texture, rashes, abscesses, or boils.
Head:	
Eyes:	Eyebrows and eyelids, movements of eyes, vision, size and equality of pupils, reaction of pupils to light, inflammation.
Nose:	Appearance, discharge, nature of discharge, bleeding.
Mouth:	Sores, bleeding, dryness.
Throat:	Inflammation, purulent exudates.
Ears:	Appearance, discharge, bleeding.
Neck:	Limitation of movement, enlarged lymph nodes.
Lungs:	Respiratory movements, breath sounds, voice sounds, bubbling.
Heart:	Pulse rate, regularity, blood pressure.
Abdomen:	General appearance, tenderness, rebound or referred pain, spasm of muscles, masses.
Genitalia:	Tenderness, masses.
Rectum:	Hemorrhoids, impacted feces, abscesses.
Back:	Tenderness, muscle spasm, limitation of movement.
Extremeties:	Pain or tenderness, limitation of movement, deformities, disproportion in length, swelling, ulcers, soft tissue injuries, lymph node enlargement, sensitivity to pin prick and light touch, muscle spasm.

OTHER CONSIDERATIONS

Examining the victim of a medical disorder is not a simple matter. Tact, diplomacy and a calm, understanding, and sympathetic manner are essential. The ability to appraise and understand the personality of the patient and to adopt an approach that instills confidence is most important. A seriously ill person does not feel well. He cannot be expected to be cheerful and understanding, or — on some occasions — even co-operative.

The patient should be made comfortable and sheltered from wind and cold. The attendant's hands should be warmed and he must be gentle. Any unnecessary discomfort increases the difficulty in obtaining diagnostic information and may aggravate the patient's disorder.

The history and physical examination should be as thorough as possible. Interruptions should be avoided, although it may be necessary to splint a broken extremity or dress a bleeding wound before the examination can be completed. Occasionally the patient may have to be moved from an area of imminent danger. However, the examination should be resumed and completed at the earliest opportunity.

RECORDS

A complete written record must be made of all findings resulting from the examination. It would be presumptuous to rely on memory alone in evaluating any changes the patient may later display. Although all abnormalities should obviously be recorded, the absence of abnormalities is frequently of equal importance. If no specific statement has been made about the presence of a sign or symptom, a physician subsequently caring for the patient may be unable to determine whether an abnormality was absent or was simply not noticed.

REFERENCE:

1. Adams, F. D.: *Cabot and Adams Physical Diagnosis, 14th Ed.,* Baltimore, The Williams & Wilkins Co., 1958. (Quoted by permission of the author and publishers.)

CHAPTER 2

General Principles of Therapy

GENERAL PRINCIPLES

THE BASIC principles of care for the victim of an accident or disease are simple.
The major objective is to permit the body to heal itself.

Rest

Rest promotes healing during an illness or after an injury in a number of
ways. Stress is eliminated; nutrients are used for healing instead of muscular
effort; damaged tissues are immobilized to prevent additional injury. The
amount of rest desirable for different types of disease is variable. Heart disease
requires almost total immobilization − complete rest or "bed rest." Obviously
the heart cannot be completely rested − it must continue beating regularly.
Therefore exercise must be minimized to avoid any extra effort by this organ.
In a hospital patients with certain types of heart disease may be confined to bed
completely, using a bedpan or a bedside toilet, and occasionally even being fed
by the nursing staff. In mountaineering circumstances such complete rest is
clearly impossible, but patients with heart disease and a few other disorders
should rest as completely as possible. Patients with other diseases such as
gastroenteritis do not need such complete rest, but often should remain in camp
to hasten their recovery, rather than taking part in vigorous hiking or climbing.

In the absence of any injury or disease involving the brain, medications
promoting sleep, such as a barbiturate, may be given every evening to promote
sleep. Healthy climbers frequently require such medications for restful sleep,
particularly at high altitudes. Rest is so essential for effective climbing that use
of such medications in moderation should not be discouraged. For some
individuals one of the benzodiazepines is more effective for inducing sleep at
high altitudes. Individuals may vary rather widely in their response to such
medications.

For the victim of a painful injury, control of pain is also necessary for restful sleep. Usually the medication given for pain, particularly morphine or meperidine has so much sedative effect that a specific drug to promote sleep is not required.

Warmth

The patient should be kept warm without over-heating. If the injury or illness has been coupled with exposure, external sources of heat may be necessary as such patients frequently are not able to maintain their body temperature. (See "Hypothermia.") Hot water bottles, heated stones, or direct body-to-body contact are effective in providing the needed warmth. (Care must be exercised when using heated objects to avoid burning the patient, particularly if he is unconscious.)

Altitude

Evacuation to lower altitudes hastens healing and permits a more complete return to normal following traumatic injuries as well as other types of disease. An altitude of approximately 10,000 feet is sufficiently low for persons acclimatized to that level. However, individuals with diseases of the lungs or heart, particularly high altitude pulmonary edema victims, should be taken as low as possible and provided with supplemental oxygen if possible.

Coughing

Patients who are immobilized with a severe injury or serious illness may have shallow respirations. In addition, breathing may be painful or difficult. As a result respiratory activity is diminished, full expansion of the lungs does not occur, and fluid and secretions tend to accumulate in the immobile pulmonary segments. These fluid collections, which are an ideal medium for bacterial growth, cause pneumonia unless they are evacuated. Such infections result in the death of many elderly persons bedridden with fractures of the lower extremities.

To eliminate fluids, expand the lungs, and reduce the danger of infection, the patient must be encouraged — or even forced — to breathe deeply and to cough at frequent intervals. Coughing may be difficult and painful for a very ill patient or the victim of a chest injury, but it is for precisely these patients that coughing is most important. The routine practiced in most hospitals is to have the patient sit up, hold his sides, and cough *deeply* — not just clear his throat — at least once every two hours. A similar routine should be adopted under mountaineering circumstances. (After the patient has recovered to the extent that he is able to be up and walking around, such measures are no longer necessary.)

Ambulation

Anyone confined to bed as a result of illness should be encouraged to sit up and, if possible, walk about a little several times a day. Exercise increases the circulation in the legs and helps prevent thrombophlebitis. (See "Diseases of the Respiratory System.") However, the exception to this rule − patients with heart disease or who have already developed thrombophlebitis must remain absolutely bedridden if possible until the disorder has completely disappeared or evacuation has been completed.

Diet

Solid food is not as important during the acute stages of an illness as an adequate fluid intake. Unless a particular type of diet is required − as in the treatment of an ulcer − the patient should be permitted to eat whatever he desires. During convalescence more attention can be given to a nutritionally adequate diet, to which should be added extra amounts of protein.

Bowel Care

Difficulties with bowel evacuation are frequent in bedridden patients. Repression of the urge to defecate, low food intake, and dehydration (due to low fluid intake, altitude, excessive sweating, or fluid loss from other sources) or a combination of these contribute to the problem. If uncontrolled, fecal impaction often results. (See "Diseases of the Gastrointestinal System.") In the absence of solid food in the diet, stool volume is reduced. Nevertheless, bowel movements should occur about every three or four days. An adequate fluid intake is the best way to insure normal elimination, although laxatives or enemas may be necessary to prevent the development of impaction in a bedridden individual.

Convalescence

Although exercise should be encouraged during convalescence, strenuous activity prior to complete recovery may delay the return to normal health, particularly at high altitudes. In addition, an individual is more susceptible to other diseases or injuries during convalescence. Therefore, it may be desirable to postpone return to full activity for two to three extra days to be certain that full recovery has taken place.

FLUID BALANCE

An adequate fluid intake is always essential, but is of particular importance during a period of illness. A person can live for weeks without food, but only a few days without water.

Fluid Loss

Fluids are lost from the body in several ways. The "sensible loss" excreted by the kidneys ranges from one to two liters per day. The "insensible loss" of perspiration and evaporation through the lungs (to moisten air which is inhaled) amounts to approximately one liter daily in temperate climates and at low altitudes. An average adult requires two to three liters of fluid daily to replace these losses.

Fluid depletion (dehydration) can result from normal losses in the presence of inadequate fluid intake, or conversely, increased loss with no increase in intake. Inability to ingest fluids may result from protracted vomiting or unconsciousness. Water shortages also reduce fluid intake.

Increased fluid losses occur in a number of ways. In hot weather, or with a high fever, several liters of water may be lost each day through perspiration. At high altitudes two to four quarts of fluid may be lost daily through the lungs. Severe vomiting or prolonged diarrhea also lead to fluid depletion. Deaths due to cholera result from the severe dehydration caused by massive diarrheal fluid loss through the intestines.

Salt (sodium and chlorine) and other chemical substances including potassium and bicarbonate are known as electrolytes and are vital constituents of body fluids. Like water, a balance between intake and loss must be maintained. The average adult's daily salt requirement is five grams. In desert climates, where large amounts of salt are lost through perspiration, needs may climb as high as fifteen grams per day.

These water and electrolyte requirements represent the needs of a normal, healthy adult. Individuals with diseases of the heart or kidneys have quite different requirements. Serious consequences can result from the administration of normal quantities of electrolytes and water, particularly salt, to persons with one of these disorders.

The kidneys are very sensitive to changes in the body's fluid balance and react immediately to conserve or eliminate water as circumstances may require. *The urine volume over a twenty-four-hour period provides the best indication of the balance between fluid intake and losses. A urine volume of less than one-half liter (500 cc) is indicative of fluid depletion; an increased volume, two liters or more, is a sign of excessive fluid intake.*

It is essentially impossible to accurately evaluate a patient's status regarding fluids without careful measurements of all intake and losses, including vomitus and watery stools. Consideration must also be given to the insensible loss. Fever, hot weather, or high altitude must be evaluated and the loss from these sources estimated as accurately as possible. These measurements, *which must be recorded*, should be totaled at the same time every day, and the fluid needs for the following day calculated.

Dehydration at Altitude

Dehydration is ubiquitous at high altitudes. Contributing to this loss of fluids are faster and deeper breathing and cold air. Air is warmed and moistened as it passes through the mouth, nose, and other major air passages so that it has a relative humidity approaching one hundred percent and the same temperature as the body when it reaches the lungs. The greater respiratory efforts required at high altitudes increase the amount of water required to moisten the air. Furthermore, cold air with a high relative humidity, when warmed to body temperature, becomes relatively dry. As a result, the cold air found at higher altitudes requires more water to provide a relative humidity near one hundred percent while in the lungs.

Mouth breathing, during which almost all of the moisture in expired air is lost, sweating with exertion, and unavailability of water for drinking also contribute to fluid shortages at altitude.

The dehydration is further aggravated by loss or dulling of the sensation of thirst which accompanies the loss of appetite, nausea, and occasionally vomiting that occurs with acute mountain sickness. It has been suggested that dehydration contributes to the depression, impaired judgment, and other psychological and intellectual changes which occur at high altitudes.

A person must consciously push himself to drink fluids, even if he is not thirsty, when at high altitude. At sea level an average individual requires about two liters of fluid per day. At altitude, particularly above 15,000 to 16,000 feet, requirements often exceed four liters per day. The adequacy of an individual's fluid intake can be judged by his urinary output, which should be at least one-half liter every twenty-four hours.

Fluid Replacement

Oral intake is the best and easiest method of replacing fluid which has been lost. Almost all fluids are suitable for this purpose, including water, fruit juices, soft drinks, and similar beverages. (Since water contains no electrolytes, fruit juices, soups, and soft drinks which do should be encouraged.) A seriously ill patient with very little appetite must be urged to drink small quantities of fluids at frequent intervals in order to get him to ingest the needed volume. A considerable amount of patience and perseverance is often required to obtain an adequate intake.

Some disorders, of which protracted vomiting and unconsciousness are most common, render a person unable to take fluids orally. If medical attention can be obtained within one or two days, the intervening fluid depletion is usually not too severe. However, longer periods without fluid or diseases such as cholera can produce severe dehydration and require the administration of fluids intravenously. (Fluids suitable for intravenous administration would only be carried by a large, well-equipped expedition, although they might be obtained by air drop. These solutions are prepared to very strict specifications; efforts to improvise would almost certainly result in disaster.)

Each day the volume of intravenous fluids to be given must be carefully calculated. A certain quantity of fluid is required to replace normal losses; to this volume must be added the fluids necessary to replace abnormal losses. Two liters of five or ten percent glucose and one-half liter of an electrolyte solution such as Ringer's lactate usually satisfy the body's daily needs when there is no abnormal loss. Fluids lost through vomiting, diarrhea, or excessive perspiration should be replaced as exactly as possible with Ringer's lactate. Excessive fluid loss through the lungs should be replaced by glucose as no electrolytes are lost with the moisture in expired air.

Example: A climber with appendicitis and severe vomiting is at a camp located at 18,000 feet. The measured volume of vomitus is 1,000 cc; urinary output for the previous twenty-four hours is 600 cc.

	Glucose	Ringer's Lactate
Normal requirements	2,000 cc	500 cc
Replacement for vomiting	–	1,000 cc
Replacement for altitude	2,000 cc	–
Total	4,000 cc	1,500 cc

Note: No effort is made to specifically replace the urine volume. The urine volume serves only as an indication — albeit an excellent one — of the presence of dehydration.

Ringer's lactate contains very little potassium. Patients with poor kidney function cannot rid themselves of excessive potassium, which may rapidly accumulate to fatal toxic levels. However, patients with normal renal function excrete potassium in the urine. As a result, blood potassium concentrations can fall to dangerously low levels during prolonged intravenous fluid therapy if the potassium is not replaced.

Therefore, individuals receiving intravenous fluids for more than two to three days, or who have large abnormal losses from diarrhea, *and* who have a normal urine volume, should receive an extra 15 to 20 mEq of potassium per liter of Ringer's lactate. The potassium is usually provided as a solution which can be added directly to the Ringer's lactate solution.

If a person with a good heart and normally functioning kidneys is provided with an adequate intake of water (as glucose) and electrolytes (Ringer's lactate), the kidneys will compensate for any imbalance which may exist. The inevitable inaccuracies inherent in measuring fluid intake and output are fully corrected. However, an individual with pre-existing heart or kidney disease or acute renal failure as a result of his disease or injury requires much more accurate therapy which usually can only be provided with hospital facilities.

CHAPTER 3

Special Problems

FEVER

FEVER, an elevation of the body temperature, is most commonly a sign of infection. However, a mild fever frequently follows traumatic injuries; sunstroke can result in a very high fever. Normal body temperature averages about 98.6° F as measured orally, but can vary as much as a full degree upward or downward over a twenty-four-hour period. Rectal temperatures are normally one degree higher than oral readings.

A patient's temperature should not arouse concern unless it exceeds 100° F orally or 101° F rectally. Lower values are within the range of normal variation. Furthermore, a serious infection will produce an obvious fever.

Oral temperature measurements are made more easily, but suffer the disadvantage of being affected by ingested food or beverages, smoking, or even talking. Therefore, oral temperatures should not be taken for at least ten minutes after eating or smoking. If rectal measurements are necessary, a rectal thermometer is preferable. It should be carefully lubricated with petroleum jelly or a similar lubricant, gently inserted about one and one-half inches into the rectum, and left for three minutes. Anyone who is delirious, restless, or thrashing about must be watched carefully and perhaps even restrained to prevent his breaking the thermometer and injuring himself, regardless of where the temperature is measured.

As long as an illness persists, the temperature and pulse rate should be measured and *recorded* every four hours (although a soundly sleeping patient rarely needs to be awakened in the middle of the night just to have his temperature taken). Fevers sometimes follow specific patterns which are diagnostically important. The temperature may go up and stay up, gradually coming down at the termination of the illness; alternately, the temperature may spike to high levels and then fall to normal or below normal every day or every second or third day. A continuous record is needed to recognize such patterns.

The heart rate is usually elevated about ten beats per minute for every degree of fever. With some infections the pulse may remain slow in spite of fever, a finding which is important in the diagnosis of certain diseases such as typhoid fever. Therefore, the pulse should be measured and recorded every time the temperature is taken.

A moderate fever, although occasionally making the patient uncomfortable, does not produce any lasting harmful effects. In contrast, a temperature above 106° F orally can cause irreversible damage if not promptly lowered. To reduce such high fevers, the patient's body and extremities should be covered with cool (tepid) wet cloths. As the cloths become warm they should be replaced. The patient can be fanned to increase evaporation and cooling. These measures should be continued until the temperature is below 103° F. Aspirin may be given orally if the patient is fully conscious or rectally if he is comatose. The patient must be very carefully watched for eight to twelve hours after the temperature has been lowered, since high fevers frequently recur quite rapidly.

Although the fever must be lowered, the patient must also be protected from any extremes of heat or cold — such as sunlight or snow and ice — in the immediate environment. After cooling he should be redressed in the clothing normally worn under the prevailing conditions. He must not be closed up in a sleeping bag, which traps the heat and can cause his temperature to go up again, unless sleeping bags are necessary for everyone else to keep warm.

CHILLS

A chill is a feeling of chilliness accompanied by shivering which is produced by small showers of bacteria or viruses entering the blood stream. Such chills accompany infections, and are frequently the first indication of the presence of such disorders. In contrast to the chills commonly resulting from exposure to cold or sunburns, chills resulting from infection are much more severe, progressing to violent, uncontrollable shaking involving the entire body. The teeth chatter, the lips and nails are purple, the skin is pale and cold, and the victim feels miserable. (In earlier hospitals a good criterion for the diagnosis of a chill was whether the patient was shaking hard enough to make the bed rattle.) The feeling of coldness persists in spite of blankets and heating pads until the chill has run its course, usually five to fifteen minutes.

A chill is usually followed in a very short time by a fever which may reach high levels. There is no specific treatment other than caring for the underlying infection. Pneumonia, meningitis, and "strep throat" are frequently introduced with a single shaking chill. Malaria, infections of the liver and bile ducts or kidneys, and generalized bacterial infections are characterized by recurrent chills.

SHOCK

Shock is not a disease entity in itself, but is caused by an underlying illness or injury. The most common cause of shock is a sudden reduction in the volume of the body's blood, usually as a result of severe bleeding. All of the constituents of the blood — blood cells and serum — are lost by hemorrhage. However, the volume of blood can also be reduced by disorders in which only the fluid portion of the blood is lost. Large volumes of serum are poured out into the damaged tissues following a severe burn. Dehydration resulting from fluid losses caused by severe vomiting or diarrhea, as frequently occurs with cholera, can cause a reduction in blood volume which is fatal if untreated.

When the blood volume is reduced — regardless of the cause — the arteries in the skin and muscles constrict, tending to direct the available blood to the vital organs. At the same time the heart begins pumping at an increased rate in order to circulate the remaining blood faster and enable a smaller volume of blood to carry the required amounts of oxygen and nutrients to the tissues. When these mechanisms can no longer compensate for the derangements in blood volume, shock results. If untreated, severe shock eventually becomes irreversible regardless of therapy, and the victim dies.

Shock also occurs in other disorders in which there does not appear to be a definite reduction in blood volume. Severe infections or heart attacks are often associated with shock. A period of shock of varying duration is characteristic of the terminal stages of any fatal disease. The mechanisms by which shock is produced in these conditions is poorly understood and efforts at treatment, other than therapy directed toward the underlying disease, are frequently unrewarding.

Diagnosis

The symptoms of shock produced by hemorrhage depend on the percentage of the total blood volume lost. A person six feet tall and weighing 175 pounds has a blood volume of about 6,000 cc. A person five feet three inches tall and weighing 110 pounds has a blood volume of about 4,000 cc. Individuals of different sizes have roughly proportional blood volumes.

The symptoms of shock are usually more severe if the patient is bleeding rapidly than they are when blood loss is more gradual.

Estimating the volume of blood lost is not easy. Most individuals with relatively little experience tend to overestimate the amount which has been lost. A small amount of blood can cover an amazingly large area.

Mild shock results from loss of ten to twenty percent of the blood volume. The patient appears pale and his skin feels cool to the touch, first over the extremities and later over the trunk. As shock becomes more severe sweating appears, the patient usually complains of feeling cold, and he is often thirsty. A rapid pulse and reduced blood pressure may be present. However, the absence of these signs does not indicate shock is not present since they may only appear rather late, particularly in previously healthy young adults.

Moderate shock results from loss of twenty to forty percent of the blood volume. The signs of mild shock are present and may become more severe. The pulse is often fast and weak or "thready." In addition, blood flow to the kidneys is reduced as the available blood is shunted to the heart and brain, and the urinary output declines. A urinary volume of less than thirty cc (one ounce) per hour is indicative of moderate shock. Urethral catheterization, if possible, may be desirable to monitor urinary output.

Severe shock results from loss of more than forty percent of the blood volume and is characterized by signs of reduced blood flow to the brain and heart. Reduced cerebral blood flow produces restlessness and agitation followed by stupor, confusion, and eventually coma and death. Diminished blood flow to the heart can produce abnormalities of the cardiac rhythm.

Treatment

Treatment is much more effective if begun before shock actually appears, but such anticipation requires considerable perspicacity. Shock would obviously be expected after severe hemorrhage. However, some fractures, particularly those involving the spine, pelvis, or thigh, and many injuries to the internal organs are associated with severe bleeding which produces no external evidence of hemorrhage. Shock should also be anticipated in some other disorders, particularly those which result in severe fluid loss.

Successful treatment of shock depends largely upon treating the cause. However, several measures should be undertaken regardless of the underlying condition. Treatment must be started as early as possible. Following any injury the first step after controlling bleeding and insuring adequate respiration should be the treatment of shock.

The victim should be lying down with his feet elevated ten to twelve inches.

Body temperature must be maintained. Blankets or sleeping bags may not be adequate if shock is so severe that the victim cannot produce enough heat to warm himself. If necessary, hot water bottles, heated stones, or direct body-to-body contact should be used, particularly in a mountainous environment. Any impairment of respiration must be corrected, and oxygen should be administered if it is available.

Pain, unpleasant emotional stimuli such as fright or the sight of blood, or movement often increase the severity of shock. If pain is present (a patient in moderate or severe shock frequently does not feel pain), and there is no evidence of a head injury or other contraindication to such medication, morphine should be administered. Since circulation to the skin and muscles of the extremities is impaired in shock, morphine injected at those sites may not be absorbed. Intramuscular injections should be given into the pectoral muscles of the chest where circulatory impairment is less severe. Subsequent injections must be only half as large and should be given at six-hour intervals as long as shock is evident. Larger doses and more frequent injections could lead to severe overdosage. If circulation to the injection site is poor, the drugs are not absorbed. Later when the patient recovers from shock and the circulation is restored, all of the injected medication could be absorbed at once, leading to severe overdosage.

Morphine also helps to allay anxiety. With or without its use, the victim should be given all possible reassurance to minimize the effects of fear and anxiety.

The victim must not be moved until all injuries have been treated, shock has been controlled, and he appears to be in stable condition.

Low blood volume from hemorrhage or other causes can be corrected to a considerable extent by the intravenous administration of Ringer's lactate. Blood plasma or plasma expanders such as Dextran may be somewhat more effective, but are also associated with potentially harmful side effects and should only be given by a physician or an individual trained in their use. The red blood cells necessary for carrying oxygen are not replaced by these fluids, thus this therapy does have limitations. Whole blood is the optimum replacement for blood loss, but preservation and cross-matching are impossible outside of a hospital with an appropriately equipped laboratory.

Fluids should be given in anticipation of shock, particularly when the appearance of shock is felt to be a certainty, as in the case of extensive burns. The fluids should be administered in amounts which approximate the volume of lost blood. However, blood loss is usually difficult to estimate accurately, particularly with injuries where most of the loss is hidden from view. An adult with no pre-existing heart disease is rarely harmed by under- or over-replacement of as much as one or even two litters . *However, if the victim does have heart disease, care must be taken that any error is on the side of under-replacement.*

The adequacy of treatment following hemorrhage can be determined by measuring the pulse rate, blood pressure (if possible), and urinary output. Pulse and blood pressure should return to normal levels within a few minutes after replacement of the lost blood volume. A urinary volume of about sixty cc (two ounces) per hour is desirable. Declining urinary output with increasing pulse rate indicates the need for re-instituting therapy. All data regarding pulse rate, blood pressure, urinary output, and all therapy which has been administered must be carefully recorded so that the course of the patient can be followed and a physician, when obtained, can have a basis for his treatment.

The treatment of shock associated with nontramautic disorders is less clear-cut and the results are often less satisfactory. Patients in shock from peritonitis or similar disorders may benefit from one or two liters of Ringer's lactate per day, but more should not be given. The victim of a heart attack who has sustained no blood loss must not be given fluids, as they increase the work load on his already damaged heart.

AIRWAY MAINTENANCE

The mouth and nose, throat, larynx (voice box), trachea, and bronchi form the passages through which air moves into the lungs and are known collectively as the airway. The mouth, throat, and tongue are so constructed that the base of the tongue can move backward and obstruct the opening to the trachea. In swallowing, the tongue and epiglottis block this airway to prevent food or fluids from entering the lungs. Partial obstruction by this means during sleep results in snoring. However, the obstruction which produces snoring is only partial because the muscles which hold the tongue and structures of the throat are not totally relaxed during natural sleep. In contrast, disorders resulting in unconsciousness can produce complete relaxation of these muscles, permitting the tongue to totally obstruct the passage of air into the lungs.

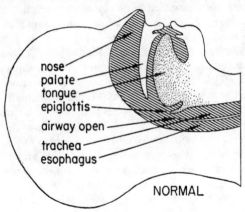

Figure 1. Structures of the mouth, throat, and airway in a normal, conscious individual.

The easiest way to prevent such airway obstruction is to tilt the victim's head back by placing one hand on the back of his neck and lifting while pushing down on his forehead with the other hand. The resulting stretching of the structures of the throat prevents the tongue from falling back far enough to produce obstruction. If there is no reason to suspect a broken neck and no other injuries which might be aggravated by turning the patient on his stomach, he may be placed in a prone position with his head turned to one side. In this position the tongue tends to fall forward instead of backward and does not block the throat. However, the head also should be extended to provide additional help in keeping the airway open.

If a broken neck is suspected, the airway can be opened by placing the fingers at the angles of the victim's jaws and pulling forward. Alternately, a finger or thumb can be hooked behind the teeth of the lower jaw and the jaw pulled forward. The neck should not be moved. If evacuation involves a long stretcher carry over rough terrain during which it may be impossible to keep the victim's airway open in this manner without moving his head, a plastic airway or tracheostomy may be necessary.

If the victim does not recover consciousness within a few minutes, a more permanent open airway must be secured, particularly if he is to be moved. Many first aid kits contain plastic airways for this purpose. These airways are flattened curved tubes which fit over the base of the tongue, allowing air to enter the larynx. (As the patient starts to regain consciousness, the tube causes him to cough and gag. At this time the tube should be removed.) Another method of keeping the airway open is to insert a large safety pin through the meaty part of the tongue and hold the tongue forward by taping the pin to the chin or anchoring it in a similar manner. Although this technique sounds and appears brutal, it is very effective and produces no permanent damage. Finally, in certain circumstances a more permanent artificial airway may require a tracheostomy which is described below.

The adequacy of the airway is very easily checked. If the victim is breathing quietly, the airway is open. Snoring or noisy breathing, labored respirations, or the absence of respiratory movements indicate partial or complete airway obstruction.

Tracheostomy

A tracheostomy is an opening in the trachea, usually in the lower portion of the neck, which allows the patient to breathe without having the air pass through the upper air passages — the mouth or nose, throat, and larynx. Although tracheostomies are quite common among hospitalized patients, they are rarely needed by the victims of mountaineering accidents or illnesses. However, accident victims with severe facial fractures may be unable to breathe through the nose or mouth due to the swelling and deformity accompanying their injuries. A crushing blow to the larynx usually produces airway obstruction. For such patients an immediate tracheostomy may be life saving. A tracheostomy may also be used to provide a more permanent open airway during evacuation of an unconscious patient, although other means for maintaining the airway are usually available.

A tracheostomy is simply a hole in the trachea and any technique for creating the hole and keeping it open may work quite well. The location of the opening has little to do with how well the tracheostomy functions except that it obviously must be below an obstructing injury. However, the site for the tracheostomy must be selected precisely to avoid damage to other structures in the neck, particularly large blood vessels which can produce a massive hemorrhage, and to minimize subsequent scarring and deformity.

Hospital tracheostomies are routinely placed just above the sternum or breast bone at the base of the neck. Nonphysicians must not use this location because the thyroid gland and the common carotid arteries (two of the body's largest) may be encountered. Instead, such individuals should place the opening for the tracheostomy in the cricothyroid membrane. The thyroid cartilage is the rather large structure which surrounds the larynx and forms the Adam's apple. The cricoid cartilage is the ring-like cartilaginous structure just below

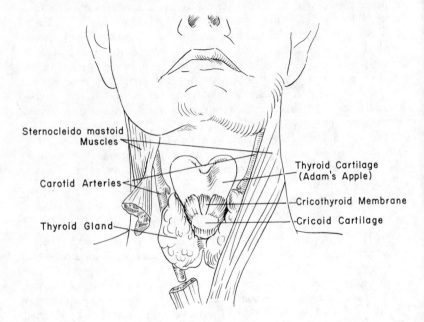

Figure 2. Location of cricothyroid membrane and carotid arteries.

the thyroid cartilage which is approximately twice as thick as the cartilaginous rings that make up the trachea below this cartilage. The cricothyroid membrane connects these two structures. (A physician's help in identifying this structure should be obtained before such knowledge is needed to care for a patient.)

To perform the tracheostomy, the patient should be lying on a flat surface, if possible, with his head extended backward to stretch the structures in the neck. The skin of the neck should be cleaned with soap and water and an antiseptic applied if time is available. The space between the thyroid and cricoid cartilages should then be precisely identified. Any kind of sharp instrument can be used to make the opening. A device (Adelson curved cricothyroidotomy cannula) produced specifically for this purpose is manufactured by Becton-Dickenson and is available through almost all of the major medical and scientific supply houses. This cannula is probably the easiest and least risky device to use, but an eight to ten gauge needle works almost equally well. A fifteen gauge needle is large enough to provide an adequate airway for most individuals if nothing larger is available. The skin can be incised first if a scalpel, razor blade, or sharp knife is available. The incision only needs to be about one-quarter inch in length, but should be right in the midline. Then the cannula or needle should be inserted into the midline of the trachea. Air can be heard moving in and out immediately.

The opening in the trachea collapses unless some kind of tube is inserted to keep it open. One advantage of using a large needle to perform the tracheostomy is that the needle can be left in place to keep the opening from being obstructed. The needle or whatever tubing is used must be anchored in place to keep it from falling out or from being jammed into the back wall of the trachea and obstructed. The needle or tubing should generally be left in place until the victim is under a physician's care. If an unconscious patient should recover enough during a prolonged evacuation not to need the tracheostomy, the needle or tubing should just be removed. The wound will close and heal with no further attention.

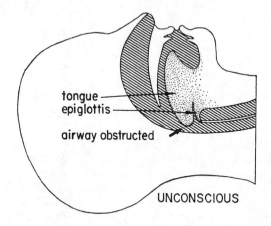

Figure 3. Position of the tongue and epiglottis in an unconscious patient.

UNCONSCIOUSNESS

An unconscious patient requires special attention to four general needs: vital functions (particularly respiration), fluid requirements, protection from the environment, and specific treatment of the underlying illness which has resulted in coma. The nature of the last two requirements depends upon the circumstances in which the victim is found; fluid requirements are discussed under "Fluid Balance."

The most obvious vital functions are those of the heart and lungs; however, little can be done to correct misfunctions of the heart in mountaineering circumstances. Furthermore, the victim of a disorder so severe that breathing ceases can rarely be kept alive by manual artificial respiration for more than a

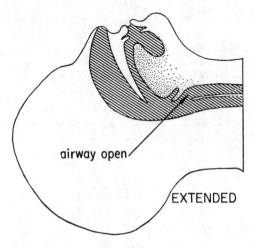

Figure 4. Position of the tongue and epiglottis in an unconscious patient with the head and neck extended to relieve airway obstruction.

few hours (see "Resuscitation"). Therefore, the specific treatment for unconscious patients in mountaineering circumstances resolves itself to the maintenance of open air passages to permit unimpeded respiration.

Disorders which produce unconsciousness are also frequently associated with vomiting. The vomitus may completely obstruct the air passages, or may be aspirated into the lungs, resulting in a severe, often fatal, pneumonia. To prevent such accidents the victim's head should be lower than his chest and turned to the side whenever he is vomiting or appears likely to vomit. If there is no reason not to do so, he can be placed on his stomach to help keep his airway open and prevent his aspirating. Unconscious persons must never be given food, fluids, or medications by mouth due to the danger of aspiration.

All medications for sleep or pain, in addition to being completely unnecessary, are quite likely to increase the depression of brain function caused by the underlying disorder and must be avoided.

The care of an unconscious patient is simple, but vitally important. Skilled treatment of other injuries or heroic rescue efforts may be completely wasted by five minutes neglect of these principles. *Regardless of the circumstances the airway must be kept open. No matter how precarious the situation, no rescue efforts can be justified until means for keeping the air passages clear during the entire evacuation have been established.* It should be obvious that an injured climber must be left in an exposed and dangerous situation if rescue attempts would cause certain death due to airway obstruction.

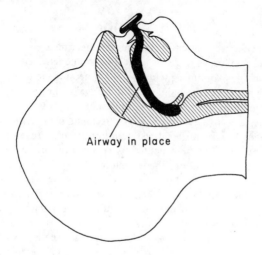

Airway in place

Figure 5. Oropharyngeal airway in place in an unconscious patient.

"Cafe Coronary"

One cause of respiratory obstruction which is becoming recognized with increasing frequency is the aspiration of a large chunk of food — usually meat. Typically the victim has been drinking, but this is not found in every instance. While eating he suddenly indicates that he is choking, usually rises out of his chair, and then collapses. *He cannot speak.* Usually, he cannot cough, or coughs very weakly and ineffectually. Death ensues within a matter of minutes if the obstruction is not relieved.

Surprisingly large fragments of food can be aspirated into the larynx. Whole radishes and similar sized chunks are typically found. The food plugs off the larynx and obstructs the airway — usually completely. Since no air can move through the larynx the individual cannot speak, cough or breathe.

Rarely the food can be dislodged by a finger inserted through the mouth. If this is not successful, the victim should be stood up if possible, grabbed from behind with both arms around his waist and the fists in the upper abdomen just below the breast bone, and squeezed suddenly and as vigorously as possible. The sudden pressure on the chest and abdomen forces air out of the lungs and often pops the obstructing food out of the larynx.

If this maneuver is not successful after two or three tries, a tracheostomy must be performed. It should be done as quickly as possible. Artificial respiration through the tracheostomy may be necessary for a short time if the victim has stopped breathing on his own.

RESUSCITATION

Occasions for effective resuscitation of mountaineering accident victims are rare. Heart attack victims, who are the most common beneficiaries of such care in urban surroundings, are infrequent in mountaineering circumstances. Victims of lightning accidents, drownings, and some avalanche victims, if reached quickly, can frequently be revived by resuscitative efforts. Even a person knocked unconscious in a relatively minor accident may temporarily stop breathing and may require artificial respiration. Furthermore, even though a patient is breathing, he may be benefited by artificial respiration if, for some reason, he appears to be breathing inadequately.

There is no point in attempting to resuscitate anyone who has received massive injuries which are obviously fatal. However, many fatal injuries do not appear so severe when first seen and may be difficult to evaluate. Furthermore, even though a considerable time passes before anyone is able to get to the accident victim, there is no sure way of knowing that breathing or the heartbeat has not ceased only seconds before the rescuers arrive. Therefore, except in obviously hopeless cases, resuscitative measures should be attempted. Certainly no harm can be done, there is little to be lost, and a great deal of benefit may be obtained.

Attempts to resuscitate anyone who has been more than fifteen minutes without breathing or heartbeat are futile. The brain can survive only about five minutes without oxygen before suffering permanent damage. After this period, deterioration sets in rapidly and by ten to twelve minutes damage is so severe that death is inevitable. However, longer periods without breathing may be survivable if the body temperature has been lowered (hypothermia). Resuscitative efforts, to be effective, must be started immediately.

The techniques of resuscitation must be practiced with an instructor before attempts to apply them if the efforts are to have a reasonable chance for success.

Artificial Respiration

Whenever an individual who appears to require resuscitation is encountered, he first should be shaken or slapped to see if he can be aroused. If the victim is truly comatose, he should be placed on a firm, flat surface and the rescuer should place his face close to the victim's mouth to listen and feel for air moving through the nose or mouth. If breathing is impaired or absent, the respiratory passages must be cleared of any obstruction. The fingers should be inserted into the victim's mouth and throat and any foreign matter or vomitous removed, particularly with avalanche or drowning victims whose efforts to breathe cause them to gulp in snow or other material.

The head should be tilted backwards by placing one hand on the back of the neck and lifting upward while pushing down with the other hand on the forehead. This maneuver places tension on the tongue and structures in the throat so that the airway is not obstructed. (See "Care of the Unconscious.") In some cases relieving such obstruction is all that is necessary for the patient to resume breathing.

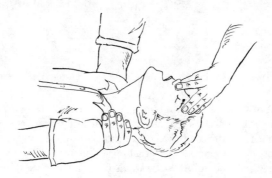

Figure 6. Positioning of the head and neck for mouth-to-mouth artificial respiration.

If artificial respiration is necessary, it should be started with the least possible delay using the mouth-to-mouth technique. The hand behind the neck holds the head forward while the hand on the forehead pushes downward and the thumb and forefinger pinch shut the nostrils. (In an alternate method, the fingers of both hands are placed behind the angles of the jaw, pulling the jaw forward while the thumbs close off the nose. This technique should be used if the victim is suspected of having a broken neck.) Rarely, the victim's jaw may be so tightly clenched that it cannot be opened. In such cases, the head must still be tilted backward to keep the airway open, and artificial respiration given by the mouth-to-mouth technique.

The rescuer should inhale, place his mouth over the victim's open mouth, and exhale with enough force to cause the victim's chest to rise. The attendant then removes his mouth and inhales again while the victim's lungs empty. Upon initiating artificial respiration the rescuer should give the victim four quick breaths without allowing time for the victim's lungs to empty. This maneuver distends the lungs, which may have been partially collapsed, and provides for more effective air exchange. Artificial respiration should be carried out at a rate of approximately twelve to fourteen breaths per minute and should be synchronized with any respiratory efforts being made by the victim.

Figure 7. Administration of mouth-to-mouth artificial respiration.

With effective artificial respiration, air can be heard moving in and out of the victim's upper air passages. Usually the victim's chest can be seen to rise and fall also. If such evidence of successful artificial respiration is not present, the airway must be examined for obstruction. Foreign matter must be removed and the head must be tipped backward as far as it will go with the jaw pulled well forward.

Figure 8. Administration of mouth-to-nose artificial respiration.

During mouth-to-mouth artificial respiration the stomach may become distended with air forced through the esophagus instead of into the lungs. This air should be removed to prevent the distended stomach from impinging on the diaphragm and interfering with respiratory movements. In children, the stomach may even rupture. Moderate pressure on the upper abdomen with the palm of the hand usually forces the air back out through the esophagus into a large belch. This maneuver may have to be repeated periodically, and the victim must be watched carefully in case he vomits at the same time.

The mouth-to-mouth method of artificial respiration is so far superior to any other method it should be used exclusively. It is almost impossible not to perform artificial respiration correctly and effectively by this technique if the precautions described are observed.

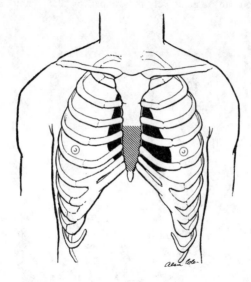

Figure 9. Area of the chest to which pressure is applied during external cardiac massage.

Cardiac Resuscitation

Following the first four quick breaths at the initiation of artificial respiration, the rescuer should determine whether the victim's heart is beating by checking the carotid pulse. The examiner can find this pulse by placing his fingers on the thyroid cartilage in the neck (Adam's apple) and moving them to either side into the groove between this cartilage (which forms a portion of the larynx or voice box) and the prominent muscle which runs from the base of the ear to the center portion of the upper chest (the sternocleidomastoid muscle). If no pulse can be felt, cardiac resuscitative measures should be instituted.

If the collapse or injury of the victim has been witnessed, and the rescuer can reach him within less than one minute, a sharp blow to the chest occasionally can stimulate the heart to resume beating. The blow should be given with the side of the hand or fist to the lower part of the chest at a point just to the left of the sternum (breast bone). A fairly hard blow is usually required to have any effect.

If no results are obtained by a single blow, cardiac massage must be begun. The normal heart pumps blood by contractions which force the blood out into the arteries. Cardiac massage accomplishes the same thing by compressing the heart from the outside. By pressing on the lower part of the sternum, the heart is squeezed between the sternum and vertebral column, forcing out the blood. Blood circulation can be effectively maintained by this technique for a considerable time.

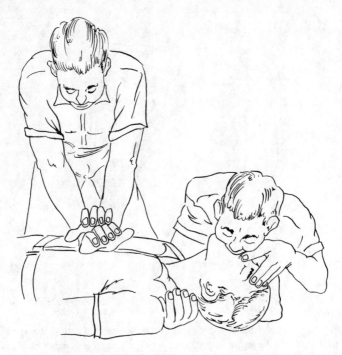

Figure 10. Administration of external cardiac massage and mouth-to-mouth artificial respiration.

The attendant should kneel over the victim, and place the heel of one hand on the lower end of the victim's sternum at a point two finger widths above the tip. The hand must not be on the tip of the sternum as this may fracture and puncture the liver, resulting in severe hemorrhage. Similarly, the fingers must be lifted from the chest wall so that only the heel of the hand is in contact with the sternum in order to reduce the probability of fracturing ribs. The second hand should be placed on top of the first and the arms should be kept straight so that force can be exerted by shifting the rescuer's weight onto his arms. The use of muscular force for cardiac massage is too tiring to be carried out for more than a few minutes. Enough pressure should be exerted to depress the sternum one or two inches. The pressure is released immediately and the maneuver repeated about sixty times a minute. The cycle should consist of approximately equal periods of time during which pressure is being applied and when no pressure is applied. The effectiveness of the massage can be checked by feeling for the pulse at the victim's neck or groin.

Pressure on the chest by cardiac massage does not move enough air into the victim's lungs to keep him alive. Therefore, mouth-to-mouth artificial respiration must be given. If a second resucer is on hand, he can give artificial respiration at a rate of one breath for every five cardiac compressions. The artificial respiration must be timed so it is given during the interval when the pressure is not being applied to the chest. The two rescuers should alternate periodically between cardiac massage and artificial respiration to avoid tiring either to the point he becomes ineffective. The switch should be made without interrupting the pattern of cardiac massage.

If only one rescuer is present he must give both cardiac massage and artificial respiration. The technique generally recommended is to give fifteen compressions of the heart at a rate of approximately eighty per minute and then two quick breaths of artificial respiration. Repetition of the cycle at this rate provides approximately sixty cardiac compressions a minute.

Other Considerations

The victim should be checked at approximately one- to two-minute intervals to determine whether spontaneous cardiac function has returned. After the victim has responded to resuscitation, he must be watched closely in case a relapse occurs. A prolonged period of unconsciousness usually follows even though he is breathing on his own. *The airway must be kept open.* If the victim is vomiting, he should be placed with his head lower than his chest and turned to the side. Shock must be anticipated and treated appropriately. Evacuation should be carried out as soon as possible.

One of the most difficult questions concerning resuscitation is when to give up. The final decision in every case must be based on consideration of the circumstances in which the accident has occurred, the extent of the victim's injuries, the treatment required and administered, the persons available for care of the victim, and the possibility of obtaining medical assistance within a short time. Artificial respiration should be kept up for anyone whose heart is still beating. On the other hand, anyone requiring cardiac massage has a poorer prognosis. If spontaneous heart action has not resumed, and the pupils of his eyes are widely dilated and do not contract when exposed to light after forty-five to sixty minutes of massage, the victim is almost certainly beyond further help.

For a majority of patients, resuscitative efforts fail. Usually the injury or disease is too severe to begin with, or resuscitation is initiated too late. However, the few individuals saved make the efforts expended on others more than just worthwhile.

REFERENCES:

1. Trunkey, D. D.: Assessment and Resuscitation of the Injured Patient (Trauma Rounds), West. J. Med. *121*: 153, 1974.

2. Rush, B. F., Richardson, J. D., Bosomworth, P., and Eiseman, B.: Limitations of Blood Replacement with Electrolyte Solutions, Arch. Surg. *98*: 49, 1969.

3. Oppenheimer, R. P.: Airway . . . Instantly, J.A.M.A. *230*: 76, 1974.

4. National Conference on Cardiopulmonary Resuscitation and Emergency Cardiac Care: Standards for Cardiopulmonary Resuscitation (CPR) and Emergency Cardiac Care (ECC), J.A.M.A. *227*: 833, 1974.

5. Ravin, M.B., and Modell, J. H.: *Introduction to Life Support,* Boston, Little, Brown and Co., 1973.

6. Stephenson, H. E., Jr.: *Cardiac Arrest and Resuscitation, 4th Ed.,* St. Louis, C. V. Mosby Co., 1974.

7. Copplestone, J. F.: The Effectiveness of Respiratory and Cardiac Resuscitation as a First Aid Measure, New Zealand J. Med. *70*: 302, 1969.

CHAPTER 4

Preventive Medicine

IN THE MOUNTAINS, where any accident or illness is often coupled with inaccessibility, the advantages of preventing such mishaps are obvious. Loss of life, permanent disability, the failure of an expedition to reach its goal must be reckoned as a high price to pay for a disability that could be avoided. Blisters can be incapacitating; frostbite may be more so; tetanus would usually be catastrophic. All can be prevented.

This chapter is limited to a discussion of protection from infectious or "communicable" diseases, encompassing immunizations, safe food and water supplies, and camp sanitation. These precautions are of obvious importance to the expeditionary mountaineer whose exposure to unusual, potentially disabling infections frequently represents the greatest single hazard in traveling to and from the mountains. The hidden hazards in many foreign cities, even in the "best" hotels, and the almost total lack of sanitary measures in areas traversed during the approach march make extensive precautions essential. However, many aspects of preventive medicine are important for mountaineering in countries where sanitary practices are reputedly more sophisticated.

IMMUNIZATIONS

The potential seriousness of any illness afflicting a member of an expedition requires that all methods of prevention be utilized. Some immunizations do not confer total immunity — typhoid fever or cholera immunization, for example — but all can decrease the likelihood of infection and lessen the severity of the disease should infection occur. For expeditions it is only logical that all members obtain immunization against all diseases likely to be encountered and for which such protection is available. (The basic principles of immunization are discussed under "Allergies.")

When traveling overseas, immunizations must be recorded on an International Certificate of Vaccination. In addition to the routine innoculations which should be obtained by everyone, travel in various parts of the world may

53

require other specific innoculations. As vaccines are improved and more experience is gained with their use, the number and size of the injections recommended for immunization changes. The U.S. Department of Health annually publishes a bulletin describing which vaccines are advisable for travel in any specific area and the latest techniques for obtaining optimum immunization. In general, if a primary series of immunizations has ever been obtained only a booster dose is required to update any particular immunization. Live virus vaccines (polio, smallpox, yellow fever) should either be given one month apart, *or* on the same day to avoid interference between the vaccine viruses.

Smallpox

At the present time smallpox vaccination is no longer required by the United States for entry into the country after travel abroad. Smallpox in the Western Hemisphere has been virtually eliminated by a vigorous vaccination campaign. However, smallpox is not uncommon in a few countries including India, Nepal, Pakistan, Bangladesh, Sudan, and Ethiopia. Travelers to those countries should be revaccinated within six months of departure regardless of the date of the last previous immunization. The site of innoculation must be observed to determine that there is a positive "take" (vesicle or blister) or a "major" or "accelerated reaction." If an "immune" or "equivocal" response occurs, vaccination should be repeated with another lot of vaccine to ensure the original vaccine was not impotent.

Tetanus

The organisms producing tetanus are widespread and infection can result from trivial wounds. The lack of effective treatment and the complete success of prevention by immunization leaves no excuse for inadequate protection against this disease. The initial series of innoculations for tetanus immunization is two injections four to eight weeks apart. A third innoculation should be obtained six to twelve months later. A booster should be obtained at least every ten years thereafter. If a booster injection has not been received within the past five years, repeat innoculation within a month of departure for overseas area and following a contaminated wound is advisable.

Diphtheria

Most adults have been immunized against diphtheria in childhood. A positive Shick skin test indicates loss of immunity and denotes the need for a booster of diphtheria toxoid. However, adult dosage requirements are less than those of children. A combined tetanus-diphtheria toxoid is available for adult use.

Poliomyelitis

Poliomyelitis is now essentially completely preventable by immunization. Trivalent oral poliomyelitis vaccine is effective for carriers of the organism as well as for nonimmune individuals and provides much longer effective immunity. Therefore oral vaccine immunization should be obtained even though prior Salk immunization has been carried out. A booster dose should be taken in preparation for an overseas trip.

Typhoid

Initial typhoid immunization is achieved by two injections four weeks apart. A booster suffices within three years of initial immunization, although yearly inoculation is desirable in areas where the disease is known to be present. Typhoid immunization is estimated to be only about seventy percent effective in preventing typhoid infection, but does significantly reduce the severity of infections which do occur.

Hepatitis

Hepatitis may appear as scattered cases or in epidemics. The causative virus is usually transmitted through fecal contamination of water supplies. No active immunization is available, but partial passive immunity may be achieved for a period of up to six months by injections of immune globulin. For expedition approach marches, injections should be given immediately prior to the first anticipated exposure and should be repeated four to six months later if the danger of infection still exists.

Yellow Fever

Yellow fever has never occurred in Asia and its introduction there would result in disastrous widespread epidemics. For that reason yellow fever immunization is required for travel in many Asian countries. This infection is endemic in many parts of Africa and South America, and immunization should be obtained before travel in these areas. A single innoculation provides effective immunization; repeat injections should be obtained every ten years. Injections must be obtained from a World Health Organization designated Yellow Fever Vaccination Center.

Cholera

Cholera immunization is required for travel in some countries in Asia, the Middle East, and Africa even though only about sixty to eighty percent immunity for a period of about six months is provided. Protection is maximal when injections are obtained shortly before departure for the endemic area. The initial innoculation should be followed by a second injection one month later. Boosters must be obtained every six months.

Plague

The effectiveness of immunization for plague is questionable. Generally this innoculation is only required for travel to areas of known plague activity such as Southeast Asia. The initial injection is followed in four weeks by a second injection, with a third injection four to twelve weeks after the second. Boosters should be obtained every three months as long as a significant danger of plague is present.

Typhus

Typhus exists in certain parts of Asia, Africa, and South America. Immunization for typhus requires an initial course of two injections of vaccine four weeks apart. A booster should be obtained every six to twelve months in the presence of the disease.

Rabies

The possibility of being bitten by a rabid animal, although remote, does exist, having been reported as an additional hazard to mountain wandering in countries such as Afghanistan. Routine vaccination of animals for rabies, although a general practice throughout the United States, is not carried out in the undeveloped countries. A duck embryo dried killed virus vaccine has been developed which can provide immunity and is also of value if administered immediately following exposure. (See "Animal Bites.") Several injections are required over a period of months, so immunization must be started early. Not everyone develops an adequate antibody response following rabies immunization, so an antibody titer determination must be obtained after the course of injections is completed.

Influenza

Polyvalent influenza vaccine given in two injections one to four weeks apart provides at least partial protection against some strains of influenza virus. Influenza immunization is not recommended for individuals under sixty-five who are in good health. However, members of an expedition, particularly to an area known to be having a high incidence of influenza, may be well advised to obtain this immunization also.

WATER

Potable water — that which is fit to drink — is not only free of bacteria and other infectious organisms, but is also reasonably clear of sediment and mineral or chemical impurities. Water obtained downstream from habitation must always be regarded as unsafe, even in areas where modern sanitation methods are practiced. Recent studies have demonstrated that almost all streams and rivers in the United States are polluted. Some high mountain streams and lakes in the western United States have been enriched with a diarrheal-causing parasite, *Giardia lamblia.*

Sterilization may be achieved by boiling, chemical treatment, or ultra-filtration; removal of sediment can be accomplished by settling or, more effectively, by filtration.

A purification technique for mountaineering parties must utilize materials which are reasonably compact and lightweight, operate efficiently, and are simple to use. During approach marches through hot terrain, water requirements may be very great (four to six quarts a day per person) and the contamination of water sources quite heavy. In such conditions, a method for supplying clean, safe, palatable water is essential for the welfare of the party.

Boiling

Simply bringing water to a boil destroys the vast majority of infectious organisms. Boiling water for twenty minutes kills all infectious organisms, including the cysts of *Endamoeba histolytica,* which are relatively resistant to destruction and may be common in some locations. Boiling is the most reliable means of destroying the viruses that cause hepatitis.

Chemical Purification

Water can be chemically purified by the addition of chlorine or iodine. Halazone (p-dichlorosulfamoyl benzoic acid) has been widely used as a source of chlorine for water purification. However, chlorine is inactivated by organic material in the water, and its action is reduced if the water is at all alkaline. Halazone is relatively slow to dissolve, and loses its potency when stored for periods of six months or longer. A brief exposure to temperatures in the range of 105° to 120°F, as may occur in a car parked in the sun, reduces potency by fifty percent. Exposure to air for two days reduces activity by seventy-five percent.

Iodine is more effective than chlorine as a water sterilizing agent. It is not inactivated by organic material in the water, is effective in cold water, and is effective in both acid and alkaline water. Tetraglycine hydroperiodide (Globaline or Potable-Aqua) is a tablet preparation which releases iodine.

Although commercially unavailable for a number of years, these tablets are now available from Wisconsin Pharmacal Company, New Berlin, Wisconsin 53131, or Badger Pharmacal, Inc., Cedarburg, Wisconsin 53012. These tablets lose their effectiveness during storage, although not as rapidly as Halazone. They lose thirty-three percent of their initial activity when exposed to air for four days.

A method of chemical water purification which has been extensively tested in military operations is the use of an iodine solution prepared from crystalline iodine. Four to eight grams of crystal iodine are placed in a one ounce clear glass bottle with a plastic top (an ordinary medicine bottle). The bottle is filled with water, shaken vigorously, and the crystals allowed to settle back to the bottom. 12.5 cc of the supernatant solution (about one-half of the bottle) is added to each quart of water, and the water is allowed to stand for fifteen minutes before consumption. One-half this volume of iodine solution can be used if the water is allowed to stand for forty minutes before it is used. If the water is unusually contaminated, it should be allowed to stand for forty minutes after addition of the full 12.5 cc. This technique has been shown to kill amoebic cysts and viruses with a resistance to disinfection comparable to hepatitis virus.

Only a small amount of the iodine crystals are dissolved each time the small bottle is filled with water. The bottle can be refilled and reused for water disinfection almost 1,000 times before the iodine is depleted. Since purified iodine is the material being used, it cannot lose its effectiveness during storage. USP grade resublimed iodine should be used for this purpose.

A few individuals are allergic to iodine and should not use this method of water purification. Individuals who have been treated for hyperthyroidism should consult their physician before using this purification system. Although iodine is widely known as a poison, in the small quantities used for disinfecting water it is not harmful. No fatality has been reported from the ingestion of less than fifteen grams of iodine, approximately twice the entire amount added to the bottle.

Filtration

Filtration not only provides the most satisfactory means for clearing murky or muddy water, but can also be utilized as a method of sterilization. A filtration system has been used by several major U.S. Himalayan expeditions since 1960. The heart of this system is a Millipore HA filter of 0.45 micron pore size, which is small enough to trap all bacteria and amoebic cysts (but not hepatitis or other viruses). These filters are available in various diameters, and are capable of supplying up to twenty or thirty gallons of water over a two-hour period.

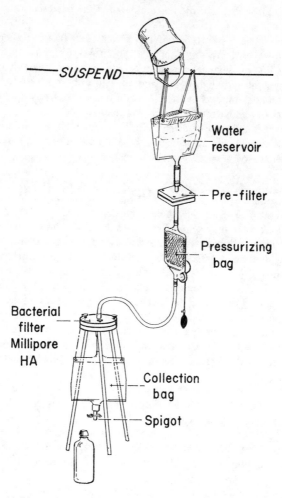

Water reservoir

Pre-filter

Pressurizing bag

Bacterial filter Millipore HA

Collection bag

Spigot

Figure 11. Diagram of the apparatus for purifying water by Millipore filtration.

The Millipore filter, along with a single glass fiber prefilter, is contained in a metal filter holder. The filter holder is sterilized by boiling each evening, then reassembled with sterile filters for the next day's use. To protect the Millipore filter from clogging with sediment, a second filter holder equipped with two glass fiber prefilters is inserted above the bacterial filter. These prefilters can be changed without sterile precautions as often as necessary. Gravity alone usually provides adequate filtration pressure, but flow through the main filter can be increased by pressurization as the pores of the bacterial filter become clogged.

A filtration system of this type provides clean water free of bacterial contaminants. However, it does not remove the viruses which cause hepatitis. Therefore, boiling or chemical treatment is required to eliminate that hazard. The system is sufficiently lightweight and efficient to be practical for expeditions with extended approach marches. In addition, it can be used without the Millipore filter to remove mud or other sediments from the water.

Obviously the final choice of a water supply system must be based on the size of the party, the area being traveled, and the contaminants present in the water from which the party members must be protected.

FOOD

Local food must be regarded with the same degree of skepticism as the water supply, particularly in undeveloped countries. Diseases commonly carried by food include the bacillary dysenteries, amebiasis, and a variety of worm infestations. Individual areas present their own unique problems. In foreign cities and during travel through inhabited countryside, the only food that can be regarded as safe from contamination is that which has been thoroughly cooked *under supervision.* Fruits must be picked above ground level, cleaned, and peeled by the eater. All other foods must be assumed to be dangerous — particularly previously peeled fruits, custards, cakes, bread, cold meats, cheeses, and other dairy products. Milk is a potential source of tuberculosis. Bottled carbonated drinks are generally safe, but any ice which might be added usually is not.

Cleaning and soaking of fresh fruits and vegetables in potassium permanganate solution is popular throughout the Far East; it is unlikely that this process is effective. Thorough cleansing of fresh foods, followed by soaking in a fairly strong chlorine or iodine solution (at least five times or more the concentration used for water purification) is more likely to produce the desired results. Brief scalding of fresh fruits and vegetables also renders them safe for ingestion.

In large cities the food and water in certain hotels may be considered safe. Nevertheless, service may not be as reported or may have subsequently deteriorated. When in doubt, all drinking water should be iodinated. Frequently tap water should not be drunk or even used for brushing teeth.

SANITATION

The basic principle for location of sites for garbage disposal and latrines is best exemplified by the word "down"; downstream, downwind, and downhill. In addition, such facilities should be located as far as possible from streams, regardless of whether the water is to be consumed in the downstream area. However, such considerations must also be balanced against convenience. Placing latrines too far from camp prevents overuse and quickly renders camp uninhabitable. Though the camp can be moved to a new location, this mode of existence poses a definite threat to the health of the entire party, as well as being esthetically unappealing. Expeditions must observe the rudiments of modern hygiene in personal care, camp cleanliness, and garbage and waste disposal if the party is to remain healthy.

Adequate personal hygiene in the field requires little more than the faithful application of daily habits of normal living: washing hands before handling food and before eating, reasonable body and oral cleanliness, and adequate waste disposal. Contact with local inhabitants presents no particular problem if good habits are observed. Almost all of the unique types of infectious disease peculiar to remote or undeveloped areas are transmitted by food, water, or hand-to-mouth contact. The hazards of airborne infection are minimal. (The possibility of tuberculosis should be recognized in persons with such suggestive symptoms as cough, fever, and wasting.)

REFERENCE:

1. Kahn, F. H., and Visscher, B. R.: Water Disinfection in the Wilderness — A Simple, Effective Method of Iodination, West. J. Med. *122*:450, 1975.

CHAPTER 5

General Principles of Care for Traumatic Disorders

TRAUMATIC injuries are the wounds produced by physical forces such as falls, falling objects, avalanches, or the cuts and bruises common in camp life. The wounds resulting from severe falls can be as devastating as those produced by bullets and explosives on the battlefield. Most mountaineering accidents are less severe, but the resulting injuries still require careful attention and proper treatment to avoid permanent disability.

EMERGENCIES

There are relatively few medical emergencies in which a matter of minutes in instituting treatment significantly affects the final outcome. In mountaineering accidents the opportunity to provide such treatment may pass before anyone is able to get to the victim. Nonetheless, a thorough knowledge of the proper methods for handling such emergencies is essential if the rare occasions in which they are encountered are to be dealt with successfully.

Priority

Upon reaching an accident victim several steps must be taken at once to prevent immediate loss of life.

1. Respiration. First, attention must be directed to establishing an open airway and covering any open chest wounds which interfere with breathing. (See "Chest Injuries" and "Special Problems.") Artificial respiration or performance of a tracheostomy should be delayed until after bleeding has been controlled.

2. Bleeding. Second, bleeding must be controlled by direct pressure — not by tourniquets. (See "Soft Tissue Injuries.")
3. Shock. Third, after good respiratory function has been established and bleeding stopped, attention should be directed to treating or preventing shock. With severe injuries treatment for shock should be instituted before the diagnostic signs actually appear. Treatment given in anticipation of shock achieves far better results than treatment instituted after its need becomes obvious. (See "Special Problems.")

DIAGNOSIS AND TREATMENT

After emergencies have received attention, the attendant should pause to review what has been done, obtain an account of the accident, and find out about any pre-existing medical condition which may require treatment. If the attendant is not a member of the party involved, he must learn the time and circumstances of the accident. If the victim was injured in a fall the attendant must determine whether the fall was completely accidental or resulted from a loss of consciousness or some other disorder. Any previous treatment or medication administered to the victim must also be ascertained.

Next, the character and extent of the victim's injuries must be determined. Although some injuries, such as fractures, may have to be cared for first, the victim must be completely and thoroughly examined. Concealed injuries must be carefully sought. A systematic routine should be used so that no areas of the body are overlooked. Although chest injuries are unquestionably more threatening than hand injuries and deserve prior attention, neglect of the hand injury can result in a crippling deformity which leaves the victim permanently handicapped.

"With a complete diagnosis, and an accurate evaluation of the general condition of the patient, the battle is half won. Many errors in care are due to incomplete diagnosis, to overlooking some serious injury while concentrating on the obvious. A systematic method of examination will obviate such errors."[1]

Examinations must be repeated, not only to watch the condition of the patient, but also to insure that all injuries have been found and treated. If the victim is unconscious at the time of the initial examination, a repeat examination must be performed as soon as he returns to consciousness.

All injuries should be treated as completely as possible before the patient is moved. Open wounds are always contaminated to some extent; further contamination should be avoided. Soft tissue injuries should be covered with a voluminous pressure dressing to provide compression and control bleeding, immobilize the injured area, minimize swelling, and help control infection. Extremities with severe injuries should be put to rest and elevated slightly. A patient with injured legs or feet should be supine with the injured extremity elevated. If evacuation requires the victim to walk or climb, frequent rest stops should be made in which the patient is able to lie down and prop up his feet.

It is particularly important that all fractures be splinted before the victim is moved. "Splint 'em where they lie" is a time-worn and well-proven adage.

The equipment necessary for the treatment of some injuries, such as injuries of the chest, would not be available on most short outings and would probably never be carried on an actual climb. However, this equipment should always be available in popular climbing areas and should be a part of the emergency gear of all mountain rescue organizations. Such treatment as can be given should be administered and more definitive care obtained as soon as possible, either by evacuating the patient or bringing the necessary materials to him.

RECORDS

A complete record of the accident and subsequent events must be written down so there can be no confusion about the victim's injuries or whether his condition is improving or deteriorating. Such records are also needed for accurately administering any treatment, particularly the proper spacing of medications to avoid omitted doses or overdosage. Finally, these records are essential for the physician who is eventually to be responsible for the victim's care.

A detailed account of the accident should be recorded at the earliest opportunity. All injuries should be carefully described. The absence of evidence of injury over major areas of the body — chest, abdomen, head, arms or legs — should also be noted. Any pre-existing medical conditions should be listed. The pulse, respiratory rate, and if possible, blood pressure should be measured and recorded at intervals of every hour or less for at least eight hours after a severe accident and every four hours thereafter. The dosage, route, and time of administration of all medications must be accurately recorded.

The written record should be kept with the patient in an easily accessible place and not tucked away in a pack or similar inconvenient location. Notations of the patient's condition or of any medication must be made immediately and not recorded from memory at a later time.

SPECIFIC ACCIDENTS

Avalanches

Most avalanche victims die as the result of the impact with large blocks of hard, packed snow or ice. A smaller number are suffocated by being buried under loose snow. The following protocol should be followed in caring for avalanche victims immediately after they have been found.

1. Determine whether victim has an obviously fatal injury.
2. If no fatal injuries are present, determine whether victim is breathing.
3. If victim is not breathing:
    a. Examine for fractured cervical spine and splint if present;
    b. Examine for penetrating chest injuries and cover if present;
    c. Institute cardiopulmonary resuscitation.
4. If victim is breathing or after CPR has been started:
    a. Examine for major open wounds and treat appropriately;
    b. Examine for fractures and splint as needed;
    c. Treat for shock;
    d. Treat for exposure.

Lightning

Lightning causes several different types of injury. Fatalities are usually the result of disruption of the electrical activity of the brain and the heart. Electrical alterations of the cerebral respiratory center can result in a cessation of respiration. Electrical changes in the heart can cause that organ to stop beating. Cardiopulmonary resuscitation should be started immediately. Prompt treatment can revive many lightning victims. (Approximately 150 to 300 persons die from lightning injury every year in the United States; many more are struck but do not die.)

Lightning may also cause burns which need to be treated just like burns from any other source. Intense blood vessel constriction can result from electrical stimulation of the nerves supplying those vessels. No definitive treatment for this condition can be given in the field, but the problem usually clears without treatment.

EVACUATION

Evacuation should be carried out rapidly, but not at the expense of providing essential care for the accident victim. Unless the environment is threatening due to the danger of avalanche, rock fall, or exposure to severe weather conditions, the patient should not be moved until initial treatment of all injuries has been completed. This initial treatment should include the establishment of an open airway with good respiration, control of bleeding and bandaging of all open wounds, splinting of fractures, and treatment for shock and hypothermia.

An effective mountain rescue requires about four dozen stretcher bearers and a good stretcher, the basket stretcher being the best available in most climbing areas. In the 1968 Winter Olympics the French army and police used an inflatable stretcher-mattress about half filled with small plastic pellets about the size of BB shot. This type of stretcher tended to mold itself to the shape of the accident victim's body so that he could not be rolled about during evacuation, and also provided some insulation from the cold. In any case, there can be little justification under almost any circumstances for rolling an accident victim with fractures of the legs, pelvis, back, or neck onto a makeshift stretcher and bouncing him along over a rough descent simply because a rigid support, such as a basket stretcher or a broad plank — and enough people to carry it — are not immediately available.

If bad weather makes evacuation urgent, it is rarely necessary to carry the victim farther than the tree line before seeking assistance to complete the evacuation in a proper manner. It may be easier and the final outcome better if sleeping bags, down filled clothing, and tents are obtained and carried to the victim rather than attempting to move him with inadequate personnel and equipment.

The four dozen stretcher bearers are essential too. Carrying an injured climber over rugged terrain is usually extremely difficult. Fewer than six individuals usually cannot handle a basket stretcher containing an adult male very smoothly. Even then, the six stretcher bearers tire rapidly and must usually be replaced every few hundred yards.

After treatment of the accident victim has been completed, the next step usually is deciding whom to send for help. If the party is small and has signed out with a Park Ranger or similar official, the wisest course may be to wait until search efforts locate the entire party. In wooded areas a fire may be built to attract the attention of fire wardens as well as provide warmth and comfort. Since at least one person should stay with the injured climber at all times, it is obvious that small parties should always register before a climb.

If the party contains more than a minimum number of people, some sort of organization should be established. The most experienced and knowledgeable individuals should be assigned positions of leadership. Party members with the greatest knowledge of medical care should stay with the accident victim or victims. The members who are the strongest climbers or hikers should go for help. Other members of the group should help with setting up a camp or carrying out any other necessary activities.

The rules for safe mountaineering are the same after an accident as before. There can be no justification for further injuries or loss of life as the result of ignoring these rules simply because one accident has already occurred. One person should not go for help alone over terrain — such as a snow covered glacier — that he would not cross by himself under normal circumstances. The recent death of one climber from hypothermia while attempting to go for help, and the subsequent rescue by a search party of the accident victim and a third uninjured climber who remained with him, point out the fundamental soundness of this philosophy.

Helicopters

The use of helicopters for mountain rescues has reduced the number of stretcher bearers needed from four dozen to about one-half dozen. Most of these can be brought in by the helicopter, along with a stretcher and any medical supplies which are needed. The helicopter also has greatly reduced the amount of time required to get the victim to a hospital or other source of definitive medical care.

The use of helicopters does require some knowledge of their capabilities and limitations. Although helicopter landings have been made at altitudes as high as 14,000 feet, most helicopters cannot land safely at altitudes much higher than 8,000 to 10,000 feet. The maximum altitude at which a helicopter can operate is determined by air density. In the morning or on a cold day the air is more dense and helicopters can operate at higher altitudes. Conversely, high air temperatures can greatly reduce the altitude at which a helicopter can safely land or take off.

Helicopters usually cannot make absolutely vertical ascents or descents. Some space for an approach and departure is needed. The most level spot which is free of surrounding obstructions, particularly electrical or telephone wires which are quite difficult to see from the air, should be selected. The wind direction should be indicated to the helicopter pilot, preferably by smoke or clothing such as a T-shirt which also indicates the wind speed.

Individuals working around the helicopter must know something of the hazards such machines present. The downward thrust from the main rotors can produce winds ranging from sixty to 120 miles per hour. Obviously a person helping to guide a helicopter to a landing should not be standing on the edge of a sheer cliff or similar drop-off.

Eyes must be protected from flying dirt and other materials. Personal equipment must be stored where it is not blown away. Strong rotor winds can tumble full packs over the ground and over a cliff or into a crevasse. Burning embers from fires can be blown about, possibly causing injuries to climbers or starting fires in the surrounding brush or forests.

The danger from the tail and main rotors would seem to be quite obvious, but a surprising number of people walk into spinning rotors every year. While the helicopter is on the ground the main rotors may be higher than a person's head, but a sudden gust of wind or slowing of their speed can bend them downward to an amazing extent; no one should stand beneath the tips of these rotors. Personnel should approach the helicopter in a crouched position, preferably from the front where the pilot can see them.

REFERENCE:

1. Committee on Trauma, American College of Surgeons, Michael L. Mason, M.D., Chairman, *Early Care of Acute Soft Tissue Injuries,* Chicago, Ill., 1957. (Quoted by permission of the publishers.)

CHAPTER 6

Soft Tissue Injuries

As GENERALLY used, the term "soft tissue" includes all of the body tissues except the bones and the specialized organs of the head and trunk. From the standpoint of traumatic injuries, the most important of these tissues are the skin and its underlying layer of fatty tissue, the muscles, and the blood vessels and nerves.

The treatment of soft tissue injuries has three objectives. First, and most urgent, is the control of bleeding. Second is the control of infection. Third is the promotion of healing, with its corollary, the preservation of function in the injured part.

CONTROL OF BLEEDING

The amount of bleeding from a wound depends upon the size, number, and type of blood vessels which have been severed. Arterial blood is under high pressure — approximately two pounds per square inch — which causes profuse bleeding following damage to an artery of significant size. The pressure in veins is only about one-twentieth that in the arteries and venous bleeding is much less severe. Blood spurts from the end of a severed artery in rhythm with the heart beat, a feature of arterial injury which can be easily recognized. This sign should be identified because a large amount of blood can be lost in a short time from arterial bleeding. Other methods of distinguishing between arterial and venous bleeding, such as attempting to recognize the difference in color, are unreliable.

Pressure is the only effective means of controlling bleeding. The severed vessels must be collapsed, obstructing the flow of blood and permitting clots to form. Venous bleeding is easily controlled because the walls of veins are easily collapsed and the clots which occlude the vessels are rarely forced out when the external pressure is released. The thicker walls of arteries make them more difficult to compress and the higher blood pressure tends to dislodge clots which are formed.

The pressure used to control bleeding should be applied directly over the wound. "Pressure points are not worth considering." [1] Bleeding from most wounds can be controlled by placing several sterile compresses directly over the bleeding points and pressing down firmly. About four to six minutes should suffice for the bleeding to be stopped completely.

In those cases where severe bleeding persists (after direct pressure has been tried at least three or four times) the wound should be packed with sterile gauze and wrapped tightly with a continuous bandage. Although this bandage should be tighter than an ordinary compression dressing, it must not obstruct circulation to the rest of the limb. Absence of pulses beyond the bandage, bluish discoloration of the nails and skin, tingling sensations, or pain in the extremity are all signs that the bandage is too tight. The entire extremity beyond the site of the wound should also be wrapped with an elastic bandage to reduce swelling and prevent damage to the previously uninjured tissues. After one or two days — with frequent, careful checking of the circulation to the remainder of the limb during the interval — this pressure bandage can be removed and replaced by a smaller dressing.

Even after bleeding is controlled movement may cause hemorrhage to start again. This recurrent bleeding is almost always less severe than that which followed the original injury and can be more easily controlled. However, an accident victim who has already lost a large amount of blood can ill afford the loss of any more. Therefore, a delay of one or two days before evacuating the victim may be desirable if severe bleeding recurs with movement. After this time fibrous tissue will have started to grow into the clots, tending to anchor them in place and thus preventing further hemorrhage. The desirability of waiting, however, must be weighed against the need for obtaining medical treatment for other injuries. If immediate evacuation is advisable, an extremity can be immobilized with a splint similar to those used for fractures.

Tourniquets are almost never necessary or even justifiable. A tourniquet inevitably cuts off the entire blood supply to the remainder of the limb, resulting in damage to all of the tissues. This damage can progress to total gangrene if the tourniquet is allowed to remain in place for too long (such as the time usually necessary to evacuate an injured climber). Tourniquets may occlude venous blood flow without totally occluding arterial outflow, resulting in more profuse bleeding than would occur with no tourniquet. Furthermore, tourniquets are rarely applied properly; permanent damage to the nerves and other structures at the site of constriction is a common result.

The only occasions when a tourniquet might be beneficial are those unusual instances in which bleeding cannot be controlled by any other method or in which no tissue is present to be damaged. An injured climber with no one to assist him might use a tourniquet on himself if he felt that he was about to lose consciousness and thus be unable to control bleeding. Similarly, if a portion of a limb is traumatically amputated, no harm would result from the use of a tourniquet immediately above the amputation site because there would be no tissues beyond that point which could be damaged. However, the tourniquet must be placed just above the point of amputation.

The tourniquet, if it must be used, should be properly applied. A large, broad piece of fabric such as a large handkerchief, a triangular bandage, or a towel should be wrapped once around the limb and tied with a single overhand knot. A short stick or similar object should be placed on top of this knot and held in place by a square knot tied in the ends of the fabric. Then the stick should be twisted until the bleeding stops — but no more — and tied or held with a strip of adhesive tape to prevent unwinding. Once a tourniquet is applied it should be left in place until the patient is in the hands of a physician.

"There are undoubtedly more deaths and loss of limbs from the use of a tourniquet than from failing to use one." [1]

CONTROL OF INFECTION

Wound infection is essentially the result of contamination, and all open wounds are contaminated to some extent. Bacteria are introduced into the wound by the object producing the injury, by dirt and other foreign material after the injury, and by the skin and clothing of the victim. Infection can also come from the fingers or instruments of the person caring for the wound. Therefore, prevention is as important as treatment in the control of infection.

Prevention

The person caring for the victim of a fresh soft tissue injury should scrub his hands vigorously, preferably with an antibacterial soap or detergent such as pHisoHex. Sterile gloves, if available, should be put on after the hands have been scrubbed. Next, the wound should be cleaned as thoroughly as possible. All fragments of dirt or foreign material should be removed with sterile forceps. Then a piece of sterile gauze should be placed over the wound while the surrounding skin, right up to the edge of the wound, is thoroughly scrubbed with a white soap, or an antibacterial soap or detergent. Next the wound itself should be rinsed, but not scrubbed, with water or saline solution. Rinsing must be thorough to ensure fragments of dead tissue, hidden dirt and debris, and — to a certain extent — bacteria are removed. With puncture wounds bleeding should be encouraged to help remove bacteria and debris. In the depths of such wounds, which are not reached by air, the bacteria which cause tetanus and gas gangrene can thrive and produce their disastrous effects.

If a wound is thoroughly washed, the value of antiseptics is questionable; if cleansing is neglected they certainly have no value. However, the use of an antiseptic is prudent, particularly with grossly contaminated wounds or animal bites. The only agent currently available which meets most of the qualifications desirable in an antiseptic for use in the care of soft tissue wounds is an aqueous solution of benzalkonium chloride (Zephiran). Zephiran is a detergent which kills bacteria without causing damage to the tissues and can be used directly in the wound. Therefore, wounds should be rather generously rinsed with this solution after they have been washed with soap and water.

The more common antiseptics, such as mercurial preparations or iodine, cannot be placed directly in a wound because they injure the tissues as well as destroying bacteria. Since all the bacteria are not killed, those that remain find the injured tissues an ideal medium in which to grow. These antiseptics do not damage the intact skin and are ideal for sterilizing the skin prior to a procedure in which the skin surface is to be opened (such as an injection). However, there is little place for such agents in the treatment of an open wound.

Soft tissue wounds never have to be closed. The primary objectives in suturing a wound are to hasten recovery and avoid formation of a scar. However, the damage done by an infection in a closed wound greatly prolongs recovery and leads to far greater scarring and deformity. Although an unsutured wound may heal more slowly, the difference is usually insignificant. Any scars which form are usually small and can easily be removed by plastic surgery if they are bothersome.

If a wound is left open the purulent material exuding from infected areas drains out onto the dressings and is discarded when the dressings are changed. This purulent material cannot escape from a closed wound. Since the skin is too tough to be penetrated, the exudate is extruded into the surrounding tissues, carrying the infection with it. The newly infected areas produce more exudate which, if the chain reaction is not interrupted, eventually invades blood vessels and spreads the infection to other parts of the body. As the infection spreads, much of the involved tissue is destroyed and is later replaced with nonfunctioning scar tissue.

If there is no infection and the edges tend to fall together, the wound is rapidly sealed by a coagulum of serum, the edges are usually closely approximated, and healing takes place with a minimum of scarring and deformity. If desired, minor injuries which appear to present no danger of infection may be closed with tape which has been sterilized by flaming, or with "butterflies." Such devices can easily be removed and the wound opened and drained should infection develop.

The danger of introducing infection, and the far greater destruction of tissue which results from infection in a wound which has been sutured, far outweigh any benefit which might be obtained by early closure.

Diagnosis

If preventive measures are unsuccessful and wound infection occurs, careful attention is required to detect the infection in time to avoid further destruction of tissue and possibly endangering the life of the patient. In order to observe the condition of the wound the dressing over any wound except a burn should be changed daily until healing is obviously underway. The victim must also be watched for signs of a systemic reaction indicating the presence of an infection.

The signs of infection found around the wound itself are primarily the signs of inflammation — pain, swelling, heat, redness, and limitation of motion. These signs are present about every wound but are much more severe in the presence of infection.

Pain is a subjective complaint and the response to pain varies greatly among individuals. Therefore, complaints of pain sometimes are difficult to evaluate. However, pain from soft tissue injuries usually begins to subside by the second or third day after injury. The persistence of severe pain beyond this period or an increase in the pain is suggestive of infection.

Redness is usually confined to a thin margin right around the wound. In infected wounds this discoloration is much more extensive. In some cases red streaks extend upwards along the limb from the site of injury, indicating that the infection has started to spread. (Although strictly speaking this is not "blood poisoning," it is one of the signs of infection to which that label is sometimes applied.)

In the presence of infection, swelling about a wound can be quite striking, even turning out the edges of the wound. The temperature of the skin immediately adjacent to any wound is usually increased, but with infection the increase is much more noticeable and covers a considerably larger area. Swelling and pain combine to cause limitation of voluntary and involuntary motion of the involved limb which is more noticeable in the presence of infection.

The systemic signs characteristic of generalized infections are also present with localized infections. An oral temperature of 100° to 101°F can be expected for one or two days after a severe injury. Fever higher than this or persisting for a longer time is suggestive of infection.

Located at various spots throughout the body are accumulations of tissue known as lymph nodes. Small vessels similar to blood vessels, called lymphatics, carry bacteria and the products of tissue destruction from a site of infection to the nearest collection of lymph nodes. Here the bacteria and other materials are trapped and destroyed. In the process the involved nodes become enlarged and tender. Since there is some tissue destruction in any injury the regional lymph nodes may be slightly enlarged with an uninfected wound. Following the onset of infection, however, the nodes become much more enlarged and tender. Furthermore, in the presence of infection more than one set of nodes is frequently found to be enlarged.

The diagnosis of a wound infection is confirmed by the finding of a purulent discharge — "pus" — in the wound or on the dressings. The discharge may be cream colored, green, or even pink or reddish in color, depending upon the

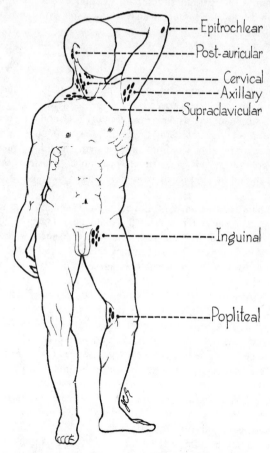

Figure 12. Location of the major collections of lymph nodes.

infecting organism. Occasionally the discharge may be clear and straw colored. A foul odor is usually present. An infected wound rarely may produce only a very scanty or no discharge, so an impression that the wound is infected is not necessarily wrong just because purulent drainage is absent.

The skin at the surface of an infected wound is sometimes sealed by coagulated serum. In these cases the exudate from the infection collects below the seal and does not appear on the dressings. If signs of infection are present, the edges of the wound should be spread apart and the wound probed with a pair of sterile forceps. If pus is present, it usually pours out when the wound is opened. If no infection is present no harm will have been done except producing pain. Although undesirable, this discomfort is a small price to pay when compared with the damage which could result from an undiscovered infection.

Treatment

The treatment for a wound infection consists of drainage and antibiotic therapy. Drainage should be carried out by opening and probing the wound with a pair of sterile forceps as described above. Care should be taken that all pockets of infection are entered and drained. If one is found, others should be sought. Gauze, preferably vaseline impregnated, should be placed in the wound to keep it open. This gauze should be changed whenever the wound is dressed, and should be kept in the wound as long as there is any evidence of infection.

Infected wounds, particularly on the extremities, benefit from the application of moist heat. The outer layer of the bandage — that which is soiled — should be removed and the injured extremity immersed in water which has been sterilized by boiling and cooled until it can be tolerated without discomfort. Alternately, warm, moist, sterile bandages can be placed directly on the wound. Moist heat should be applied three to four times a day for twenty to thirty minutes. Afterwards, the old dressing should be removed, the skin dried, and a fresh dressing applied. The wound must be covered with dry materials to avoid maceration of the skin from continuous dampness. Moisture softens the coagulum which tends to form in the wound and permits more thorough drainage. The heat causes the blood vessels in the area to dilate and promotes healing and eradication of the infection. Once the infection has disappeared and healing is underway, soaking should be discontinued.

The bandage on a draining wound should be changed as frequently as necessary to keep the skin around the wound dry. The skin can be cleansed with alcohol-soaked sponges during dressing changes.

Antibiotics should be administered for major wounds and badly contaminated wounds with a high risk of infection before signs of infection appear. Wounds which do not produce significant disability should not be treated with prophylactic antibiotics, since the risk of developing an allergy to the medications or other side effects is so high and such therapy is almost never needed. After an infection is established, antibiotic therapy is necessary.

If antibiotics are administered they should be given in large dosages and for at least six to eight days to prevent the emergence of infectious bacterial strains which are resistant to the antibiotics. If the patient is not allergic to penicillin, he should be given a penicillinase-resistant penicillin. In addition he can be treated with a cephalosporin. Therapy should be continued for two or three days after wound healing is clearly underway or all signs of wound infection have disappeared.

BANDAGING

A bandage should perform several functions: covering and protecting the wound to aid in the control of infection, providing compression to help control bleeding and swelling, and immobilizing the injured area to reduce pain and promote healing.

Antisepsis

The dressings covering a wound must be sterile to prevent infection or, if infection has occurred, to limit it to the organisms already present. A clean, but not necessarily sterile, bandage is placed over the dressings to keep them dry and prevent them from being soiled. Water or perspiration seeping into the wound from the outside inevitably carries in bacteria.

Dressings on infected wounds absorb the discharge resulting from the infection. Enough sterile gauze should be placed over the wound to prevent this discharge from reaching the surface of the bandage and contaminating the clothing or other wounds.

Dressings which are contaiminated by purulent drainage must be handled with forceps or similar instruments which can be sterilized. Such dressings should never be touched with the fingers, and should be disposed of by burning. If more than one wound or more than one accident victim is to be cared for, the infected wounds should be put off until last. The attendant must scrub his hands thoroughly after dressing each wound to prevent the spread of infection between wounds or individuals.

Compression

For the first three to four days after injury all major wounds should be covered with a compression bandage to control bleeding and swelling and to provide immobilization. A number of gauze pads should be unfolded, crumpled, and placed over the dressing which covers the wound. Then the dressings and crumpled gauze should be wrapped with a continuous bandage which applies moderate pressure over the wound. The bandage should be snug but not tight — not nearly as tight as the type of bandage used to control hemorrhage. Only gentle compression is desired; there must be no constriction if the wound is on an extremity.

Splinting

Splinting of soft tissue wounds is best accomplished by the application of a compression dressing. Injured hands should be splinted in the position of function.

Protection

Enough dressings must be included in the bandage to protect the wound from further trauma — either striking against some object or simply being irritated by clothing. The bandage also must be secured so that it does not become dislodged.

Bandaging Materials

Lacerations may be covered by one of the plastic dressing materials such as "Telfa" which do not stick to the wound and are therefore much less unpleasant to remove. Abrasions, puncture wounds, some avulsions, and all infected wounds require gauze which has been impregnated with petroleum jelly to prevent it from adhering to the wound surface. With all wounds, sterile gauze pads four inches square should be placed over the initial layer to absorb any drainage and provide cushioning.

For bandaging, materials such as "Kling" which have a certain amount of elasticity are much more satisfactory than plain gauze rolls. Elastic materials are easier to use, stay in place better, and exert a modest pressure on the wound. A two- or three-inch elastic bandage can be used for this purpose and offers the advantage of serving a number of other useful purposes as well.

If there is a chance of the wound being wet, it can be covered with waterproof tape. Otherwise waterproof tape should not be used since perspiration accumulates underneath, tending to macerate the skin and also causing the tape to come loose.

The skin on which tape is to be placed should first be swabbed with tincture of benzoin. During subsequent dressing changes the tape should not be removed. If the tape is clipped off at the edge of the dressing and the new layer of tape placed on top of the old, the skin irritation associated with repeatedly stripping off the tape can be avoided.

SPECIAL INJURIES

Lacerations

Lacerations, which are produced by cutting or tearing injuries, may be clean and straight, like an incision, or ragged and irregular. These wounds should be treated for bleeding and infection as previously described. Small tags of skin or other tissue in ragged lacerations should be snipped off with sterile scissors. Removal of these fragments causes little pain or bleeding and helps prevent infection.

A severe laceration may damage blood vessels, nerves, or tendons as well as the skin. Any attempt to repair these structures in the field would almost inevitably lead to further damage and increase the danger of severe infection. The wound should be bandaged as usual, the patient evacuated, and restoration of the damaged structures left to surgery at a later date.

Puncture Wounds

Puncture wounds which have only a small external opening may extend deeply into the underlying tissue. Deeper structures may be damaged and infection can develop in the depths of the wound. Bleeding should be encouraged in order to wash out any foreign material and debris. A small piece of gauze should be inserted in the opening of the wound to prevent it from being sealed and to permit the exudate from infected areas to drain to the outside. In remote areas where evacuation requires several days or more, antibiotic therapy may be desirable. Foreign bodies may be removed from the wound if they are superficially located and extraction does not require probing; otherwise foreign bodies should be left in place to be removed later.

The greatest danger from puncture wounds is tetanus. The organisms which produce this disease grow in wounds where they are not reached by air. However, the disastrous effect of tetanus can be prevented by prior innoculations with tetanus toxoid. Such innoculations should be obtained every five to ten years, but particularly before a major expedition to a remote area.

Abrasions

Abrasions are produced by forceful contact with a rough surface and although usually superficial, can extend quite deeply and produce serious damage. Since abrasions rarely produce severe bleeding, the main objectives of treatment are to prevent infection and to promote healing. All large fragments of foreign material should be removed from the wound with sterile forceps. However, the removal of numerous small embedded particles usually aggravates the injury and should not be attempted. Most foreign material is extruded during healing. The rest, if bothersome, should be removed under more propitious circumstances.

The wound should be covered with a single layer of sterile gauze impregnated with petroleum jelly. Then a bandage with several layers of sterile gauze should be applied to absorb the exudate always produced by such open wounds. During subsequent dressing changes the petroleum gauze should not be removed unless it spontaneously separates from the surface of the wound. Crusts which form should be left in place unless infection supervenes, in which case they should be removed to permit drainage.

Infection can be recognized in abrasions by the copious, purulent exudate. This type of exudate is easily distinguished from the scanty, watery exudate normally produced by such wounds. The exudate associated with infection usually floats the petroleum gauze off the wound. If infection occurs, the petroleum gauze should be replaced with a fresh layer and the wound bandaged with a thick dressing.

Avulsions

Avulsions are wounds in which tissues are pulled or torn away. The loss most commonly involves only a small area of skin with a little of the subcutaneous tissue. Frequently the skin is not severed along one side, creating a tissue flap. In contrast the most severe injury of this type is a traumatic amputation in which a limb is completely severed.

Avulsions in which the tissue is completely lost should be treated in the same manner as an abrasion. (There is no sharp dividing line between a superficial avulsion and a deep abrasion.) However, wounds in which the full thickness of the skin is lost do not heal without skin grafting. Obviously the victims of such injuries must be evacuated to a hospital.

If a flap of skin remains, it should be thoroughly cleaned and replaced in its original position. The wound should be bandaged with a bulky compression dressing and the entire limb should be splinted. This flap of skin is, in effect, a skin graft. In the absence of infection the injured area may heal without further difficulty.

Any muscle or fatty tissue adherent to the bottom of the flap usually dies following the injury and should be trimmed from the skin flap if possible. If the fragment of adherent tissue is large, the base of the wound should be covered with petroleum impregnated gauze, and the flap with the attached fat or muscle replaced. Then the injury should be bandaged with a compression dressing, and the victim rapidly evacuated.

If all of a skin flap does not survive, either as a result of infection, movement, inadequate blood supply, or other factors, the nonliving portion of the flap turns black after seven to ten days. This black tissue may be trimmed away with sterile scissors. (If bleeding is encountered the tissue is still alive and may be saved.) In the event of death of all or a large part of the flap the victim must be evacuated.

For major injuries antibiotic therapy should be started at once. Infection can be minimized in wounds with skin flaps remaining, thus promoting healing without grafting. Although wounds in which the tissue is totally lost are almost certain to eventually become infected, damage by the infection can be minimized.

Contusions

Contusions or bruises are injuries in which the tissues are crushed, producing bleeding into the damaged areas. Usually the subcutaneous tissue and muscle are injured and there is no break in the overlying skin.

The ideal treatment for a severe contusion is immediate rest for the injured area until bleeding has ceased. However, such treatment may be impractical in some mountaineering circumstances. Cessation of bleeding requires six to eight hours. After that much time has elapsed, the injured muscles may be so stiff and painful that the victim is unable to walk, even though he had not been particularly disabled immediately following the injury. Therefore the recipient of a severe contusion should make every effort to get out of a remote area without stopping to rest for more than a few minutes, unless he has adequate supplies to tide him over for a period of three to four days. The alternate prospects are either being stranded for this time or being carried out by his companions.

If circumstances do not require immediate evacuation, the area of injury should be elevated and put to rest. If extensive or progressive swelling develops, a pressure dressing can be applied. The dressing should encompass the entire limb, from the finger tips or toes to well above the area of the injury, but must not occlude the circulation. After twelve to eighteen hours, movement of the injured area may be resumed, if tolerated, in order to speed resorption of the blood. Heat in the form of hot packs, heated and padded stones, or a hot water bottle may help to accelerate blood resorption and to relieve some of the discomfort.

Cold applications — snow, ice, or wet clothes — to a contusion immediately after injury may have some benefit. Cold applications do have a tendency to reduce the pain, and also cause the blood vessels in the area to constrict, reducing the hemorrhage into the tissues. Care must be exercised to avoid cold injury (frostbite), particularly on the extremities. Also cold application may hasten the appearance of disabling pain and stiffness with severe contusions and its use must be tempered by consideration of the circumstances in which injury has occurred and the need for rapid evacuation.

Stiffness persisting for more than two weeks in a muscle which has been severely bruised may herald the onset of calcium deposition in the injured tissues. This process continues until the entire clot has been transformed into bone — about twelve to eighteen months. Although such calcium deposits cause little disability, the muscle should be rested as much as possible while the process is active to minimize the extent of calcification. Diagnosis depends upon x-ray demonstration of the calcium deposits.

Wounds of the Hands and Feet

Wounds of the hands or feet are of particular importance because these structures are so anatomically complex. All wounds in these areas must be thoroughly cleansed, but no tissue should be cut away unless it is obviously dead. In bandaging, care must be taken that the fingers or toes are separated by

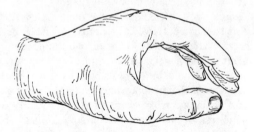

Figure 13. "Position of function" of the hand.

gauze to prevent maceration from the continuous dampness produced by perspiration. A bulky pressure dressing should be applied and the hand should be splinted in the "position of function." Antibiotic therapy should be instituted at the time of injury and evacuation begun immediately, particularly for hand injuries.

Neck Injuries

Neck injuries require special attention because vital blood vessels and respiratory passages are locacted there. The danger from injury to these structures is so great that severe wounds in this location should not be treated in the same manner as soft tissue wounds elsewhere. No effort should be made to wash out the wound, remove foreign bodies, or disturb any blood clots. The wound should be covered with a bandage which does *not* encircle the neck and the victim evacuated immediately. (Superficial wounds which do not involve vital structures do not require special treatment.)

Respiratory obstruction must be avoided by ensuring an open airway. Cervical fractures, head wounds, or chest wounds associated with the injury must receive appropriate attention.

Vascular Injuries

Blood vessel injuries cannot be repaired in the field. However, vascular surgery has recently been developed to the point that many such injuries can be successfully treated if surgery is begun early enough. Time is most important for those injuries in which the remaining blood supply to the rest of the extremity is just barely adequate to permit survival of the limb. A limb with an injury of this kind should be kept lower than the rest of the body so that gravity assists the flow of blood beyond the site of the injury. However, the dependent position also causes fluid to collect in the tissues, producing swelling which tends to prevent blood from reaching the tissues. Therefore, in caring for such

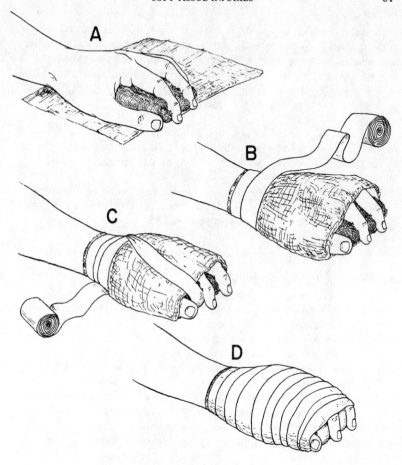

Figure 14. Technique for bandaging the hand in the "position of function."

injuries, the limb must be maintained in the lowest position in which swelling does not occur. A number of adjustments in the position of the limb are usually necessary before the best level is found.

A limb with impaired circulation must be carefully protected from any subsequent injuries. Inadequacy of the blood supply prevents normal healing in such tissues. Furthermore, since any bacteria in the wound would not be destroyed by the body's defenses in the usual manner, the limb could be lost from infection.

Blisters

The most common complaint of inexperienced hikers is blisters, and the most common cause is new or ill-fitting boots. A common mistake is to buy boots that are too loose in the instep which allows the foot to jam forward in the boot going down hill, producing "downhill blisters." Hiking boots should hold the instep securely to prevent the foot from pushing forward. "Uphill blisters" are common over the heel or the tendon at the back of the ankle (Achilles tendon).

Blisters can be avoided by (1) buying properly fitting boots, (2) breaking them in prior to long walks or climbs, (3) putting adhesive tape over areas that blister prior to starting the walk, and (4) wearing a light, thin pair of socks under the heavy wool socks.

Once a blister is formed, further injury to the area should be prevented by covering it with tape, moleskin, or a doughnut of felt. Ruptured blisters should be treated in the same manner as an abrasion. The feet should be kept meticulously clean with soap and water to prevent infection.

Swollen or Tingling Hands

After a day of backpacking the hands may be swollen due to the constant dependent position of the arms. Constricting backpack straps around the shoulders may contribute by obstructing the venous return of blood from the hands. No therapy except reassurance is needed.

Some people with the so-called "thoracic outlet syndrome" develop numbness or tingling along the inner (little finger) side of the hand after backpacking. Such symptoms are caused by pressure of the ribs on the nerves to that part of the hand when the shoulders are thrown back. They are more common after carrying an older type backpack with shoulder straps and no frame than one with which the weight of the pack is carried primarily on the hips. No therapy is needed for such tingling or numbness and no permanent damage results.

REFERENCE:
1. Kennedy, R. H. in Committee on Trauma, American College of Surgeons, *Early Care of Acute Soft Tissue Injuries,* Chicago, 1957. (Quoted by permission of the publishers.)

CHAPTER 7

Fractures and Related Injuries

MOUNTAINEERING accidents usually involve the impact of a body against a solid surface such as rock, snow, or ice when one or both are moving at a considerable speed. It is not surprising that such accidents often injure the rigid framework of the body. The care for fracture victims presents a challenging problem requiring an understanding of the nature and possible after effects of bone injuries if further damage is to be prevented.

Fractures may be *simple,* in which there is a single, clean break, or *comminuted,* in which the bone is shattered into numerous fragments. Most fractures are *closed,* with no break in the overlying skin. If the skin is broken, either by the ends of the broken bone or the object which caused the injury, the fracture is called *open* or *compound.* The two bone ends resulting from a simple fracture may be driven into each other (impacted), resulting in a fracture which is rather stable with little displacement or deformity and little damage to the surrounding tissues. In contrast, some comminuted fractures produce the sensation of handling a structure with no bone at all. Damage to the surrounding tissues is often severe and further injury may occur, even rupture of the skin, during efforts to splint the fracture.

Any bone or joint injury is serious, particularly in mountaineering circumstances. If other vital structures are damaged the results can be disastrous: injuries of the major blood vessels can produce severe hemorrhage or gangrene of the extremity; disruption of the skin can lead to severe bone infections; damage to nerves may result in a paralyzed, useless extremity.

DIAGNOSIS

The cardinal signs of a fracture are:

1. Pain and tenderness
2. Swelling and discoloration
3. Deformity

Pain at the point of the fracture is usually quite severe and is aggravated by any movement or manipulation. The area of injury is typically exquisitely tender. Swelling and discoloration are present around the site of the fracture although both may extend for a considerable distance several days after the fracture. All of these signs, although suggestive of a fracture, are not diagnostic as they may occur with sprains and occasionally with simple contusions.

Obvious deformity is diagnostic of a fracture; the grating of the ends of the broken bones as they rub together is of similar significance. One or both ends of the bone can occasionally be seen in open fractures. A less obvious but definite sign of fracture is shortening of the extremity in which the fracture is located. With fractures of the thigh or hip, the affected leg is usually one to two inches shorter than the uninjured leg due to the over-riding of the bone ends. (In a few individuals such shortening may have been previously present as a result of an old injury.)

Loss of function of the injured extremity is significant if present. However, a limited amount of function of the injured area may persist with some fractures, particularly those of the small bones of the feet and hands, or those in which the bone ends are impacted. If the patient is permitted to continue using the injured extremity, damage to the bone and surrounding tissues may be greatly increased.

Being certain that a fracture exists is desirable, *but is not essential*. Manipulation of the bones to test for the presence of a fracture almost inevitably produces further injury. The bone ends must never be moved to test for grating. If signs suggest the presence of a fracture, its existence should be assumed until x-ray examination proves otherwise. Occasions may arise, particularly with ankle injuries, in which an extremity is severely injured but does not appear to be fractured. In situations where the victim cannot be evacuated for three to five days, the absence of a fracture may become apparent. If the possible fracture site is kept immobilized and slightly elevated, such a delay rarely has any adverse effect on the final outcome.

TREATMENT

Immobilization

The treatment for any fracture is immobilization; additional measures are necessary for open fractures and fractures associated with massive blood loss. Immobilization prevents further damage to surrounding tissues by the bone ends, reduces pain, and decreases the risk of shock. However, the proper alignment of the bone fragments necessary for healing cannot be obtained in the field and should not be attempted.

Immobilization of a fracture in an outdoor setting is occasionally a challenge because material for splints is difficult to obtain. However, rope or nylon webbing and wood are usually available in mountaineering circumstances, and many climbers carry triangular bandages. Any material that stabilizes the fracture area can be used. A folded newspaper is particularly effective for fractures of the forearm and wrist. A pack of brush, pillow, sleeping bag, or even a heavy piece of clothing can be used with satisfactory results. A well-prepared expedition should carry several inflatable, plastic splints. These splints are lightweight, easy to apply, and help control hemorrhage by applying pressure over the leg when the splint is inflated. (The air should be temporarily released from the splint every one to two hours to allow circulation to return to the skin areas.) Standard splints are readily available in most downhill ski areas. The cross-country skier should remember that a ski is an excellent splint and two make a sled.

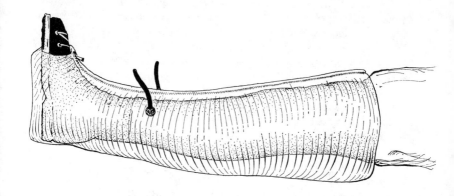

Figure 15. Inflatable splint for fractures of the lower leg and ankle.

For a splint to provide effective immobilization, both the joint above and the joint below the fracture must be immobilized. With a fracture of the forearm, the wrist and elbow should be included in the splint. If the break occurs at the level of the thigh, both knee and hip motion must be controlled. In addition, as can be seen by examining an outstretched leg (which illustrates the position in which a splint is usually applied), the knee can be moved by rotating the ankle. Thus stabilization of the foot is also necessary to provide immobilization of the thigh or hip. Boney prominences, especially at the wrist, elbow, ankle, and knee, should be padded to prevent discomfort from pressure by hard materials used for splints.

Attempts by inexperienced personnel to manipulate fractures have damaged more arms and legs than they have helped. Blood vessels or nerves can be injured; the contaminated ends of bone fragments protruding through the skin can retract, leading to severe infection; the fibrous sheath and blood vessels which provide nutrients for the bone can be damaged, causing a serious delay in healing or even death of the damaged bone. Therefore, under most circumstances, no attempt should be made to straighten a deformed, fractured limb.

However, there are two exceptions to this rule. If many hours or days will elapse before medical assistance can be obtained (which is frequently the case in mountaineering accidents), an attempt to straighten the extremity may be made. The other indication for manipulation is loss of the blood supply to the extremity beyond the fracture site. A patient with this complication usually has severe pain, numbness, and coldness in the affected limb, which is cyanotic or pale and swollen. If the bone ends are only pressing against the artery or vein, restoration to normal position may relieve the obstruction. However, if the vessel is actually torn such manipulations are usually unsuccessful. Loss of sensation may also be due to injury of a nerve, in which case unskilled manipulation can increase the damage which has already occurred.

To straighten the extremity, strong traction should be applied by pulling on the end of the limb while someone holds the body from above. Restoration to the normal position should be attempted *only* when the fracture surfaces are separated by the pull and any necessary rotation can be performed gently and easily. These maneuvers can be carried out more readily immediately after the fracture has occurred. Later, muscle spasm and swelling tend to restrict motion and increase deformity.

Bleeding

Hemorrhage occurs with all fractures. The sharp, jagged ends of some broken bones cause extensive destruction of the surrounding tissues, resulting in severe blood loss. The hemorrhage can be so great that shock or even death results and yet the site of the injury may present little evidence of bleeding. Severe bleeding usually occurs following fractures of the trunk or lower extremeties. *Anyone caring for a fracture patient must be aware of the threat of shock and be prepared to administer any necessary treatment.*

Open Fractures

The danger of infection makes open or compound fractures much more serious problems than closed fractures. Osteomyelitis, an infection of bone, often produces extensive bone destruction, usually hinders or completely prevents healing of fractures, and frequently leads to permanent crippling deformities. The infection is often difficult to eradicate, even with antibiotic therapy, and occasionally persists for years, producing widespread debilitating effects.

Any fracture is considered to be "open" if the skin is broken, regardless of whether the skin was damaged by the jagged bone ends or by the object which produced the injury. A penetrating wound which damages a bone is considered an open fracture because the skin is no longer able to prevent bacteria from gaining entrance to the injured tissues.

An open fracture should be treated like a contaminated soft tissue injury. All dirt and foreign material must be carefully and completely washed away. Then the wound should be left open, bandaged, and splinted. The patient should be evacuated as rapidly as possible. If evacuation can be completed in a few hours or one or two days, antibiotics should not be administered unless they can be given intravenously. If evacuation requires a longer time, high doses of intravenous or oral antibiotics should be given. The antibiotics administered should combine a penicillinase-resistant penicillin and one of the cephalosporins.

Control of Pain

Pain resulting from a fracture is greatly reduced by immobilization. If the fractured extremity is splinted very shortly after the injury, no medications are usually needed during splinting. Later, a strong analgesic such as morphine or meperidine may be required for splinting or any similar maneuvers. Analgesics may also be required to relieve the pain of the unavoidable jolts encountered during evacuation over rough ground.

Morphine should be injected intramuscularly every four hours as necessary. However, absorption of the drug from the injection site is reduced in the presence of shock. Repeated or large doses can lead to overdosage when normal circulation is restored. If needed in the presence of shock, morphine should be injected into the muscles of the chest, should be given at six-hour intervals, and, after the first injection, should be given in amounts only half as large as the usual dose.

TRANSPORTATION

Treatment for fractures and all other injuries must be completed before the victim is moved unless the site of the accident is in imminent danger from hazards of terrain or weather. Bleeding must be arrested, shock brought under control, all fractures splinted, and any other injuries cared for before the subject is transported any farther than is necessary to remove him from such danger. A complete examination must be made to prevent seriously aggravating any undetected injuries during evacuation.

Individuals with fractures of the upper extremity, collar bone, or ribs and some persons with head injuries can walk under their own power. These patients must be closely attended since weakness and instability can result from the injury or from drugs given for pain. Subjects with fractures of the lower extremities, pelvis, or vertebral column, and the victims of severe head injuries must be carried. Considerable ingenuity, resourcefulness, and sheer determination are often required to evacuate individuals with these injuries without aggravating the injury.

SPECIFIC FRACTURES OF THE UPPER EXTREMITY

Hand and Fingers

The hand and fingers can be immobilized by bandaging the hand with a wad of material held in the palm. A rolled-up pair of socks fits the hand well and serves nicely for this purpose. If the fracture involves the portion of the hand adjacent to the wrist, a splint should be applied to the entire hand and forearm to prevent motion of the wrist. Splints of this type are more comfortable when placed along the palm and the underside of the forearm. A forearm sling should be used to keep the hand elevated.

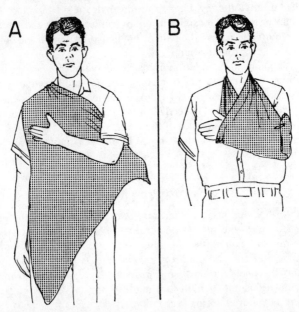

Figure 16. Application of a forearm sling.

Forearm

Most wrist fractures and all forearm fractures require inclusion of the hand and elbow in the splint. After splinting, the injured arm should be suspended in two slings as described for fractures of the upper arm.

Elbow, Upper Arm, and Shoulder

Immobilization of fractures of the elbow, upper arm, and shoulder is best achieved by the use of two slings. The first is tied behind the neck and supports the elbow, forearm, and hand. The second is tied around the chest and holds the upper arm against the body. Should numbness of the little and ring fingers develop, padding of the elbow to prevent pressure on the nerve there may be necessary. If only one triangular bandage is available, rope, nylon webbing, or some other material can be substituted for one of the slings. Rope can replace the chest sling if the fracture involves the elbow or forearm. If the upper arm or shoulder is injured, the forearm can be supported by a carefully padded rope extending around the neck and tied to the wrist.

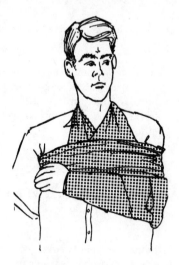

Figure 17. Forearm sling with an upper arm binder.

Collar Bone

Fractures of the collar bone (clavicle) are less uncomfortable if the individual holds his shoulders back. The shoulders can be splinted in this position by passing a bandage or rope over the shoulder and under the armpit on one

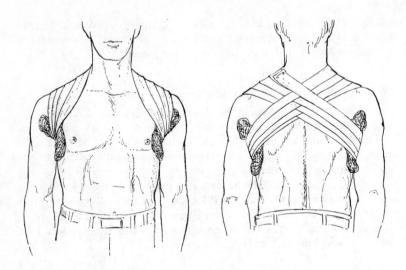

Figure 18. Figure-eight bandage for splinting a fractured collarbone.

side, across the back, and then over the shoulder and beneath the armpit on the opposite side, forming a figure-eight. The bandage should be applied over the victim's clothing and the shoulders and armpits must be heavily padded. The coils should be applied while the shoulders are thrown back and should be just tight enough for the victim to be able to relieve pressure on his armpit by holding his shoulders back.

SPECIFIC FRACTURES OF THE LOWER EXTREMITY

Foot and Toes

Injuries of the toes and foot are best splinted by a good boot. Since the boot is usually in place at the time of injury, fractures below the ankle are uncommon among well-equipped climbers or skiers. Some fractures of the small bones of the foot result from accidents which seem insignificant at the time and are associated with relatively little pain. However, if pain persists for several weeks, the victim should consult a physician.

Crippling fractures of the heel bone (calcaneus) can result if a person falls some distance and lands on his feet. Pain prevents bearing weight on the injured heel during evacuation.

Ankle

Fractures of the ankle, which are more common than fractures of the foot, require immobilization by splints encompassing the foot and knee. Two splints should be used, one on each side of the leg. The splints should be padded and held in place by tape, bandages, rope, or a similar material. If the area of the fracture is still painful when the victim is moved, the outer splint should be extended above the hip. Some straightening may be necessary before a badly distorted ankle can be splinted, but such manipulation must be held to a minimum. A patient with an ankle fracture may be able to move short distances with his uninjured leg and firm support on each side. However, evacuation for distances greater than a few hundred yards usually requires a stretcher of some kind.

Leg and Knee

Fractures of the lower leg can be immobilized in a manner similar to that used for injuries of the ankle. Fractures involving the knee require immobilization of the foot, ankle, knee, and hip.

Kneecap

A fracture of the kneecap alone may prevent the victim from using the lower leg because the tendons which pull the leg forward are severed. Patients with such fractures should have a splint placed behind the leg, extending from the level of the ankle to the hip. With the leg and thigh snugly bound to this splint the victim may be able to walk short distances.

Thigh

For immobilization of a fracture of the long bone in the thigh (femur) traction to overcome the pull of the strong thigh muscles is desirable. These muscles tend to cause the bone ends to override at the point of the fracture, producing severe damge in the surrounding tissues. A Thomas splint, or one of its modifications, is probably the best means for obtaining traction for a broken femur in mountaineering circumstances. However, these splints are applied incorrectly so often that their use is being discontinued in many areas.

The Thomas splint consists of a padded ring attached to a metal frame. In use the ring fits snugly against the buttock and is held in place by a belt, strap, or similar device which passes over the front of the leg at the level of the groin. The frame is composed of two metal rods which extend along both sides of the leg and are joined a few inches beyond the foot by a cross-piece.

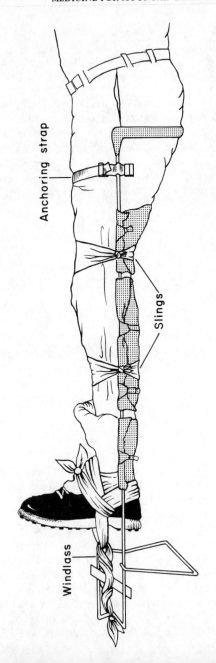

Figure 19. Fractured thigh immobilized with a Thomas splint.

In applying a splint of this type the boot should remain in place and the ankle must be carefully padded to prevent obstruction of the blood supply to the foot. A traction hitch similar to the figure-eight bandage used for sprained ankles is placed over the boot and padded ankle. Next, the leg is lifted gently by pulling on the foot and the splint slipped into place. After the splint is secured at the level of the groin, the hitch should be tied to the cross-piece of the metal frame. A rod or stick is then inserted in the hitch (between the cross-piece and the foot) and twisted to apply traction on the leg. The pull should only be strong enough to prevent the foot and leg from sagging when the splint is lifted, but the hitch may have to be tightened one to two hours after the splint is applied as the thigh muscles relax and lengthen.

Extra bandages should be used as hammocks to support the leg in the splint and a circular bandage must be added to prevent the leg from swinging from side to side. In addition, the lower end of the splint should be elevated so no pressure is placed on the patient's heel.

Pain in the foot after the splint has been applied indicates the blood supply to the foot has been impaired. The traction hitch must be disassembled *at once* and the ankle more carefully protected. Permanent damage to the foot, which usually would be more crippling than the fracture, frequently results if adequate precautions are not taken to prevent obstruction of the circulation. In view of this danger, Thomas splints probably should not be used if evacuation is going to require more than a few hours or in cold weather.

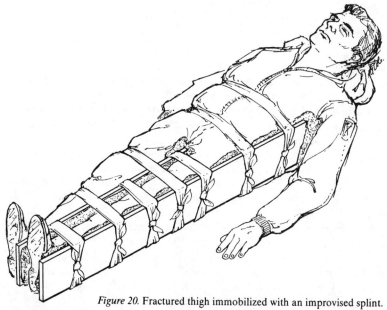

Figure 20. Fractured thigh immobilized with an improvised splint.

A makeshift Thomas splint can be made from two ski poles in an emergency. The wrist straps are hooked together and slipped up against the buttock like the half ring of a Thomas splint. A handkerchief or similar item is used to tie the hand grips together across the front of the thigh like the belt on the Thomas splint. Bandages tied between the poles support the leg, and the hitch around the ankle is hooked to the baskets or ends of the ski poles.

Two splints can be applied as described for the ankle and lower leg. The outside splint must extend up to the level of the armpit and the inside splint must extend to the groin. In addition, both legs should be bound together so that the uninjured leg can be used as an additional splint. Padding placed between the thighs reduces discomfort from the inner splint. If both thighs are fractured the legs should still be bound together to increase the stability of the independent splints.

Hip

Fractures of the hip require no splinting other than binding the legs together. However, the victim must not be permitted to walk on the injured leg.

SPECIFIC FRACTURES OF THE TRUNK

Pelvis

Fractures of the pelvis should be suspected following severe accidents if side-to-side or back-to-front pressure over the pelvis causes pain. Blood loss with pelvic fractures is inevitably severe, but is rarely evident when the victim is examined. The volume of blood lost in the tissues around the fracture is commonly enough to cause the victim to go into shock, and may be sufficient to cause death. Therefore, therapy for shock should be instituted if a pelvic fracture is suspected.

Splinters of bone from pelvic fractures frequently damage the organs within the pelvis, particularly the urinary bladder. This complication should be suspected if the victim fails to void or passes only a few drops of bloody urine after the injury. (Injuries of the bladder are discussed in the chapter "Abdominal Injuries.")

No splinting is required for pelvic fractures since the muscles around the pelvis hold the bone fragments in place. The patient should be placed on a stretcher in a supine position and should be evacuated without being permitted to sit up or stand.

No one with a pelvic fracture should be permitted to walk unless absolutely necessary; pain prevents any motion by most victims. However, some individuals may be able to move slowly and carefully with such injuries if circumstances make it essential. Injuries of the back of the pelvis are less dangerous than those in front if walking is necessary.

Vertebral Column Fractures

Fractures of the vertebral column in the back and neck are always accompanied by the possibility of injury to the enclosed spinal cord. The higher the level at which the fracture occurs, the greater is the risk of serious nervous system damage and the more grave are the consequences of the injury.

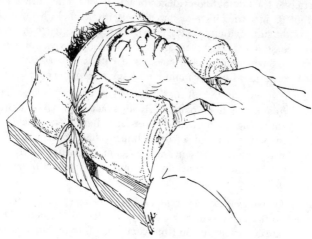

Figure 21. Technique for immobilizing the head for patients with fractured cervical vertebrae.

Pain or tenderness along the spine or anywhere in the neck following a fall should arouse concern about the possibility of a vertebral fracture. Occasionally such fractures present areas of swelling or discoloration similar to fractures elsewhere. Unusual prominence of one of the vertebral spines is sometimes found. However, if pain alone is present, the existence of a fracture should be assumed.

Signs of spinal cord damage include pain which radiates around to the front of the body or down the arms or legs, numbness, tingling, and partial or complete paralysis. However, the absence of spinal cord damage is by no means evidence that a vertebral fracture has not occurred. The vertebral column is commonly fractured without injuring the underlying cord. To risk cord damage by improper treatment is to take a chance of turning an unfortunate accident into a genuine catastrophe. Paralysis resulting from a spinal cord injury is frequently permanent.

During evacuation of a patient with a confirmed or suspected vertebral fracture the body must be firmly secured so that it does not roll or twist if it is jostled while going over rough terrain. The patient should be transported on a firm support such as a metal basket or a broad wooden board. A rolled up jacket or a similar object should be placed under the small of the back to support the spine in that area. With injuries of the neck, padding must be placed on both sides of the head and neck to prevent the head from rolling from side to side.

There possibly are mountaineering situations, particularly in extremely exposed and hazardous locations, in which it may be safer to allow an individual with a vertebral fracture but no evidence of spinal cord injury to walk slowly and carefully on his own. His spine may be better protected when splinted by the spasm of the surrounding muscles, than it is when subjected to the jolting of an improvised stretcher. However, any movement by the victim should be risked only under extreme circumstances and with a full realization of the danger of severe injury from such minor mishaps as stepping on a loose stone.

An accident victim with spinal cord damage and paralysis requires special attention during evacuation, particularly if evacuation takes more than twenty-four hours. The victim should not be moved until a complete examination has been performed and all other injuries have been treated. Good respiratory function must be present and the victim should preferably not be in shock. Finally, adequate personnel and equipment for proper transportation must be on hand.

During prolonged evacuation special care must be given to the areas which support the body's weight — heels, buttocks, shoulders, and elbows. The pressure on these areas prevents blood from circulating through the tissues. Normally such deprivation of the blood supply results in pain. However, patients with spinal cord injuries are not able to feel pain in areas supplied by nerves which originate below the site of injury. The associated paralysis would prevent them from adjusting their position even if they could appreciate the pain. After a few hours of being deprived of blood the tissues in these areas die, eventually resulting in extensive ulcers known as "bed sores." To avoid this complication the pressure points, particularly the heels and buttocks, must be carefully padded. Furthermore, this padding should be rearranged every two hours, day and night. The prevention of bed sores, which heal very poorly and are difficult to cure, requires diligent and devoted nursing care.

Most vertebral fractures which damage the cord paralyze the bladder and large intestine. Bladder care requires repeated catheterizations at least every eight hours or the insertion of an indwelling catheter. The care of bowel paralysis necessitates enemas about every three days and close observation to prevent the development of a fecal impaction. (See "Gastrointestinal Diseases.")

OTHER FRACTURES

Rib fractures are discussed under "Thoracic Injuries." Skull fractures and fractures of the face and jaw are discussed under "Head Injuries."

OTHER INJURIES OF BONE AND RELATED STRUCTURES

Dislocations

A dislocation is an injury in which the normal relationships of a joint are disrupted. Frequently the bone is forced out of its socket, as occurs in dislocations of the shoulder, elbow, or hip. For other joints there is no definite socket and the two joint surfaces are simply displaced. Fractures of the associated bones and injuries of adjacent nerves, blood vessels, and other structures may be present.

The signs of a dislocation are similar to those of a fracture: pain which is aggravated by motion, tenderness, swelling, discoloration, limitation of motion, and deformity of the joint. The findings are localized to the area around a joint, but comparison with the opposite, uninjured joint is often necessary to be certain that a definite abnormality is present. Frequently the dislocated joint appears larger than normal due to overlapping of the bone ends.

Correction of a dislocation is technically difficult and unskilled efforts can easily damage blood vessels and nerves or even produce fractures. Pain and muscle spasm can prevent the use of the extremity for climbing. Some injured joints must be splinted or even placed in a cast for three to four weeks or more to give the injured ligaments and tendons about the joint time to heal. However, an attempt to correct the deformity is justified in certain circumstances or in relatively remote areas. Pain, pallor or cyanosis, swelling, numbness, or the absence of pulses beyond the dislocation are indicative of interference with the blood supply. Prompt action may be required to save the extremity from gangrene. A steady, firm, but gentle pull in the direction of the long axis of the extremity, while an assistant pulls in the opposite direction from above, may correct the dislocation or at least relieve pressure on the blood vessels.

The chance of success decreases and the risk of further injury increases with the passage of time after injury. Therefore, the attempt at reduction must be made as quickly as possible, if at all.

Dislocations of the fingers, which occur most commonly at the second joint, may be corrected quite easily immediately after the dislocation by pulling on the injured digit. The injured finger can then be splinted effectively by taping it to an adjacent, uninjured finger. Dislocations of the thumb are usually accompanied by a fracture of the bone at the base of the thumb. Such injuries are

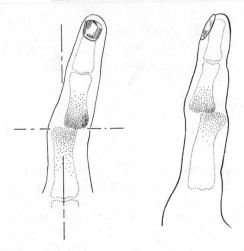

Figure 22. Dislocation of the finger.

seldom stable when corrected by manipulation alone and are best treated in the field by total immobilization.

A dislocated shoulder may be reduced to its normal position rather easily if the joint has been dislocated on previous occasions. Some individuals have permanently damaged shoulder joints which frequently become dislocated with almost insignificant trauma. However, restoration to proper alignment can be achieved almost as easily. The attendant should push his stocking foot which is on the same side as the injured shoulder (i.e. left foot for left shoulder, right foot for right shoulder) against the ribs in the patient's armpit while pulling on the arm at the same time. Replacement of the bone into the shoulder socket usually occurs readily — but so can damage to blood vessels and nerves or fracture of the surrounding bones. Therefore, such heroic treatment is best reserved for circumstances where days may pass before medical help can be obtained.

A safer, somewhat simpler, but more prolonged method of reducing shoulder dislocations is to place the victim face down on a table or similar surface so that the injured arm can dangle straight down without encountering any obstruction. A ten- to twenty-pound weight should be attached to the arm with tape. After one-half to two hours the constant pull by the weight tires the muscles surrounding the shoulder, causing them to relax and frequently permitting the bone to slip back into its socket. If reduction does not occur within two hours, traction should be discontinued and the victim evacuated.

On rare occasions an individual may become so completely relaxed while asleep that his jaw falls downward and slips out of its socket. When the subject awakens he finds that he cannot close his mouth. In a remote area, the resulting inability to swallow could lead to serious difficulties. Usually such complete relaxation follows the use of sleeping pills or over-indulgence in alcohol.

Disclocations of the jaw are rather easily and safely reduced. The attendant should insert both thumbs over the molars of the patient's lower jaw and press directly downward. A considerable force may be required to overcome the spasm in the jaw muscles, which are quite strong, but the jaw should slip back into place without too much difficulty. (The thumbs should be heavily padded to prevent serious "bites" as the jaw pops back into its socket.) After reduction, a bandage should be placed over the point of the chin and tied over the top of the head. This bandage should permit the jaw to be opened slightly for eating and talking, but should be tight enough to prevent repeated dislocations. The bandage should be worn continuously for about a week and while sleeping for a month. If pain persists in the joint, which is located just in front of the ear, a physician should be consulted.

The reduction of any dislocation is facilitated by the administration of medications to relieve pain. Approximately fifteen minutes should be allowed for the drug to take effect. Finger dislocations can be reduced so easily that such drugs are not necessary.

After any dislocation is reduced, the injured area should be splinted in the same manner as a fracture of that area. The injured extremity may be useless for climbing for at least two to three weeks — often longer.

Contusions of Bone and Subperiosteal Hematomas

A direct blow to a bone which does not result in a fracture or dislocation may still cause sufficient damage to produce swelling in the tissue covering the bone (periosteum) or bleeding between that tissue and the rigid portion of the bone (subperiosteal hematoma). The injured person complains of localized pain, the area is quite tender, and the bone may appear or feel larger than normal.

Treatment consists of application of cold packs and a pressure bandage during the first twenty-four hours following injury, together with splinting to prevent motion of the involved area. After twenty-four hours, local heat rather than cold should be applied and activity can be allowed to the limits of pain tolerance. However, if a fracture or dislocation cannot be ruled out, immobilization should be continued.

Sprains and Strains

Sprains and strains, which are tearing, avulsing, or severe stretching injuries of tendons and muscles, often cannot be differentiated from fractures except by x-ray. The injury may be fully as damaging as a broken bone to the function of an extremity. The signs are similar to a fracture, although grating of broken bone ends and deformity are not present. Swelling is often quite marked and discoloration may also be present. If an injury is obviously severe, the wisest course is to treat it as a fracture.

The application of cold immediately after injury reduces hemorrhage and swelling. (Care must be exercised to avoid cold injuries.) Later the reduction of swelling can be aided by compression, such as applying an elastic bandage. (The circulation must not be impaired.) The blood and damaged tissue are resorbed more rapidly and healing promoted somewhat if the injured area is elevated slightly above the level of the rest of the body. Motion and use speed healing but only when resumed after the initial reaction — primarily swelling and hemorrhage — has subsided and healing has already begun spontaneously.

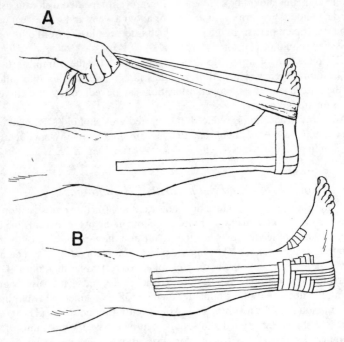

Figure 23. Technique for taping a sprained ankle after healing has begun. (The foot should be held perpendicular to the leg while the tape is being applied. The ankle should be taped for only the first three or four days of use after healing is underway.)

Sprained ankles are the most common injuries of this type, and circumstances frequently require that the subject walk (or hobble) from the climbing or skiing area. In such situations the ankle should be supported by a figure-eight bandage put on over the boot. The loops of the figure-eight should pass around the back of the heel and under the sole of the foot, crossing on top of the foot. However, the person can no longer rely on the injured ankle to perform normally and the risk of further, more severe damage is great. The victim should return to camp and rest until it becomes evident that no fracture is present and the injury does not require evacuation. On the ski slope, this type of injury should terminate the day's skiing and could possibly require several days' rest before activity is resumed.

The most common skiing injury involves the tendons and ligaments of the knee, and occasionally damages the cartilage which covers the joint surfaces. A person with this injury should not be permitted to walk on his injured leg (he rarely can do so). The knee should be splinted as if it were fractured and the victim evacuated by sled or stretcher. Such injuries frequently require a cast and four to six weeks or more to heal.

Muscle and Tendon Tears

Exertion of a sudden, strong force with the related bones and joints fixed in position, such as can occur at the end of a fall, may tear a muscle from its insertion, or may completely rupture the body of the muscle or tendon. Muscle tears or "pulls" can also result from sprinting at top speed, or sudden movements or changes of direction. A penetrating injury may partially or completely sever a muscle or tendon. A complete separation of the muscle, or its tendon and attachments, results in a loss of the ability to perform the movements produced by that muscle. An incomplete interruption seldom results in loss of function but does predispose the structures to later complete separation.

Frequent sites of tendon or muscle insertion injuries are the fingertips below the nails, the elbow, and the ankle. Ruptured muscles and tendons more commonly occur in the calf of the leg, the front and back of the thigh, and the upper portion of the arm and shoulder. Pain, tenderness, swelling, and loss of motion are the usual findings. Sometimes a defect in the muscle or tendon can be felt.

Treatment consists of the application of cold and immobilization. If possible, rapid evacuation should be accomplished since definitive repair of these injuries is most successful if done within the first twenty-four hours following the accident.

Bursitis, Tendonitis, and Shin Splints

Bursitis, tendonitis, and shin splints are characterized by inflammation of the tendons or the flattened, fluid-filled, cyst-like bursae which cushion and lubricate the movements of the tendons. These disorders are characterized by the gradual onset of pain and stiffness, which is usually related to the unaccustomed use of a muscle or group of muscles for an extended length of time. Frequently the pain is first noticed upon awakening in the morning following such activities. The gradual onset and the lack of any relation to a single traumatic incident serve to distinguish these disorders from fractures, dislocations, and sprains.

Splinting may relieve the immediate discomfort but often prolongs the problem. Moist heat, such as a warm, moist towel, and aspirin every four hours provide some relief. In some instances cold application may be more effective than heat. The pain, which is rarely disabling, may persist for a long time. Continued use of the joint throughout the full range of motion is important to prevent chronic stiffness and pain.

BACK INJURIES

Strain

Back pain is produced by a wide variety of disorders. Simple strain, which is one of the most common causes, can result from carrying heavy loads, working in an unaccustomed stooped position, or sleeping in an awkward position. However, treatment of a strained back is frequently frustrating. The measures which provide the greatest relief are sleeping on a firm support, such as a mattress with a sheet of plywood underneath, and applying heat to the affected area. When sleeping out-of-doors a mat should be used which provides insulation but little padding. Warm moist towels or a hot water bottle applied to the painful area helps relieve the muscle spasm. Aspirin can be taken to mask the pain; codeine may also be necessary on some occasions.

Ruptured Disc

The vertebrae of the spinal column are separated by cushions of cartilagenous material which absorb the force from the numerous jolts to which the body is subjected. A ruptured disc is an extrusion of this semi-solid material into the spinal canal, resulting in compression of the spinal cord or the nerves coming from the cord. The basic defect consists of degeneration and weakening of the ligaments which normally hold this cushion in place. Trauma is only the final incident in producing a ruptured disc. Unless this basic defect is present, trauma alone usually fractures the vertebra instead of causing the disc to rupture.

The nature and location of symptoms in this condition are highly characteristic. Pain begins in the lower back, radiates to one side, and passes through the buttock and down the back of the leg. The pain may also involve the outside of the leg, but is rarely present in the front or inner portions of the leg. The discomfort frequently causes the victim to walk with a decided limp. Excruciating back pain when moving to and from a supine position is also characteristic.

Examination of the patient reveals that the vertebral column in the lower back does not bend when he leans as far as possible to either side. This immobilization is produced by spasm in the muscles in the area of injury, resulting from the pain associated with movement. This muscle spasm can usually be palpated by an examiner's fingers. Loss of sensation to pin-prick or the light touch of a wisp of cotton may be present over the foot and lower leg on the affected side.

The treatment for a ruptured disc is the same as for strain of the back muscles. However, the two conditions should be differentiated since each has a quite different prognosis. Strain, which is rarely disabling, usually clears up in a few days — or perhaps a few weeks — with rest and proper treatment. In contrast, a disc may be incapacitating. Furthermore, the pain of a ruptured disc, although occasionally disappearing in a similar period of time with complete rest, is usually much more prolonged and may be relieved only by surgery. Finally, even though symptoms disappear rather promptly, a recurrence is likely at any time. Under expedition circumstances these prognostic factors must be considered in making any plans for future climbing.

Individuals with a previous history of a disc problem should consult an orthopedist or neurosurgeon before undertaking further climbing activities, particularly if evidence of sensory impairment is present.

Muscle Compartment Compression

A few muscles are enclosed in a firm fibrous sheath which forms a tight nondistensible envelope. Injuries to such muscles which result in bleeding or swelling can increase the pressure within that sheath to such a level that the circulation of blood to the muscle is impaired or totally blocked. As a result the muscle dies and is replaced with nonfunctioning scar tissue, usually resulting in a permanent crippling disability of that extremity.

The muscle most commonly involved in this type of compartmental compression is the muscle to the outside of the shin bone in the front of the lower leg. The patient usually has a definitive, obvious injury of his leg. Subsequently, he slowly but steadily develops excruciating pain and tenderness over the entire muscle, extending from the knee to the ankle. Such pain is usually accompanied by coldness and numbness of the foot.

In order to prevent permanent incapacitating damage to the muscle, immediate evacuation for surgical opening of the compartmental space is required.

CHAPTER 8

Burns

THE SEVERITY of a burn depends upon the size of the area it covers, the depth to which it extends, and its location on the body. Few individuals survive burns which involve more than fifty percent of the body surface. In contrast, few burns covering less than twenty percent of the body prove fatal if given proper care. Burns of the face and neck, hands, arm pits, and crotch are frequently more incapacitating because specialized organs and complex anatomical structures are involved or the areas are difficult to keep clean.

Burns are classified as first, second, or third degree according to the depth to which damage extends. First degree burns are superficial, do not kill any of the tissue, and only produce redness of the skin. Second degree burns cause death of the upper portion of the skin, resulting in blisters. Third degree burns produce death of the full thickness of the skin and may extend deeply into the underlying tissues. Third degree burns, if more than one inch in diameter, do not heal unless covered by skin grafts, and can produce extensive, deforming scars.

An extensive, deep burn incurred in a remote mountainous area can be a catastrophe, particularly if the fluids needed to replace those lost into the burned tissues are not available. Evacuation must be carried out at once by the fastest means available.

First degree burns may require no treatment. Therapy for more severe burns consists of both care for the local injury and treatment of the effects of the burn on the entire body.

LOCAL THERAPY

Immediately after the burn is incurred all clothing and jewelry covering the injury should be removed. If the burn is small and very deep, immersion in cold water helps reduce the pain. Cold injury must be avoided. The burned area should be carefully washed with sterile cotton soaked with warm, previously boiled water and liquid soap. All debris, dirt, and fragments of loose skin must be removed. (These measures are surprisingly painless if carried out gently.) The burn should be covered with a layer of a sterile dressing made of material (such as gauze impregnated with petroleum jelly) which does not stick to the wound. A thick, bulky dressing should be placed on top of this layer. This dressing should be held in place by a snug bandage which applies a moderate amount of pressure to the damaged area. Ointments or creams should *never* be placed on a second or third degree burn. These materials have no benefit whatsoever, greatly increase the danger of infection, and make the wound difficult to clean. (Gauze impregnated with petroleum jelly is a prepackaged, sterile dressing obtainable from the manufacturers of dressings and bandages, not ordinary gauze on which some petroleum jelly has been smeared.)

If the burn occupies less than fifteen percent of the body surface area and does not involve the face, neck, hands, or genital area, the patient may not need to be evacuated. The bandage must be left in place without being disturbed for at least six to eight days. Changing the bandage prior to this time introduces the danger of infection without benefiting the patient. Only after about a week has elapsed can an accurate distinction between first, second, and third degree burns be made. If a third degree burn is present, the patient usually should be evacuated, although a small third degree burn would not always require interruption of an outing scheduled to end within a week or ten days.

If the burn is found to be only first degree or superficial second degree with no blisters present when the bandage is removed, no further treatment is required. Even bandaging is not necessary unless the area requires protection from trauma.

If blisters, either intact or ruptured, are present, the wound should be redressed with a similar bandage to protect any intact blisters and prevent infection. This dressing can be changed every three or four days until healing is complete.

Third degree burns at six to eight days are covered by a thick, leathery layer of parched, dead skin which may range in color from white to dark brown or black. This area is completely insensitive to touch. In cases in which there is some doubt about the depth of the injury, gentle testing for anesthesia with a sterile object is a good way of determining whether the burn has extended through the full thickness of the skin.

If a third degree burn is found, the injury should be covered with an identical bandage and plans begun to evacuate the patient. If the burn is small and does not particularly incapacitate the victim there is no urgency about evacuation. However, these burns do not heal without skin grafts. Some eight to ten days after injury the layer of dead skin begins to crack and loosen around the edges. Infection inevitably follows, even under optimal circumstances, and can have dire consequences.

If the burn is incapacitating from the onset, either from its extent or location, the victim should be evacuated at once without waiting to determine the depth of the wound.

GENERAL THERAPY

Burn Shock

Any burn which covers more than fifteen percent of the body surface is accompanied by a serious threat from shock — "burn shock." Blood serum and fluids from the surrounding tissues pour out into the burned area, reducing the volume of the blood and producing the usual signs and symptoms of shock. In addition the urine volume falls to very low quantities — a highly significant sign.

The percentage of the body area covered by the burn can be estimated from the accompanying chart. Anyone with a second or third degree burn covering

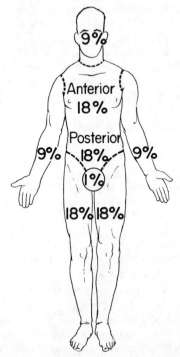

Figure 24. Percentage of total body surface area of various portions of the body.

more than fifteen percent of the body area must be evacuated immediately. If evacuation requires more than twelve to eighteen hours and signs of shock appear, appropriate fluid therapy must be instituted.

A procedure known as the Evans formula has been devised for determining the proper amount of fluids to be administered. According to this formula the percentage of the body surface covered by the burn, multiplied by the body weight in kilograms (2.2 pounds = 1 kilogram), yields a figure which is the volume of plasma (or plasma substitute) to be given during the first twenty-four hours after the burn. An identical volume of Ringer's lactate should also be administered, as well as the usual daily fluid requirements.

For example, the fluid requirements calculations for the first twenty-four hours for an eighty kilogram man (176 pounds) with a thirty percent burn would be as follows:

(30 X 80 = 2,400)	
Plasma or plasma substitute	2,400 cc
Ringer's lactate	2,400 cc
Five to ten percent glucose	2,000 cc
	—————
Total in the first twenty-four hours	6,800 cc

Some important details about such therapy are:

1. One-half the fluids should be given intravenously during the first eight hours after the burn. The remainder should be spread over the next sixteen hours.
2. The administration of plasma and saline should be alternated — one liter of plasma followed by one liter of saline, etc.
3. If a burn covers more than fifty percent of the body area, the fluid requirements should be computed for a fifty percent burn. Use of a larger figure yields a volume of fluid too large for the heart to handle in one twenty-four hour period.
4. The patient's urine volume must be carefully measured. If it is greater than fifty cubic centimeters per hour, the intravenous fluids must be administered more slowly or even reduced in quantity.
5. The patient with a severe burn is usually thirsty. This thirst should be combatted by the use of intravenous fluids since fluids given orally usually cause vomiting during the immediate post-burn period. (Any fluids lost by vomiting must be replaced with Ringer's lactate.)

During the second twenty-four hours after the burn, one-half the original volume of plasma and lactate should be administered along with 2,000 cc of five or ten percent glucose to meet fluid requirements. After the first forty-eight hours the patient is usually able to maintain his fluid intake orally. Fruit juices, which have a high potassium content, should be avoided for several days, since the blood already contains an excess of potassium due to the destruction of red blood cells by the burn.

After two to three days, as the swelling about the burn disappears, the urine volume becomes very large. This high urinary output is to be expected as the body must rid itself of the extra fluids administered (necessarily) immediately after the burn.

Other Considerations

Penicillin should be administered every six hours until the patient is in the hands of a physician or obviously well on his way to healing.

The pain experienced by burn victims is variable. Superficial burns may be almost painless once they are covered and not exposed to air. Deeper burns may destroy the nerves and produce anesthesia in the area of injury. Shock tends to dull the pain that is present. The pain should be controlled, but with as little medication as possible. Aspirin and codeine alone should be used if they are effective. If morphine or meperidine are necessary, smaller doses (one-half to three-fourths the usual dose) should be tried before resorting to a full dose. If the patient is in shock, the medications for pain should be injected into one of the muscles of the trunk so they will be better absorbed. However, morphine and meperidine have a somewhat depressive effect on the body and may aggravate the general effects of the burn.

The victims of burns incurred at high altitudes should be given oxygen until they are evacuated to lower levels. Oxygen may be life-saving for a patient with an extensive burn at high altitude.

Burns around the face and neck are particularly dangerous because the flames may be inhaled. The victim of this type of injury must be evacuated with extreme urgency. If the upper respiratory tract has been burned, swelling soon occurs, obstructing the passage of air and causing the victim to suffocate. Treatment of this complication requires a tracheostomy. If the flames reach the lower portion of the respiratory tract and the lungs are seared there is probably nothing anyone can do. If the victim survives the initial injury, the burn causes fluid to collect in the lungs in large quantities, causing death.

Dehydration of the patient following a burn, caused by the outpouring of fluids into the tissues, creates a considerable danger of thrombophlebitis. This complication should be watched for and appropriately treated if it occurs. However, prevention by administering the required fluids and thus avoiding dehydration is far more desirable.

CHAPTER 9

Injuries of the Head and Neck

BRAIN INJURIES

BRAIN injuries are probably the most common cause of death in mountaineering accidents. The treatment of such injuries must include special attention for the vital functions dependent upon central nervous system control.

Unconsciousness following a blow to the head is a definite sign that the brain has been injured. The severity of the injury correlates roughly with the duration and depth of coma. A patient who responds in some fashion when called by name, or responds to pinching or similar painful stimuli usually has not incurred serious brain damage and often regains consciousness in a short period of time. Deeper coma, in which the victim is completely flaccid and has dilated pupils, a slow pulse rate, and irregular respirations, is indicative of a more severe injury. Widely dilated pupils which do not contract when exposed to light are indicative of a degree of brain damage which few survive. Bleeding from within the ears is a sign of fracture of the base of the skull which also is often fatal.

Occasionally a person who has received a blow to the head may regain consciousness only to lapse into coma again later as the result of continued bleeding within the skull (see "Subdural Hematoma"). Considerable perspicacity is required to recognize the subtle changes of this type of disorder at a time when effective treatment can be instituted.

Treatment

No specific treatment can be given for a brain injury in the field. The patient must be evacuated to the care of a neurosurgeon. Close attention must be given to the maintenance of an open airway during evacuation if the victim is unconscious. *There is no point in attempting to evacuate an unconscious individual if the airway is not kept open.*

Evacuating a comatose subject can be so difficult that waiting until the subject has regained consciousness is often highly desirable. In a particularly exposed and hazardous situation, such as on a sheer rock wall, a delay of five to six hours is fully justified. However, if the victim is not awake at the end of this time or shows signs of deepening coma, he cannot be expected to regain consciousness without medical treatment. The absolute necessity for maintaining an airway during evacuation, and the difficulty in doing so during descent from such a position, may require that the victim be left on the wall with one individual to care for him while the rest of the party goes for help.

All injuries to other areas of the body must be found and treated. Diligence is required to avoid overlooking injuries if the patient is unconscious and is not able to point out areas which are painful. Any lucid interval must be utilized to re-examine the patient and insure that no injuries have been missed.

Many serious injuries are neglected for long periods because the victim is lying on his back and no one has examined this area. Since shock rarely results from brain injury alone, the presence of shock should prompt examination for other injuries, particularly damage to the intra-abdominal organs and fractures of the legs and pelvis. In addition, approximately fifteen percent of all severe head injuries are associated with a broken neck, necessitating careful handling and appropriate splinting during evacuation.

Oxygen, if available, should be administered to all brain injury victims regardless of the altitude. With such injuries respiratory function is depressed at a time when an adequate supply of oxygen for the brain is particularly important.

During evacuation the victim should be transported in the supine position with his head slightly elevated if possible to promote the drainage of venous blood from the brain and help reduce swelling and congestion. However, if the victim is vomiting, his head must be lower than the rest of his body to prevent aspiration of the vomitus. The presence of severe facial fractures may require that the victim be transported in a face down position or that a tracheostomy be performed in order to maintain an open airway.

A record of pulse, respiration, and if possible, blood pressure should be made at hourly intervals for the first twelve hours after injury and then every four hours until evacuation is completed.

If the victim is not hospitalized, either because the injury does not appear to be of sufficient severity, or circumstances prevent hospitalization, he should be closely watched for at least a week after his injury. A blood clot may be formed within the skull which produces no signs or symptoms at the time of the accident but can prove fatal a few days or weeks later.

SUBDURAL HEMATOMA

The brain is unique among the body's organs in that it is encased in a snugly fitting envelope of bone. Bleeding or swelling, which accompany injuries to any organ or tissue, compress the brain within this rigid covering and frequently

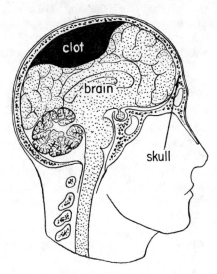

Figure 25. Subdural hematoma.

produce damage and dysfunction quite out of proportion to the size and severity of the original injury. A minor hemorrhage, which would not be of any significance with a wound anywhere else, is often sufficient to cause death when confined within the skull.

Occasionally a blow to the head, although not severely injuring the brain at the time, breaks some of the blood vessels around the brain. Blood from the torn vessels pours out into the narrow space between the brain and the skull and produces a clot which compresses the brain. Death is usually the final outcome in untreated cases or in cases in which treatment is obtained too late.

The speed with which this clot develops depends on the number and size of the blood vessels which have been damaged. Following severe injuries the evidence of bleeding may become apparent within a few hours. In other cases, signs of injury may not appear for two or three weeks or occasionally even longer. (Even though the bleeding stops the clot continues to enlarge through the absorption of water due to osmotic pressure created by the breaking up of the red blood cells.) The prognosis for the patient correlates fairly well with the speed with which the hematoma becomes evident. An acute subdural hematoma which develops within twenty-four to forty-eight hours carries a very poor prognosis. A chronic subdural which develops two to three weeks after injury carries a much more favorable prognosis.

An epidural hematoma is a similar disorder which usually follows a fracture of the skull. The clot is located between the bone and its covering fibrous membrane, but the effect on the brain is the same. The damaged blood vessels producing an epidural hematoma are usually medium sized arteries rather than the smaller veins which produce a subdural hematoma. Therefore, signs of an epidural hematoma usually come on faster and are more severe.

Diagnosis

In a typical example of subdural hematoma the victim receives a blow to the head, is unconscious for about thirty to sixty minutes, and then returns to consciousness and apparent normality. Some time later he begins to exhibit signs and symptoms of a brain injury. Eventually, after a variable period of time, he lapses into unconsciousness.

The victim is in critical condition when coma occurs the second time and must be evacuated immediately if he is to have any chance for survival. A much more favorable outcome is usually possible and evacuation is certainly much easier if the signs of the developing clot can be recognized before unconsciousness ensues.

Few cases of subdural hematoma develop following an injury which renders the victim unconscious for less than twenty minutes. Occasionally this disorder does follow less severe injuries and may rarely develop after a blow which does not produce unconsciousness at all. Therefore, the recipient of any blow on the head must be closely watched. However, the period of twenty minutes is a good reference point in evaluating the seriousness of a head injury. Anyone unconscious for a longer time must be considered to be in significant danger of developing a subdural hematoma.

The intellect is the highest function of the brain and is frequently the first to be impaired in central nervous system disorders. Changes in personality — particularly irritability — confusion, and irrational speech or behavior are all signs of cerebral dysfunction. Anyone knocked unconscious may be mildly confused or irrational for a few hours after regaining consciousness. However, such signs are indicative of a serious disorder if they persist for more than twenty-four hours or begin to get worse.

Headache and nausea, with or without vomiting, frequently result from brain injuries. Stumbling, loss of coordination, loss of the ability to stand with the eyes closed, and weakness are more serious signs of a cerebral disorder. Inequality of the pupils is a definite and important sign of brain injury which must be carefully sought.

None of these signs in itself is diagnostic of the presence of a subdural hematoma; most can be produced by diseases of other organs. However, deterioration in the victim's condition, an increase in the severity of any signs and symptoms of brain injury, or the concurrence of several such signs following a head injury is highly significant and should prompt immediate evacuation. Paralysis, loss of sensation, disturbances of vision or hearing, and loss of consciousness are signs that develop later in the course of the disorder. Evacuation should not be delayed until these late signs have appeared.

Treatment

Treatment for a subdural hematoma consists of its surgical removal, which cannot be performed in the field. The only recourse is evacuation of the patient to the care of a neurosurgeon. The more quickly evacuation is accomplished the better are the victim's chances for complete recovery.

A rapidly developing subdural hematoma in a remote area is of such grave danger and the difficulties in evacuating an unconscious subject from such a situation so great that the occurrence of a head injury to a member of a weekend outing or similar short trip is more than adequate justification for cutting short the outing while the victim is able to walk to a location where medical care is available. On a more extended expedition, the victim should at least be returned to a point where further evacuation can be readily accomplished should signs of increasing injury develop.

SKULL FRACTURE

Skull fractures are often surprisingly difficult to diagnose. Nonfatal fractures may occur with relatively little brain injury and no detectable deformity. (In contrast, fatal brain injuries occasionally occur without fracturing the bones of the skull.) A few fractures may result in a small portion of the skull being depressed into the brain. Larger depressed fractures and fractures accompanied by other obvious deformities are usually immediately fatal.

The other signs of a fracture — pain, tenderness, swelling, and discoloration — are masked by contusions or lacerations of the scalp which produce swelling and bleeding in the tissues overlying the skull. Occasionally the signs characteristic of fracture are present on the opposite side of the head from the point of impact. In this location such findings are often indicative of the presence of a fracture. This injury — the so-called *"contre-coup"* fracture — is produced by the coincidence of the forces created by the impact at a point on the opposite side of the skull. Paradoxically, the skull may not be fractured at the point where the blow actually landed.

Fractures of the base of the skull frequently produce bleeding from the ears or nose. (The attendant should make certain the blood is coming from within the ears or nose and not from a laceration of the surrounding skin.) Similarly, the clear, straw-colored fluid which surrounds the brain — cerebrospinal fluid — may leak from defects in the bones of the ear or nose resulting from a skull fracture. However, many of the fractures which produce these signs are also associated with brain injuries which prove fatal immediately or within two or three days.

Fractures of the base of the skull may also involve the bony orbit of the eye. The eye on the injured side drops back into its socket and appears sunken when compared with the opposite eye.

The safest course is to assume that any head injury which has resulted in unconsciousness has also fractured the skull. X-ray examination should be obtained to determine whether a fracture is present. Under expedition circumstances, the persistence of headache for more than two or three days, the appearance of other signs of brain injury, or the presence of blood or cerebrospinal fluid leaking from the nose or ears should prompt immediate evacuation to an area where x-ray studies can be made and definitive treatment instituted.

No specific treatment for skull fracture can be given in the field. The victim should be evacuated promptly with special precautions to prevent further head injuries. Injuries to other parts of the body should receive appropriate attention. Unconsciousness requires the maintenance of an airway and the usual treatment for coma resulting from any disorder. If blood or cerebrospinal fluid is leaking from the nose or ears, penicillin should be given every six hours to reduce the possibility of infection spreading from these areas to the brain.

SCALP INJURIES

Scalp injuries differ from other soft tissue injuries in two respects. First, the scalp contains a large number of blood vessels which produce rather severe bleeding from otherwise minor injuries. Secondly, infected scalp wounds are potentially more dangerous due to the proximity of the brain and the danger of spread of the infection to that organ. Fortunately, the scalp is more resistant to infection than most of the other soft tissues.

The treatment of scalp injuries is similar to the care for soft tissue injuries located anywhere else on the body. Bleeding can be controlled by pressing down firmly with the finger tips or with a gauze pad on both sides of the injury. Special care must be taken to flush all loose foreign material out of the wound.

A foreign body embedded in the skull or brain must not be disturbed. The wound should be bandaged with the object in place, thick dressings applied to prevent dislocation of the object during transport and the victim evacuated immediately. If evacuation requires more than a day the patient should be given penicillin or nafcillin, intravenously if possible, in twice the usual dose every six hours.

During the cleansing of a scalp wound the underlying bone should be examined, but not probed, for evidence of a fracture. If a fracture is found or suspected, similar antibiotic therapy should be given and the patient evacuated.

FACIAL INJURIES

Soft Tissue Injuries

The tissues of the face have a greater blood supply than most other areas, tend to heal faster, and have greater resistance to infection. Fragments of skin in facial wounds should not be trimmed away unless they are so badly damaged that survival is obviously impossible. Many such skin fragments can be saved and may reduce the need for skin grafting at a later date. Scarring is also reduced by preserving these fragments.

Fractures

Facial fractures are uncomfortable, but do not require splinting and seldom interfere with locomotion. Delayed treatment is often the preferred method of caring for hospitalized patients with such injuries. Therefore, specific treatment for facial fractures is rarely an urgent problem. However, such fractures can create serious problems in the maintenance of an open airway, particularly in unconscious patients. A fractured jaw may permit the tongue to drop back into the throat, completely obstructing the passage of air. Blood from fractures about the nose runs back into the throat where it is often aspirated, causing obstruction of the smaller air passages in the lung.

Brain injuries, skull fractures, and fractures of the vertebral column in the neck frequently accompany facial fractures, and must be cared for if present.

Fractures should be suspected after any severe blow to the face. Pain, tenderness, swelling and discoloration are signs which tend to confirm such suspicions. Facial fractures rarely cause any gross deformity, except for occasional fractures of the nose or jaw, but some discontinuity of the bones can occasionally be felt. A broken nose frequently produces rather profuse nose bleeds. Double vision is frequently a sign of fractures of the bones about the eye.

Except for fractures of the lower jaw, facial fractures do not require splinting as do most other fractures. A broken jaw should be splinted by a bandage which passes under the chin and over the top of the head, binding the lower jaw to the upper. The patient is required to subsist on a liquid diet since he is unable to chew solid food.

The maintenance of an open airway in a patient with facial fractures may require diligence and perseverance. The victim frequently must be transported in a face down position, particularly if severe bleeding or swelling is present. Fractures of the jaw should not be splinted if the victim needs to breathe through his mouth. A finger should be swept through the mouth of any unconscious patient with a broken jaw to remove any teeth or bone fragments which have broken off and prevent them from blocking the airway. Obviously his face must be kept free of pillows or sleeping bags, and the stretcher while he is in this position. A hole can be cut in the stretcher for the victim's nose and mouth.

Nose Bleeds

Nose bleeds are very common following minor injuries to the nose; fractures of the nasal bones are usually accompanied by rather severe bleeding. Nose bleeds without any antecedent trauma are even more common and may be severe. Anyone with repeated or severe nose bleeds should consult a physician since such incidents may be signs of a serious disorder.

The patient should be placed in an upright position with his head leaning forward. He must not be allowed to sit with his head leaning backwards or to lie down on his back, as this permits the blood to drain back into the throat where it is usually swallowed and frequently produces nausea and vomiting.

Pinching the nostrils together along their full length may stop the bleeding.

If bleeding persists, a cotton pledget can be moistened with phenylephrine nose drops or spray and formed into an elongated roll. After both nostrils have been blown clear to remove any clots or mucous, the cotton roll should be inserted in the side which is bleeding. The nose should be held closed with gentle pressure for three to five minutes. After the pressure has been released another two to three minute interval should be allowed to pass. Then the cotton roll can be gently removed. If bleeding persists, this procedure may be repeated as often as necessary until the bleeding is controlled. This technique is usually effective eventually even with nasal fractures.

EYE INJURIES

Injuries to the eye must always receive immediate and careful attention. Even the most trivial injury can result in total loss of vision if not cared for properly.

Penetrating Injuries

Eye injuries are usually obvious, but may be easily overlooked in an unconscious patient. Such injuries must always be suspected in the presence of head or facial injuries or injuries of the opposite eye.

The various types of eye injuries include lacerations, in which there is obvious damage to the structure of the eye, contusions which produce hemorrhage within the eye and loss of vision but no external signs of injury, and injuries of the nerves and muscles of the eye or the bone surrounding the eye, which result in double vision, or occasionally loss of vision.

The eye is located within a socket of bone which protects it from most injuries. As a result, those injuries which do occur are usually associated with injuries of the surrounding bone and soft tissues. Eyelid injuries, which are discussed below, can be almost as devastating as injuries of the eye itself.

The treatment for all eye injuries consists of bandaging the eye, administering antibiotics, and evacuating the victim to an ophthalmologist. Attempts to remove foreign bodies or any other manipulations almost inevitably result in further damage. Extensive experience has demonstrated that a delay of ten to fourteen days in obtaining treatment for such injuries usually makes no difference in the final results.

All dirt and debris should be washed away as gently as possible with lukewarm clean water or saline solution. No attempts should be made to remove blood clots attached to the eye, since it is impossible to distinguish between blood clots and fragments of the inner structures of the eye which have been extruded through a wound. Eyelid injuries should also receive appropriate care.

During evacuation the eye should be covered with a bandage or patch. The uninjured eye should be covered with a shield of cardboard or similar opaque material with a small hole in the center. This type of shield permits the patient to see only straight ahead and minimizes eye movements, thereby tending to splint the injured eye.

Penicillin should be given orally every six hours if evacuation requires more than one day. Aspirin and codeine or morphine may be given every four hours to reduce pain; medications for sleep may also be required because such injuries often cause the patient much anxiety. The patient should be kept quiet during evacuation. He must not be permitted to touch his injured eye or finger its bandage.

Eyelid Injuries

Injuries of the eyelids can be as threatening to vision as injuries of the eye itself. If the eye is not continuously moistened by the tears which the lid spreads over its surface, it rapidly dries. Drying causes death of the superficial layers of cells of the eye, resulting in scarring and blindness.

The torn or lacerated eyelid, after being washed free of all dirt and foreign material, should be returned as closely as possible to its original position. The eye must be completely covered. A snugly fitting bandage should be applied to hold the fragments in place. Both eyes should be bandaged to prevent blinking or other movements which would disturb the alignment of the injured lid.

Rarely the entire lid may be ripped away. If the lower lid is lost the upper lid can usually be pulled down with adhesive tape to cover the entire eye. If the upper lid or both eyelids are lost, the exposed eye should be covered with a thick layer of an ophthalmic ointment. A sterile dressing, preferably of soft material, should be placed over the eye and held in place with a snug bandage.

Patients with such severe eyelid injuries should be evacuated as fast as possible. Antibiotics are not necessary and should not be given unless the injury is unusually contaminated. The tears contain a substance — lysozyme — which is antibacterial and is quite capable of eliminating most bacteria.

Minor lacerations, scratches, or abrasions which do not penetrate the eyelid, avulse portions of the lid, or damage the underlying eye are not such serious injuries. They should be treated in the same manner as similar skin injuries anyplace else, and do not require any special consideration.

Foreign Bodies

Foreign bodies in the eye are very common, are usually easily removed, and are rarely followed by any serious consequences. These objects are usually adherent to the inner surface of the eyelids and can be removed by pulling one eyelid over the lashes of the other. If necessary, the eyelid can be folded outward over a match stem or similar object and the foreign material brushed away with the edge of a clean handkerchief or a wisp of sterile cotton.

A foreign body may become embedded in the superficial layer of the eye itself. A physician should preferably remove the offending object, but in circumstances where a physician is not available attempts can be made to brush the object away with a sterile cotton swab or the corner of a folded handkerchief. If the object cannot be brushed away, it can occasionally be removed by using the tip of an eighteen or nineteen guage injection needle. Obviously great care must be exercised. If these measures are not successful, the eye should be bandaged and medical assistance obtained. Foreign objects which appear to actually penetrate the eye should *never* be disturbed by anyone other than an opthalmologist.

Occasionally the foreign material produces a mild conjunctivitis which should be treated as described in "Diseases of the Eye, Ear, Nose, and Throat." Individuals with a foreign object imbedded in the eye should receive the same treatment regardless of whether signs of conjunctivitis are present.

EAR INJURIES

Ear injuries are infrequent. Most are simple skin injuries which should be treated like similar injuries located any place else. More severe injuries are often associated with severe head or brain injuries.

One important cause of ear injuries is the use of keys, toothpicks, hairpins, or almost anything to clean the canals of water or wax. Nothing should ever be used to clean the ear in this manner. The old adage "never put anything in your ear smaller than your elbow" is a wise one. If accumulations of wax, or more rarely a foreign body such as a small insect, cause problems, they should be removed by irrigating the ear with lukewarm water, preferably using a soft rubber bulb designed specifically for this purpose.

Occasionally a traumatic injury causes a hematoma or blood clot to develop in the external portion of the ear. If the clot is large enough to cover one-third or more of the ear and is allowed to persist, it can cause permanent scarring resulting in a cauliflower ear deformity. Such clots should be incised and drained to avoid this type of scarring. First the skin should be cleaned and an antiseptic applied. Then one or more small incisions should be made, and the blood expressed with gentle pressure. Removal of all the blood is not necessary and would probably aggravate the underlying injury. The ear should then be covered with a sterile bandage.

NECK INJURIES

Injuries to the neck can cause serious damage to the many structures contained in that area. Many large blood vessels are present and can produce massive hemorrhage. Hoarseness, coughing up blood, or the development of a diffuse swelling of the neck which feels spongy or crepitant to palpation is an indication of injury to the air passages in the neck. Patients with such injuries should be evacuated without delay. Swelling associated with the injury may result in the later development of airway obstruction, so the patient must be carefully watched and preparations for performance of a tracheostomy should be made.

BAROTRAUMA

The middle ear and the paranasal sinuses consist of numerous small chambers lined by thin mucous membranes and filled with air. These chambers have narrow connections to the nose or throat through which air can move to equalize the pressure of the air within the chamber with that of the external atmosphere. For the middle ears this tube enters the throat and is known as the eustachean tube.

If the pressure within the chambers is not equalized, a sense of fullness develops and hearing is diminished. Swallowing or yawning may open the eustachean tube rather suddenly so that a "pop" is heard as the pressure is suddenly equalized. As atmospheric pressure decreases, such as during the ascent to higher altitudes, air leaves these chambers without difficulty. However, during a descent to a lower altitude more active measures such as swallowing or yawning are required to open the eustachean tube and permit the pressure to equalize.

Occasionally a cold or nasal allergy causes the mucosa around the openings of the eustachean tube and the ducts into the nasal sinuses to swell and plug off these tubular openings. At a pressure differential of ninety millimeters (which represents a change in altitude of about 3,750 feet) the eustachean tube can no longer be opened by swallowing. As the pressure differential increases the sensations of fullness in the ears and nose become more and more painful. Involvement of the ears can cause sensations of noise, lightheadedness, and hearing loss. If sufficiently severe the ear drum can be ruptured. However, pressure differentials of such severity can only develop when descent is made rapidly, as occurs in unpressurized aircraft or sometimes in automobiles on steep mountain roads.

As soon as an individual becomes aware of symptoms in his nose or ears he should begin making efforts to equalize the pressure. Subjects with colds or hay fever should be aware of their increased risk from barotrauma and should be prepared with decongestants to help reduce the mucosal swelling. A phenylephrine spray or similar preparation is usually adequate. Care must be taken to apply the spray a second time after an interval of several minutes so the spray can enter the deeper recesses of the nose and back into the throat. A systemic decongestant such as Actifed can also be taken in advance of the descent, although this drug should not be used if drowsiness is likely to create problems.

If precautions are not successful or are neglected, or the individual is unconscious, an aerotitis media or aerosinusitis may develop. These disorders are usually quite painful. However, they rarely cause any other problems, and the pain usually disappears within twenty-four hours or less. The patients should be given a systemic decongestant such as Actifed to promote drainage of the ears or sinuses. Aspirin with codeine may also be given to help relieve the pain.

REFERENCES:

1. Javid, M.: Head Injuries, New Eng. J. Med. *291*: 890, 1974.
2. Hoff, J.: Evaluation of the Patient with Head Injury (Trauma Rounds), West. J. Med. *121*: 435, 1974.

CHAPTER 10

Chest Injuries

CHEST injuries are of particular importance because they interfere with the vital function of respiration. At high altitudes, where the oxygen content of the air is low, even minor injuries to the chest may assume major importance. In contrast to abdominal injuries, however, definite help can be given the victim of a chest injury in mountaineering circumstances.

THE MECHANICS OF RESPIRATION

The function of the lungs is to provide oxygen for the body and to dispose of carbon dioxide. During inspiration the chest is expanded by the muscles in the chest wall. Simultaneously, the muscle in the diaphragm contracts, pulling this structure downward. Air is drawn into the lungs by the negative pressure created through the bellows action of the chest and the diaphragm.

Expiration is essentially a passive action involving no muscular contractions. The lung tissue is stretched by the expansion of the chest during inspiration. When the muscles relax at the end of inspiration, the chest wall and diaphragm are pulled back into their original positions by the elasticity of the lung.

Each lung is enveloped by a thin membrane called the visceral pleura. Another membrane, the parietal pleura, lines the inner surface of the rib cage. The space between these two layers of pleura is called the pleural cavity. Normally the lungs fill the entire thorax so that the two layers of pleura are in intimate contact with each other. If the chest wall is perforated or the lung is punctured, air enters the pleural space. The elasticity of the lung causes it to collapse, extruding or pulling more air into the pleural space, depending on the site of the opening. Subsequent expansion of the chest cavity serves only to pull air in through a hole in the chest (or to pull air out through a hole in the lung) into the pleural cavity and does not expand the lung itself. This condition is known as pneumothorax. At high altitude, where great demands are already being made on pulmonary function, the resulting loss in pulmonary capability may well prove fatal.

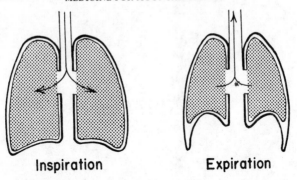

Figure 26. Normal pulmonary function. (Figs. 26, 27, 28, 30, 32, and 60 are adapted from *Surgery of the Chest,* 3rd ed., by Julian Johnson and Charles K. Kirby. Copyright 1964, Year Book Medical Publishers, Inc. Used by permission. Drawings by Edna Hill.)

CLOSED CHEST INJURIES

Broken Rib

A severe blow to the chest may break one or more ribs, but the ribs are so enmeshed by muscles that they do not need to be splinted or realigned as is necessary with other broken bones. Other than producing discomfort, most rib fractures are not serious injuries. However, pain from the fracture can interfere with movement of the underlying lung. Fluid and secretions then collect in the immobile segment of lung, producing congestion or even pneumonia. Very rarely a broken rib may be displaced by the force producing the fracture. The displaced bone end can puncture the lung or, if low in the chest, be associated with kidney, liver, or spleen injury.

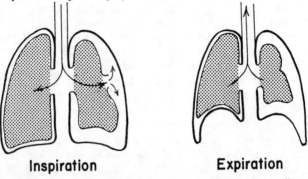

Figure 27. Pulmonary function with a punctured lung and intact chest wall. (Adapted from *Surgery of the Chest,* 3rd ed.)

A broken rib should be suspected after any blow to the chest followed by pain and tenderness over the area of injury, particularly if the pain is aggravated by deep breathing. Usually a defect cannot be palpated at the point of fracture since the ends of the rib are held in position by their surrounding muscles.

The victim should rest for a day or two, as dictated by the degree of pain. Adhesive strapping over the rib is not advisable at high altitudes (over 10,000 feet) since such immobilization of the chest wall produces even more interference with movement of the lung on that side. Impaired function in the segment of lung underlying the fracture could have serious effects under such conditions. At lower elevations, if the pain cannot be controlled with moderate doses of codeine, four or five strips of one- or two-inch adhesive tape can be applied to the chest to minimize movement of the injured area. The strips of tape should lie over and parallel with the fractured rib and should run from the mid-line in front past the vertebral column in back. Taping usually gives some relief from pain, but must be removed in two to three days. Similar immobilization can also be provided by wrapping the chest with an elastic bandage, but since both sides of the chest are restrained, this technique must not be used at high altitudes.

Flail Chest

If a number of ribs are broken in several places, a sizable plate of chest wall can become loosened, destroying the rigid integrity of the chest wall. Such injuries require immediate treatment since respiratory function is usually severly impaired.

The bellows action of the diaphragm and chest walls pulls air into the lungs during inspiration by creating a negative pressure within the rigid thoracic cage. Multiple rib fractures can produce a mobile section of chest wall which

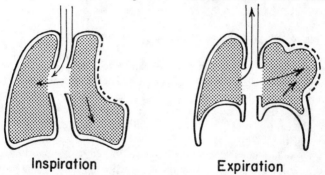

Inspiration **Expiration**

Figure 28. Pulmonary function with a flail chest. (Adapted from *Surgery of the Chest,* 3rd ed.)

moves back and forth during respiration — a flail chest. When the chest is expanded, the negative pressure pulls the loosened portion of the chest wall inward rather than pulling air into the lung. If the area of flail chest is large, ventilation may be so impaired that death ensues. If the damaged area is smaller, severe respiratory insufficiency results.

The victim typically has a history of having received a severe blow to the chest followed immediately by pain and difficulty with breathing. He is usually fighting for air and breathing very rapidly; his lips, skin, and nails may be cyanotic due to poor oxygenation. Careful examination of the chest discloses a mobile segment of chest wall which moves paradoxically with each respiration. (When the rest of the chest expands on inspiration, the loosened segment of chest wall is pulled inward.)

Flail chest must be differentiated from a simple broken rib which produces pain with breathing but does not interfere with the movement of air. Traumatic pneumothorax, which is discussed below, must also be anticipated.

The treatment of flail chest centers upon immobilization of the loosened segment of chest wall, thus re-establishing normal respiratory function. In an emergency the victim can simply lie on the injured side with a rolled-up parka or other piece of clothing beneath the loose segment of rib cage. The pressure effectively immobilizes the loosened portion of the chest wall and thus allows more adequate respiration. Such a simple measure may often prove life-saving.

Figure 29. Patient lying on a rolled-up garment to support a flail chest.

More permanent fixation of the rib cage can be achieved with adhesive tape immobilization of the loose fragment of chest wall or through external pressure on the broken rib segments by a sand bag or even a smooth rock properly padded. The loosened segment of chest wall must not be allowed to move; any reasonable means of providing such immobilization benefits the patient's respiratory function.

The lung underlying a flail chest is usually bruised and is poorly aerated. Fluid secretions often accumulate in the damaged lung, since proper drainage of the lung is impaired. To avoid pneumonia the patient must be encouraged to clear his lungs frequently by coughing.

The need for oxygen therapy can be determined by the degree of respiratory distress and the general condition of the patient. If the patient has a severe degree of flail and cannot be moved to a physician's care, penicillin should be given every six hours to reduce the danger of bacterial pneumonia. At altitudes over 10,000 feet, both antibiotic and oxygen therapy should be administered, even for relatively minor chest injuries that would not require such vigorous therapy at lower altitudes.

The advisability of emergency evacuation depends on the situation and the condition of the patient. Even with an extensive injury the chest wall becomes relatively stable within about one week. However, during this period pneumonia and progressively poor oxygenation (hypoxia) of life-threatening proportions can develop. If there is any evidence of such complications associated with fractured ribs, flail chest, or pneumothorax, oxygen should be administered and the patient evacuated. He must be hospitalized where he can be placed on a mechanical ventilator if such is required.

Following any chest injury in which breathing is difficult and oxygenation marginal, propping the patient in a sitting position gives some relief. While lying down, the heavy abdominal organs press on the diaphragm and squeeze the lungs into the upper part of the chest. Such encroachment is more likely to occur in fat people. Sitting up pulls down on the diaphragm, gives the lungs more room for expansion, and improves ventilation. Even rolling a fat person on his side helps, for the weight of his belly and abdominal organs rest on the ground, not pushing against his lungs.

Pneumothorax

On occasions a broken rib may be displaced and puncture the underlying lung. Air enters the pleural space through the injury, causing the lung on that

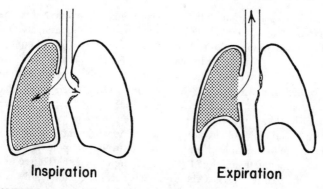

Inspiration   **Expiration**

Figure 30. Pulmonary function with a tension pneumothorax. (Adapted from *Surgery of the Chest,* 3rd ed.)

side to collapse. The tear in the pleura often allows air to enter but not to escape from the chest, thus building up a considerable pressure in the involved pleural space (tension pneumothorax). As a result the lung is further collapsed and respiration is severely impaired.

The patient usually has received a severe, nonpenetrating blow to the chest which is followed by respiratory distress. (Pneumothorax occasionally occurs spontaneously, the onset marked by the sudden appearance of chest pain and respiratory difficulty.) Pain and tenderness is present over the fracture, as with an uncomplicated rib fracture, but chest wall instability or flailing is usually absent. Listening to the chest — preferably with a stethoscope — reveals greatly diminished or absent breath sounds over the entire chest on the side of the injury — a highly significant diagnostic finding. The pressure within the pleural space may push the heart to the opposite side, causing the point at which the heart beat is felt to shift away from the injured side. Also the trachea in the lower part of the neck may be pushed to the side opposite the pneumothorax.

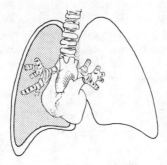

Figure 31. Collapse of the left lung and shift of heart and trachea to the right with left pneumothorax.

Although oxygen partially alleviates symptoms of pneumothorax, the only definitive treatment is to remove the air trapped in the pleural cavity and to allow the lung to re-expand. This procedure should be performed under sterile conditions in a hospital where the chance of infection is minimal. If, however, the patient appears to be in critical condition, tube thoracostomy may have to be performed in more primitive circumstances. Only a person who has witnessed — or preferably practiced — thoracostomy under the tutelage of a physician should attempt tube drainage of the chest. The possible dangers — infection, puncture of the heart or a major blood vessel, missing the chest and puncturing the liver or spleen, and others — outweigh the potential benefits in the hands of the totally untrained. (See "Technique for Tube Thoracostomy.")

Within the past few years a chest tube has become commercially available which is fitted with a one-way flutter valve (Heimlich valve) which permits air and blood to leave the chest, but stops air from re-entering. This apparatus does not require underwater bottle drainage and therefore is well adapted to use in the mountains in the occasional case where tube thoracostomy is necessary. The Heimlich valved tube can be used in a patient who is being evacuated — a great advantage over older techniques.

Decompression of a pneumothorax produces immediate relief of respiratory distress. However, considerable hazard for the patient still exists. The presence of a tube in the chest wall creates an opening through which infection can be introduced into the pleural space. To combat this danger the area around the tube must be kept clean and covered with a sterile bandage. Penicillin may be administered every six hours if the risk of infection appears great.

Usually the hole in the lung seals within one to four days, at which time air no longer bubbles from the end of the tubing when it is placed under water. When no bubbles have been seen for six hours or more, the tube should be clamped. The patient must be watched closely for several hours to see whether respiratory distress returns. If he remains in satisfactory condition, the tube should be left clamped for twenty-four hours. If no air bubbles from the tube when the clamp is released at the end of this time, the tubing may be withdrawn. If bubbles are seen, the entire procedure should be repeated twenty-four hours later. The patient must be closely attended during the time the tube is clamped so that the clamp can be released if respiratory difficulty develops.

To repeat, tube thoracostomy is not to be undertaken lightly and should be attempted only if the victim appears to be dying and the proper equipment is on hand. *The person performing the procedure must have had prior experience with the technique under the guidance of a surgeon.* However, since the technique may prove life-saving, particularly in cases of traumatic pneumothorax at high altitude, it should be utilized if adequately trained personnel and proper equipment are available.

Hemothorax

An injury to the chest may damage blood vessels in the chest wall or in the lung, resulting in bleeding into the pleural space, particularly if a rib is fractured and displaced. The danger of hemothorax, as such a collection of blood in the chest is called, lies in (1) the consequent collapse of the lung as the blood fills the chest; (2) the occasional instances in which the blood loss is sufficiently large to produce shock or — more rarely — death; (3) the tendency of the clot to become infected; and (4) constriction of the lung as the clot retracts weeks or months after the injury.

Blood accumulating in the chest after an injury should be removed; however, removal can wait until the patient is evacuated. The desperate respiratory disturbance that occurs with a tension pneumothorax rarely occurs with hemothorax and there is little danger that the patient will bleed to death into his chest.

Hemothorax usually follows a severe, nonpenetrating injury to the chest and may produce signs and symptoms which simulate pneumothorax. However, tapping on the bare chest produces a dull, solid sound over the accumulating blood instead of the resonant sound heard over air-filled lungs. If the patient can be placed in a sitting position, breath sounds may be absent over the lower part of the chest and yet present over the upper portion. (The breath sounds may be difficult to hear without a stethoscope.)

The bleeding into the chest cavity usually stops spontaneously within a few hours. If shock does appear it should be treated in the appropriate manner. Nothing can be done to stop the bleeding without surgical intervention, and even that is impossible in hospitals which are not equipped to handle chest surgery. Evacuation should be carried out as soon as the patient's blood pressure, pulse rate, respiratory rate, and his general condition look as though he can tolerate being moved.

If a patient is in such a remote area that he cannot be evacuated for several days or weeks, and bleeding is so severe that removal of the blood is necessary to allow proper expansion of the lung, tube thoracostomy may be necessary to remove the blood from the chest.

PERFORATING CHEST INJURIES

A fall onto a sharp or pointed object, such as an ice ax (particularly during an ice ax arrest), may actually punch a hole in the chest wall, producing one of the few medical emergencies in which minutes will determine success or failure. A hole in the thoracic wall permits air to be sucked through the wound into the pleural cavity, causing collapse of the lung. Subsequent respiratory efforts move air back and forth through the hole in the chest rather than through the trachea. Air does not reach the portion of the lungs in which oxygen and carbon dioxide are exchanged and the patient rapidly suffocates.

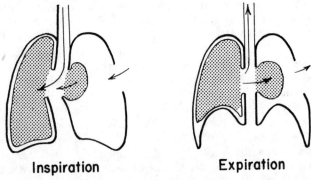

Inspiration   **Expiration**

Figure 32. Pulmonary function with a punctured chest wall. (Adapted from *Surgery of the Chest*, 3rd ed.)

The victim almost always has an obvious penetrating injury of the chest wall, producing a so-called "sucking wound" since air is sucked in through the wound during inspiration. Due to the impairment in respiration the patient begins fighting for air almost immediately and soon becomes cyanotic, loses consciousness, and goes into shock if untreated.

The hole in the chest must be tightly closed at the earliest possible moment in order to restore respiratory function. The best method of closing such a wound is with sterile, fine mesh, vaseline impregnated gauze and an outer, thick, sterile dressing. However, the cleanest available substitute must be utilized immediately: a clean handkerchief, or even a parka can be stuffed over the opening. *The hole must be closed immediately or without exception the patient will die.* A more ideal dressing may be applied later, but air must not be permitted to enter the chest while the coverings are being switched.

Oxygen therapy should be instituted at the earliest opportunity and discontinued only when the patient's condition has definitely stabilized. Decompression of the chest as described for pneumothorax may be necessary. Shock almost invariably accompanies a large penetrating wound of the chest, and should be anticipated and treated. Penicillin or a penicillinase-resistant penicillin should be given every six hours until evacuation is completed if the patient is not allergic to penicillin.

All patients with penetrating injuries of the chest must be evacuated at the earliest possible moment so that the hole in the chest wall can be permanently closed by surgery.

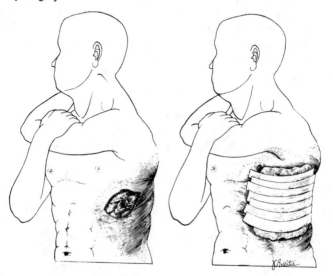

Figure 33. Open chest wound before and after bandaging.

CHAPTER 11

Abdominal Injuries

THE DEFINITIVE treatment for a severe abdominal injury consists of surgery, which is out of the question in mountaineering surroundings. Therefore, management of severe abdominal trauma in such situations consists of recognizing the severity (or triviality) of an injury and deciding whether immediate evacuation is required. As with all injuries, a conservative approach should be adopted; if there is any question about the diagnosis, the worst should be assumed.

Under no circumstances should pseudoheroic attempts at surgical intervention be made. The results would be uniformly fatal without proper anesthesia, sterile operating conditions, or the proper instruments. Even the most severe trauma can occasionally be successfully managed without operation. Furthermore, operative intervention under primitive conditions would be more deadly than most injuries.

DIAGNOSIS

Before any decision can be made concerning the care of an accident victim, an accurate diagnosis must be made. The first step is obtaining an account of the accident. Exact details of the injury, including the site and direction of a blow to the abdomen, are helpful in diagnosing the nature of the intra-abdominal injury. A blow to the left upper quadrant of the abdomen or lower part of the chest may rupture the spleen; on the right side a blow to the same area would injure the liver; trauma to either flank or the back may damage a kidney.

The abdomen must be carefully examined as described in the chapter "Acute Abdominal Pain." Close attention should also be given to blood pressure, pulse rate, respiratory rate, color of skin and fingernails, and other signs of shock. The urine should be examined for blood. However, attention should not be focused on the abdomen to the extent that other injuries are overlooked or neglected.

If the patient is to be evacuated to a physician, a written account of the accident and all diagnostic findings, along with a detailed record of subsequent events, should accompany him. The exact time of the accident, all medications and the time they are administered, hourly measurements of pulse and respiratory rates, and observations about the victim's general condition must be carefully recorded.

TREATMENT

Most abdominal injuries occur out of camp. Since the victim may require immediate evacuation to a surgical facility, he should be carried with all reasonable haste to base camp. The sooner such patients are brought to a camp or evacuation point, the better they withstand the subsequent rigors of bleeding or peritonitis which result from the accident. Patients with severe abdominal injuries usually require litter evacuation of some kind.

Abdominal trauma frequently produces rather severe pain. (The pain may not be proportional to the severity of the injury. Even minor abdominal trauma may be quite painful at first, although the discomfort usually subsides in the hours that follow.) In general, the patient should be kept comfortable by the administration of codeine or morphine. However, these drugs may not be properly absorbed if shock is present, and over-dosage may occur after the circulation is restored. The patient should be made comfortable but not "snowed under." If the patient is to be evacuated promptly to a surgeon, morphine should not be given since such medications tend to mask some vital diagnostic signs. If evacuation is not necessary or must be delayed, more liberal use can be made of morphine.

Severe abdominal trauma may produce bleeding into the peritoneal cavity, rupture of abdominal organs, or both. Peritonitis inevitably results, although the inflammation following hemorrhage is due to irritation by the blood rather then infection. Gastric distension, absence of bowel sounds, nausea and vomiting, and other signs of peritonitis are usually present. (The treatment for peritonitis is described in "Acute Abdominal Pain.")

Shock usually follows abdominal trauma, particularly when intra-abdominal hemorrhage results, and should be anticipated and treated.

NONPENETRATING INJURIES

Blunt or nonpenetrating injuries to the abdomen may produce:

1. Contusion of the abdominal wall;
2. Internal bleeding due to a ruptured spleen, liver, or kidney;
3. Rupture of other internal organs such as the urinary bladder, or rarely, the intestines;
4. Any combination of the above.

Contusion of the Abdominal Wall

Any blow to the abdomen causes a bruise which may be very painful. However, although the area of impact may be quite tender, the abdomen around it is not so painful. If the internal organs have been injured, tenderness is usually diffuse. In the first hour after injury deciding whether a severe blow has produced merely a bruise or serious intra-abdominal damage may be quite difficult. Therefore, a delay of several hours may be necessary before a diagnosis can be made with certainty. A large black-and-blue area may blossom forth twenty-four to thirty-six hours after the injury as blood lost at the time of the accident works its way out under the skin. This discoloration is of no significance, does not require treatment, and subsides spontaneously in time regardless of its extent.

After a tumbling fall — as may occur on a steep ice slope — bruises often appear in areas that the victim had not realized were injured. Frequently the subject feels far more sore and stiff the day after a fall than he did immediately after the injury. If there is no other associated injury, the patient usually recovers after a few days of rest and mild analgesia with aspirin and codeine every four to six hours.

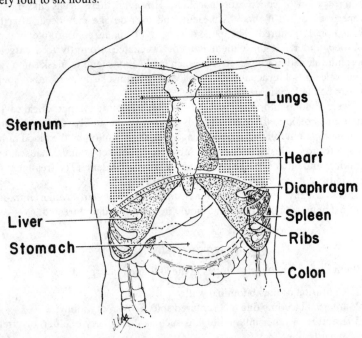

Figure 34. Location of the liver and spleen in relation to the lower ribs anteriorly.

Internal Bleeding

A blow to the abdomen may rupture the liver, spleen, kidney, or a combination of the three. Rupture is more likely if the blow falls immediately over the organ. The liver lies in the right upper quadrant; the spleen in the left upper quadrant. Both are tucked under the rib cage and can be injured by blows to the upper abdomen or to the lower part of the chest. The kidneys, which lie on either side of the backbone, may be damaged by a blow from the back. These organs are solid and may shatter when hit directly. Blood from an injured liver or spleen flows unimpeded into the abdominal cavity. The hemorrhage usually does not stop without surgical intervention. The kidney is enveloped in a tough sheath so that the bleeding is contained. However, blood from a ruptured kidney does appear in the urine.

Ruptured Kidney

A ruptured kidney is usually manifested by:

1. A history of a blow in the flank;
2. Pain, tenderness, and discoloration at the point of injury;
3. Blood in the urine.

Most kidney injuries cease bleeding spontaneously; rarely the kidney must be removed to stop the hemorrhage. The presence of large amounts of blood in the urine for more than six hours, a drop in blood pressure, or a consistently elevated pulse rate are indications that bleeding has assumed dangerous proportions. The patient should be treated for shock and evacuated as rapidly as possible. If the bleeding does stop, the victim must still wait ten to fourteen days before resuming vigorous activity.

Ruptured Liver or Spleen

The patient characteristically has a history of having received a blow to the upper abdomen or lower chest. Pain, tenderness, and evidence of contusion are usually found in the area of impact and one or more ribs may be broken. Shortly after the injury intra-abdominal pain appears, first in the region of the injury and later more diffusely throughout the abdomen. The pain is usually aggravated by breathing deeply and may be associated with pain in the shoulder.

A patient with either of these injuries typically appears in reasonably good condition at first. As hours go by his condition deteriorates. The pulse becomes weak and rapid, and pallor, restlessness, and other signs of shock appear. With the spread of pain, the abdomen becomes tender and rebound tenderness, distension, absence of bowel sounds, and other signs of peritonitis develop.

A patient with an injury of the spleen may recover from the initial accident only to bleed massively when a clot breaks loose from the splenic surface several days or even a week later. The signs of intra-abdominal hemorrhage appear rapidly following this development.

Patients with such injuries must be evacuated to the care of a surgeon as rapidly as possible. The hemorrhage very rarely stops spontaneously; most victims bleed to death if they do not receive surgical treatment. The sooner an operation can be performed, the better are the chances for survival.

During evacuation shock must be anticipated, if it is not already present, and appropriate therapy begun. Pulse, respiratory rate, and blood pressure should be recorded every hour to assist the surgeon who is to assume care of the patient.

Ruptured Abdominal Organ

Severe blunt abdominal trauma may rupture one of the hollow intra-abdominal organs such as the intestines or the urinary bladder. The contents of

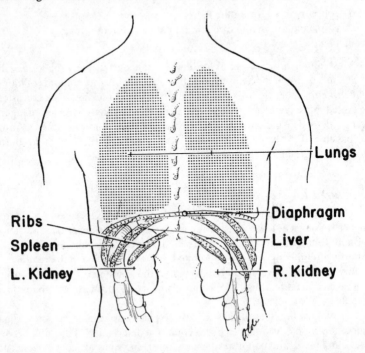

Figure 35. Location of the liver, spleen, and kidneys in relation to the lower ribs posteriorly.

the damaged organ are spilled into the abdominal cavity, producing peritonitis. Rupture of the urinary bladder usually occurs only if the patient is injured when his bladder is full, and is usually associated with a fractured pelvis.

Following injury the pain gradually becomes worse and spreads over the entire abdomen as peritonitis becomes generalized. Diffuse tenderness, abdominal distension, vomiting, and fever soon appear. If the bladder is ruptured, no more urine is voided except for a few drops which are mostly blood.

Treatment is the same as described for peritonitis in the chapter on "Acute Abdominal Pain."

PENETRATING ABDOMINAL INJURIES

Perforating injuries of the abdomen, which are rare in mountaineering, are occasionally caused by a skewering ski-pole, an aberrant ice ax, or even a gunshot wound. These injuries are extremely serious and require operative treatment. Not only are the abdominal organs injured, but the abdominal cavity is contaminated from external sources, causing severe peritonitis.

The diagnosis is usually quite obvious. However, a perforating abdominal wound may be overlooked following a shotgun injury. Attention must not be limited to the area of most obvious injury. The patient should be stripped of all clothes and the entire abdomen and back carefully checked for bullet or pellet holes.

Evacuation should be carried out as quickly and rapidly as possible. During evacuation the patient should be treated for peritonitis. Shock should be anticipated and treated.

A sterile dressing should be placed over the wound. In contrast to the usual care given soft tissue injuries, the wound should not be washed or cleaned up since such efforts only introduce more infection. Any loops of bowel protruding through the wound should be pushed back into the abdomen with the cleanest technique possible. The dressing over the wound should be sufficiently snug to prevent the bowel from popping back out again. This dressing should not be changed once it is in place since further contamination of the wound would result and no benefit can be expected.

CHAPTER 12

Medical Problems of High Altitude

MEDICAL PROBLEMS due to high altitude include a number of uncomfortable symptoms and some potentially dangerous conditions, all resulting from a decrease in the oxygen concentration in the blood caused by the low atmospheric pressure at high altitudes.

PHYSIOLOGY

Altitude effects result from the lower oxygen content of the air, not the lower barometric pressure. At 18,000 feet the atmospheric pressure is half that at sea level and any given volume of air contains half the amount (by weight) of oxygen it does at sea level. However, the proportion of oxygen in the atmosphere does remain constant at approximately twenty percent. The body requires just as much oxygen at high altitude as at sea level, but cannot store oxygen as it stores water or nutrients.

Acclimatization

Man's survival and effective function at 18,000 feet and toleration of 28,000 feet without supplemental oxygen is an example of adaptation or acclimatization. The most important processes in acclimatization are:

1. *Increase in respiratory rate and volume (ventilation).* This change usually begins at about 3,000 feet and may not reach a constant value until several days after arrival at high altitude. Its effect is to deliver more oxygen per minute to the air sacs of the lung for absorption by the blood in the lung capillaries. The increase in ventilation is most obvious during exercise and is experienced by the new arrival at high altitude as undue shortness of breath during even moderate exertion.

2. *Changes in the pulmonary circulation.* During exposure to any type of low oxygen atmosphere, including high altitude, the pressure in the pulmonary arteries is elevated and the capillaries of the lung are more fully perfused with blood, increasing the capacity of the circulatory bed of the lung to absorb oxygen.

3. *Increased number of red blood cells.* Shortly after arrival at high altitude a slight increase in the number of red blood cells in the blood occurs due to loss of water from the fluid portion of the blood. Later, red blood cell production by the bone marrow is increased so that the blood contains more red cells than at sea level. Since the red cells carry oxygen, the increased number of red cells permits each unit of blood to carry more oxygen. This process reaches its maximum level after about six weeks.

4. *Increased cardiac output.* During the first few days at high altitude, the volume of blood pumped by the heart per minute is increased, which increases the rate of oxygen delivery to the tissues.

5. *Changes in capacity of blood to deliver oxygen.* Red blood cells contain 2,3 diphosphoglycerate (DPG) which facilitates release of oxygen from the cells. The concentration of DPG in the blood increases rapidly during ascent to high altitudes. This increase, along with changes in the acidity of the blood, allows oxygen to be released to the tissues more easily.

6. *Changes in tissues of the body.* Prolonged residence at high altitude is accompanied by changes in the tissues which consume oxygen, particularly muscle, which permit normal function at very low oxygen pressures. These changes include an increase in the number of capillaries within the tissue, and an increase in the concentration of enzymes which consume oxygen, as well as an increase in the number of mitochondria, which are the cellular structures within which these enzymes are located.

The time required for the different adaptive processes is variable. The respiratory and biochemical changes are complete in six to eight days. The increase in the number of red blood cells is about ninety percent of maximum at six weeks. In general, about eighty percent of adaptation is complete by ten days, and ninety-five percent is complete at six weeks. Longer periods of acclimatization result in only minor increases in high altitude performance.

Acclimatization is lost about as rapidly as it is gained after return to sea level — about six to ten days — but some altitude tolerance may be retained for six weeks or longer.

The Heart and Altitude

High altitude is not dangerous for the heart. Heavy exercise puts a greater strain on the heart at sea level than it does at high altitude. Maximal exercise at sea level is limited by the heart's ability to pump blood. At high altitude

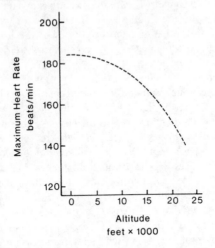

Figure 36. Decline of maximum heart rate with altitude.

exercise is limited by the ability of the chest muscles and diaphragm to move air in and out of the lungs. Thus lung function limits exercise at high altitude before maximal stress is placed on the heart. The amount of exercise that can be performed at high altitude is less than at sea level and the heart rate reached during maximal exercise is less, indicating less cardiac work. Maximal exercise capacity decreases progressively with higher altitudes.

Lung Function and Altitude

At sea level the lungs' capacity to deliver oxygen to the blood maintains a normal blood oxygen concentration even during exhausting exercise. During heavy exercise at high altitude this capacity of the lungs can be exceeded and the oxygen concentration of the blood can fall. The magnitude of the fall in oxygen concentration is related to the severity of the exercise and the altitude and is an important factor in limiting exercise performance at very high altitude.

Work of Breathing

Breathing requires work by the muscles connecting the ribs and by the diaphragm. The oxygen required for this work is small, accounting for only about three percent of the total body oxygen consumpton. At high altitude the work of breathing, especially during exercise, is greatly increased. The increase in the rate and depth of breathing requires the use of muscles of the neck,

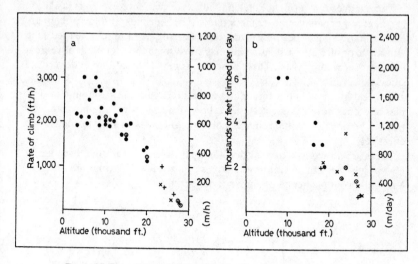

Figure 37. Rate of ascent and daily altitude gain at various altitudes.

shoulders, and abdomen. With heavy effort at very high altitudes the oxygen required for breathing may be so great that it significantly reduces the amount left for climbing. Supplemental oxygen at very high altitude helps prevent a fall in oxygen concentration during exercise and also decreases the amount of oxygen required for the work of breathing, making more available for climbing.

ACHIEVING ACCLIMATIZATION

In a practical sense, acclimatization can be attained in one of three ways: (1) going to high altitude and spending the first two to four days in light activity; (2) going to an intermediate altitude for two to six days and then moving up to a higher altitude; or (3) climbing 500 to 1,000 feet each day, interrupted by an occasional rest day. Most climbing parties, by intent or due to the terrain, use the third method of adaptation which does appear to give the most protection against altitude illness and allow maximum climbing performance.

Acclimatization requires continuous exposure. The amount of acclimatization achieved by several weekend sojourns above 10,000 feet is minimal. Since acclimatization is lost at about the same rate it is gained, an acclimatized individual can spend a few days at sea level and then return to high altitude without much loss of tolerance. However, if the sea level stay is longer than two weeks, problems of high altitude occur just as frequently as during the initial ascent.

There is anecdotal evidence that individuals over twenty-five years in age are less likely to experience acute mountain sickness or high altitude pulmonary edema than younger persons. It has also been observed that prolonged high altitude exposure at yearly intervals may have some long-term adaptive benefits over succeeding years. These conclusions may not stand up under critical study, however.

Physical fitness does not confer any protection against acute mountain sickness and does not facilitate acclimatization. A physical training program carried out before high altitude climbing does permit the individual to climb more effectively.

There are no artificial or pharmocologic aids to acclimatization. Breathing a low oxygen mixture several times daily is of no value. No drugs are of value. Vitamins or supplemental iron are not beneficial.

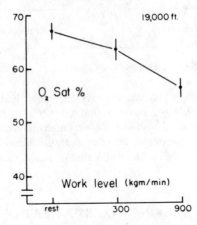

Figure 38. Blood oxygen content (saturation) under varying working conditions at 19,000-foot altitude.

ACUTE MOUNTAIN SICKNESS

Acute mountain sickness is not a specific disease, but is a term applied to a group of rather widely varying symptoms caused by altitude. The primary cause is undoubtedly the decreased oxygen in the blood which is related directly to the altitude attained. (Some of the symptoms may be related to the low carbon dioxide content of the blood which results from the increase in respiration.) However, the mechanism by which the reduced oxygen produces the varied features of acute mountain sickness is uncertain. The evidence presently available suggests some alteration of the cells lining small blood vessels is present which allows water to leave the vessels and accumulate in the tissues in an abnormal manner. This change apparently is associated with a reduction in water excretion by the kidneys.

The symptoms of acute mountain sickness depend on the height attained and the rate of ascent, usually begin within a few hours of ascent, and begin to decrease in severity on about the third day. Common symptoms include headache, dizziness, fatigue, shortness of breath, loss of appetite, nausea and vomiting (particularly in children), disturbed sleep, and a general feeling of being unwell (malaise) which has been compared to "feeling as if I had the flu" or having a hangover. Drowsiness and frequent yawning are common. Anxiety attacks and hyperventilation may occur. Cheyne-Stokes breathing may be present during the day, and is common at night, when it may interfere with sleep.

A cerebral form of mountain sickness due to the effect of oxygen lack and possibly abnormal fluid collection on the brain may have as the principal symptoms, headache, dizziness, memory loss, confusion, and a decrease in mental acuity. The decrease in mental acuity may be indicated by memory loss, forgetfulness, or the inability to solve simple problems, such as reading a watch or clock from a mirror. In severe cases disturbances in gait, nerve paralysis, psychotic behavior, hallucinations, or coma may be seen. High altitude pulmonary edema may be present in this type of acute mountain sickness and may not be suspected. The cerebral form of acute mountain sickness is more commonly observed at altitudes in excess of 14,000 feet. Prompt treatment is important and consists of oxygen administration and evacuation to a lower altitude.

Acute mountain sickness occurs with increasing frequency at higher altitudes. Between 8,000 and 10,000 feet occasional individuals have symptoms; above 14,000 feet most have symptoms.

Individuals with acute mountain sickness should avoid heavy exertion, drink extra fluids, and eat a light, high carbohydrate diet. Aspirin can be used for headache. Tobacco and alcohol should be avoided. Light outdoor activity is preferable to complete rest. Sleep is definitely not helpful since respirations are slower during sleep, which may make symptoms worse. Sedatives should be avoided since they also decrease respirations, but some individuals may require such drugs for restful sleep.

Some individuals with more severe acute mountain sickness may be forced to rest and may require low flow oxygen (two liters per minute through a plastic mask which covers nose and mouth). To obtain full benefit from oxygen, it should be used continuously for at least fifteen minutes. Oxygen is of no value if it is inhaled for only a few minutes a few times a day. If the supply is adequate, it can be used for twelve to forty-eight hours. If severe symptoms persist despite oxygen or if oxygen is not available, descent to a lower altitude usually results in prompt relief, even if the descent is only 2,000 to 3,000 feet.

Occasionally, an individual who has recently arrived at high altitude may become unusually sleepy and drowsy or very weak. He may rest in a semi-sleeping condition, becoming increasingly cyanotic and beginning to hallucinate or behave in an irrational manner. Recovery can be quickly achieved by awakening the individual, helping him walk around in the open air, and encouraging deep breathing. During sleep, respirations are decreased and the oxygen concentration in the blood can fall to low levels. The oxygen concentration increases rapidly when the individual is awake, active, and breathing deeply.

Some relief from symptoms of acute mountain sickness can be achieved by voluntarily taking ten to twelve successive deep breaths every four to ten minutes. This maneuver provides only temporary relief from symptoms and if overdone may cause dizziness and tingling of the lips and hands due to blowing off too much carbon dioxide.

Acute mountain sickness can be prevented by gradual acclimatization at intermediate altitudes or a gradual ascent over a period of four to six days. There is some experimental evidence that a high carbohydrate diet taken for several days prior to ascent and continued for the first three days of altitude exposure minimizes the symptoms of acute mountain sickness.

Acetazolamide (Diamox) has been found to be of limited value for acute mountain sickness in several well controlled studies. A physician should provide the prescription since there are medical contraindications to this drug, such as kidney or liver disease. The usual dose is 250 mg twice daily beginning one or two days before ascent and continued for three to five days after arrival. Side effects, especially if acetazolamide is taken for more than five days, include tingling of the lips and finger tips, blurring of vision, and alteration of taste. The symptoms subside when the drug is stopped.

There are no physiologic tests that can determine in advance whether an individual will develop acute mountain sickness, nor are there any specific measurements which identify the presence or severity of the disorder. Psychological factors and suggestibility may affect symptoms of acute mountain sickness to a considerable degree.

Generalized Edema at High Altitude

Edema at high altitude is a harmless disorder occurring during the first week at high altitude which is probably caused by the increased permeability of small blood vessels and reduced kidney function resulting from reduced concentrations of oxygen in the blood. Fluid retention can cause a weight gain of four to twelve pounds. The excess fluid can also produce swelling of the face and eyelids (usually observed upon arising in the morning) or swelling of the ankles and feet (usually observed at the end of the day). Urine output may be scanty in spite of adequate fluid intake. Upon returning to a lower elevation, large volumes of urine are passed as the accumulated fluid is lost. Recurrences with each altitude exposure are common. The condition may be somewhat more common in women during the premenstrual period.

Such edema can be prevented or minimized by a low salt diet and the use of a diuretic, but these measures may easily cause greater problems than the disorder they are used to treat.

Retinal Hemorrhages

Hemorrhages into the layer of sensitive light receptors in the back of the eye apparently occur fairly commonly at high altitudes. Usually such hemorrhages can be detected only by examining the interior of the eye with an ophthalmoscope. However, a recent report has described climbers who were aware of visual defects due to such hemorrhages while on a climb and who had permanent damage as a result. The frequency of such severe hemorrhages may be quite low, but retinal hemorrhages in general may not be preventable by slow acclimatization. [1-3]

High Altitude Pulmonary Edema

High altitude pulmonary edema is probably the most dangerous of the common types of altitude illness. This disorder results from filling of the air sacs (alveoli) of the lungs with fluid which has oozed through the walls of the pulmonary capillaries. As more alveoli fill with fluid, oxygen transfer from air to the pulmonary capillaries is blocked. A marked drop in the oxygen concentration in the blood results, producing cyanosis, interference with cerebral function, and ultimately death by suffocation.

The causes of high altitude pulmonary edema are not clearly understood. Studies have established that patients with this disorder develop a much greater increase in pulmonary artery pressure than usually occurs as part of altitude acclimatization. However, the increase in pulmonary artery pressure alone is not an adequate explanation for the fluid collection. Similar pressure increases occur in other disorders associated with reduced oxygenation of the blood, but are not associated with edema. Therefore it appears that some alteration of the small blood vessels which allows the fluid to leak into the air spaces must take place.

High altitude pulmonary edema is not due to heart failure or pneumonia. However, prior to the recognition of this disorder in 1960 most episodes of high altitude pulmonary edema occurring in climbers were erroneously diagnosed as pneumonia.

High altitude pulmonary edema severe enough to cause physical incapacity is usually associated with rapid ascents by unacclimatized individuals who engage in heavy physical exertion after arrival at high altitudes. (Episodes of high altitude pulmonary edema resulting in only mild symptoms and spontaneously subsiding without specific treatment may also occur, but their incidence and related features are unknown.) More rapid ascents and higher altitudes are associated with a greater incidence of this disorder. However, high altitude pulmonary edema occurs as low as 8,000 feet — rarely even lower.

The risk of developing high altitude pulmonary edema has been variously reported as one-half to eight percent, and there appears to be a somewhat higher incidence in children and adolescents. This type of pulmonary edema may also occur during re-ascent when acclimatized individuals spend more than fourteen days at sea level and then return to high altitude.

Symptoms of high altitude pulmonary edema usually begin one to four days after arrival at high altitude and consist of undue shortness of breath with moderate exertion, a sense of "tightness in the chest" or a feeling of impending suffocation at night, and weakness and marked fatigability. The individual with pulmonary edema is typically much more tired than other members of the climbing party. Headache, loss of appetite, nausea, and vomiting are frequently present. Coughing is an important early sign, although it is probably more frequently caused by drying of the throat than pulmonary edema. The cough is usually dry and nonproductive at first, but with pulmonary edema becomes persistent with white, watery or frothy sputum being coughed up. Later the sputum may be streaked with blood.

The pulse rate is usually rapid (110 to 160 per minute) even after several hours of rest, and is associated with rapid respirations (twenty to forty per minute). The lips and nail beds are often cyanotic, but the skin may be pallid and cold. Bubbling or crackling sounds may be heard over the chest with the unaided ear or a stethoscope. The symptoms and signs often become worse during the night.

An important indication of the severity of high altitude pulmonary edema is the level of mental acuity. Confusion, delirium, and irrational behavior are caused by pronounced reduction of the oxygen supply to the brain and are signs of severe pulmonary edema. If the patient becomes unconscious, death may follow within two to six hours.

The most important method of treatment is to assist the patient to a lower altitude. If he cannot easily walk, litter evacuation may be necessary. Even a descent of 2,000 to 3,000 feet may result in prompt improvement. After arriving at a lower altitude the patient should rest in bed for two to three days. Physical activity increases the severity of high altitude pulmonary edema, and several days are required for the fluid to be re-absorbed from the lungs.

If oxygen is available it should be administered without delay. Rescue parties — including helicopter evacuation units — should bring oxygen to the victim and begin using it at once. Deaths have occurred during evacuation when oxygen has not been carried.

The flow rate for the oxygen should be four liters per minute for the first

Table 1. An Analysis of Thirty-Three Instances of High Altitude Pulmonary Edema in Climbers

	Mean	*Range*
Age	30 years	20 to 43 years.
Altitude of Occurrence	13,670 ft.	8,600 to 24,000 ft.
Duration of Ascent	3.9 days	1 to 11 days
Interval Before Onset of Symptoms	3 days	1 to 11 days
Most Common Features	Cough (24) Shortness of Breath (20) Fatigue (16) Confusion, Mental Changes (16) Gurgling in Chest (14)	
Pulse Rate	115 per min.	96 to 170 per min.
Duration of Edema	5.2 days	2 to 10 days
Prior Episodes of High Altitude Pulmonary Edema	4 (12 percent)	
Deaths	9 (27 percent)	

fifteen minutes, but then can be reduced to two liters per minute to conserve oxygen. A snug fit of the face mask must be ensured.

Improvement is usually rapid after oxygen is begun, but its administration should be continued for six to twelve hours before efforts are made to assist the patient to a lower altitude. Oxygen should be given during rest stops and upon arrival at the lower elevation. Twenty-four to forty-eight hours of low flow oxygen therapy (two liters per minute) may be required for prompt and complete recovery. Oxygen should not be given for less than fifteen minutes; continuous low flow oxygen for six to twelve hours is more beneficial than intermittent short periods at high flow rates.

As soon as the victim reaches a medical facility a chest x-ray should be obtained since diagnostic pulmonary densities may persist for several days after apparent recovery. Residual weakness and fatigue may persist for one to two weeks after descent and treatment.

The following case reports illustrate the typical features of high altitude pulmonary edema: A thirty-eight year old healthy and experienced mountaineer was climbing in the Cordillera Blanca of Peru. In three days he climbed from 9,000 to 14,000 feet over a series of ridges — one of which was 16,000 feet high — with a heavy pack. On the evening of the third day he was more tired than other members of the party and had Cheyne-Stokes respirations. The following day he engaged in little activity, but on the fifth day engaged in steep climbing to a higher camp with a heavy pack. He was far more short of breath than other members of the party, and upon arrival at the 16,000 foot camp was tired and listless and could not eat. He began to cough and one of his companions stated that he "obviously had fluid in his lungs." He was comfortable only in a seated position. Because he was thought to have pneumonia, he was given penicillin. His breathing rapidly became more labored and his cough more severe and frequent. His companion, who was not a physician, wrote in his diary "the next few hours his breathing became progressively more congested and labored. He sounded as though he were literally drowning in his own fluid with an almost continuous loud bubbling sound as if breathing through liquid." During the night his breathing became far worse and he lost consciousness. He died at dawn on the second day of his illness. His companion stated in his diary "a couple of hours after his death, when we got up to carry on the day's activities, I noticed that a white froth resembling cotton candy had appeared to well up out of his mouth." An autopsy performed five days after death disclosed findings compatible with severe pulmonary edema. At the time of this incident high altitude pulmonary edema had not been recognized, so prompt evacuation to a lower altitude — which might have been life-saving — was not carried out.

A thirty year old salesman from the San Francisco Bay Area was an avid weekend skier. He skied nearly every weekend from late November to the middle of April in the Tahoe area. A late snowfall in May enticed him to ski over the Memorial Day weekend. On May 26 he drove to Lake Tahoe (6,300 feet) and the following day he skied at Heavenly Valley (altitude 8,000 to 11,000 feet). He then drove to Mammoth Lakes (8,000 feet) where he spent the next two nights. He skied the next two days on Mammoth Mountain between 8,000 and 11,000 feet. On the afternoon of the second day at Mammoth he noted increasing shortness of breath, fatigue, and weakness. He continued to ski even though he barely could climb up the loading ramp to get on the chairlift. That night he developed a cough and more intense shortness of breath, and noted gurgling sounds in his chest. Early in the morning he coughed up bloody sputum and a doctor was called. He was given an injection of penicillin and advised to drive home. The following day, eighteen hours after arrival at sea level, he still felt weak and short of breath and saw his family doctor. He had a respiratory rate of twenty-four per minute and a heart rate of ninety-two. Persistent crackling sounds were present in the lower portion of the right lung. A blood count and an electrocardiogram were normal. A chest x-ray disclosed fluid in the lower portions of both lungs. The patient was hospitalized and treated with oxygen, a diuretic, and penicillin. He improved rapidly and was discharged four days later with complete clearing of the pulmonary fluid. (This report illustrates several important aspects of high altitude pulmonary edema: (1) Three days of skiing between 8,000 and 11,000 feet and two nights of sleeping above 8,000 feet were sufficient to produce pulmonary edema in this physically fit man. A shorter period of skiing or sleeping at a lower elevation probably would have prevented the episode. (2) Heavy physical effort was continued on the third day of skiing in spite of symptoms, a frequent factor leading to severe high altitude pulmonary edema. (3) Symptoms became worse at night, a common occurrence probably caused by lower blood oxygen concentrations during sleep which have been observed in normal subjects at high altitude.)

Many drugs have been employed in the prevention and treatment of high altitude pulmonary edema, including digitalis, diuretics, antibiotics, cortisone, and morphine. At the present time no clear evidence of benefit which would justify the use of any of them has been presented. Furosemide (Lasix), a diuretic, has been recommended by several climbers, and anecdotal reports of successful treatment of high altitude pulmonary edema have been published. However, treatment failures are usually not reported. Until clear evidence of benefit is available, it appears best to avoid the use of furosemide or other diuretics since large doses may result in a decrease in blood volume with resultant weakness and a fall in blood pressure when standing.

Preventive measures for high altitude pulmonary edema are similar to those for acute mountain sickness — gradual ascent and acclimatization. Heavy physical exertion should be avoided for the first few days after a rapid ascent to high altitude. Individuals with a prior history of this disorder must be particularly careful with preventive measures.

Climbers must be aware of the early symptoms and signs of high altitude pulmonary edema. Climbing leaders must be alert for these signs, and should enforce rest or an early descent. Some climbers may conceal or deny symptoms until they collapse unexpectedly. Failure to eat, a rapid resting pulse rate, and a dry cough — particularly at night — are early warning signs of pulmonary edema.

PERSISTENT MOUNTAIN SICKNESS

Two varieties of persistent mountain sickness have been recognized: a mild form termed "subacute," and a severe form termed "chronic." In the subacute type control of breathing is normal and the lungs are fully ventilated. Symptoms are similar to those of acute mountain sickness. In the chronic variety ventilation of the lungs is inadequate because neural respiratory control is abnormal.

Subacute Mountain Sickness

The physical deterioration of mountaineers spending several days or weeks above 18,000 to 20,000 feet is typical of subacute mountain sickness. At such altitudes even a fully acclimatized individual cannot provide adequate blood concentrations of oxygen for the body tissues. Due to this limitation, no permanent human habitations exist above 18,000 feet. Subacute mountain sickness can occur at lower altitudes — from 10,000 to 14,000 feet for some individuals.

Most symptoms of subacute mountain sickness are similar to those of acute mountain sickness. Inability to obtain sound, restful sleep is common. The severity ranges from mild insomnia to an almost total inability to sleep, forcing the victim to return to lower altitudes. Cheyne-Stokes respiration is responsible for only a few cases of sleeplessness. Nocturnal restlessness, awakening after short intervals of sleep, and disturbing dreams are more common.

A particularly difficult problem for individuals with subacute mountain sickness is the decreased capacity for sustained physical work. Fatigue persists throughout the day and recovery does not occur with sleep. Weakness and lethargy are common and undue shortness of breath during exertion may be troublesome. Loss of appetite and insomnia are largely responsible for the characteristic weight loss of ten to twenty pounds experienced by nearly everyone spending a significant amount of time at high altitude. Distaste for tobacco may accompany the loss of appetite.

Some subjects exhibit predominantly neurologic symptoms and signs. Headaches, which are usually in the back of the head, can be intense and are occasionally associated with neck pain. Ringing in the ears, areas of numbness and tingling sensations, particularly in the extremities, or severe pain in the extremities, joints, or low back areas may appear. Paralysis of the extremities and paralysis of the arm and leg on one side of the body have occurred. Depression, inability to carry out sustained mental work, forgetfulness, and a decreased ability for conceptual thinking are frequent. Irritability and personality changes are occasionally noted.

Methods of ameliorating the severity of subacute mountain sickness include adequate prior acclimatization, periodic visits to lower altitudes for recuperation, oxygen administration, proper diet and fluid intake, and the judicious use of drugs to assure restful sleep. No therapy can completely eradicate or prevent subacuate mountain sickness.

Chronic Mountain Sickness

Chronic mountain sickness is a disorder entirely separate from the more common acute and subacute varieties. It is characterized by marked cyanosis of the lips and nails, and episodes of pronounced sleepiness and mental depression. Swelling of the feet and abdomen due to heart failure may be present. Chronic mountain sickness may suggest the presence of a serious underlying disease of the lungs or heart, but complete recovery usually occurs within six weeks or less if the individual is returned to sea level. (Rarely this disorder appears for the first time in individuals living at sea level. In such cases it is known as the "alveolar hypoventilation syndrome" rather than chronic mountain sickness, but the disorder is apparently identical to that occurring at high altitudes.)

The basic disturbance in chronic mountain sickness is inadequate aeration of the lungs for proper oxygenation of the blood at high altitudes. For some reason the body's chemical receptors fail to detect the lowered blood oxygen, and do not stimulate faster and deeper respirations.

Once an individual has experienced chronic mountain sickness, it would probably recur if he returned to high altitude. However, chronic mountain sickness is only observed in persons who have lived at a high altitude for many years and apparently never occurs in mountaineers, even after weeks at high elevations.

NUTRITION AT ALTITUDE

The maintenance of an adequate food and water intake is particularly difficult at high altitudes. Appetites are always poor and climbers usually eat and drink much less than they need under such conditions. Much of the physical fatigue and weakness experienced at high altitudes is due to in-adequate nutrition, dehydration, and possibly potassium loss accompanying very high energy expenditure. British Himalayan parties have reported that the average caloric intake during approach marches was 4,200 calories per day. However, intake fell to 3,200 calories between 19,000 and 22,000 feet and to 1,500 calories above 24,000 feet. The American party which ascended the west ridge of Mount Everest attributes a large part of its success to continuous conscious efforts to consume adequate amounts of food in spite of a lack of appetite. There is some evidence that food absorption by the intestine is less efficient at very high altitudes than at sea level, which may contribute to the weight loss observed in climbers at very high elevations.

Climbers often go hungry at high altitude rather than eat food which they do not crave. Menus should consist largely of foods known to be enjoyed by all the party members, but special foods to satisfy individual tastes must also be carried. Diets should contain large amounts of sweets which are usually con-sumed in large quantities at high altitudes. Fatty foods or highly condensed rations may not be tolerated. There is no scientifically acceptable evidence that a high vitamin intake or the use of special vitamins such as Vitamin E or B complex vitamins is of any benefit to physical performance at high altitude (or anywhere else). On prolonged expeditions where fresh vegetables and fruits are not available, Vitamin C deficiency can be corrected by the use of ascorbic acid, but most packaged drinks such as lemonade or orange juice have Vitamin C added. If vitamin intake appears inadequate, two multivitamin tablets per day can be taken. There is no value in taking more than the body requirement of vitamins, as the excess is simply excreted in the urine. Excess Vitamins A and D — and possibly others — may definitely be harmful.

FLUID BALANCE AT ALTITUDE

Dehydration is ubiquitous at high altitudes. Contributing to this loss of fluids are faster and deeper breathing and cold air. Air is warmed and moistened as it passes through the mouth, nose, and other major air passages so that it has a relative humidity approaching one hundred percent and the same temperature as the body when it reaches the lungs. The greater respiratory efforts required at high altitudes increase the amount of water required to moisten the air. Furthermore, cold air with a high relative humidity, when warmed to body temperature becomes quite dry. As a result, the cold air found at higher altitudes requires more water to provide a relative humidity near one hundred percent while in the lungs.

Mouth breathing, during which almost all of the moisture in expired air is lost, sweating with exertion, and unavailability of water for drinking also contribute to fluid shortages at altitude.

The dehydration is further aggravated by loss or dulling of the sensation of thirst which accompanies the loss of appetite, nausea, and occasionally vomiting that occurs with acute mountain sickness. It has been suggested that dehydration contributes to the depression, impaired judgment, and other psychological and intellectual changes which occur at high altitudes.

A person must consciously push himself to drink fluids, even if he is not thirsty, when at high altitude. At sea level an average individual requires about two liters of fluid per day. At altitude, particularly above 15,000 to 16,000 feet, requirements often exceed four liters per day. The adequacy of an individual's fluid intake can be judged by his urinary output, which should be at least one-half liter every twenty-four hours.

Fluids may be taken as water, tea, coffee, lemonade, soups, or other beverages. If salt loss through perspiration is not severe and soups are an important part of the diet, salt tablets are usually not necessary. Upon returning from an extensive stay at high altitude, the intake of soup and salty foods should be limited to prevent swelling of the face, eyelids, feet, and abdomen. However, such swelling soon disappears. Aside from producing a somewhat unpleasant appearance, it does no harm.

REFERENCES:

1. Rennie, D., and Morrissey, J.: Retinal Changes in Himalayan Climbers, Arch. Ophthalmol. *93*:395, 1975.
2. Wiedman, M.: High Altitude Retinal Hemorrhage, Arch. Ophthalmol. *93*:401, 1975.
3. Shults, W. T., and Swan, K. C.: High Altitude Retinopathy in Mountain Climbers, Arch. Ophthalmol. *93*:404, 1975.
4. Houston, C.: Acute Pulmonary Edema of High Altitude, New Eng. J. Med. *263*:478, 1960.

5. Hultgren, H. N., Spickard, W. B., Hellriegel, K., and Houston, C. S.: High Altitude Pulmonary Edema, Medicine *40*:289, 1961.

6. Hultgren, H. N.: Treatment and Prevention of High Altitude Pulmonary Edema, Amer. Alpine J. *14*:363, 1965.

7. Singh, I., Khanna, P. K., Srivastava, M. C., Lal, M., Roy, S. B., and Subramanyan, C. S. V.: Acute Mountain Sickness, New Eng. J. Med. *280*:175, 1969.

8. Roy, S. B., Guleria, J. S., Khanna, P. K., Manchanda, S. C., Pande, J. N., and Subha, P. S.: Haemodynamic Studies in High Altitude Pulmonary Edema, Brit. Heart J. *31*:52, 1969.

9. Houston, C. S.: One Price of Acrophilia, New Eng. J. Med. *285*:1318, 1971.

10. Houston, C. S.: High-Altitude Pulmonary and Cerebral Edema, Amer. Alpine J. *18*:83, 1972.

CHAPTER 13

Hypothermia

A DECREASE in core body temperature to a level at which normal muscular and cerebral functions are impaired is known as hypothermia. Normal body temperature is within one degree of 98.6°F. At body temperatures between 93° and 95°F muscular incoordination appears; at lower temperatures cerebral function deteriorates. Death due to cessation of effective heart function occurs between 78° and 82°F. It is now well recognized that most deaths which would formerly have been attributed to exposure or exhaustion are due primarily to hypothermia.

PHYSIOLOGY

Heat loss from the body occurs by four routes:

1. Radiation — direct heat transfer to the environment by emission of energy.
2. Convection — air next to the skin is warmed and is carried away to be replaced by cool air (when air temperature is cooler than skin temperature). Wind greatly accelerates heat loss by this means. A similar process occurs during immersion in cold water.
3. Evaporation — evaporation of sweat from the skin results in considerable heat loss due to the high heat of vaporization of water. Inspired air is warmed, saturated with vapor at body temperature, and expired, resulting in transfer of heat from the body to the environment. Heat loss by sweating and from the lungs is increased by exercise.
4. Conduction — heat is conducted directly away from the body when it is in contact with cold water, snow, or a cold ground surface.

Several physiologic mechanisms maintain body temperature in a cold environment:

1. Constriction of blood vessels in the skin and extremities — when skin blood vessels constrict, the skin and underlying tissue layers cool and tend to form a protective shell which decreases heat transfer to the environment. The temperature of the outer skin layers may be close to that of the ambient air. Constriction of blood vessels in the hands and feet results in reduced blood flow and reduction of the temperature to a level close to that of the environment, reducing heat loss.
2. Shivering — heat production by the body is increased by shivering, which consists of involuntary, rapid muscular contractions that produce heat by increasing metabolism. The increase in body metabolism associated with shivering is approximately equal to that of a fast walk or jog.
3. Increased energy cost of physical activity — individuals exercising in cold conditions burn up more energy than when performing similar exercise in a warm environment. While this energy consumption increases heat production and helps maintain body temperature, it also leads to more rapid exhaustion than the same amount of work in warmer conditions.

STAGES OF HYPOTHERMIA

If protective mechanisms fail and the core body temperature falls, progressive muscular, cerebral and circulatory failure occur at the temperature levels indicated:

98° - 95°F Sensation of chilliness, skin numbness; minor impairment in muscular performance, especially in use of hands; shivering begins.

95° - 93°F More obvious muscle incoordination and weakness; slow stumbling pace; mild confusion and apathy.

93° - 90°F Gross muscular incoordination with frequent stumbling and falling and inability to use hands; mental sluggishness with slow thought and speech; retrograde amnesia.

90° - 86°F Cessation of shivering; severe muscular incoordination with stiffness and inability to walk or stand; incoherence, confusion, irrationality.

86° - 82°F Severe muscular rigidity; semiconsciousness (barely arousable); dilatation of pupils; inapparent heart beat and pulse.

82° - 78°F Unconsciousness; death due to cessation of heart action.

The presence and severity of hypothermia must be assessed by these symptoms and signs in most situations. Ordinary clinical thermometers are of no value since they do not register low temperatures.

CAUSES OF HYPOTHERMIA

Hypothermia occurs most rapidly in a cold, wet, windy environment. Studies of survival in cold water immersion due to boating accidents have shown that the duration of survival is related to several factors:

1. Water temperature — at a water temperature of 32° death occurs in fifteen minutes, while at 70° survival for as long as forty-eight hours has been observed.
2. Clothing — persons wearing heavy clothing survive longer since the clothing traps a layer of warm water close to the body and reduces cooling by convection, conduction, and radiation.
3. Physical activity — victims who do not swim or struggle in the water have a longer survival time due to lower evaporative heat loss from the lungs and slower depletion of energy stores which maintain body heat.
4. Body build and sex — obese individuals and women have a longer survival time as the result of the insulating properties of subcutaneous fat.

The same general principles apply to hypothermia on land. A wet, cold, windy environment removes body heat rapidly. Exposed skin is the most important source of heat loss by radiation, convection, evaporation, and conduction. Heat loss from an uncovered head or bare hands may account for as much as fifty percent of the total body heat loss at air temperatures below 40°F. Dry clothing traps a layer of warm air which is an efficient insulator. The high thermal conductivity of water (over 200 times that of air) greatly reduces the protective value of clothing when it becomes wet. Experimental studies carried out by Pugh in Great Britain clearly demonstrated the decrease in protection from cold occurring when clothing became wet.[2] Subjects were dressed in 1.8 clo units consisting of a parka, wool jersey, cotton string undershirt, cotton shorts, socks, shoes, and gloves. (A clo unit is equivalent to an ordinary businessman's summer clothing; arctic flying suits are rated at 3.5 clo units.) When the subjects' clothing became wet its cold protective effect dropped to 0.18 clo units. With waterproof rain gear the protective effect for wet clothing increased five times to 1.0 clo units.

Heat loss, especially from wet skin, is greatly increased by wind. The "wind chill" factor is an important guide to the probability of cold injury or hypothermia. The accompanying table summarizes this effect.

Heavy physical exercise increases heat loss by increasing evaporation from the lungs and sweating, which also deplete body fluids. Exercise in a cold environment requires more energy stores and a higher water intake than equivalent exercise in a warm environment. Fluid loss results in a decrease in blood volume and blood pressure and increases the tendency for weakness, apathy, and collapse to develop when hypothermia occurs.[2]

Table 2. Wind Chill Chart

Wind Speed (MPH)	Temperature (Thermometer Reading, Fahrenheit)										
	50	40	30	20	10	0	-10	-20	-30	-40	-50
	Equivalent Temperature										
5	48	37	27	16	6	-5	-15	-26	-36	-47	-57
10	40	28	16	4	-9	-24	-33	-46	-58	-70	-83
15	36	22	9	-5	-18	-32	-45	-58	-72	-85	-99
20	32	18	4	-10	-25	-39	-53	-67	-82	-96	-110
25	30	16	0	-15	-29	-44	-59	-74	-88	-104	-118
30	28	13	-2	-18	-33	-48	-63	-79	-94	-109	-125
35	27	11	-4	-21	-35	-51	-67	-82	-98	-113	-129
40	26	10	-6	-21	-37	-53	-69	-85	-100	-115	-132

Wind speeds greater than forty miles per hour have little additional effect.

In a survey of eighty-eight episodes of hypothermia in Britain, of which twenty-five were fatal, the following causes were present:[2]

1. Bad weather — setting out in extreme weather conditions or being overtaken by bad weather, especially blizzards.
2. Being benighted — more episodes occurred in individuals who pushed on to exhaustion and were out all night than in those who bivouacked in a sheltered area.
3. Being wet or having unsufficient clothing — inadequate protection against wind, at least over the lower half of the body was a feature of all clothing assemblies recorded.
4. Exhaustion — physical exhaustion was a contributing factor in the more serious cases.
5. Inexperience and lack of training.

PREVENTION OF HYPOTHERMIA

Awareness of the causes of hypothermia and the rapidity with which fatal hypothermia can develop is the most important aspect of prevention. On any trip — even a one-day excursion — where sudden changes in weather can occur, clothing adequate to protect as much exposed skin as possible must be worn or carried. Long trousers, a long sleeved shirt or sweater, a windbreaker, and a cap are the minimal essentials. Wool provides more effective insulation than cotton. A windbreaker and wind pants that allow perspiration to escape are excellent for protection against cold wind and dry snow. A bivouac sac is the most compact, easily carried protection in the event of a forced overnight stay. A light tent, sleeping bag, and sleeping bag cover offer even better protection. Extra items of dry clothing and sleeping bags should be stowed in plastic bags since packs and stuff bags may leak or be soaked by a fall into a stream.

Alertness for the early symptoms and signs of hypothermia is the responsibility of all climbers, particularly trip leaders. Early signs may be undue fatigue, weakness, slowness of gait, apathy, forgetfulness, and confusion. These symptoms must not be negligently ascribed to fatigue or altitude. In hypothermia shivering may not occur, especially during heavy physical activity.

The time course of hypothermia may be short. In bad weather, hypothermia usually becomes evident five to six hours after starting, but in very poor weather with heavy exertion and inadequate clothing, symptoms may appear within one to two hours. The interval between the onset of symptoms and collapse may be as short as one hour, and the interval between collapse and death may be only two hours.

In deteriorating weather a party should retreat or bivouac in a suitable shelter before the appearance of signs or symptoms of hypothermia in members of the group. When muscular incoordination or mental impairment are present, hypothermia is already serious. Confused, clumsy hypothermic climbers who cannot use their hands are unable to perform the functions essential for survival. At this point the game may already have been lost.

A bivouac shelter should provide protection from wind, precipitation, and surface water. Insulation from the ground, snow, or ice should be prepared. All available clothing and rain gear should be put on and a tent, tarp, or rain cover should be used for protection. Several persons huddling together conserve heat more effectively than individuals alone in separate shelters. In addition, weaker members of the group can be constantly observed and treated more efficiently. Sleeping bags should be used if available. Even if clothing or sleeping bags gradually become damp or wet, they should not be discarded since the inner layers tend to stay warm and transfer of body heat to the environment is retarded. It is usually wiser to stay in a wet bag in a shelter than to try to make a run for a warmer spot in bad weather.

In addition to prevention of heat loss, adequate water and food intake are essential for survival. Water intake during mild exertion should be at least two quarts per day; considerably larger quantities are required with heavier exertion or at high altitude due to greater water loss from the lungs. Continued water loss by perspiration, respiration, and urine production without replacement of fluid and salt results in dehydration, which is associated with a decreased volume and an increased concentration or thickness of the blood. Dehydration may be accompanied by weakness, fatigue, dizzyness, and a tendency to faint when standing; constriction of peripheral blood vessels, increasing the danger of frostbite; a tendency to develop severe shock following even minor injuries; and a tendency to form clots in the veins with the resulting danger of pulmonary embolism (see Thrombophlebitis in "Diseases of the Respiratory System").

Since thirst is usually not experienced during dehydration, a conscious effort to consume adequate fluids may be necessary. Water intake can rarely be maintained by eating snow or ice, and additional body heat is required to warm water from such sources to body temperature. Hot liquids should be consumed if they are available. An adequate fluid intake is indicated by a urine volume of one pint or more daily.

Arctic survival studies have shown that an increased salt intake reduces the dehydration in an exposure situation. Salt is present in high concentrations in soups, most tinned meats, salt fish, and salted nuts. Table salt can be added to drinking water (one teaspoon per pint).

Food replenishes body energy stores which are essential for continued heat production to maintain body temperature as well as for physical effort. Fruit or fruit drinks, candy, salted nuts, and tinned meats should be carried as emergency rations. Eating small amounts of food at frequent intervals rather than eating three large meals (or two small meals with a large meal at the end of the day) helps prevent depletion of body energy stores during the day. Starvation, in its usual sense, is not a cause of death in an exposed situation, but definitely contributes to depletion of body energy stores which predisposes to the development of hypothermia. Starvation may also result in an increased acidity of the blood (ketosis and acidosis) which aggravates the effects of fatigue and hypothermia. Eating small quantities of food at one to three hour intervals also helps prevent the development of ketosis and acidosis, even if the quantities consumed are not large enough to fully replace the body stores. In an emergency situation any available food should be consumed, even wild animals such as birds or rodents which may have to be eaten uncooked.

Body energy stores should be conserved by reducing physical activity to a minimum and trying to keep warm. Involuntary shivering increases energy requirements substantially. Often a choice between resting and shivering or performing light work and not shivering is necessary. Since the energy cost is the same, the latter is usually preferable since it is better for morale.

Frostbite is common in exposed bivouacs and in many instances may be due to dulled mental acuity resulting from hypothermia and high altitude. Climbers must be sure that hands and feet and bare skin areas are well covered and protected from freezing.

Drugs are of no value in a survival situation. Stimulants such as Benzedrine or Dexedrine may provide temporary increased alertness and energy, but are followed by a period of greater depression and weakness. Sedatives such as barbiturates are dangerous because they tend to produce coma or irrational behavior. Alcohol causes dilatation of skin blood vessels and increases heat loss. Also, dehydration is increased by alcohol.

It is common in bad weather for a party to be confined to a temporary shelter for several days. Experience has shown the desirability of keeping a party intact under these conditions and the danger of sending individuals for help unless weather conditions are safe. After several days in an emergency bivouac, muscular weakness, fatigue, and dizzyness on standing may be severe and the ability to hike substantial distances may be greatly reduced. A climber must not overestimate his capacity to reach a place of safety. It is usually safer for a party to remain together and signal for help than to try to reach a roadhead with uncertain physical ability.

TREATMENT OF HYPOTHERMIA

One or two members of a party may rapidly become hypothermic due to inadequate clothing or a fall into a stream. One party — perhaps a rescue party — may come upon another group with many or all of its members suffering with hypothermia. Unless the situation is unusually hazardous due to the threat of avalanches or a similar danger, or a warm, permanent shelter such as a cabin is *very* near, a shelter should be set up and treatment begun without delay. Even after external warming has begun, core body temperature may continue to fall for one or two hours. For this reason, early recognition of the existence of hypothermia, prompt institution of therapy, and continuation of treatment until normal body temperature is restored before evacuation are essential.

Wet clothing should be removed and replaced with warm, dry garments, and the victim must be warmed. Rewarming cannot be carried out effectively simply by placing the hypothermic patient in a sleeping bag. A sleeping bag only provides insulation — not heat. A hypothermic patient with no source of heat is only capable of warming the bag to his own depressed body temperature. Some external source of heat must be supplied. Placing a second person with normal body temperature in the bag to provide warmth by direct body-to-body contact has been found to be one of the most effective methods of rewarming. Warm stones or bottles filled with hot water can also be placed in the bag. Care must be taken not to burn the patient if he is not fully conscious.

Since hypothermic patients feel little or no pain and already have cold extremities, they are very susceptible to frostbite. The hands and feet and any exposed areas such as ears or nose must be protected. An unconscious patient or one in severe hypothermia with no sensations of pain must also be carefully examined for fractures or other injuries if he has fallen.

The presence and severity of the hypothermia must generally be determined from the symptoms and signs displayed by the patient. Ordinary clinical thermometers do not register low temperatures and are of no value. A low temperature clinical thermometer which reads as low as 20°C (68°F) is available from Zeal G. H., Ltd., 8 Lombard Street, S. W. 19 London, England. A thermometer for measuring air temperatures can be used as a rectal or oral thermometer (depending upon the patient's state of consciousness) to provide a rough indication of the severity of the hypothermia. Such thermometers are rarely accurate within more than three to five degrees, but the amount of inaccuracy and whether it is above or below the true temperature can be gauged by taking the temperature of a normal member of the party.

Patients in deep hypothermia are often erroneously thought to be dead, but a feeble heart action may persist and revival may be possible. Heart sounds may be inaudible, pulses may not be palpable, and respirations may appear to have ceased. If doubt exists, mouth-to-mouth resuscitation should be started along with rewarming.

Recently a warming blanket utilizing circulating warm water has been developed and appears to be an effective method for rapidly rewarming hypothermia victims. Such units should be a valuable adjunct to other methods of treatment (although probably not replacing them) and increased use of this device should be encouraged.[3]

After evacuation, management of the victim should be supervised by a physician since intravenous fluids, cardiac monitoring, assisted respiration, and other special procedures may be required. Some physicians have recommended rapid rewarming by immersion in a tub of warm water. Others consider such rapid rewarming undesirable since it may increase shock by diverting the blood flow to the skin and extremities. The question is still being debated. If rapid rewarming is employed, it must be done in a medical facility where a physician's supervision is available and materials for the treatment of deeper shock, if it occurs, are available.

A remarkable report from Lapland illustrates some of the features of successful survival in snow. Evert Stenmark was hunting alone on cross country skis in mid-January. He lost control of his skis and fell into a gully. With his skis caught in brush and buried by snow, he could not get out. By moving his body and using his ski pole he was able to clear an air space around his chest and head and poke an air hole in the surface of the snow. He ate snow and ice regularly and consumed his four ptarmigans. He tied a handkerchief to his ski pole and poked it above the surface of the snow, moving it periodically to attract attention. Two severe snowstorms occurred on the first and fourth days. On the eighth day he was rescued. He suffered no injury except minor frostbite. He was wearing about three clo units with a cap, two pairs of wool gloves with leather shields, two pairs of wool socks, and heavy boots.

REFERENCES:
1. Bangs, C.: Survival in Winter, Off Belay, p. 12, December 1974.
2. Pugh, L.: Accidental Hypothermia in Walkers, Climbers and Campers: Report to the Medical Commission on Accident Prevention, Brit. Med. J. *1*:123, 1966.
3. Dayton, L., and Arnold, J.: Hydraulic Sarong, Off Belay, p. 2, June 1975.
4. Lathrop, T.: *Hypothermia: Killer of the Unprepared,* Portland, Mazamas, 1972.
5. McGeary, G.: Accidental Hypothermia, Summit, p. 2, March 1969.
6. Hunter, W.: Accidental Hypothermia, Northwest Med. *67*:569, 735, and 837, 1968.
7. Hudson, L. D., and Conn, R. D.: Accidental Hypothermia: Associated Diagnoses and Prognosis in a Common Problem, J.A.M.A. *227*:37, 1974.
8. *Cold Injury,* Dept. of Army Technical Bulletin, TB Med 81, March 30, 1970.
9. Rogers, T., Setliff, J., and Klopping, J.: Energy Cost, Fluid and Electrolyte Balance in Subarctic Survival Situation, J. Appl. Physiol. *19*:1, 1964.
10. Ripjägaren: Ekenstam Skid och Friluftsfrämjandets, Årsbok, 1956.

CHAPTER 14

Frostbite

FROSTBITE is an injury produced by cold in which the affected tissues are frozen. The hands and feet, which are farthest from the heart and have a more tenuous blood supply, and the face and ears, which are usually the most exposed portions of the body, are the areas most commonly involved.

The principal effect of cold is to impair the circulation of blood to the affected area. When the body is chilled, the blood vessels in the skin contract, particularly in the extremities, reducing the amount of heat lost by radiation into the surrounding atmosphere. Thus, body heat is conserved at the expense of lowering the skin temperature. Under such circumstances blood vessel constriction may become so severe in areas which are more severely chilled that circulation almost totally ceases. Cold also damages the capillaries in the affected areas, causing blood plasma to leak through their walls, thus adding to the tissue injury and further impairing circulation by allowing the blood to sludge inside the vessels.

As the circulation becomes severely impaired all sensation of cold or pain is lost. Unless the tissue is rewarmed promptly, the skin and superficial tissues actually begin to freeze. With continued chilling the frozen area enlarges and extends to deeper levels. Ice crystals form between the cells, and then grow by extracting water from within the cells. The tissues may be injured physically by the ice crystals, and by dehydration and the resulting disruption of osmotic and chemical balance within the cells.

Prevention

Frostbite can occur in any cold environment, but is usually associated with an overall body heat deficit resulting from inadequate clothing or equipment, reduced food consumption, exhaustion, injury, or a combination of such factors. "Wind-chill," rather than temperature alone, determines the rate of heat loss (see "Hypothermia"). If a person is cold, the blood vessels of the skin are constricted, and the skin temperature is reduced, making the superficial tissues, especially those of an extremity, much more susceptible to cold injury.

Adequate clothing and equipment, particularly boots and mittens, are essential for any cold weather outing. Boots must be well broken in and large enough to fit comfortably with several pairs of socks. Laces, particularly at the top, should not be tight. Gaiters or overboots should be worn if deep snow is anticipated. Gloves, or preferably mittens, should be of good quality and in severe conditions should be tied to the climber. Dry socks and glove liners should be carried, since moisture greatly reduces the insulation value of any clothing. For the same reason, clothing should be adequately ventilated to avoid dampness from excessive perspiration.

Heat production, resulting from exercise or the protective mechanism of shivering, is just as important as clothing in maintaining body temperature. Frequently the second man on a rope, sitting quietly while belaying the leader up a long pitch, is the one who suffers frostbite. An accident victim, lying immobilized, may suffer frostbite even though he appears to be more than adequately clothed for the existing weather conditions.

An inadequate food intake or exhaustion can reduce the body's stores of nutrients to a level at which the body temperature can no longer be maintained. Both conditions are not uncommon at high altitudes. Under such circumstances relatively minor injuries may produce shock, which also predisposes the victim to the development of cold injuries.

In a cold environment, alcohol and tobacco should be strictly avoided. Alcohol dilates the blood vessels of the skin and may temporarily warm the skin, but eventually results in an increased loss of total body heat. Smoking, in contrast, tends to constrict the blood vessels in the skin and may be sufficient to initiate frostbite in a threatened area.

Diagnosis

The earliest signs of frostbite are a sensation of cold or pain and pallor of the skin in the affected area. As freezing progresses, the tissues become even whiter in appearance and all sensation is lost. With deep frostbite the tissues become quite hard.

During and following thawing the injured area is often extremely painful. One to three days after thawing the site of injury appears red and is severely blistered — first with small blebs and later with large, coalescing blisters. In more severe injuries, or when rewarming has not been properly performed, the tissue has a dull, ashen-gray color; later it may turn black and appear dried and shriveled. However, in many cases the early appearance suggests a much more severe injury than actually exists. The victim should not be allowed to become alarmed about his condition as even mild cases of frostbite have a frightening appearance during the stage of blistering.

Treatment

In recent years most of the older methods of treatment for frostbite have been shown to be ineffective or even harmful. Rubbing the injured area briskly with snow or ice "to restore the circulation" only increases the injury. (In view of the nature of the damage to the blood vessels and tissues, further cold or trauma would be the worst possible treatment.) Gradual rewarming has also been advocated but is no longer recommended. Drugs which prevent the blood from clotting (and thus obstructing the circulation) or dilate the blood vessels are of unproven value and should not be used in mountaineering circumstances.

The preferred treatment is rapid rewarming. However, *rewarming must not be attempted until the victim has reached a place where his entire body can be kept warm during and after treatment, and from which he can be evacuated without having to use the injured extremity.* Trauma to frozen tissues is certain to do some harm, but such trauma would be tremendously more damaging after rewarming. Furthermore, as soon as the tissue is rewarmed it must have the best possible blood supply. If the patient is cold, the blood vessels remain constricted and circulation is inadequate. Walking on a frozen foot for twelve to eighteen hours or even longer produces less damage than inadequate warming or warming in circumstances in which the victim's entire body cannot be warmed.

Rewarming should be carried out in a water bath between 100° and 108° F. (Higher temperatures produce further damage to the already injured tissue. The water must not be hot enough to feel uncomfortable to the attendant's hand.) Rewarming in a water bath of large size offers the advantage of warming the frozen extremity more rapidly, resulting in less tissue loss in many cases, particularly where frostbite has been deep and extensive. A large container also permits more accurate control of the temperature. If a tub, large wastebasket, dishpan, or similar container is not available, a plastic bag supported inside a cardboard or wooden box can be used.

During rewarming hot water must usually be added to the bath occasionally to keep the temperature at the desired level. The injured extremity should be removed from the bath and not returned until the water has been thoroughly mixed and the temperature measured. An open flame must not be used to keep the water bath warm. The frostbitten extremity may come in contact with the area to which heat is applied and, since sensation would have been lost due to the injury, be seriously burned.

For rewarming the extremity should be stripped of all clothing and any constricting bands, straps, or other objects which might impair the circulation. The injured area should be suspended in the center of the water bath and not permitted to rest against the side or bottom. Warming should be continued for about thirty minutes even though the frostbitten tissues become quite painful.

Aspirin and codeine, or morphine or meperidine if needed, may be given during rewarming or afterwards for pain.

Following rewarming the patient must be kept warm. The injured area should be elevated and must be protected from any kind of trauma or irritation. Blankets or bedclothes should be supported by a framework to avoid pressure or rubbing on the injured area. Every effort should be made to avoid rupturing the blisters once they have formed.

Subsequent care should be directed primarily toward preventing infection. Cleanliness of the frostbitten area is extremely important. The extremity should be soaked daily in a water bath at body temperature, to which a germicidal soap containing hexachlorophene has been added. If contamination of the water supply is a possibility, the bath water should be boiled (and allowed to cool) before use. Water temperature must always be tested with a thermometer or, at worst, the hand of an uninjured individual. Water baths help to keep the frostbitten area clean and to remove any dead tissue. Whirlpool baths are very beneficial if available. Dead tissue should not be cut or pulled away; the water baths remove such tissue much more efficiently.

Only sterile, soft, dry material should be used to dress the frostbitten tissues. A small amount of dry sterile cotton may be placed between the fingers or toes to avoid maceration. Antibiotics should not be given routinely, but if infection appears to be present ampicillin or cloxicillin should be administered every six hours until a physician's care is obtained. A tetanus toxoid booster shot, or human antitoxin if the patient has not been previously immunized against tetanus, should also be given at this time. The patient should have complete rest and a good diet high in proteins. Smoking should be strictly prohibited since it reduces the already deficient blood supply to the affected area. Moderate movement of the limb should be encouraged, but should be limited to movements which can be carried out without assistance, either from others or through manipulation by the patient. Considerable reassurance and emotional support may be required by the patient, particularly if the appearance of the injured areas is at all alarming.

An individual who has sustained frostbite in the past is usually more susceptible to subsequent cold injury because the blood vessels in the injured area are permanently damaged.

Other Types of Cold Injury

Severe cold injury can be sustained at temperatures above freezing, particularly after prolonged exposure in a damp or wet environment. Such injuries are called "shelter leg," "immersion foot," or "trench foot" depending on the circumstances of exposure. Although the problem of thawing the extremity does not exist, treatment (rest, maintenance of overall warmth, warm baths, and prevention of infection) is essentially the same as that described for frostbite.

REFERENCES:

1. Washburn, B.: Frostbite: What It Is—How to Prevent It—Emergency Treatment, New Eng. J. Med. *266*:974, 1962. (The same article also appears in.The American Alpine Journal *13*:1, 1962.)
2. Hanson, H. E., and Goldman, R. F.: Cold Injury in Man: A Review of its Etiology and Discussion of its Prediction, Milit. Med. *134*:1307, 1969.
3. Miles, W. J.: Frostbite and Hypothermia—Current Concepts, Alaska Med., p. 26, March 1973.
4. Kyösola, K.: Clinical Experiences in the Management of Cold Injuries: A Study of 110 Cases, J. Trauma *14*:32, 1974.
5. Sumner, D. S., Criblez, T. L., and Doolittle, W. H.: Host Factors in Human Frostbite, Milit. Med. *139*:454, 1974.
6. Snider, R. L., and Porter, J. M.: Treatment of Experimental Frostbite with Intra-arterial Sympathetic Blocking Drugs, Surgery *77*:557, 1975.
7. Akers, W. A.: Paddy Foot: A Warm Water Immersion Foot Syndrome Variant. Part I. The Natural Disease, Epidemiology, Part II. Field Experiments, Correlation, Milit. Med. *139*:605 and 613, 1974.

CHAPTER 15

Injury from Solar Radiation

SUNLIGHT is commonly held to be beneficial to health, but many harmful effects can be produced by excessive exposure. Sunburn is well recognized; less well known are the long term effects of repeated overexposure which produces degenerative changes in the skin that can eventually lead to skin cancer. In the spectrum of solar radiation energy, much of the energy is of shorter wavelength (ultraviolet) or longer wavelength (infrared) than visible light. Most biological damage is caused by ultraviolet radiation of wavelengths less than 4,000 Å (1 centimeter $= 10^8$ Ångströms (Å)).

Ultraviolet exposure in mountaineering may be much greater than at sea level for several reasons. At high altitudes there is less filtering of sunlight by the earth's atmosphere, particularly in the harmful ultraviolet wavelengths. In addition, glaciers and snowfields reflect about seventy-five percent of the incident ultraviolet radiation so that mountaineers are exposed to reflected as well as direct rays of the sun. Under certain conditions, such as in a cirque, reflection can cause a manifold increase in total radiation. Wind also increases the effect of ultraviolet radiation.

Even if a climber is shielded from the direct rays of the sun, much ultraviolet radiation may still reach him due to atmospheric scattering. This "sky radiation" may contribute half of the total ultraviolet radiation and tends to be greater when high, thin cirrus clouds are present. Indeed, total ultraviolet radiation may even be greater on an overcast day than on a cloudless day. This can be a particularly dangerous hazard since it is so inapparent.

SUNBURN

Variation in sensitivity to sunlight between individuals is considerable. Blue-eyed redheads and blondes are more susceptible to sunburn than are brunettes; children are more susceptible than adults. Sensitivity to sunlight may also be increased by a number of drugs and other substances. (Agents increasing sensitivity to sunlight include sulfonamides and their derivatives; oral antidiabetic agents; certain diuretics — phenothiazines, thiazides (Diuril and similar drugs); most tetracyclines, particularly Declomycin; barbiturates; biothionol (used in soaps and many first aid creams and cosmetics); many plants and grasses (fig leaf, certain meadow grasses, wild parsnip, celery, and others); certain dyes used in lipstick; green soap; and coal tar or coal tar derivatives.)

Excessive exposure to ultraviolet radiation of 2,900 to 3,200 Å damages the tissues of the superficial skin layers. An exposure of thirty minutes produces redness of the skin along with slight swelling. More prolonged exposure may cause pain and blistering. In severe cases chill, fever, or headache may develop. Sunburn of the lips is often followed by painful herpes simplex infections (fever blisters, cold sores), which may cover most of the surface of the lips.

If the skin is also exposed to longer ultraviolet wavelengths (3,200 to 4,200 Å), an increase in pigment results, producing a suntan. Suntan has a protective value due to the screening effect of the increased pigmentation and the thickening of the outer layer of the skin.

Prevention

Mountaineers must take unusual care to prevent sunburn. Whenever possible, exposure should be gradual at first to permit natural tanning and thickening of the skin. For some light-skinned individuals adequate tanning is impossible. Such persons may benefit from the use of methoxsalen, followed by brief exposure to the sun or an ultraviolet lamp. However, this treatment must be undertaken only under the direction of a dermatologist or other physician.

Protective creams or lotions are especially important when climbing on snow or at high altitude. They should be applied liberally and frequently, particularly when excessive sweating and wiping of the neck and face tend to remove the preparation. The nose, cheeks, neck and ears are most frequently sunburned; the lower surfaces of the nose and chin are frequently burned by reflected radiation and should not be neglected.

Products currently marketed in the United States for use with sun exposure fall into three different groups. The first, and perhaps the largest, is the group of popular remedies which contain no sunscreens and provide no protection at all from ultraviolet radiation. Baby oil, mineral oil, olive oil, lanolin, and coconut oil are among the products in this category. These agents may provide some relief from the discomfort of sunburn after it has occurred, but do nothing to protect the skin.

Products in the second group contain effective sunscreens which filter out the ultraviolet radiation of wavelengths 2,900 to 3,200 Å which damage the skin, but permit radiation of longer wavelengths to pass through and produce tan-

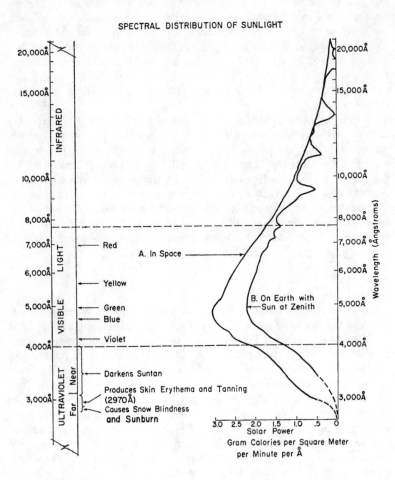

Figure 39. Quantity of light of different wavelengths in sunlight.

ning. The most effective of these sunscreens is para-aminobenzoic acid (PABA). A solution of five percent PABA in fifty to seventy percent alcohol provides excellent protection from sunburn. PABA sunscreens stay on longer than other products when exposed to moisture from sweating or swimming. Rarely PABA products cause contact dermatitis (see "Allergies") and they may also leave a yellow stain on clothing which is not removed by washing. Products containing PABA are PreSun and Pabanol.

Esters of PABA also provide good protection against sunburn, do not stain clothing, and resist moisture fairly well, although they are more easily removed than nonesterified PABA sunscreens. Products containing PABA esters include Block Out, Eclipse, Pabafilm, Sea & Ski, and others.

The third group consists of products which block out all ultraviolet radiation. The best known of these agents contain opaque pigments such as titanium dioxide (A-Fil) or zinc oxide (Zincofax Cream). Such agents are used on the nose, lips, ears, or similar areas which tend to become easily sunburned and are not covered by clothing.

Products containing benzophenones, such as Uval and Solbar, also screen out all ultraviolet radiation, but are easily removed by sweating. Such agents were developed primarily for individuals with certain skin diseases which require such complete protection.

Treatment

If prevention has been neglected or has been inadequate, application of cold, wet dressings soaked in boric acid solution (one teaspoonful per quart of water) or a one to fifty solution of aluminum acetate may relieve discomfort. Soothing creams may be helpful if swelling is not severe. Steroid preparations, such as one-half percent hydrocortisone ointment or an aerosol spray containing prednisolone such as Meti-Derm, are helpful in reducing inflammation if applied early. However, steroid preparations must be used sparingly if at all. Reducing the inflammation may reduce pain somewhat, but probably slows the processes of healing and repair following the burn and may increase susceptibility to infection. Extensive or unusually severe sunburn may have to be treated as a second degree burn (See "Burns").

SNOWBLINDNESS

The surface of the eye (cornea and conjunctiva) absorbs ultraviolet radiation just as the skin. Excessive exposure can result in sunburn of these tissues, producing snow blindness (photophthalmia). Any source of ultraviolet radiation including sun, ultraviolet lamps, and electric welding equipment, may produce photophthalmia. During the actual period of exposure there is no sensation other than brightness to warn the individual. Symptoms may not develop until as much as eight to twelve hours after exposure. The eyes initially feel simply irritated or dry, but as symptoms progress, the eyes feel as though they are full of sand. Moving or blinking the eyes becomes extremely painful. Even exposure to light may cause pain. Swelling of the eyelids, redness of the eyes, and excessive tearing may occur. A severe case of snow blindness may be completely disabling for several days.

Prevention

Snow blindness can and should be completely prevented by the consistent use of proper goggles or sunglasses. Any lens transmitting less than ten percent of the erythemal band of sunlight (below 3,200 Å) is satisfactory. Glasses should be large and curved or have side covers to block most of the reflected light coming from below and from the sides. Under severe radiation conditions (as on a concave, high-altitude snowfield) goggles are safer, even though they are less comfortable and tend to steam up. If only glasses are available, a sunscreen should be applied to the eyelids to prevent burning. Spare goggles should be carried, but in an emergency lenses made of cardboard with a thin slit to see through may be used. The eyes may be covered alternately so that only one eye at a time is exposed to the sunlight.

Eye protection is just as necessary on a partly cloudy or moderately overcast day as it is in full sunlight. Snow blindness can even be produced during a snow storm if the cloud cover is thin.

Treatment

Snow blindness heals spontaneously in a few days; however, the pain may be quite severe if the condition is not treated. Cold compresses applied to the eyes and a dark environment may give some temporary relief. Early and frequent applications (hourly) of an *ophthalmic* ointment or drops containing cortisone or some other steroid can provide relief from pain, lessen the inflammatory reaction, and shorten the course of the illness. The individual must not rub his eyes. Local anesthetic agents should not be employed since they rapidly lose their effectiveness and may lead to damage of the delicate corneal surface.

CHAPTER 16

Heat Injuries

THE HUMAN body temperature is maintained at an almost constant level of approximately 98.6°F. This constant temperature results from sensitive control of the balance between heat produced or absorbed by the body and heat lost to the environment.

Heat is produced within the body by the metabolism of nutrient substances. Exercising muscles consume large quantities of such nutrients (primarily glucose) and produce considerable amounts of heat. The heat produced by metabolism generally ranges between 2,000 to 5,000 kilocalories per day, depending largely upon the state of nutrition of the individual and the amount of physical activity in which he engages. The body must get rid of this heat to prevent an increase in body temperature and the resulting ill effects. Although some heat may be absorbed through radiation from the atmosphere or rocks heated by the sun if they are warmer than the body, a hot environment tends to cause heat illnesses primarily because it interferes with heat elimination.

Heat is eliminated from the body principally through the skin. Blood is warmed as it passes through exercising muscles or other tissues where metabolism is taking place. When the warmed blood circulates through the skin, heat is lost by convection to the surrounding atmosphere, or by conduction if the individual is in contact with water, snow, or cold rocks. The cutaneous blood vessels may dilate also, increasing blood flow in the skin and so increasing the rate of heat loss.

Perspiration promotes heat loss by cooling the skin through evaporation. Evaporative cooling results from the large amount of heat that is required to change water from its liquid form to a vapor. This heat is removed from the adjacent skin (or respiratory passages) and from the blood flowing through the region. The evaporation of one cubic centimeter (1 cc or one-thirtieth of an ounce) of perspiration removes enough heat to lower the temperature of 575 cc of blood about 1°C or 1.8°F. In practical terms this means that one pint of sweat can remove a bit over 200 kilocalories of heat or about two-thirds the amount of heat produced during one hour of moderate exercise. Maximal exercise can result in more than 600 kilocalories per hour of heat production, the equivalent of the heat lost with two or three pints of sweat. This approaches the maximum sweating rate for individuals not acclimatized to heat.

Acclimatization to heat takes about one week and results in an increased tolerance for exercise in a hot environment. This type of acclimatization depends on mechanisms which increase the maximum sweating rate and reduce the amount of salt lost in a given volume of sweat. Water deprivation does not accelerate heat acclimatization, despite the persistence of this fallacy.

PREVENTION OF HEAT INJURIES

Most heat injuries can be prevented by an adequate fluid and salt intake. An active climber produces heat at the rate of hundreds of kilocalories per hour. If he is in a hot environment, he may also be absorbing more heat from the air and the rocks. In such circumstances the only possible avenue of heat loss is through the evaporation of body surface moisture. Staggering amounts of water and salt can be lost through perspiration under such severe conditions. Up to two quarts of fluid may be lost in a single hour. Enough water and salt must be consumed during the course of the day to make up for this loss.

The magnitude of the fluid and salt requirements under such severe conditions is illustrated by the precautions taken during a recent military exercise in the deserts of Southern California and Arizona. The expected average temperature was between 100° and 110°F. Every man participating in the operation was *ordered* to drink eight quarts of water every day and to take three to five grams of extra salt. Since thirst or hunger for salt would not alone result in an adequate intake, each person in a command position was held responsible for ensuring that his men met the daily intake requirements.

In addition to adequate fluid and salt consumption, more obvious preventive measures, such as rest in the shade during the hottest part of the day, are quite important. In situations where high temperatures are combined with high humidity (which reduces evaporation from the skin) shelter from the sun and inactivity during the day to minimize metabolic heat production may be the only means of avoiding heat injury. Travel at night may be necessary. The use of plastic sweat clothes during strenuous exercise under hot conditions should be avoided for the same reasons. This is not a safe way to lose weight under extreme conditions.

A number of factors can increase the risk of heat injury. Individuals with any kind of cardiovascular disease or a chronic disease such as diabetes are more susceptible, as are patients with fever due to infection or some other cause. Large doses of amphetamines as well as LSD have been implicated in some deaths from heat stroke.

TYPES OF HEAT INJURIES

Heat Exhaustion

Heat exhaustion, which can involve individuals in excellent physical condition, is caused by prolonged physical exertion in a hot environment. In such situations the blood vessels in the skin can become so dilated that the blood supply for the brain and other vital organs is reduced to inadequate levels. Dehydration may also cause a mild reduction in blood volume. The result is a physiological disorder which is similar to fainting and is rarely serious unless complicated by some coexisting disease. Lack of acclimatization to heat, or even minor degrees of dehydration or salt deficiency make an individual more susceptible to heat exhaustion.

At the time of onset the victim feels faint and is usually aware of a rapid heart rate. Nausea, vomiting, headache, dizziness, restlessness, or even loss of consciousness are not uncommon. Most important from a diagnostic standpoint, *the patient's temperature is not significantly elevated and may be below normal.* The presence of sweating and the skin color are variable.

Treatment consists of rest in a comfortable environment and the administration of salty fluids (after the patient returns to consciousness). Recovery can be expected in a very short time, but steps should be taken to prevent a recurrence. Any underlying heart or vascular disease or other predisposing illnesses must be appropriately treated.

Heat Stroke

Heat stroke (also called "sunstroke") results from inadequacy of the sweating process. For normal individuals exercising in a hot environment, the rate of sweating decreases steadily. After a number of hours of uninterrupted work under such conditions the rate of perspiration can reach very low levels. In heat stroke this normal reduction in sweating progresses to the complete breakdown of the sweating and heat regulatory mechanisms.

The sweating deficiency appears to result from exhaustion of the sweat glands. This disorder rarely occurs if some relief from sweating, such as cool nights or air-conditioned sleeping quarters, is afforded during some part of each twenty-four hours.

The onset of heat stroke is often very rapid. The victim may be previously aware of extreme heat, but then quickly becomes confused, incoordinated, delirious, or unconscious. Characteristically, *the body temperature is above 105°F, the skin is hot, and sweating is completely absent.* (Some infections, such as meningitis, can also cause temperatures of 104° or higher. An obvious exposure to extreme heat, however, would be indicative of heat stroke.)

Treatment must be instituted immediately. All untreated cases are inevitably fatal due to brain damage; the degree of residual damage in nonfatal cases is directly related to the amount of elapsed time before treatment is begun. *Heat stroke is one of the few true medical emergencies.* The body must be cooled as rapidly as possible. Total immersion in tepid (not cold) water should be employed if available. Otherwise the victim should be covered with cloths soaked in water or alcohol and fanned to promote evaporation. Ice packs or chemical cold packs may cause cold injury and probably should not be applied. The limbs should be vigorously massaged to prevent stagnation of the circulation in the extremities and accelerate cooling of the vital organs. (This adjunct is frequently overlooked, but is of vital importance.)

Cooling can be stopped when the temperature reaches 102°F, but may have to be reinstated if high fever recurs. The victim's temperature may be quite unstable for several days and must be carefully watched. Aspirin should be avoided as it is rarely of any benefit and may be harmful. A physician's care should be obtained if possible.

Persistent coma after cooling has been achieved is indicative of brain damage and requires immediate evacuation. Some heat stroke victims develop acute renal failure. Some residual intolerance for heat can be expected in individuals who recover without any apparent disability.

Heat Cramps

Muscle cramps are severe, spasmodic contractions of one or more muscles, which most frequently involve the legs or abdominal muscles. The cramps may last up to fifteen minutes or, on rare occasions, even longer. The involved muscle is sometimes sore for several days afterwards.

Frequently cramps can be stopped almost instantly by stretching the involved muscle. For example, a cramp in the calf muscles can often be abolished by extending the leg and pointing or pulling the toes upward as far as possible. Kneading or pounding the muscle is less effective and may contribute to the residual soreness.

No etiology can be identified for most muscle cramps, although salt deficiency is a common cause. Under circumstances in which increased loss of salt could occur, muscle cramps — heat cramps or salt cramps as they would then be called — are indicative of salt depletion. Oral administration of salt and water should provide prompt relief from repeated episodes of cramps. Recurrences can be prevented by providing a daily supplement of ten to fifteen grams of salt and a generous fluid intake.

Prickly Heat

Prickly heat is a condition in which sweating is impaired due to obstruction and inflammation of sweat glands. The best treatment is to provide relief from the heat. This disorder is usually not serious, but is irritating and can result in complications such as infection of the affected skin. The discomfort is aggravated by the friction of clothing and by most creams and ointments.

REFERENCES:

1. Baetjer, A. M.: Chapter 25 in *Preventive Medicine and Public Health*, Maxcy, Ed., New York, Appleton-Century Crofts, 1956.
2. Kleiber, M.: *The Fire of Life*, New York, John Wiley and Sons, 1961.
3. Lee, D. H. K.: Terrestrial Animals in Dry Heat: Man in the Desert, *Handbook of Physiology, Section 4: Adaptation to the Environment*, Baltimore, Waverly Press, Inc. 1964.
4. Lee, D. H. K.: Heat Regulation, *Heat and Cold Effects and Their Control*, U.S. Public Health Service Publication No. 1084, Washington, U.S. Government Printing Office, 1964.
5. Marie, Sister M., and Ferguson, M.: Heat Illness, GP *22*:1, 1960.
6. *Sunstroke, Heatstroke, Heat Prostration*, U.S. Public Health Service Publication No. 176, Washington, U.S. Government Printing Office, 1961.
7. Knochel, J.: Environmental Heat Illness, Arch. Int. Med. *133*:841, 1974.

CHAPTER 17

Animal Bites

THE DANGER of infection following the bite of any animal is very great. The mouths of all animals — including humans — contain numerous bacteria which are introduced into the wound at the time the bite is inflicted. Human bites tend to produce particularly virulent infections.

Bites should be treated as contaminated soft tissue injuries. The wound should be washed with copious quantities of soap and water. After thorough rinsing with water, aqueous Zephiran should be poured into the wound, particularly if the bite was inflicted by a possibly rabid animal. Under no circumstances should the wound be sutured. A sterile dressing should be applied and the patient and his wound closely observed for evidence of infection. Appropriate therapy should be instituted if infection does develop.

RABIES

Rabies is caused by a viral infection; the harmful effects are the result of infection of the brain. Rabies has been known and deservedly feared since antiquity. Until recently, not a single human patient with proven rabies had ever survived. At the time this is written, two people with rabies have survived, but one of those is reported to have rather severe residual brain damage.

Within the United States rabies has been controlled to a considerable extent through the vaccination of domestic animals. Dog rabies has diminished from over 5,000 cases in 1946 to just 180 in 1973. Human rabies has concomitantly declined from more than twenty cases a year in the 1940s to less than two cases a year in the 1970s. In 1973 seventy-nine percent of all confirmed animal rabies was in wildlife, primarily skunks, foxes, bats, and raccoons. (Rabies is not endemic in rodents. Bites by rats, mice, chipmunks, squirrels, rabbits, or other rodents have never been proven to produce human rabies.) Bat rabies is endemic in all areas, both urban and rural, within the continental United States.

Outside the United States, particularly in underdeveloped countries, vaccination of domestic animals for rabies is practiced on a very limited basis or not at all. Therefore, the risk of contracting rabies from pets or other animals in these areas is considerably higher.

Essentially all carnivorous animals are susceptible to rabies and capable of transmitting the infection. The virus involves the salivary glands and is present in the saliva. Transmission of the infection occurs through a wound which is contaminated with the saliva of the rabid animal. The virus cannot penetrate intact skin, but can enter through a scratch, bite, or other break in the skin, or through an intact mucous membrane such as lines the mouth, nose, or eyelids. Therefore, the infection can be transmitted by licking without a bite having been inflicted. Infection has been transmitted by breathing aerosolized rabies virus in a medical laboratory, and can probably be transmitted by breathing the air in caves inhabited by rabid bats.

Diagnosis

If rabies is to be prevented it must be recognized in the attacking animal so that the human victim can be treated before symptoms develop. Treatment begun after the victim begins to show signs of rabies is almost always totally ineffective.

The diagnosis of rabies is generally made by killing the suspected animal, removing its head, and shipping the head under refrigeration to an appropriate laboratory. (In the United States, public health laboratories generally are responsible for transporting the head to a central laboratory.) In the laboratory the animal's brain is examined for the presence of the rabies virus (using a fluorescent antibody technique). In the United States the results of such examinations are highly reliable. In other countries they may not be.

If the animal cannot be killed or captured, it should be assumed to be rabid. The only exceptions are for bites inflicted in those areas where rabies does not occur. (Hawaii is considered to be free of all forms of wildlife rabies. All animals brought into the islands are quarantined for prolonged periods to prevent the introduction of this infection. In contrast, within the continental United States all bat bites should be considered to have been inflicted by a rabid animal if the bat escapes.)

For bites from normally behaving dogs or cats which have been previously vaccinated and which can be captured after the bite is inflicted, treatment can be withheld while the animal is held in captivity for a period of ten days. If the animal does not become ill during this period of observation, no antirabies treatment is needed for the bite victim. If it does become ill, the head should be sent for examination and treatment started while awaiting the results.

Rabies in animals follows a highly variable course. The well-known "mad dog" foaming at the mouth is almost never seen. Unprovoked attacks are the

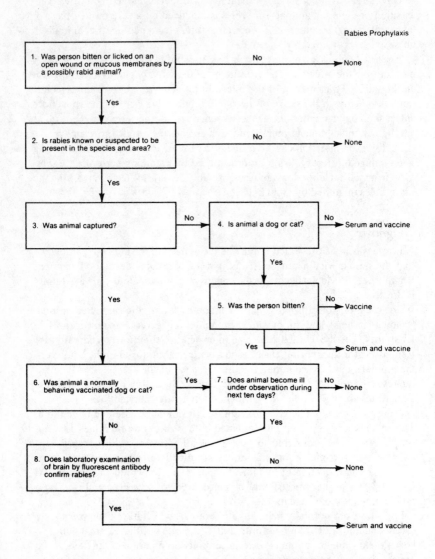

Figure 40. Postexposure rabies prophylaxis algorithm. (From J.A.M.A., April 21, 1975, vol. 232, no. 3. Used by permission.)

most common indication of rabies. (Bites incurred while feeding an unknown animal are considered provoked.) Occasionally the only outward sign of rabies is the lack of fear of man, which may even appear to be a show of friendliness. Animals such as skunks, which usually scurry away from any threatening situation, may actually pursue a supposed attacker.

Treatment

Treatment of the wound produced by the animal bite is a vital part of the care for patients exposed to rabies. The severity and speed of onset of infection is dependent to a certain extent upon the number of viruses introduced. Washing saliva out of the wound helps to reduce the number of viruses which can enter the tissues.

The wound should be thoroughly washed with large quantities of soap and water. After thoroughly rinsing away the soap, the wound should be flushed with aqueous Zephiran (which can actually kill some of the viruses). Immediate washing is of such urgency that it should be instituted without delay. If soap or Zephiran are not available, anything on hand — including whiskey or other alcoholic beverages — should be used.

Specific treatment for rabies consists of administering vaccine to build up immunity to the rabies virus during the incubation period between the bite and the appearance of signs of the disease (see "Allergies"). In most circumstances serum from an animal already immune to rabies — antirabies serum — is also administered. The accompanying chart, adopted from recommendations of the Viral Diseases Division, Bureau of Epidemiology, Center for Disease Control, Public Health Service, U.S. Department of Health, Education, and Welfare, depicts the type of therapy that should be administered following different types of rabies exposure.

The rabies vaccine currently available in the United States is prepared from viruses grown on duck embryos and is free from many of the serious side effects which were common with treatment with the older nerve tissue vaccines. However, treatment is not totally free of side effects, particularly allergic reactions including anaphylactic reactions (see "Allergies"). The injections are almost always painful.

Vaccine injections should consist of 1 cc of vaccine injected into the subcutaneous tissue of the back, abdomen, or thighs. Each injection should be made at a different site. Vaccine injections should be given every twelve hours for seven days, followed by injections every twenty-four hours for the next seven days. Booster injections should be given twenty-four and thirty-four days after the series of injections is started.

The most widely available preparation of antirabies serum is prepared in horses. Many people are allergic to horse serum and should not be treated with this preparation. A careful questioning about such allergy, and skin testing if possible (described under treatment for poisonous snake bite) should be carried out before treatment with horse serum is begun. Antirabies serum prepared from human volunteers is now available within the United States for everyone who needs treatment. It probably is not available at all outside the United States at the present time (1975).

The dosage of antirabies serum is 40 international units per kilogram of body weight (approximately 20 units per pound). Up to fifty percent of the antiserum should be infiltrated around the bite and the remainder injected intramuscularly.

During the course of vaccine injections, antihistamines can be administered to counteract some of the side effects. Steroids should not be administered since they tend to inhibit the desired immune response.

Vaccination

The duck embryo vaccine has proven suitable for human vaccination against rabies prior to actual exposure. Such vaccination has been used for veterinarians, animal handlers, and laboratory workers who have a high risk of exposure. In view of the wide distribution of rabies in bats and the risk of infection by breathing the air in the caves they inhabit, cavers and others frequently exposed to this source of infection should probably be vaccinated. Climbers visiting countries in which rabies is a significant danger may also be well advised to obtain pre-exposure vaccination.

POISONOUS SNAKE BITE

Poisonous snake bites are unquestionably serious, potentially deadly accidents. Nonetheless, the danger from a single bite has been greatly exaggerated by overly dramatic literary presentations and superstition. In the United States an average of about twenty people die each year as the result of a bite by a poisonous snake. Many more bites occur, but less than three percent prove fatal. Even the accepted fatality rate of three percent is probably too high since almost all fatal bites are recorded, but many nonfatal bites go unreported, even though the victims are hospitalized for observation or treatment. In a compilation of over 400 well documented copperhead bites occurring in eastern North Carolina over a period of years, only two deaths could be found. In both cases the unfortunate victims had been bitten simultaneously by three or more snakes.

Such statistics are an adequate cause for optimism on the part of a snake bite victim and his attendants and should encourage a conservative approach in the treatment of such accidents. However, they in no way justify a lack of preparation for informed, rapid, and vigorous therapy when such is needed.

Unfortunately the treatment of poisonous snake bites remains a subject of considerable confusion and misunderstanding. The authoritative publication of untested personal opinions or the results of poorly designed and inadequately controlled animal experiments, compounded by a sometimes sensationalist press, have produced widespread misinformation. These results are particularly unfortunate when the basic principles of poisonous snake bite treatment are so well known.

The only methods for treating poisonous snake bites which are of clearly proven value are incision and suction and antivenin administration.

Diagnosis

An accurate diagnosis is vitally important in the treatment of snake bite and is not as simple as might be expected. Every year a number of people die from fright or unnecessary treatment following the bite of a nonpoisonous snake. In India, where snake bites are quite common, deaths resulting from treatment for nonpoisonous snake bites are reported to number in the thousands every year.

The first step in diagnosis is identification of the snake. If possible the snake should be killed so it can be closely examined.

Poisonous snakes of the world include the *Elapidae,* the *Viperinae,* and the *Crotalinae.* Within the family *Elapidae* are found the North American coral snake, the Indian krait found in India and Pakistan, the tiger snake of Australia, the death adder of Australia and New Guinea, the Indian cobra found in most of Southeast Asia including Indonesia and Formosa, the Mamba found in East Africa, and the Ringhals found in South Africa. The *Viperinae* include the puff adder found in most of Africa and southern Arabia, the saw-scaled viper found in northern and western Africa to northern India and Ceylon, the Palestine viper of the Middle East, and Russell's viper found from West Pakistan to Formosa. The *Crotalinae* family includes all of the North American rattlesnakes as well as the copperhead and cottonmouth moccasin, the fer-de-lance and neotropical rattlesnake found from Mexico to Argentina, the Jararaca of tropical South America, and the Habu found in the Ryuku Islands with closely related species in Formosa and the southeastern part of the People's Republic of China.

The poisonous snakes of the United States are the rattlesnakes, copperhead, cottonmouth or water moccasin, and the coral snake. All North American poisonous snakes except the coral snake are pit vipers and have a characteristic triangular head and a heavy body. However, the body markings are usually not specific enough for identification to be made by the markings alone. These snakes are called "pit vipers" because they have a small pit located between the eye and the nostril, a feature found only in these poisonous species. The pit vipers are also characterized by having single scales reaching across the undersurface of the body posterior to the anus; most other snakes have double scales. If fangs are present, the snake is undoubtedly poisonous. However, the

HARMLESS

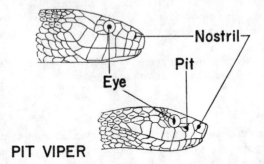

PIT VIPER

Figure 41. Comparison of the heads of pit vipers and non-poisonous snakes.

fangs may be folded back against the roof of the mouth, making them difficult to identify. One or both fangs may be broken off; three or four are sometimes found. The presence of rattles is of obvious significance, but the absence of rattles may only mean that they have recently been broken off.

The coral snake is a small, thin, brightly colored snake, quite different from the pit vipers. It can be identified by the adjacent red and yellow bands. The king snake and several other harmless species with similar coloration have adjacent red and black bands. A helpful mnemonic is:

> "Red and yellow — kill a fellow;
> Red and black — venom lack."

The coral snake has very short, immovable fangs unlike those of the pit vipers. It is limited by its size to biting fingers, toes, or loose folds of skin, and must bite and hold on rather than making a lightning-fast strike like the pit vipers.

After examining the snake, the site of the bite should be inspected. If only the fangs strike the victim, one or two small puncture marks are produced, a reliable indication that the snake is a poisonous variety. However, the converse sign, a U-shaped row of small punctures resulting from the other teeth in the snake's mouth, is not so reliable. Supposedly the U-shaped bite is found only following the bite of a nonpoisonous snake which lacks fangs. However, the marks from the fangs of a poisonous snake may be hidden among the marks from his other teeth if he has succeeded in embedding his fangs so deeply that the other teeth have also reached the skin. Even when the fangs alone have entered the skin, a U-shaped row of teeth marks from the bottom jaw may be present.

The reaction following the bite is one of the best indications that the snake was poisonous. This reaction, which is usually quite severe following the bite of

POISONOUS   NON-POISONOUS

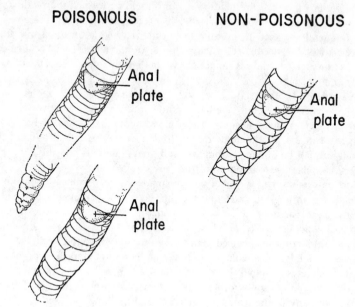

Figure 42. Comparison of the scales on the under-surface of tails of poisonous and non-poisonous snakes.

a pit viper, occurs within a few minutes after the victim is bitten. The onset is marked by intense pain or burning at the site of the bite which is accompanied or followed shortly by swelling and purplish or greenish discoloration. Soon the victim becomes weak and dizzy with cold, clammy skin and a weak, thready pulse. Other signs of shock may also be present.

The reaction to the bite of a coral snake is less intense. Pain is often not as severe, and swelling is usually absent.

If no reaction follows the bite, no treatment should be instituted. Poisonous snakes occasionally strike their victims without injecting any venom. Occasionally the snake lacks venom as a result of having just bitten some other animal.

Treatment

The treatment for all snake bites, regardless of the species, consists of incision and suction combined with the administration of antivenin. Both procedures used together produce considerably better results than either used alone. Treatment should be started as soon as possible to obtain optimum results.

Before any incisions are made, the skin should be washed thoroughly and swabbed with an antiseptic. Such obvious precautions against contamination are frequently neglected, resulting in infections which are responsible for a large part of the residual damage resulting from snake bites. The bacteria which cause tetanus and gas gangrene have both been isolated from the mouths of poisonous snakes.

A sterile razor blade should be used to make *linear* incisions one-eighth to one-quarter inch deep and one-half to three-quarters inch long overlying the fang marks. Another incision can be made about six inches higher if the swelling spreads up the limb quite rapidly. However, significant benefits usually cannot be obtained from any additional incisions and the danger of infection or damage to important structures is quite high.

Incisions on the hands or feet must be made with extreme care and should extend only through the skin and the thin layer of subcutaneous tissue. The hands and feet are marvelously complex anatomical structures. Deep incisions can sever tendons, nerves, or blood vessels and produce permanent crippling.

A tourniquet may be placed about the limb just above the swelling, but it must *never* hinder the circulation of blood in the injured limb. The purpose of the tourniquet is to hinder the movement of venom in the subcutaneous tissue spaces. The blood supply to the limb is reduced to a precarious state by the snake bite; any further impairment may result in gangrene. *Pulses must be present beyond the site of constriction.* A broad piece of cloth such as a hand-kerchief should be used for the tourniquet; the shoe-string-like tape provided in some snake bite kits frequently damages underlying nerves and other structures, particularly if applied tightly. If any question exists about the way the tourniquet should be placed, it should not be used at all.

Suction over the incisions is best performed by suction cups such as those in snake bite kits. Suction by mouth can be used but is not as effective. Furthermore, the danger of introducing wound infection is much greater, and the danger of self-envenomation is not inconsiderable. If enough suction cups to cover all the incisions are not available, the cups can be rotated at intervals of three to five minutes. Suction should be maintained for an hour and then discontinued; little additional venom can be extracted after this time.

Antivenin

The only antivenin produced for general use in the United States is made from horse serum and supplied by Wyeth Laboratories, Inc. This antivenin is available throughout the country and is effective to some extent against all North and South American poisonous snakes. (Travelers to other continents should obtain appropriate anti-sera from manufacturers located there.)

Unfortunately a number of people are allergic to horse serum. In allergic individuals the damage from the horse serum antivenin frequently exceeds the damage from the snake venom. Therefore, tests for allergy (hypersensitivity) must be made before the antivenin is used.

The Wyeth antivenin comes in a small kit containing the necessary syringes and needles for administration. The antivenin itself is in crystallized form and retains its potency for a period of five years without refrigeration. The kit also contains ten cubic centimeters (10 cc) of sterile water for mixing with the crystallized antivenin to prepare it for injection.

In addition a small vial of horse serum is enclosed for testing for "sensitivity" or allergy. For the test, one-tenth cubic centimeter (0.1 cc) of this serum is injected into (not under) the skin of the forearm in such a fashion that a small blister is raised. If no reaction to this intradermal test occurs within twenty minutes, the antivenin can be administered. If more than a slight redness of the skin appears at the site of the test, the victim is allergic to horse serum and needs to be desensitized.

If the victim *is not* hypersensitive to the serum, the antivenin can be injected into a large muscle farther up the limb. As many as four or five vials of antivenin may be required for the bite of a large snake. (The severity of pit viper bites can be estimated by the amount of swelling which occurs, the rapidity with which swelling progresses, and the general condition of the patient.)

If the victim is allergic to horse serum, desensitization must be carried out, preferably by a physician. The procedure for desensitization is described in detail in the instructions which accompany the antivenin and must be followed precisely.

Antivenin therapy is much more dangerous than incision and suction, even though the latter is much more dramatic. The administration of antivenin (without prior desensitization) to an individual who is allergic to horse serum would usually have catastrophic results. Desensitization is a tedious procedure, consuming a large amount of time which can be more effectively used in evacuating the victim. Furthermore, efforts to desensitize a patient to horse serum are frequently unsuccessful, even in expert hands. Therefore, unless the victim has been bitten by several snakes, or by a very large snake, or by a species with particularly potent venom, and appears to be in severe distress or actually approaching death, he should not be given antivenin if he is allergic to horse serum. The same restrictions should probably also be applied to the treatment of individuals who are not allergic to horse serum.

Cold Therapy

A form of treatment mentioned only to strongly advise against its use is packing the extremity in ice, snow or cold water, or using ethyl chloride spray to cool the limb. Individuals recommending this type of treatment (cryotherapy) have assumed that most of the active components of snake venom are enzymes. Generally speaking raising the temperature of the medium in which an enzyme is acting 10° C doubles the activity of the enzyme; lowering the temperature a similar amount reduces enzyme activity by half. Cooling the tissues in which the venom has been injected is supposed to reduce the activity of the enzymes so the body's defense mechanisms can eliminate the enzymes before much damage is done.

This assumption, upon which cryotherapy of poisonous snake bite is based, is fallacious for two reasons. First, a large portion of the active toxins in snake venoms are peptides — not enzymes. Peptides are substances similar to many proteins but of smaller molecular weight. The activity of these peptides is not affected by temperature as is the activity of enzymes.

Second, the enzymes produced in any animal body generally are optimally active at that animal's average body temperature. Snakes are cold blooded animals. Enzymes produced by cold blooded animals — whether in venoms, digestive juices, or elsewhere — are active at low temperatures. Some components of snake venom are not inhibited at all by the amount of cooling which can be obtained by the techniques used in this form of therapy.

In contrast, man is a warm blooded animal. His enzymes are optimally active at his body temperature of 37° C and are inhibited by cooling.

The body's principle detoxifying mechanism appears to be the action of antibodies against the venom. Lowering the temperature causes constriction of blood vessels, and definitely retards access of the antibodies to the toxins.

Snake venom severely damages blood vessels, injuring vessel walls, which allows serum to escape into the surrounding tissues, and causing clots to form within the vessels. As a result of the clots and compression of the blood vessels by the fluid in the surrounding tissues, blood flow to the extremity beyond the bite is severely compromised. Further reduction of the blood flow through constriction of the blood vessels caused by cooling the limb could be — and commonly has been — disastrous.

Other Considerations

The victim of a snake bite must be kept quiet and not be permitted to walk or move about. Physical activity increases the rate of circulation of the blood and thus increases the rate of spread of the venom. However, the effects of activity are frequently worse than would be expected from this consideration alone.

If the victim cannot be evacuated for several days, antibiotics may be needed to combat wound infection. A barbiturate every four to six hours helps keep the victim quiet and allay anxiety. Drugs for pain, such as morphine or meperidine increase the toxicity of venom and must not be used. Alcohol increases absorption of the venom and physical activity by the victim and must also be avoided.

Most snake bite fatalities result from shock, regardless of the species of snake or whether the venom is primarily toxic to the blood and blood vessels (the pit vipers) or to the nervous system (coral snake and cobras). This complication must be anticipated and treated appropriately.

Every case of snake bite is different and the treatment must be tailored to fit each case. Children and elderly persons tolerate poisonous snake bites poorly and require more vigorous treatment in order to survive. Bites occurring in the spring, when the snake has just emerged from hibernation and its venom is more concentrated, are more severe than bites occurring at other times of the year. Bites about the head or trunk are more dangerous than bites on the extremities and require more intensive treatment.

SPIDER BITE

The black widow (*latrodectus mactans*) is the only spider found in the United States which is capable of routinely producing serious illness by its bite. The "tarantula" which is native to the Southwest bites only after extreme provocation. Its weak and ineffective fangs can only penetrate thin skin on the sides of the fingers and the effects of the bite are no worse than an insect sting. However, large hairy tarantulas found in other areas such as Brazil or Peru can produce effects identical to those of the black widow with their bites.

The brown spider (brown recluse or violin spider — *Lososceles reclusa*) has been publicized as the cause of "necrotic arachnidism." Following the bite of this spider a blister surrounded by an area of intense inflammation about one-half inch in diameter appears. Pain, which is mild at first, may become quite severe within about eight hours. Over the next ten to fourteen days the blister ruptures and the involved skin turns a dark brown or black color. Eventually the black, dead tissue falls away, leaving a crater which heals with some scarring.

A few deaths have occurred in children as the result of the bite of the brown recluse spider. The most common complication has been the need for a small skin graft to cover the ulcer left by the bite. Antihistamines and steroids may relieve symptoms following the bite. For severe reactions treatment for shock may be necessary. Antivenin for the bite of this spider is not available in the United States.

Jumping spiders, trapdoor spiders, orbweavers and spiders of the *Chiracanthium* species among others have been reported to produce mild local reactions. All spiders are venomous, but most have fangs which are too delicate to pierce the skin.

The black widow alone is capable of causing a significant number of deaths among its victims. Even so, fatalities from the bite of this spider are limited almost entirely to small children or elderly individuals in poor health. In healthy adults, the bite may cause severe pain and prostration for two to four days, but complete recovery almost always follows.

The female black widow is coal-black and has a prominent, globose abdomen. The body may be as large as one-half inch in length (not including the legs). On the undersurface of the abdomen is a red or orange figure which usually resembles an hour-glass but may be round or have some other configuration. Markings of the same color but in varying patterns are sometimes present on the back. However, only the under-surface markings are characteristic for the species. (The male of this species, which is smaller and has a dirty brown color, is completely harmless.)

The black widow weaves a coarse, crudely constructed web in dark corners, both indoors and out. (Nearly half the black widow bites reported in the medical literature in the first four decades of this century were inflicted on male genitalia by spiders lurking underneath the seats of outdoor toilets.) However, this spider is timid and prefers to run away rather than attack an intruder.

Diagnosis

At the time the bite is inflicted the victim may feel a slight pain similar to a pin prick, slight burning, or nothing at all. Small puncture wounds, slight redness, or no visible marks at all may be found at the site of the bite. Within fifteen to sixty minutes severe pain develops in the area around the bite and spreads rapidly to involve the entire body. The characteristic pattern of spread is by continuity — that is, from a bite on the forearm the pain would spread to the elbow, then to the shoulder, and then over the rest of the body, including the legs.

The pain is very severe and the victim frequently writhes in agony. The abdominal muscles are characteristically rigid and hard, although actual abdominal tenderness is not present. Spasms of other muscles also occur. The victims are often covered with perspiration; dizziness, nausea, and vomiting are common. Signs of shock are frequently present. Breathing may be labored, speech blurred, and coordination impaired, often closely resembling alcoholic intoxication.

If the spider or its bite have not been noticed, these signs and symptoms may lead to the erroneous diagnosis of an acute abdominal emergency.

Treatment

Specific antivenin for black widow bites is available in the United States from Merck, Sharp and Dohme, Inc. The antivenin is prepared from horses and should not be given to anyone allergic to horse serum. Careful testing for such allergy should be carried out before the antivenin is administered. Treatment consists of one ampule of serum (2.5 cc) injected intramuscularly. A second ampule may be given but is almost never necessary. In fact, the first ampule is probably not necessary for most healthy adults and certainly should not be given to anyone allergic to horse serum.

In addition to antivenin, nonspecific therapy should be directed towards relieving muscle spasms. On a mountaineering expedition, drugs for the relief of such spasms would probably not be carried. However, hot baths may be of some help. Calcium gluconate (10 cc of a 10 percent solution) can be injected intravenously every four hours as long as the pain persists. Therapy with analgesics such as morphine may be helpful, but usually will not provide complete relief from the pain.

Incision and suction as performed for snake bite must not be attempted. These techniques are ineffective in removing the spider venom and introduce the danger of infection. If the site of the bite is painful an ice cube can be applied, but should be removed after antivenin therapy is given.

The pain and prostration following a spider bite usually disappear in two to four days, but complete recovery may require several weeks.

SCORPION STINGS

Scorpions are found throughout most of the United States, but the species lethal to man are limited to Arizona and Southern California. However, in this area scorpions are a serious problem. Sixty-nine deaths from scorpion stings occurred in Arizona between 1929 and 1954 compared with twenty deaths from rattlesnake bites.

Scorpions are eight-legged arachnids which range in length from three to eight inches and have a rather plump body, thin tail, and large pinchers. They are found under rocks and logs, buried in the sand, in collections of lumber, bricks, or brush, and in the attics, walls, or understructures of houses or deserted buildings.

Scorpion stings can usually be avoided by exercising care when picking up objects such as stones or logs under which scorpions like to hide during the days. Since scorpions are nocturnal, walking barefooted after dark should also be avoided. Shoes and clothing should be shaken vigorously before putting them on.

The lethal species of scorpions are often found under loose bark or around old tree stumps. They have a yellow to greenish-yellow color and measure three inches in length and three-eighths inch in width when of adult size. One species has two irregular dark stripes down its back.

The sting of a non-lethal scorpion is similar, although somewhat more severe, to that of a wasp or a bee and should be treated in an identical manner.

The lethal scorpion stings are much more severe but fatalities are limited almost entirely to small children or elderly persons in poor health. (The large number of scorpion deaths in Arizona is undoubtedly related to the tendency for scorpions to dwell in the vicinity of human habitation where children are frequently playing.)

Diagnosis

The sting of one of the lethal species of scorpions produces a pricking sensation. Pain follows shortly and may become severe. The area soon becomes quite sensitive so that tapping it lightly with a finger produces a tingling or prickly feeling which travels up the extremity toward the body. This increased sensitivity occurs only with stings from the lethal species and is a highly significant diagnostic finding.

In severe scorpionism the entire extremity becomes numb and a feeling of tightness in the throat appears. The patient becomes restless and jittery and, in fatal cases, convulsions and respiratory difficulty follow.

Usually nothing abnormal can be seen at the site of the sting at any time during the disorder. Nevertheless, this is the last part of the body to recover in non-fatal cases and may remain abnormally sensitive for one to two weeks.

Treatment

Specific scorpion antivenin prepared from goats (which avoids the problem of allergy to horse serum) is available from the Antivenom Production Laboratory, Arizona State University, Tempe, Arizona. However, it is generally only needed by children or elderly or debilitated persons.

High doses of barbiturates (200 to 300 mg of secobarbital every four to six hours) can be used to counteract the restlessness and jitteryness which accompany stings by lethal species of scorpions. Chlorpromazine may be somewhat superior for this purpose, but in view of the occasional severe side effects produced by this drug its use should be limited to physicians. Other symptoms such as excessive salivation may be relieved by atropine, but this drug also should probably only be administered by a doctor.

A few patients develop shock following a sting by one of these lethal scorpion species. If signs of shock appear, appropriate care should be instituted.

The application of ice to the site of the scorpion sting may help relieve local symptoms. Cold injury must be avoided.

REFERENCES:

1. Corey, L., and Hattwick, M.A.W.: Treatment of Persons Exposed to Rabies, J.A.M.A. 232:272, 1975.
2. Boys, F., and Smith, H.: Poisonous Amphibians and Reptiles, Springfield, Ill., Charles C. Thomas, 1959.
3. Gennaro, J. F.: Observations on the Treatment of Snakebite in North America, in Venomous and Poisonous Animals and Noxious Plants of the Pacific Region, Keegan, H. L., and Macfarlane, W. V., Ed., New York, The MacMillan Co., 1963.

4. Russell, F. E., Carlson, R. W., Wainschel, J., and Osborne, A. H.: Snake Venom Poisoning in the United States: Experience with 550 Cases, J.A.M.A. *233*:341, 1975.

5. Thorp, R. W., and Woodson, S. D.: *Black Widow,* Chapel Hill, N.C., The University of North Carolina Press, 1945.

6. Stahnke, H. L.: *Scorpions, 2nd Ed.,* Tempe, Ariz., Poisonous Animals Research Laboratory, Arizona State College.

Chapter 18

Diseases of the Respiratory System

THE RESPIRATORY system moves air in and out of the lungs to provide oxygen for the body and to eliminate carbon dioxide. The components of this system are:

1. The nose and mouth, trachea, bronchi, and bronchioles which form the passages through which air moves into the lungs;
2. The mucous membranes lining the air passages which remove foreign material, humidify the air, and raise or lower its temperature to that of the body;
3. The alveoli, composed of delicate, one cell thick membranes, which make up the largest portion of the lung tissue and in which oxygen and carbon dioxide are exchanged between blood and air;
4. The thin, membraneous pleura which covers the lungs, lines the inner surface of the chest wall, and facilitates the movement of the lungs within the chest;
5. The chest wall and diaphragm which, acting like a bellows, move air in and out of the lungs;
6. The receptors which respond to chemical changes in the circulating blood and transmit impulses through various nerve networks to control the rate and depth of respiration (chemoreceptors).

The rate and depth of breathing are controlled by a complex system of receptors throughout the body. Chemical receptors respond to an oxygen deficiency, an accumulation of carbon dioxide, or a decrease in the acidity of the blood (which normally is maintained at a slightly alkaline pH) to bring about faster, deeper breathing. Under ordinary resting conditions approximately one-half quart of air is inspired with each breath. The normal respiratory rate is ten to twelve breaths per minute. The respiratory volume is decreased as much as twenty to thirty percent during sleep, which further

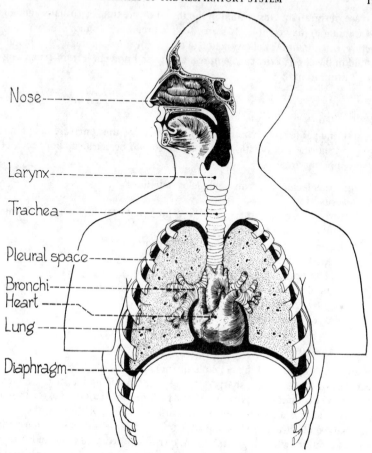

Figure 43. Anatomy of the respiratory system.

decreases the oxygenation of the blood at high altitude and thereby probably explains the aggravation of symptoms of altitude sickness during the night. Exertion, by increasing the need for oxygen and also by producing more lactic acid and carbon dioxide which stimulate the respiratory center in the brain, increases the respiratory volume, occasionally to as much as 150 quarts per minute during violent exercise. Even at very rapid respiratory rates, oxygen is taken up by the blood and carbon dioxide given off with extraordinary efficiency.

Many different disorders can affect the respiratory system at different levels. Head injuries or diseases of the brain usually slow or stop, but occasionally increase, respiration. Obstruction in the throat or the trachea (usually sudden and traumatic) may completely stop effective breathing. Injury, even without fracture, can impair the bellows action of chest wall and diaphragm. Air, blood, or fluid in the chest cavity can compress a lung and prevent it from expanding during inspiration.

Symptoms

The principal symptoms produced by diseases of the lungs are coughing, pain, and shortness of breath. Details which should be clarified about each of these symptoms are:

Pain: Exact location and any change or radiation;
  Severity;
  Nature — stabbing, sharp, dull, crushing, continuous, or intermittent;
  Onset — sudden or gradual;
  Relation to respiration, movement, and exertion;
  Relation to onset of other symptoms.
Cough: Dry or productive (sputum is coughed up);
  Color and consistency of material which is coughed up;
  Coughing up blood.
Shortness of Breath: Relation to position;
  Factors which cause aggravation or provide relief;
  Time and nature of onset.

Pain due to diseases of the lung, pleura, or chest wall is related to breathing; deep inspiration causes a sharp stabbing pain. An irritating, dry, frequent cough is very common at high altitude due to drying and irritation of the throat, and is not always an indication of lung disease. (See "Diseases of the Eyes, Ears, Nose and Throat.") The cough due to lung disease is deeper, and usually produces sputum which is green, yellow, or rust colored, and thick and stringy in the case of infection. Sputum may be thin, watery, and pink or bloody in the case of high altitude pulmonary edema. (See "Medical Problems due to High Altitude.") In the case of pulmonary embolism (see below) the sputum is usually bloody. Chest pain, shortness of breath, and thin, pink sputum may be symptoms of heart disease and heart failure. (See "Diseases of the Heart and Blood Vessels.")

Physical Examination

The entire patient must be examined even though the principal site of disease is in the lungs. An elevated pulse rate and fever are indicative of significant disease. Fever is usually a sign of infection but may be seen with other disorders such as pulmonary embolism. The patient should be examined for obvious breathing difficulty, irregularities of respiratory rhythm, and subtle differences in the movements of the two sides of the chest during respiration. The signs of respiratory difficulty include forced or labored breathing, rapid respirations, shallow or irregular breathing, noisy breathing, cyanosis (a purple discoloration) of the lips, nails, or skin, or even the complete absence of respiration. The respiratory rhythm can be observed while measuring the respiratory rate. Minor changes of rhythm are of no significance; important irregularities are quite obvious. Differences in the movements of the two sides of the chest should be sought during quiet respiration and during deep breathing.

Auscultation consists of listening to the sounds made by air passing in and out of the lung. The unaided ear, closely pressed against the chest is adequate for this purpose, but a stethoscope is more convenient and easier to use. Quiet breathing in normal lungs produces sounds so faint that they are barely audible. Therefore, the patient must breathe fairly deeply through his mouth during the examination so that these sounds may be heard. All portions of the lungs should be examined to be sure no abnormalities are missed and the extent of the diseased area is recognized.

Many diseases of the lung cause fluid to collect in the small bronchi and alveoli producing bubbling or crackling sounds known as rales. Such fluid accumulations are typical of infection or pulmonary edema. Wheezing is more indicative of asthma or some other form of small airway obstruction. Wheezing that can be cleared by a single cough is rarely significant. With severe pneumonia or pulmonary embolism a portion of the lung is often consolidated due to fluid and infection in the alveolar sacs. On listening to the chest over these areas, the breath sounds heard may be quite different — harsher and louder — than over normal lungs.

If no sounds whatever are heard over a portion of the chest, there is probably fluid or air in the space between the lung and the chest wall. Rarely, the absence of breath sounds may be due to obstruction of a large airway leading to that portion of the lung.

Auscultation of the lung, although requiring practice and experience, is not too difficult to learn and can be a valuable diagnostic aid.

CHRONIC LUNG DISEASE

Chronic lung disease can be the result of chronic infection (such as tuberculosis), slow growing tumors, small airway infection (bronchiectasis), or chronic obstructive disease. Emphysema (dilatation of the alveolae and formation of small or large cysts due to destruction of the alveolar walls) is the result of longstanding chronic lung disease, most often obstructive disease. Both obstructive disease and emphysema commonly result from long exposure to air pollution, particularly cigarette smoking.

Most individuals with chronic lung disease are aware of their problem, and are not likely to venture into the mountains. However, in the early stages of these diseases, they may not be detectable except with severe exertion or at altitude. The first signs of chronic obstructive lung disease or of emphysema may be a decrease in the respiratory reserve. This reserve is the extra breathing capacity which is called on during exertion. Respiratory reserve is also called upon during activity at high altitude, or whenever infection of part of the lung, shock, or loss of blood decrease the availability of oxygen to the body. Persons who know they have impaired respiratory reserve should be cautious about altitude and particularly about exertion at altitude.

DISORDERS OF RHYTHM

Cheyne-Stokes Respiration

Above 13,000 feet almost everyone has Cheyne-Stokes (or periodic) breathing; it is not rare as low as 8,000 feet. The pattern of respiration begins with a few shallow breaths, increases in depth to very deep, sighing respirations, and then falls off rapidly. Respirations can cease entirely for a few seconds. (An observer may fear that the person is dead.) Then the shallow breaths resume and the pattern is repeated.

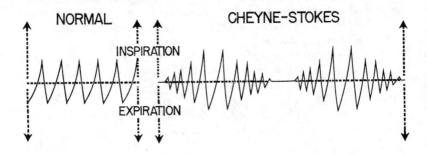

Figure 44. Diagrammatic comparison of normal and Cheyne-Stokes respiration.

This type of irregular breathing is so common at high altitudes that it should not be considered abnormal. Cheyne-Stokes breathing may be present on some occasions and not on others. It may be a sign of serious illness if it occurs for the first time during an illness or after a significant injury.

During the period when breathing has stopped the person often becomes restless and sleep may be broken. Occasionally the individual awakens with a rather distressing sense of suffocation. A mild sleeping medication usually prevents the frequent wakenings. Aminophyllin given by rectal suppository at bedtime is frequently quite beneficial if the respiratory irregularity prevents adequate rest.

Hyperventilation Syndrome

Hyperventilation — overbreathing — is usually not due to disease or injury, which may be confusing to the observer who watches a patient breathing very deeply and very rapidly. The "hyperventilation" syndrome is most commonly of emotional origin, and the observer aware of this possibility may be helped in the diagnosis by questions about or previous knowledge of the patient's emotional state.

As the victim breathes rapidly and deeply, an abnormally large amount of carbon dioxide is lost through the lungs, altering the acid-base balance and the pH of the blood and producing the typical symptoms. Individuals who develop the hyperventilation syndrome are usually nervous, tense, and apprehensive. However, the disorder can occur in apparently stable persons. Among beginning climbers apprehension about climbing or fear of exposure might well initiate such a reaction.

The first signs are *shortness of breath,* rapid pulse, dizziness, faintness, sweating, apprehension, and a sense of suffocation. The victim often complains "the air doesn't go down far enough." He, or more frequently she, breathes in gasps or takes frequent deep sighs. As the blood becomes more alkaline numbness or tingling around the mouth and in the fingers appears. These symptoms may subsequently increase to painful cramps or spasms of the fingers and hands. Spasms of the muscles of the hands and forearms are particularly frightening to the victim, who believes he is paralyzed.

The shortness of breath is puzzling since the regulatory mechanisms of the body would be expected to correct the hyperventilation. However, in this condition, these mechanisms are overridden by the emotions.

When the hyperventilation syndrome is suspected, one should first make sure that no other problem is present. Then reassurance and explanation usually are sufficient to reverse the disorder. The patient should be instructed to slow or stop his breathing. A mild tranquilizer such as one of the benzodiazepines or a barbiturate may be given. If these measures are not successful, the patient should be told to breathe gently in and out of a large paper or plastic bag held snugly over the mouth and nose. This measure permits exhaled carbon dioxide to accumulate in the lungs and blood, and usually relieves the symptoms promptly. Once recovered, the patient may feel weak and shaky, and may have a headache. The mechanism of the disorder should be explained to him in some detail to help prevent recurrences.

INFECTIOUS DISORDERS

Tracheitis

The trachea, the large airway leading from the throat to the middle of the chest where it divides into the two main bronchi, is often inflamed and occasionally infected. Usually the patient describes pain in his throat below the tonsils, or beneath his sternum, which becomes worse with breathing. Coughing may cause pain in the same area, and may produce thick sputum. Treatment of tracheitis is the same as described below for bronchitis.

Bronchitis

Bronchitis, or more properly tracheobronchitis, is an infection of the major air passages to the lungs. Such infections are rarely disabling but can progress to pneumonia. This disease frequently comes on during or after a cold, causing the disorder to be called a "chest cold" or "cold in the chest." However, a cold is a viral infection. Although the trachea and bronchi may be infected by the same virus, bronchitis is usually a bacterial infection which supervenes during the viral infection. Bronchitis can also occur without a preceding viral infection.

The predominant symptom of bronchitis is a persistent, irritating cough which may be dry, but frequently becomes productive after one or two days. The sputum is usually green or yellow and is thick and tenacious. Slight pain may be associated with the coughing and the victim may notice easy fatigability, particularly at high altitudes. However, he usually does not appear severely ill, and has only a slight fever or none at all. If the infection involves the larynx (voice box) he may be hoarse. A few wheezes and rales may be heard throughout the chest but these tend to disappear with coughing.

Treatment for tracheitis or bronchitis begins with adequate hydration. The patient should drink lots of fluids, particularly warm liquids. If possible he should inhale steam from a boiling kettle or pot. Antibiotics should also be administered, particularly if there is any fever. Tetracycline or erythromycin are the drugs of choice. For individuals not allergic to penicillin, ampicillin is more broadly effective. Rest in a warm place, and a mild pain reliever, if needed, are helpful. Also helpful is the old-fashioned remedy of rubbing oil of wintergreen into the skin over the painful area, or an old-fashioned mustard plaster if available. The patient need not rest, but should not strenuously exert himself. If the condition persists for several days, descent to low altitude may be necessary.

Pleurisy

Pleurisy is an inflammation of the thin membranes which cover the lungs and inner chest wall. The inflammation most commonly originates in the lung as part of some other process, often pneumonia, but occasionally a virus infection of the pleura itself, a bruise of the pleura due to injury, or irritation due to pulmonary embolism. Viruses occasionally cause infections limited solely to the pleura. These disorders are of short duration and are not severely disabling. They are rather uncomfortable, particularly at high altitudes or similar situations in which the victim is required to breathe more rapidly and deeper than normal.

The primary symptom — usually the only symptom — is pain with respiration. This pain is usually a rather sharp, stabbing sensation, limited to a rather small area in one side of the chest. Deep inspiration elicits a particularly severe twinge.

Physical signs are slight or absent. Motion on the affected side may be somewhat limited and a few wheezes or rales may be heard over the involved area. The patient may be more comfortable when lying on the affected side, thus limiting the motion of that part of the chest. The general appearance of the patient is important. If pleurisy alone is present the patient rarely appears seriously ill. If the fever is high, the pulse rate rapid, or the patient seems quite sick, some underlying condition such as pneumonia or embolism should be suspected.

Pleurisy unaccompanied by another disease, though painful, usually clears up in three or four days, and requires little treatment other than splinting with tape or an elastic bandage, and rest. Antibiotics should be given if pneumonia is suspected. It is also important to take the patient to a lower altitude if an underlying disease is suspected. Severe pain of pleurisy can be alleviated by adhesive tape tightly applied to the affected area. Wide strips of tape should be placed from one to two inches beyond the spine and beyond the sternum over the painful area. It is helpful to paint the skin with tincture of benzoin before applying the tape, and to remove the tape after three days, replacing it if necessary. In the absence of tape, a snugly bound elastic bandage may be equally helpful.

Pneumonia

Bacterial and viral pneumonia are due to infections of the lung tissue, notably the alveoli. Persons weakened by fatigue, exposure, or disease elsewhere in the body are particularly susceptible. The alveoli fill with infected fluid, impairing the exchange of carbon dioxide and oxygen. The respiratory rate and pulse rate increase. The fever associated with infection increases the body's needs for oxygen as the infection itself decreases the supply of oxygen. If a large amount of lung is involved the oxygen lack combined with the toxic substances may cause death. Pneumonia should always be taken seriously and descent to medical facilities accomplished as soon as possible.

The symptoms of pneumonia vary with the causative organism and the severity of the infection. All pneumonias usually cause a fever of more than 102°F (oral) and a rapid pulse and respiratory rate. Bacterial pneumonias are often ushered in by one or more shaking chills, followed by a high fever. The patient appears quite sick and may be very weak.

Coughing is a prominent symptom of all lung infections. The cough may be dry at first, but usually becomes productive after one or two days. The sputum, which is usually green or yellow but sometimes has a rusty color, is thick and mucoid and frequently has an appearance resembling pus.

Some bacteria tend to localize in a single segment of the lung, producing consolidation in the involved tissues. The signs of disease are limited to that area of the lung. The overlying pleura is often involved by the infection and, as when only the pleura is inflamed, stabbing pain on breathing may be severe. Not infrequently pleurisy is an early and sometimes the first indication of underlying infection. Since the pain varies with the depth of respiration, the chest tends to be involuntarily splinted and respiratory movement is reduced on that side.

Lobar pneumonia, usually caused by the pneumococcus and limited to one or two lobes of the lung, has become much less frequent in recent years for reasons not completely understood. At the same time other infections have become more common. Viruses, fungi, yeasts, and other microorganisms are identified as the cause of pulmonary infections more frequently now than several years ago. Each of these infecting organisms produces a somewhat different type of infection and differing signs and symptoms. Most of them cause poorly localized, widely scattered small areas of infection, which rarely produce signs of consolidation or pleurisy. These infections, called bronchopneumonia, viral pneumonia, or diffuse pneumonitis, often begin rather insidiously, become severe only after a longer period than do the lobar or bacterial pneumonias, and are consequently harder to diagnose and often unsuspected. So-called "walking pneumonia" is generally due to a virus. It creeps up on the individual, is difficult to treat and resistant to most antibiotics, and usually disables the patient for a longer period of time. If this type of insidiously developing pneumonia is suspected, it would be wise to take the patient to a lower altitude. Pneumonias due to the rarer organisms are more difficult to diagnose, and usually require special tests in a well-equipped hospital.

The patient suspected of pneumonia or bronchitis presents a therapeutic dilemma. If the individual appears seriously ill, the onset has been rapid, and signs suggesting lobar pneumonia are present, antibiotics should be begun immediately. The choice of antibiotics depends on many circumstances. If the patient is not allergic to penicillin, then ampicillin is preferred, and should be given four to six times a day, usually after a "loading dose" of twice the usual dose. If penicillin is used, the same dose schedule should be followed. If there is any question about allergy to penicillin, then an antibiotic such as tetracycline or erythromycin is preferred. Treatment should consist of a loading dose followed by a regular dose every four hours. Whatever medication is given should be continued for at least seven, and preferably ten days. It is not only useless, but often leads to a relapse, to stop antibiotics after a shorter period of treatment.

Once the patient has reached a hospital, considerable difficulty in diagnosis may result because the antibiotic may obscure the identity of some less common infecting organisms. Consequently, some physicians urge that no treatment be given until the organism has been identified. However, if hospitalization must be delayed for more than two or three days, or if the patient is quite ill, it is much better to start treatment and wait for diagnosis later.

A patient with any type of pneumonia is oxygen deficient above 8,000 feet. When oxygen is available it should be given freely while transportation is arranged. (Some oxygen may be reserved for the patient who appears more ill or more lacking in oxygen than his companions.) The combination of fever and infection increases the demand for oxygen while impaired lung function decreases the supply. Evacuation to a lower altitude as soon as possible should be the rule when pneumonia is suspected.

Recovery depends entirely on the severity of infection and type of organism. It is rare that the patient with pneumonia can resume climbing for several weeks.

OTHER PULMONARY DISORDERS

High Altitude Pulmonary Edema

Although high altitude pulmonary edema was first clearly described over sixty years ago, only in the last fifteen years has it been recognized as a major problem for mountaineers. Cases which occurred prior to 1960 were usually disagnosed as pneumonia, and there are resemblances between acute pulmonary edema and pneumonia. This important and serious mountaineering problem can occur and has been fatal as low as 9,000 feet, although it is rare below 12,000 feet. It is fully described in the chapter "Medical Problems Due to High Altitude."

Asthma

Asthma is a disease of the bronchi caused by allergy. Contact with the substance to which the individual is allergic (the allergen) increases the secretion of mucous into the bronchi. Simultaneously the muscles in the walls of the bronchi go into spasm, constricting these air passages. The narrowed bronchi, filled with excess mucous, obstruct the passage of air and cause respiratory difficulty.

Asthma may be very mild, severe, or even fatal (fortunately, very rarely). A first attack may occur at any time and any place, although most frequently the patient is aware of his asthma long before he takes up mountaineering.

Asthma is a recurring disease; a climber with this disorder would usually have suffered a number of previous attacks. He should be under the care of a physician from whom he should obtain the medications necessary to care for himself during an asthmatic attack. However, individuals with mild asthma are not particularly limited in the extent to which they can partake in mountaineering.

The most significant sign of asthma is difficulty in breathing, particularly in expiration. The expiratory phase of respiration, which normally requires less time than inspiration, is considerably prolonged and may require conscious effort on the part of the patient.

An incessant, irritating cough is often present. Towards the end of an asthmatic attack the patient may cough up considerable quantities of very thick mucous. Fever is usually absent but the pulse rate may be moderately increased. The respiratory rate is usually faster than normal in spite of the difficulty in breathing.

When the patient is examined the chest is often found to be more expanded than normal at the end of expiration. Loud wheezes and some bubbling and crackling sounds are usually audible throughout all parts of the lung.

The keystone of asthma treatment is adequate fluid intake. Whatever medication is used, doubling the intake of liquids will benefit the patient. Often steam inhalations are beneficial. Mild asthma responds well to one of the oral theophylline preparations. Attacks of moderate severity can often be controlled by an orally administered isoproterenol (Isuprel) solution. More severe attacks require subcutaneous injections of 0.3 cc of 1:1,000 solution of adrenalin, which can be repeated every five to ten minutes for several doses. The pulse rate rises, often to an uncomfortably high level following adrenalin. If more than a few injections are given, or if the series is repeated after several hours, pulse and blood pressure should be recorded after each injection. Aminophyllin by rectal suppository is often beneficial, but requires twenty to thirty minutes to take effect. Inhalation of nebulized medication has become popular in recent years and, when used only occasionally and only for severe attacks, is dramatically effective. It should not be used more than every one or two hours, and rarely used for more than one day. Many asthmatics carry a nebulizer or at least know which one is effective.

Since asthma further limits the amount of oxygen available to the body, oxygen inhalation is usually helpful at altitude, but any mucous blocking the airways must be coughed up or the oxygen will be ineffective. The best way to insure such obstructions are eliminated is to provide plenty of liquids and the most appropriate medication.

Prevention of asthmatic attacks is important. Patients with allergies which cause severe asthma should be aware of their susceptibility and avoid the allergens whenever possible.

Severe asthmatics should obtain detailed instructions and all necessary medications required for their care from their personal physician before embarking on mountaineering outings. Since persons who have long-standing severe asthma tend to have chronic pulmonary disease as well, it may be unwise for them to venture above 8,000 feet. Some physicians have the impression that persons with asthma tend to be more susceptible to high altitude pulmonary edema, but this predisposition can neither be proven nor disproven. Persons with asthma are well advised to be more cautious with altitude and to allow more time for acclimatization.

Thrombophlebitis and Pulmonary Embolism

Clotting of the blood in the leg or arm veins is not uncommon in mountaineers. Thrombophlebitis, as the presence of such clots is called, was seldom reported in mountaineers before 1950, but it is now known to occur not infrequently and complications are common.

The principle danger from thrombophlebitis lies in the tendency for the blood clots which form in the veins to break off and be carried back through the heart into the lungs where they lodge in the arteries (pulmonary embolism). Large clots may lodge in the major pulmonary arteries. In either location they obstruct the blood flow and decrease oxygenation of the blood.

Increased coagulability of the blood and stasis (decreased speed of blood flow in the veins) favor the development of thrombophlebitis.

Factors increasing the tendency of the blood to clot are:

Dehydration — inadequate fluid intake causes the blood to become thicker and more viscous;

Increase in the number of red blood cells due to high altitude — this normal mechanism of acclimatization also increases the viscosity of the blood;

Stress — the stress of climbing and a hostile environment produces a reaction which causes the blood to clot more readily than normal;

Oxygen lack — blood clots more readily at altitude due to mechanisms which are poorly understood.

Factors predisposing to stasis are:

Prolonged immobility — a storm-bound party may spend days in a small tent, immobile and resting in cramped, awkward positions;

Low temperature — decreased blood flow in cold extremities, due to arterial contraction to preserve heat, reduces the volume of blood to be returned to the heart through the veins;

Heavy packing or long standing – climbing with heavy loads increases stasis in the legs, but even more dangerous is a long stance in difficult ice steps on complicated and difficult climbs;

Tight clothing – the veins with their low blood pressure are easily constricted and obstructed.

Oral contraceptive drugs also promote the development of thrombophlebitis and pulmonary embolism. Women taking such drugs should discontinue them several weeks in advance of any mountaineering outing during which a stay of more than two or three days at altitudes higher than 12,000 to 14,000 feet is anticipated, particularly when cold or other conditions may lead to circumstances predisposing to the development of thrombophlebitis.

The most common symptom of thrombophlebitis is a deep, aching pain in the calf, inner side of the thigh, or back of the knee, which frequently comes on suddenly and is aggravated by walking. When the thrombosed vein is located in the calf – as it most frequently is – the overlying muscles are tender. Flexing the foot upward also causes pain in the calf. Red, tender, slightly swollen streaks along the arms suggest the possibility of thrombophlebitis in the arm veins, but an acute infection with lymphangitis also must be considered.

Swelling of the affected leg usually occurs and can be most easily detected by measuring the circumference of both legs at identical five-inch intervals from the ankle to upper thigh. Differences in circumferences of one-half inch are frequent and are of no significance; greater differences are cause for concern. The extremity may be pale, is sometimes cyanotic, and may have diminished arterial pulsations. Redness is sometimes visible along the course of a superficial thrombosed vein. Fever of 100° to 102° F is sometimes present and persists an average of seven to ten days.

Pulmonary embolism is manifested by the sudden onset of pain in the chest. Cough, shortness of breath, and a rapid pulse usually accompany the pain. Later the pain becomes pleuritic – that is, aggravated by respiration, particularly deep breathing. White, frothy material is coughed up at first, but the sputum becomes obviously bloody within a few hours. The respiratory rate and pulse rate are moderately increased and there is frequently a slight fever. Signs of consolidation may appear over the involved areas a day or so after onset.

If the embolus is large, the initial symptom may be the sudden onset of a sense of suffocation rather than pain. Severe shortness of breath, cyanosis, distension of neck veins, and signs of shock follow shortly. Pulse and respiratory rates are elevated as well as the temperature. Pleuritic pain, cough, bloody sputum, and signs of solidification usually develop a few hours later, although pleurisy may be completely absent if the blood clot is large and lodges in a

Table 3. Diagnostic Features of Various Severe Pulmonary Diseases

	Pneumonia	High Altitude Pulmonary Edema	Heart Failure	Pulmonary Embolism
ONSET	Gradual	Gradual, 12-36 hours after reaching high altitude	Gradual	Sudden
CHILLS	Frequently present at onset	Absent	Absent	Absent
FEVER	Usually present; frequently high	Absent or low	Absent or low	Moderate; may be absent
SPUTUM	Thick, stringy; green, yellow, or rusty	Frothy; white or pink	Frothy; white or pink	Frothy at first; later grossly bloody
PAIN	Pleuritic; sometimes absent	None	None	Pleuritic
PHYSICAL FINDINGS	Localized or diffuse; may be slight	Diffuse or in lower portions of lungs	Diffuse or in lower portions of lungs	Localized if present
OTHER FEATURES	May follow a cold, bronchitis, or exposure	No history of heart disease; usually preceded by rapid ascent to high altitude (over 9,000 feet)	Previous evidence of heart disease	Evidence of thrombophlebitis

central part of the lung. The signs and symptoms are much more severe and the patient is more gravely ill, but he may have no pain.

A massive pulmonary embolus can produce collapse and death, frequently within seconds, or may lead to such respiratory difficulty that the patient dies from oxygen lack, particularly at altitude.

Prevention is important but difficult. If confined to a tent by a storm, care should be taken to exercise the feet and ankles for a few minutes every hour and to avoid tight, constricting clothing. It is extremely important that an adequate fluid intake be maintained. Persons with varicose veins should either avoid high altitude climbing or receive special instructions and possibly surgical treatment from their physician.

Aspirin has a tendency to decrease clotting of blood, particularly at altitude. Therefore aspirin should be administered when thrombophlebitis or pulmonary embolism is first suspected. Anticoagulant treatment is routinely used in thrombophlebitis with or without embolism, but must be reserved for hospital use since the consequences of over-dosage are too risky to allow such therapy without laboratory control.

Once thrombophlebitis develops the patient must be completely confined to bed. Walking or any other movement may cause the clots to break off and embolize. The feet should be elevated slightly, the clothing kept loose, and awkward positions avoided. Aspirin and codeine may be given for pain if necessary but no other medications are needed. Immobilization should be continued until all signs of thrombosis have been absent for four to five days.

Ace bandages wrapped snugly (but not tight enough to obstruct circulation) around both legs are desirable. Such bandages are a good preventive measure if the patient is immobilized by frostbite or injury at altitude. It should be noted that frostbite predisposes to thrombophlebitis and may lead to pulmonary embolism.

The party with a patient who has thrombophlebitis on a mountain expedition is faced with a difficult decision. It is desirable to keep the patient quiet, his leg bandaged, and to hydrate him carefully, but it is often difficult to stay long in a mountain camp and the temptation is to transport the patient. The dilemma is far greater once pulmonary embolism has occurred and life is threatened by subsequent emboli. Evacuation is essential, but the patient should be carried as much as possible. If climbing is unavoidable, the affected leg or arm should be carefully bandaged, particularly if embolism has occurred. It is simply too risky not to get these patients to hospital care, but every precaution must be taken to ensure that minimum activity and stress result.

CHAPTER 19

Diseases of the Heart and Blood Vessels

THE HEART and blood vessels circulate the blood, which transports oxygen, carbon dioxide, nutrients, and wastes to and from the body tissues. The heart consists of a four-chambered pump — right auricle, right ventricle, left auricle, and left ventricle. Blood is pumped from the left ventricle into the aorta, the body's main artery. This vessel gives off many branches which divide into smaller and smaller arteries and finally into capillaries barely large enough to permit the passage of one red blood cell at a time. In the capillaries oxygen diffuses into the tissues, carbon dioxide diffuses into the blood, and nutrients, waste products, and other substances move freely back and forth between the blood and the tissues. From the capillaries the blood flows into larger and larger veins and returns through the right auricle into the right ventricle. The blood is then pumped from the right ventricle to the lungs, where it picks up oxygen and gives off carbon dioxide, and is returned through the left auricle to the left ventricle. The control of the blood flow is vested in sensitive receptors which dictate the output of the heart and the amount of blood supplied to various areas of the body.

PHYSICAL EXAMINATION

Simple methods of physical examination can provide important information regarding the function of the heart and circulatory system in an acute cardiac emergency, even though an exact diagnosis may require a physician's skill and experience. The physical examination should include: (1) determination of heart rate and rhythm; (2) evaluation of arterial and venous pressure; (3) evaluation of the peripheral circulation, cyanosis, pallor, edema; (4) auscultation of the chest.

The heart rate is most easily counted by feeling the radial pulse at the wrist. Carefully palpating the outer edge of the wrist at the base of the thumb with the first two fingers usually reveals the pulsations of the radial artery. Finger pressure should be gentle so that the artery is not totally occluded. The pulsations should be counted for fifteen to thirty seconds and multiplied by four or two to obtain the rate per minute. In some subjects the radial artery may be small or the pulsations may be too weak to count. In such conditions the carotid or femoral pulse should be palpated. The carotid pulse can be found in the groove between the thyroid cartilage (Adam's apple) and the prominent strap muscle of the neck. The femoral pulse can be found in the groin about midway between the center of the pubic area and the lateral bony edge of the hip. Clothing should be removed from the area before palpating the femoral pulse.

If no pulses can be felt, the heart rate can be determined by using a stethoscope placed on the chest between the left nipple and the sternum (breastbone). Each heart beat is accompanied by two heart sounds of slightly different tone (lub-dup, lub-dup). While heart sounds in normal subjects can be heard with the unaided ear pressed against the chest, the heart sounds may be faint in shock and a stethoscope must be used. A little prior practice — even listening to one's own heart — is useful in emergencies. When listening to the heart sounds, the carotid pulse can be palpated and the two sounds observed to accompany the pulsations of the carotid artery.

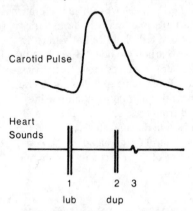

Figure 45. Relationship between carotid pulse and heart sounds.

The normal resting heart rate varies between sixty and eighty per minute. In well conditioned individuals heart rates as low as fifty per minute may be present. The heart rate is lower during sleep. At high altitude the resting heart rate may be as high as one hundred per minute during the first few days of acclimatization.

Normally the heart rhythm is perfectly regular. In teenagers the heart rate may change with respiration – increasing during inspiration and slowing during expiration. This is normal and can be identified by having the subject hold his breath during which the rhythm should be perfectly regular.

Arterial pulses are usually equal in both wrists, both sides of the neck and both sides of the groin. Absence of a pulse on one side of the body may indicate arterial obstruction or injury. When the pulse in these areas are barely palpable, the blood pressure is usually low. Good strong "bounding pulses" usually indicate a normal blood pressure and normal heart action. When most normal subjects are lying flat, the neck veins can be seen partially or fully filled from just above the middle of the clavicle (collar bone) to just below the lower edge of the jaw. When the subject is sitting upright or partially upright (semi-recumbent) the neck veins should not be filled above the clavicle. Tense filling of the neck veins in these positions is abnormal and may indicate heart failure or obstruction of venous flow to the heart.

Accurate measurement of systolic blood pressure requires a sphygmomanometer and stethoscope. The cuff of the sphgymomanometer is wrapped smoothly and firmly (but not tightly) around the upper arm well above the elbow. The cuff pressure is inflated to about 180 mm or until the radial pulse disappears. With the arm extended, the stethoscope should be placed over the bend of the arm and the cuff pressure allowed to fall slowly. As the cuff pressure drops, a thumping sound synchronous with the pulse can be heard. The pressure at which the sound first appears is the systolic blood pressure. As the cuff pressure continues to fall, the pressure at which the sound completely disappears is the diastolic blood pressure. If the radial pulse can be felt and a stethoscope is not available, the systolic blood pressure can be approximated by inflating the cuff and allowing the pressure to fall until the radial pulse first appears. This pressure is ten to twenty mm lower than the pressure determined by a stethoscope, but the method is reliable in emergency situations. Normal blood pressure varies from 105 to 140 mm systolic and 60 to 80 mm diastolic.

Normally the lips, tongue, and nail beds are pink, but when the oxygen concentration of the blood is low, they may be blue or purple. This discoloration (cyanosis) is commonly noted at high altitude and may be severe in high altitude pulmonary edema. At lower elevations cyanosis usually indicates inadequate oxygenation of the blood by the lungs such as occurs in airway obstruction, pneumonia, or chest injury. When the blood pressure is low and blood flow to the extremities is decreased, the nail beds may be cyanotic, the lips and tongue may be a blue-gray color. This type of cyanosis is due to decreased blood flow and may occur even though oxygenation of the blood in the lungs is normal. It is commonly seen in shock.

Edema is a general medical term for excess accumulation of water in the tissues. It is not uncommon in women during the first few days at high altitude. The face may be puffy in the morning, mild swelling of the feet or ankles may

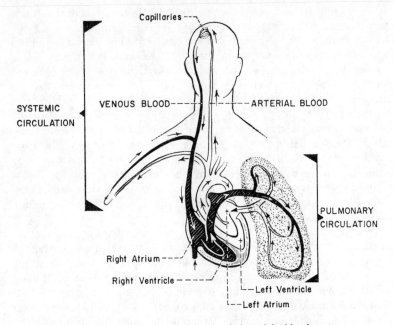

Figure 46. Diagram of the circulation of the blood.

be noted, and a weight gain of four to twelve pounds may occur due to the retention of salt and water by the body. More severe degrees of edema, especially if progressive and lasting for more than a week, may indicate heart failure or kidney disease and should be investigated.

Individuals who have marked difficulty in breathing during ordinary effort, or who have shortness of breath when lying flat which is relieved by sitting up, may have excess fluid accumulation in the lungs (pulmonary edema). At high elevations high altitude pulmonary edema should be suspected, but at lower elevations heart failure may be the cause. Auscultation of the chest in a patient with pulmonary edema from either cause usually reveals crackling or gurgling sounds with each breath. Bronchial asthma usually produces squeaking or groaning sounds, especially during expiration. (Auscultation of the lungs is discussed in "Diseases of the Respiratory System.")

CLIMBERS WITH HEART DISEASE

Heart disease is very common in our society. Many patients with heart disease live long, active, useful lives. Modern management of heart disease encourages physical activity within specified limits, particularly among older people who are participating more frequently in climbing and backpacking.

No patient with heart disease should climb unless he has his physician's approval. He should follow the instructions and provide his own medications recommended by his physician. The outing leader should be familiar with these recommendations and should be alert for complications that require treatment or evacuation. The patient's physician − not the trip leader − is responsible for his continuing medical management. For longer trips or expeditions the leader should be supplied with a letter from the physician outlining the nature of the patient's condition, restrictions on activity that should be observed, medications to be taken, and a description of any signs or symptoms that require additional therapy or evacuation.

MAJOR HEART DISEASES

Angina Pectoris

Angina pectoris is a particular form of chest discomfort caused by narrowing of the coronary arteries that supply the heart muscle with blood. The narrowing is the result of arteriosclerosis, which consists of deposits of lipids (cholesterol and other fats) in the inner lining of the arteries. Rupture of these fat deposits or clotting in the narrowed artery may cause the onset of angina, an increase in the severity of pre-existing angina, or an acute myocardial infarction (heart attack or coronary thrombosis).

The discomfort of angina pectoris consists of a pressure-like sensation or a deep seated pain beneath the breastbone (sternum) which appears on effort and disappears after a few minutes of rest. The discomfort may be described as a sensation of squeezing, a weight on the chest, a band around the heart, or a deep burning sensation. The discomfort may be felt in the neck, jaws, or arms. If effort is continued, the discomfort increases. Angina pectoris on effort may frequently be accompanied by shortness of breath which subsides as the chest discomfort eases.

Patients with mild angina pectoris may be permitted by their physicians to hike or climb provided they follow instructions and carry nitroglycerine tablets to relieve more severe episodes of pain. Such patients should not be permitted on long trips or expeditions.

Individuals who develop angina for the first time or who experience unusually frequent or severe attacks of angina should be placed completely at rest (lying down) and given nitroglycerine for relief. A nitroglycerine tablet should be held under the tongue until it has dissolved. Several tablets may be necessary to obtain relief. Nitroglycerine tablets should be kept in their original brown bottle and should not be kept longer than six months after purchase. Cotton wads should not be kept in the bottle, and the bottle should be tightly capped to avoid loss of potency of the tablets. Absolute rest with sedation should be provided for six to eight hours until the patient has no further episodes of angina. The patient should then be evacuated with as little exertion as possible. Angina is an indication of severe heart disease and may be a prelude to a more serious heart attack.

Myocardial Infarction

Myocardial infarction is a serious, acute medical emergency which may lead to sudden death. Chest pain is the most common initial symptom, and may appear at rest or during effort. The pain resembles angina pectoris but is usually more severe, may last for one to six hours, and is not usually relieved by nitroglycerine. Frequently other symptoms and signs are present, including nausea, vomiting, difficulty in breathing, weakness, sweating, pallor, cyanosis and cold extremities. The blood pressure may be low; the heart rate may be slow and occasionally irregular.

Myocardial infarction is due to a complete obstruction of a coronary artery with death (necrosis) of the heart muscle supplied by that artery.

The patient should be immediately placed completely at rest. Nitroglycerine should be given to relieve pain. If the pain is not relieved in ten to fifteen minutes, meperidine or morphine should be given every two hours until pain is relieved. If the patient is agitated, a barbiturate can be given every four hours. If oxygen is available, four to six liters per minute should be given with a plastic face mask. If the patient is coughing, short of breath, and wants to sit up to breathe more easily, he should be permitted to do so. Administration of oxygen should be continued. Prompt evacuation by helicopter is essential. A physician should accompany the helicopter since cardiac resuscitation may be necessary at any moment.

Cardiac Dyspnea

Cardiac dyspnea is undue shortness of breath with exercise due to heart disease. It may occasionally occur at night and awaken the patient with a sense of suffocation, causing him to sit up or move out into fresh air to obtain relief. Examination usually discloses a rapid heart rate, rapid respirations, and anxiety. Auscultation of the chest may reveal rales or crackling sounds indicating the presence of fluid in the lungs. If the patient has a history of heart disease, a heart murmur, or treatment for heart failure, the diagnosis of cardiac dyspnea should be made. Complete rest, sedation, and the administration of a diuretic (furosemide twice daily for two days) are required. The patient should be evacuated after twelve to twenty-four hours of rest with as little effort on his part as possible. If the dyspnea is severe, oxygen and meperidine or morphine should be given.

At high altitude, high altitude pulmonary edema should be considered, particularly if the subject has no history of heart disease and has recently arrived at high altitude. If high altitude pulmonary edema is suspected, rest, oxygen, and assisted transport to a lower altitude are necessary.

Valvular Heart Disease

Patients may have deformities of heart valves that cause heart murmurs and yet be capable of heavy physical effort without difficulty. However, heavy activity may produce complications for patients with some varieties of valvular heart disease. Such complications include cardiac dyspnea, cardiac pulmonary edema, atrial fibrillation and stroke. Any individual with a heart murmur or valvular heart disease should be examined by his personal physician who should decide whether or not the patient should be permitted to climb. This information should be given to the outing leader along with recommendations regarding limits of activity, medications to be taken, and complications that might be expected.

NONCARDIAC CHEST PAIN

Most individuals who complain of chest pain do not have heart disease, but unfortunately, many think they do. Several common types of chest pain not related to heart disease are: (1) Chest aches and soreness due to muscular effort. After unaccustomed physical work involving the arms and shoulders, such as climbing, cross-country skiing, carrying a heavy pack, or cutting wood, soreness and aching of the upper chest muscles may be present for two to three days. The ache is usually constant and may be worsened by motion, and the muscles may be tender. Aspirin and rest is effective treatment. (2) Chest discomfort due to anxiety. Nervous, anxious, fearful individuals may notice a pressure-like sensation across the chest associated with a sense of suffocation, trembling, dizziness and occasionally numbness of the lips and fingers. The heart rate may be increased. Reassurance, rest and mild sedation should be employed. (See Hyperventilation Syndrome in "Diseases of the Respiratory System.") (3) Aching or sticking pain over the heart. After heavy climbing or hiking some individuals may note an aching pain or sticking, sharp pains over the left nipple area. The pain may be constant or intermittent and is often worse at night. Reassurance, rest, and aspirin are all that is usually needed. (4) Heart burn. A burning, constant pain below the end of the breast bone and extending behind the breast bone up into the throat may be noted after a heavy meal, excessive consumption of strong coffee, tea, or alcohol, or the use of carbonated beverages. The discomfort may be aggravated by drinking hot liquids and relieved by milk or belching. The discomfort is not related to effort and may last for one to three hours. Heartburn should not be mistaken for angina. Rest, reassurance, and the administration of milk or antacids are appropriate methods of management.

DISORDERS OF CARDIAC RHYTHM

Paroxysmal Tachycardia

This impressive term is used for a disorder characterized by the sudden onset of a very rapid heart rate with associated symptoms of pounding in the chest, weakness, dizzyness and shortness of breath. The heart rate is very rapid (150 to 220 per minute) and perfectly regular. The pulses may be so weak that a stethoscope applied to the chest is required to count the rate. Victims may have experienced similar previous attacks. The patient should rest until the attack stops spontaneously. If the attack does not stop within ten to fifteen minutes, a few simple maneuvers may be tried. The patient can be asked to forcefully blow up a paper bag or an air mattress. Holding his breath as long as possible may be tried. Putting a tongue blade or a spoon handle in the back of the throat so the patient gags may stop the attack. If these measures fail, the right carotid artery should be located and massaged, at first gently and then firmly. The patient may immediately notice the cessation of the attack. Since episodes of tachycardia tend to recur, the patient should be evacuated if it is his first attack or control has been difficult.

Atrial Fibrillation

Atrial fibrillation refers to a rapid, irregular heart beat. The heart rate may be 100 to 180 per minute. The attack may appear suddenly and resemble an attack of paroxysmal tachycardia. The important difference is that with atrial fibrillation the rhythm is totally irregular. Careful palpation of the pulse and auscultation of the heart may be necessary to be sure of the irregularity of the rhythm since with fast rates exceeding 160 per minute any irregularity is difficult to detect. Bed rest and sedation should be instituted; frequently normal heart action will return spontaneously after a few hours. Maneuvers employed in paroxysmal tachycardia are of no value in atrial fibrillation. If the attack does not respond to rest and sedation after twelve to twenty-four hours, evacuation to a physician's care should be carried out.

Digitalization

If someone with medical experience is available and evacuation of the patient with either of the above rhythm disturbances is difficult or likely to be delayed, digitalis may be necessary. If the attack has not stopped after twelve to twenty-four hours, digoxin 0.25 mg may be given every two hours for a total dose of 1.5 mg (six 0.25 mg tablets). (The attendant must be certain that the patient has not taken any digitalis the previous week.) If the irregularities persist, digoxin 0.25 mg may be given daily. The patient should be kept at rest and sedated. Adequate fluids should be given to prevent clot formation in the heart which may cause embolism or a stroke. If nausea, vomiting, or slowing of the heart rate below sixty per minute occur, digoxin should be stopped since these are common signs of overdosage.

Cardiac Syncope

Cardiac syncope is loss of consciousness due to heart disease. Two general forms are recognized — exertional syncope and arrhythmic syncope. In exertional syncope, loss of consciousness or a "blackout spell" occurs during a burst of heavy effort such as hurrying uphill. Unconsciousness may occur suddenly or may be preceded by a "gray out" sensation or severe dizzyness or weakness. Convulsive movements may occur. Exertional syncope most frequently occurs in patients with aortic stenosis (a narrowing of the outlet valve from the left ventricle). It is occasionally seen in patients with arteriosclerotic coronary artery disease. Treatment for unconsciousness should be administered, the blood pressure should be measured and the heart rate and rhythm should be determined.

Arrhythmic syncope occurs as the result of a sudden abnormal increase in heart rate (tachycardia) or a marked slowing or temporary cessation of the heart beat (heart block). The episode may occur suddenly, without warning, and the patient may fall and injure himself. Convulsive movements may occur. General measures for an unconscious patient should be instituted. The blood pressure should be measured, and the heart rate and rhythm should be determined. If a very slow heart rate is present and persists after recovery, Isuprel glossetts should be administered every hour.

Cardiac syncope can usually be distinguished from simple fainting. In a simple faint there is usually an obvious cause such as the sight of blood, an overheated room, or prolonged standing. Fainting usually has a more gradual onset, does not occur during effort, and the heart rhythm is regular with a rate rarely below sixty per minute.

Any individual with evident or suspected cardiac syncope should be treated with rest and sedation for six to twelve hours and then evacuated to the care of a physician since cardiac syncope may be an early warning sign of heart disease which can cause sudden death.

MINOR DISTURBANCES OF CARDIAC RHYTHM

Sinus Tachycardia

Anxious individuals after heavy exertion or at high altitude may be aware of a pounding sensation in their chest due to a rapid, forceful heart beat and may be fearful of heart disease. If the heart rate does not exceed 140 per minute and gradually slows to a lower rate with rest and sedation, a diagnosis of harmless sinus (normal) tachycardia may be made. No specific treatment except rest and reassurance is necessary.

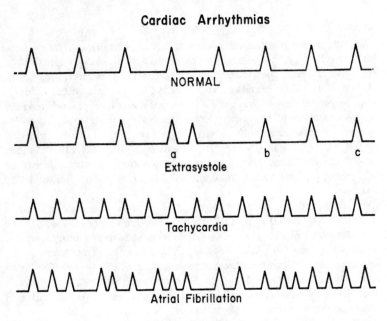

Figure 47. Diagrammatic comparison of normal and abnormal cardiac rhythms. (Note: interval ab = interval bc.)

Extrasystoles or "Skipped Beats"

Normal individuals may occasionally notice occasional irregular thumping sensations in their chest, especially at rest or during the night. They may feel their pulse and notice occasional pauses between normal beats. Such irregular beats are called extrasystoles and are of no significance unless the patient clearly has a heart disease, such as angina, myocardial infarction or cardiac dyspnea. Rest and reassurance are usually the only measures needed. Avoidance of stimulants such as coffee or tea, or tobacco may entirely eliminate the extrasystoles.

If a bothersome irregularity of the heart beat persists, if the skipped beats occur more than five times per minute, and if they have never been experienced before, evacuation to a physician's care is desirable.

HIGH BLOOD PRESSURE

Since about ten to twenty percent of people in the United States over forty have an elevated blood pressure, it is evident that many individuals with high blood pressure are climbers. The following general guidelines should be followed: (1) Individuals with high blood pressure should climb only with the consent and advice of their physician. (2) Patients with severe high blood pressure and those who have had complications of high blood pressure should not climb. Complications of high blood pressure include strokes, heart failure, coronary artery disease (angina), decrease in visual acuity, and kidney failure.

Individuals with moderate degrees of high blood pressure who climb may experience complications in the mountains with which outing leaders should be familiar. These include: cardiac dyspnea, angina pectoris, stroke, and severe headache. The occurrence of any of these complications is an indication for prompt evacuation to a physician's care.

Some patients with high blood pressure may have episodes of marked elevation of blood pressure associated with severe headache, confusion, forgetfulness, visual impairment, and other neurologic symptoms such as slurred speech. The blood pressure should be measured if such symptoms appear and the patient should be treated with complete rest and sedation. If the systolic pressure exceeds 200 mm Hg, nitroglycerine should be given every hour to reduce the pressure. Evacuation to medical care should be arranged after six to twelve hours of rest and treatment.

Some patients with high blood pressure who are taking medication to regulate their pressure may be permitted to climb by their physicians. Such patients should supply their own medication and follow their physician's recommendations carefully. Fluid intake should be adequate and their diet should be low in salt and protein.

VASCULAR DISEASE

Claudication

Older individuals with arteriosclerosis of the arteries of their legs may experience pain or cramps in their calves, hips, buttocks or thighs while walking uphill, especially when carrying a heavy load. The pain occurs during effort, becomes more severe as effort is continued, and is relieved by rest. The medical term for this condition is claudication.

Claudication should be distinguished from the more common type of leg cramps which typically occur at rest or during the night and are accompanied by painful spasm or contraction of the muscles — usually in the calf or foot. If claudication is mild, a slower pace and a light load may permit the individual to continue climbing. Smoking increases the severity of claudication and should be avoided. If claudication is severe or appears suddenly, the patient should rest and should be evacuated with minimal effort to a physician's care.

Varicose Veins

The veins of the extremities have numerous small valves within them to ensure that the blood flows only in the direction of the heart. The pressure in the veins is so low that the increase in antrathoracic or intra-abdominal pressure associated with straining or strenuous exercise would cause reversal of the venous blood flow if these valves were not present.

In some individuals the valves in the veins of the legs become incompetent. As a result the veins become markedly dilated and tortuous (varicose) and the return of venous blood from the limb to the heart is impaired. Persons with varicose veins frequently complain of aching in their legs, particularly after they have been on their feet for a prolonged period. The condition should be corrected surgically because it can lead to ulceration of the skin and other complications. The earlier correction is undertaken the more satisfactorily it can be carried out.

The importance of varicose veins in mountaineering lies in the tendency for this disorder to increase the fatigability of the legs and limit endurance. In addition, the blood vessels just beneath the skin are greatly enlarged. Relatively minor injuries, which might go unnoticed, can penetrate one of these veins and produce a severe hemorrhage. Although the bleeding can be easily controlled, a person with varicose veins should be aware of this danger.

REFERENCE:
1. Selzer, A.: The Heart. *Its Function in Health and Disease.* University of California Press, 1966.

CHAPTER 20

Gastrointestinal Diseases

THE GASTROINTESTINAL tract consists of the esophagus, stomach, small and large intestine, liver, gallbladder, and pancreas. This system ingests food, breaks it down into forms which can be utilized by the body, and finally excretes the residual waste material.

The esophagus aids in swallowing and propels the food rapidly into the stomach, where it remains thirty to sixty minutes while being digested by hydrochloric acid and several enzymes. The food is then passed into the upper part of the small intestine (duodenum) where different enzymes secreted by the intestinal mucosa and the pancreas further modify the partially digested food, preparing it for absorption. Bile salts, which are secreted by the liver and stored in the gallbladder, emulsify fats so that they can be absorbed. Absorption takes place in the middle and lower segments of the small intestine. In the large intestine, water is extracted from the residual wastes which are then excreted. Before traveling to the rest of the body, all of the blood from the small intestine goes to the liver where a fantastic number of complex biochemical reactions convert the absorbed nutrients to substances needed by the other tissues and organs of the body.

Diseases of many organs produce symptoms referable to the alimentary tract, particularly nausea and vomiting. In addition, the majority of gastrointestinal illnesses cannot be exactly diagnosed in the field. Even when the cause of a disorder is known, there is often no specific therapy. Therefore, the treatment for most gastrointestinal diseases is directed solely toward eliminating or alleviating the patient's symptoms.

The signs and symptoms produced by diseases of the gastrointestinal system are nausea and vomiting, diarrhea, constipation, bleeding, jaundice, and pain. Pain which comes on suddenly and unexpectedly is such an eminent problem that it is discussed in a separate chapter entitled "Acute Abdominal Pain." The physical examination of the abdomen is also described in that chapter.

VOMITING

The causes of vomiting are legion. A partial list includes such widely varying disorders as acute gastroenteritis, motion sickness, head injury, various metabolic diseases, numerous bacterial and viral infections, pregnancy, environmental heat, strenuous exertion, and appendicitis.

If the patient is stuporous or unconscious, a single bout of vomiting can be disastrous. The vomitus can be aspirated into the lungs, resulting in a severe, often fatal pneumonia. Death from respiratory obstruction may occur if the volume of aspirated material is large. At the first sign of vomiting, a comatose patient's head should be lowered and turned to the side. He may be lifted by the waist about twelve to eighteen inches if no other injuries are present. The head down position must be maintained until vomiting has ceased and the vomitus cleared from his mouth. *Every effort must be made to prevent the patient from aspirating the vomited material.*

Protracted vomiting sometimes causes a small to moderate amount of blood to appear in the vomitus due to the rupture of small blood vessels in the lining of the esophagus or stomach. Such bleeding is fairly common when vomiting is the result of excessive alcohol consumption and usually subsides promptly when the vomiting ceases.

Vomiting caused by minor disorders usually stops without any treatment. After the first bout the individual often feels better and is able to resume limited activities. If vomiting does not stop within a few hours without treatment, a serious underlying disease must be considered. Successful treatment of vomiting with drugs may mask one of the principal signs of brain injury, an acute abdominal disorder such as intestinal obstruction or appendicitis, drug overdose, or some other disease, and result in delay in obtaining definitive care.

When no underlying disease can be identified, vomiting must be cared for in a nonspecific manner. If any orally administered medication can be retained, cyclizine (Marezine) tablets should be administered every six hours as long as the patient feels nauseated. If oral medication is not possible, cyclizine rectal suppositories should be administered every six hours. Frequently treatment can be continued by mouth after the first suppository. Treatment for more than twenty-four hours should be avoided if possible. While under treatment the patient must not take part in any activities in which drowsiness, a common side effect of cyclizine and all drugs used for treating vomiting, could result in injury.

Following recovery the diet should be bland and preferably liquid for about twenty-four hours. Fluids which have been lost should be replaced as soon as possible to prevent dehydration.

If vomiting is prolonged, the body becomes depleted of fluid and salt. Rarely, medications alone cannot stop the vomiting until the fluid and salt are replaced. Thus treatment for intractable vomiting may require intravenous therapy. If the proper fluids for intravenous therapy are not available, the patient must be evacuated.

Motion Sickness

Symptoms of motion sickness can sometimes be reduced by lying down with the eyes open. Sitting over the wing of an airplane or near the center of a ship reduces the motion experienced by the subject.

Treatment is most effective when started thirty minutes before the motion is encountered. Cyclizine tablets may be given every four to six hours, but no more than four should be taken in any twenty-four hour period. Dimenhydrinate (Dramamine) is a similar drug which is equally effective and probably more readily available. One tablet should be taken every four hours.

DIARRHEA

Of the many causes for diarrhea, the most common is a change in food or surroundings. Most other causes are equally benign, although a few diseases characterized by diarrhea are quite severe.

The common causes of diarrhea are listed below according to the seriousness of the underlying disease and not the severity of the diarrhea.

Mild
    Acute (Acute Gastroenteritis)
        Staphylococcal Enteritis
        Food Allergy
        Viral Enteritis
        Traveler's Diarrhea
    Chronic
        Emotional Colitis
        Irritable Colon Syndrome
        Change of Food or Surroundings
        Diseases of Other Organs

Severe
    Acute
        Cholera
        Bacillary Dysentery
    Subacute
        Typhoid Fever
    Chronic
        Amebiasis

This classification is of value because the treatment for all of the diseases within most of the groups is similar. However, the time between contraction of the disease and the onset of symptoms is not the same for acute diseases of the mild and severe groups. Furthermore, any of the diseases of the severe group may produce only mild symptoms. Indeed amebiasis is usually accompanied by very mild symptoms, but is included in the severe group because very serious complications can result.

ACUTE GASTROENTERITIS

Acute gastroenteritis ("stomach flu") is characterized by rapidly developing generalized abominal distress culminating in waves of cramps and diarrhea. During spasms of pain the patient typically draws his knees up against his abdomen for relief. However, the periods between spasms are relatively free of pain. Nausea is frequent and may be accompanied by vomiting. Sometimes nausea and vomiting are the dominant features of the illness.

Mild generalized abdominal tenderness is commonly present, particularly in the lower part of the abdomen, and the bowel sounds are usually much louder than normal. Mild chills and fever may be present in severe cases, but usually are absent.

The diarrhea is frequently explosive in onset and is characterized by the passage of copious, watery, foul-smelling stools. The number of stools varies from three or four to as many as twenty. Mucous is occasionally present in the stool, and prolonged diarrhea may rarely produce slightly bloody stools, but blood and mucous are usually absent. The disorders with a more rapid onset are usually more severe but are of much shorter duration. These diseases have been called "ptomaine poisoning," a term which is no longer used because it included several different diseases. Four types of acute gastroenteritis — staphylococcal enteritis, food allergy, viral enteritis, and traveler's diarrhea — are discussed individually below.

Staphylococcal Enteritis

Staphylococcal enteritis results from the ingestion of a toxin produced by staphylococcal bacteria which contaminate food or the utensils in which food is prepared. This toxin is heat-resistant and may not be destroyed by cooking. The bacteria are present almost everywhere and cannot be avoided. However, ordinary caution in cleaning cooking utensils and the refrigeration of all foods from the time of preparation until they are consumed reduces the number of staphylococci present and prevents the formation of significant amounts of the toxin.

The incubation period for this disorder is one to six hours, averaging three hours, and the onset is frequently explosive. However, the disorder rarely lasts more than five or six hours. Characteristically more than one person develops the disease — usually most of the individuals who have eaten the contaminated food.

Food Allergy

Food allergy is a rare disorder which results from allergy to a food which is completely normal and causes no symptoms in others. The onset is characteristically sudden — frequently explosive — and comes on within a few minutes to three or four hours after ingestion of the offending product. Nausea and vomiting frequently predominate. The disease disappears within a few hours or as soon as the causative food is eliminated by vomiting or diarrhea. Very rarely is more than one person affected, and that individual may have a history of a similar reaction to the same substance.

Viral Enteritis

Viral enteritis is caused by a number of viruses which are transmitted primarily by fecal contamination of water or hands, but may be spread by other means including personal contact. The incubation period is one to five days, averaging three days. Fever may be present along with other symptoms suggestive of influenza. The acute illness usually lasts only about one day but loose stools may persist for a week. Usually more than one person contracts this disorder.

Traveler's Diarrhea

Most of the cases of acute gastroenteritis occurring in visitors to tropical areas are classified as "traveler's diarrhea." This group of disorders has been labelled with many highly descriptive names such as the Aztec two-step, the Inca curse, the Hong Kong dog, the Delhi belly, Montezuma's revenge, or simply "turista." Although the cause for traveler's diarrhea has long been an enigma, recently evidence has begun to accumulate implicating enteropathogenic *Escherichia coli* in many cases. *E. coli* are normal bacterial inhabitants of the bowel found in everyone. However, certain strains have been found to produce a toxin which causes diarrhea, and these strains have been isolated from many patients with traveler's diarrhea.

Many other causes for traveler's diarrhea have been found, including salmonellosis, an infection with bacteria similar to those which cause typhoid fever, and rarely parasites such as *Giardia lamblia*. Precise identification of the causative agent in cases of traveler's diarrhea requires fairly sophisticated bacteriological laboratory facilities, and even then frequently is not possible.

The infection is usually spread by fecal contamination of the water used for drinking or cooking, usually as a result of improper sewage disposal combined with inadequate water purification. Inhabitants of many underdeveloped countries are continuously exposed to these organisms, build up resistance to them, and are not bothered by their presence in the water. However, outsiders who have not developed this resistance usually become unpleasantly (and occasionally severely) ill from such infections. Water harboring these organisms is more frequently found in populated areas where the volume of sewage is greater and storage of the water prior to distribution provides an opportunity for both contamination and multiplication of the bacteria.

The incubation period is six to forty-eight hours and the illness usually lasts two to five days. The onset is not so explosive as the disorders with shorter incubation periods. Chills and fever are rare, and the stools usually do not contain blood or mucous. Usually more than one person develops the disease if they have not exercised adequate precautions to avoid infection.

Treatment

The treatment for all types of acute gastroenteritis consists of fluid maintenance and the relief of symptoms. These disorders are rarely so severe that they produce dehydration, but occasionally this does occur. The tendency for dehydration at high altitudes would definitely be aggravated by severe vomiting and diarrhea. The urine volume must be watched to be certain that the patient does not become dehydrated. All fluids are helpful in replacing those which are lost and can almost always be administered orally after vomiting has stopped. Juices or similar beverages, particularly salty broths or soups, have the additional advantage of replacing salt as well as water. A bland diet should be given if the patient can eat.

The treatment of the patient's symptoms is somewhat controversial. Administration of drugs to control diarrhea may mask the patient's disease without curing it. Occasionally fever and toxicity may actually increase if the diarrheal stool is still being produced but is being retained within the large intestine, perhaps allowing some of the toxic products to be absorbed. On the other hand, the drugs which are administered for this purpose are rarely sufficiently effective to really hide a severe diarrhea. A compromise which appears safe is to administer medications only to control severe cramps, and then only at intervals of at least four hours or more. Such medications should be stopped if they appear to increase the patient's fever or to make him more ill. Paregoric (tincture of opium), diphenoxylate (Lomotil), and codeine are the most effective drugs for treating diarrheal cramps. These drugs vary in their effectiveness with different individuals. The most effective for the patient should be administered; if one is not effective, the others may be tried.

Antibiotics are of no benefit for most patients with traveler's diarrhea. However, patients who have fever, muscle pains, and profuse cramps may benefit from the administration of ampicillin every six hours if they are not allergic to penicillin.

The amount of rest required by the patient varies widely. Some victims are able to continue climbing; few feel the need for rest in bed.

CHRONIC MILD DIARRHEA

A mild diarrhea, consisting only of soft stools and a moderately increased frequency of bowel movements, may result from many different causes. A change in food, water, or surroundings is the most common. Emotional disturbances such as excitement or anxiety frequently produce similar symptoms. Diseases of other organs are often accompanied by a mild diarrhea.

These disorders are classified as chronic because they may last for days or even several weeks. However, the diarrhea is only mildly bothersome, almost never incapacitating, and usually clears up spontaneously without any therapy. Usually no treatment is necessary. Diphenoxylate three or four times a day may help reduce the number of bowel movements and tend to return the stools to normal consistency. Antibiotics or other medications should be avoided.

Irritable Colon Syndrome

The irritable colon syndrome (also known as mucous colitis, spastic colon, or unstable colon) is a very common disturbance of large intestinal function which may result in diarrhea or constipation. This syndrome is emotional in origin and its appearance is directly related to periods of emotional stress. Therefore, this type of dysfunction could be expected to appear during mountaineering outings.

Most patients have some abdominal pain, which may suggest some other disorder. The pain is most common in the upper abdomen or the left lower quadrant. Some patients may have severe pain in the left flank which may radiate to the chest over the heart, the left shoulder, and down the inner surface of the left arm. This pattern is suggestive of the pain encountered with angina or a coronary thrombosis (see "Diseases of the Heart and Blood Vessels"). The pain may be relieved by the passage of gas or feces.

Such patients usually have other symptoms not directly related to the large intestine. Loss of appetite, nausea, belching, and occasionally vomiting indicate involvement of the upper gastrointestinal tract. Headache, sweating, flushing, shortness of breath, sighing respirations, and hyperventilation (see "Diseases of the Respiratory System") may be observed.

The stools are usually small, regardless of whether the patient has diarrhea or constipation, and a considerable amount of mucous is usually present.

Treatment consists principally of recognizing the nature of the disorder and reassuring the patient. If treatment of diarrhea is desirable, an anticholinergic drug is usually most effective. Drugs such as paregoric or diphenoxylate are usually not effective and should not be used. However, drug therapy of any type is usually not required. The disorder disappears as soon as the source of the stress is eliminated, although repeated episodes with subsequent stress are characteristic.

SEVERE DIARRHEAS

The severe diarrheas are all of infectious origin and are most frequently transmitted by fecal contamination of drinking water. In areas where these diseases exist all water must be carefully sterilized. Persons dwelling in cities where the public water supply is of uncertain cleanliness should drink bottled water or other beverages. All foods should be thoroughly washed in a strong solution of chlorine and peeled if possible. Contamination of food during preparation should also be avoided. If possible, stool cultures for bacteria should be obtained on the native personnel in large expedition parties, particularly those engaged in preparing meals, in order to detect carriers of infectious diseases.

Strict precautions are necessary to avoid spread of the infection. A patient who has contracted one of these diseases should be isolated from the other members of the party as much as possible. The number of attendants should be limited to two or three, preferably party members who have been previously immunized against the patient's illness.

The attendants must ensure all possible measures to avoid spreading the infection are taken. They should wear protective rubber or plastic gloves if these are available. They must scrub their hands vigorously, preferably with an antiseptic soap such as pHisoHex, after any contact with the patient. All feces and vomitus should be mixed with an antiseptic such as one percent Cresol, if such is available, and buried deeply in a spot where contamination of water is unlikely. All utensils and other instruments should be immersed in boiling water. Indispensible items such as clothing or sleeping bags which cannot be boiled, should be aired in bright sunlight for at least two or three days after the patient is recovering and the danger of spreading the infection has passed.

Cholera

Cholera, once a scourge throughout the world, is now rare where modern sanitation and water purification methods are practiced, and when accurately diagnosed, can be easily and effectively treated. However, cholera is still common in certain areas. Epidemics, which claim many lives among the very young and the elderly and infirm, still occur in parts of India and other Southeast Asian countries.

Cholera is caused by a bacterial infection which is transmitted primarily through contaminated water, but may also be contracted from food, particularly items which are not cooked. A vaccine has been developed, but is of questionable value, only providing partial immunity for a period of about six months. All persons entering or passing through areas in which cholera is known to exist probably should receive this vaccine beforehand, and revaccination should be obtained every six months. However, the principal value of vaccination may be to facillitate travel through countries which require prior vaccination for individuals who have been visiting or residing in an area where cholera is endemic. Work towards developing more effective vaccines is continuing.

Fortunately, the cholera organism cannot survive for long periods outside the human body. Therefore most cases of cholera occur near areas of significant population and thus in areas where hospital care is available. However, some cases of cholera cause no more symptoms than one of the mild diarrheas and thus may go undiagnosed. Also carriers, although much rarer than in diseases such as typhoid fever, do appear occasionally. Thus, cases of cholera can occur at some distance from medical aid. The severity of the disease and its rapid onset may prevent evacuation of the patient, making treatment in the field necessary.

The incubation period for cholera is one to three days, during which time the victim may notice mild diarrhea, depression, and lassitude. The onset at the end of the incubation period is explosive. The patient has voluminous diarrhea, copious vomiting, and is prostrate. The disease can become overwhelming with amazing rapidity, leaving the patient severely dehydrated and in shock just from diarrheal fluid loss within one to three hours.

The gastrointestinal tract is quickly emptied and the stools lose their feculant character and are not foul smelling. The patient is constantly dribbling stools consisting almost entirely of water containing flecks of mucous. The name "rice-water stools" has been given to the material which is passed because the mucous looks like grains of rice floating in water. However, the stools rarely contain blood.

Frequently no warning of the need to defecate is felt, resulting in repeated, almost uncontrollable bowel movements. Similarly, vomiting may occur without antecedent nausea, although vomiting is rarely present after the onset of the illness. As the patient becomes dehydrated, fever and a high pulse rate appear. The features become gaunt, the eyes shrunken, and the skin shriveled and dry. The blood pressure frequently drops below normal and the pulse may be difficult to feel. Urinary output falls to nothing.

The treatment for cholera consists of fluid replacement. The entire volume of stool and vomitus must be replaced with Ringer's lactate solution. These volumes must be measured if replacement is to be accurate. Intravenous administration of fluids is often necessary during the early stages of the disease, and may be lifesaving if the patient is severely dehydrated and in shock. Two to four liters of Ringer's lactate may be required in the first hour, and as much as eight or more liters during the first day. However, after dehydration has been corrected and the patient is no longer in shock, he usually is able to take fluids orally. Fluid losses can be replaced orally with a solution containing 4.0 gm of sodium chloride, 4.0 gm of sodium bicarbonate, 1.0 gm of potassium chloride, and 20 gm of glucose per liter of water. Ordinary maintenance fluids — two liters of five to ten percent glucose and one-half liter ·of Ringer's lactate, or similar volumes of other liquids if taken orally — must also be administered in addition to the replacement fluids.

Victims of cholera are severely ill and obviously require bed rest. A canvas cot with a hole in the center through which the patient can defecate without having to move helps make him more comfortable and facilitates the collection and measuring of the stools during the first few days of the illness.

Tetracycline every six hours helps reduce the duration of diarrhea, but is only an adjunct to therapy and must not be substituted for fluid and electrolyte replacement. Sedatives only make care of the patient more difficult and should be avoided.

Cholera is not very contagious, and is spread principally through fecal contamination. Strict sanitary measures regarding the disposal of feces and vomitus and the cleansing of all contaminated articles, including clothing, bedding, and utensils, should be observed to avoid further spread of the disease.

The acute phase of the disease rarely lasts more than three to five days. The patient usually is able to eat a bland diet by the third day. However, several weeks may be required to fully regain his strength.

Bacillary Dysentery

Bacillary dysentery, or "Shigellosis," is caused by bacteria of the genus *Shigella* and occasionally by other organisms. These organisms are widespread, being found in temperate as well as tropical areas. However, the more severe cases of bacillary dysentery appear most frequently in tropical or semitropical climates. The infection is spread by contaminated water and food. Crowded living conditions and inadequate sewage disposal increase the likelihood of infection.

The incubation period varies from one to six days with an average of forty-eight hours. The onset is usually rather abrupt and is characterized by symptoms quite similar to acute gastroenteritis. Severe, intermittent abdominal cramps are followed by copious diarrhea which soon produces watery, foul stools. The symptoms of dysentery are much more severe and disabling than acute gastroenteritis, however. The onset of the disease is usually associated with fever and chilly feelings or frank, shaking chills. The patient is obviously ill and may be prostrate. The stools contain large amounts of mucous and pus and occasionally moderate amounts of blood, particularly four to five hours after the onset. Nausea is common but vomiting frequently does not occur. Abdominal tenderness may be severe, is most marked in the lower portion of the abdomen, and is frequently accompanied by spasm of the abdominal muscles.

After six to eight hours the symptoms abate somewhat, but the disease may take seven to ten days to run its course.

Bacillary dysentery may be indistinguishable from acute gastroenteritis. However, with dysentery the symptoms are usually more severe, the patient is more obviously ill, pus and blood are present in the stools, and the disease runs a longer course.

The patient should be placed in bed and given fluids to prevent dehydration. Intravenous fluids may be necessary in the more severe cases. A bland diet may be given if it can be tolerated by the patient. A hot-water bottle or other warming device placed on the abdomen may reduce some of the pain and tenderness. Morphine or drugs to stop the diarrhea should not be given for cramps because these drugs tend to produce intestinal paralysis which prevents the patient from taking fluids orally. They also may make the fever and overall disability worse.

Ampicillin should be given orally every six hours; the first dose should be twice as large as the usual dose. This drug frequently produces a marked improvement in twenty-four hours or less, but should be continued for at least three or four days or until all symptoms have disappeared.

The victim of bacillary dysentery frequently requires seven to ten days to recover his strength after the symptoms of his disease have disappeared. Isolation and prevention of spread of the infection are essential.

Typhoid Fever

Typhoid fever is an infection caused by bacteria which produce a generalized infection as well as diarrhea. After food or water contaminated by these bacteria has been ingested, the organisms invade the wall of the small bowel, multiply there, and then enter the blood stream.

Occasionally people who have recovered from typhoid fever may continue to harbor the organisms in the gastrointestinal tract and excrete them in the stools (carriers). The bacteria can survive for weeks or months under natural conditions. Uncooked foods, salads, raw milk, and water contaminated by sewage are the most important sources of infection.

After an incubation period of ten to twelve days, malaise, headache, and fever gradually appear. The fever goes up and down daily, eventually reaching levels of about 103°F by the third week of the illness. At this time headache, lack of appetite, abdominal discomfort, and occasionally nosebleeds may be present. Chills and sweats can occur. At later stages delirium and diarrhea may occur if the fever is sustained at a high level for a long time.

Usually no diagnostic physical signs are present in the first week. During the second or third week a rash may appear for two to three days. This rash consists of crops of red, round, slightly elevated spots three millimeters in diameter which are most common on the upper abdomen and lower chest and blanch on pressure. The pulse is often slow in relation to the fever. A pulse rate of eighty-five may accompany a temperature of 104°F. Vague, diffuse abdominal tenderness may also be present.

In the treatment of typhoid fever, rest and maintenance of fluid balance are important. Aspirin may lower the temperature, but can also make the patient feel worse and should not be administered. Chloramphenicol is the antibiotic of choice for treating typhoid fever. However, the diagnosis of typhoid fever without laboratory facilities is unreliable, and the side effects of chloramphenicol therapy can be devastating. Therefore, this drug should only be administered by a physician. Ampicillin is usually effective for treating typhoid fever and is free of the unfortunate side effects of chloramphenicol. This antibiotic should be used just as it is in the treatment of bacillary dysentery.

Prior to travel to an area where tyhpoid may be encountered, immunization for typhoid fever should be carried out. Although immunization does not completely prevent infection, it does reduce the severity of the disease and reduces the incidence of complications. Sources of infection and contamination of food by carriers should be avoided.

Amebiasis

Amebiasis is caused by the protozoan *Endamoeba histolytica,* a larger and more complex organism than the bacteria. Although generally thought of as a tropical disease, amebiasis is by no means limited to such areas.

These organisms invade the wall of the large intestine where the adult parasites form cysts which are passed in the feces of the host and are responsible for the spread of the infection. These cysts are most commonly ingested with contaminated water. Food which has been fertilized with human excreta, carelessness in food preparation, and insects — particularly flies — are other sources of infection. Chlorine added to drinking water does not kill the cysts; iodine and boiling destroy them quite effectively.

Amebiasis is usually quite mild in its early stages and symptoms may be entirely absent. More commonly a mild diarrhea with soft stools and a moderately increased number of bowel movements occurs. Occasionally patients develop constipation rather than diarrhea. A few patients have more severe symptoms which are suggestive of acute gastroenteritis, including numerous watery stools which contain mucous or even blood, and abdominal cramps. However, a period of mild gastrointestinal dysfunction usually precedes the onset of the more severe stage of amebiasis. Easy fatigability, a low fever, and vague pains in the muscles, back, or joints are frequently present. Nervousness, irritability, and dizziness occasionally develop. In a typical patient no abnormality can be found by physical examination, although slight tenderness in the right lower quadrant of the abdomen is sometimes present. The diagnosis is suggested by the chronicity and mildness of the diarrhea and a history of exposure to conditions in which infection is likely. Laboratory facilities are required to make a certain diagnosis.

If amebiasis is suspected, tetracycline should be given four times a day for one week. This antibiotic occasionally causes diarrhea itself, but this side effect disappears after the course of therapy is completed. However, tetracycline may not completely eradicate the infection.

Table 4. Characteristics of Diseases Causing Diarrhea

Disorder	Incu- bation Period	Fever	Chills	Number of Stools*	Blood in Stool	Mucus in Stool	Duration	Appears Ill	Common in U.S.A.
MILD									
Food Allergy	0-3 hours	No	No	0-4	No	No	2-3 hours	No	Moderately
Staphylococcal Enteritis	1-6 hours	No	No	4-20	No	Rare	4-6 hours	No	Yes
Viral Enteritis	1-5 days	Occ.	No	4-20	Rare	Rare	1-7 days	Slightly	Yes
Traveler's Diarrhea	6-48 hours	Rare	Rare	4-20	Rare	Rare	2-5 days	Occ.	No
Chronic Diarrhea	Varies	No	No	0-4	No	Rare	Varies	No	Yes
SEVERE									
Cholera	1-3 days	Yes	Occ.	Innumerable	No	Large amounts	7-21 days (3 days)**	Usually prostrate	No
Bacillary Dysentery	1-6 days	Yes	Occ.	4-20	Occ.	Yes	7-10 days (6-8 hrs.)**	Yes	No
Typhoid Fever	10-12 days	Yes	Yes	4-20	Occ.	Occ.	3-4 weeks	Yes	No
Amebiasis	Varies	Rare	Rare	0-4	Rare	Rare	Varies	Usually not	No

Occ. = Occasional

*The number of stools is only an approximation given to indicate the nature of the diarrhea.

**The figures in parentheses indicate the duration of the earlier, more severe phase of the disease.

All persons visiting an area in which amebiasis is prevalent must be examined for this disease upon their return. The amoebae may lie quietly within the large intestine for years, producing no symptoms, and then spread to the liver where they form abscesses and occasionally even invade the lung. This form of the disease is very serious and has a high mortality rate. Fortunately it can be easily prevented by early diagnosis and treatment.

CONSTIPATION AND RECTAL PROBLEMS

Healthy adults rarely need to be concerned about constipation. The concept that normal individuals should have a bowel movement every day is a myth perpetrated on bowel-conscious people by herb peddlers. Bowel rhythm can vary widely. For some individuals three stools a day is normal; others normally have one stool every three days.

The type of food consumed plays a large part in determining the character and frequency of stools. Foods which are almost completely absorbed, such as milk or candy, cannot be expected to produce a copious stool; the reverse is true for foods with a large unabsorbed residue such as bran or many leafy vegetables.

Constipation is more accurately defined as the passage of hard, dry stools rather than a specified frequency of bowel movements. Dehydrated foods, infrequent stops, disruption of normal schedules, and reduced intake of water and fluids all tend to cause constipation. An adequate fluid intake — at least two quarts per day — and the inclusion in the diet of fruits and other foods which loosen the stools help to maintain normal bowel function.

In general, laxatives have very little prophylactic or therapeutic value. If, in an unusual situation, laxatives become necessary, the best and safest is Milk of Magnesia, one or two tablespoonfuls or two to four tablets at bedtime.

Fecal Impaction

Under conditions in which the urge to defecate is resisted, such as weather that confines climbers to their tents, or more commonly during recovery from an injury or disease, the normal bowel reflexes may become insensitive and permit stool to accumulate in the rectum. Conditions producing dehydration, such as a high fever, inadequate fluid intake, high altitude, or a combination of such factors, may cause the normal fluids in the stool to be reabsorbed with such avidity that a bulky, hard residue remains which cannot be evacuated in a normal manner.

The best way to determine whether impaction has occurred is to insert a moistened or lubricated and (if available) gloved index finger into the rectum. If a mass of hard stool is found it must be extracted. The mass of stool should be broken up with the index finger and the fragments removed as gently as possible. Injury of the rectal and anal tissues must be avoided. Following manual removal of the impaction, an enema should be given and the causes of the impaction corrected.

Although breaking up and extracting a fecal impaction is esthetically un-pleasant, no alternative exists. Enema fluids will not enter the solidified fecal mass; laxatives have no effect on the dilated, flaccid rectal wall. Paradoxically, fecal impaction may be accompanied by the passage of a number of small, watery stools — the only material which can get past the impacted mass.

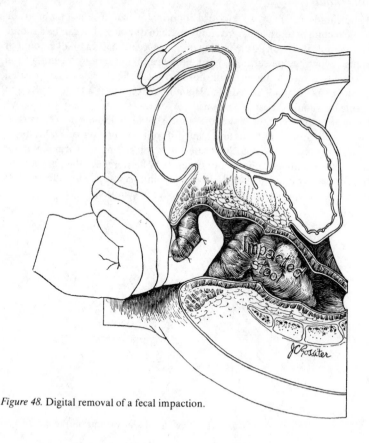

Figure 48. Digital removal of a fecal impaction.

Anal Fissure

With constipation the stool may become so hard and bulky that its passage causes a small tear (fissure) in the lining of the anus. Subsequent bowel movements are painful and may be associated with a small amount of bleeding.

Relief of the constipation sometimes permits the fissure to heal. Mineral oil, one tablespoon twice a day, lubricates the stool and reduces the pain with bowel movements. (Mineral oil is not a true laxative — only a lubricant.) A bland anesthetic such as dibucaine ointment may be applied to the anus if the pain is bothersome. The area should be cleaned gently after each bowel movement and wiping, scratching, and rubbing should be avoided.

Hemorrhoids

Hemorrhoids (or "piles"), which are abnormally dilated veins that protrude from the rectum or anus, are more annoying than disabling, but can be a source of considerable irritation due to itching or pain. Occasionally a small amount of bleeding follows the passage of a hard, bulky stool, but serious bleeding from hemorrhoids is rare. Climbers with hermorrhoids should have them treated surgically before a major expedition. Hemorrhoidectomy is a minor operation requiring only limited hospitalization.

If hemorrhoids are bothersome, the stools should be loosened by the ingestion of large quantities of fluids and plenty of fruit. Mineral oil, one tablespoon twice a day, may be taken to lubricate the stool. Sitting in warm water for fifteen to thirty minutes three or four times a day helps relieve the burning and itching. A bland ointment such as dibucaine ointment applied to the anus, or hemorrhoidal suppositories often provide relief of symptoms.

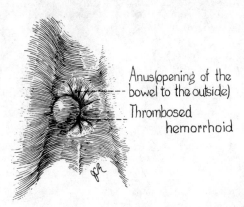

Anus(opening of the bowel to the outside)

Thrombosed hemorrhoid

Figure 49. Anus with a thrombosed hemorrhoid.

Thrombosed Hemorrhoid

Occasionally the blood within a hemorrhoid clots, causing moderately severe pain. The pain may come on gradually or suddenly, and the victim usually has noted prior symptoms attributable to the presence of hermorrhoids. A swollen, tender, purple nodule can be seen protruding from the wall or opening of the anus.

After washing the area with soap and water, an incision can be made in the top of the thrombosed hermorrhoid and the clot evacuated. Relief of pain is frequently dramatic and many days of distress can be avoided if the thrombosed hemorrhoid is large. Aspirin and codeine can be given for pain prior to incision; a local anesthetic can be injected if available. Sterile pads should be left in the intergluteal cleft for several days to reduce soiling of clothing and irritation of the incision site. Warm baths or packs help relieve pain and anal muscle spasm.

Rectal Abscess

Abscesses in the tissues surrounding the rectum and anus usually follow chronic anal disease which should be corrected before a prolonged mountaineering outing is undertaken. Abscesses in this location are not basically different from abscesses elsewhere in the body.

The cardinal sign of rectal abscess is throbbing pain in the region of the anus. Malaise, fever, and chills are commonly present and the patient may appear acutely ill. Examination usually reveals the characteristic signs of an abscess — redness, tenderness, increased heat, and swelling. The abscess may point in the skin adjacent to the anus. A few rectal abscesses are located deeper beneath the skin and can only be detected as a moderately firm mass felt during digital examination of the rectum.

Rectal abscesses require the same treatment as abscesses anywhere — incision and drainage. If the abscess points in the skin about the anus, an incision should be made in the center of the fluctuant area. If a deeper abscess is felt, the patient should be evacuated, since drainage of such abscesses must be carried out by a physician. Serious complications can follow an abscess in this location if it is not properly treated. If the patient has a fever, ampicillin or a penicillinase-resistant penicillin should be administered every six hours during evacuation.

PEPTIC ULCER AND RELATED PROBLEMS

A peptic ulcer is a crater in the lining of the stomach or intestine produced by the digestive action of the enzymes and acids in the stomach. The cause of peptic ulcers is not well understood. However, emotional factors clearly play a part in their development.

An uncomplicated ulcer is not usually disabling, although the pain can be severe. However, an ulcer is dangerous because serious complications can occur, most importantly hemorrhage and perforation. These complications are disabling, life-endangering conditions requiring immediate evacuation to a medical center. Perforation is discussed in "Acute Abdominal Pain."

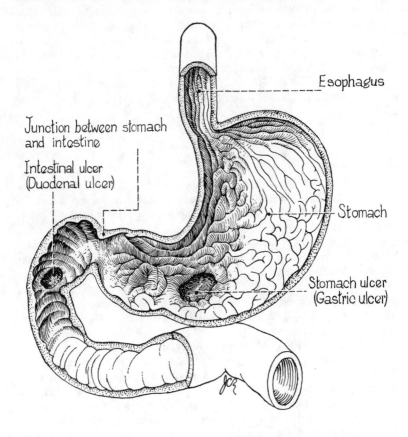

Esophagus

Junction between stomach and intestine

Intestinal ulcer (Duodenal ulcer)

Stomach

Stomach ulcer (Gastric ulcer)

Figure 50. Gastric and duodenal ulcers.

The characteristic symptom of an ulcer is a gnawing or sharp pain, usually located high in the upper portion of the abdomen near the midline. The pain typically comes on one to four hours after eating or between midnight and two o'clock in the morning. Bland food, milk, or an antacid usually relieves the pain fairly promptly.

The pain is thought to be caused by the effects of stomach acid on the ulcer. Food and antacids tend to neutralize the acid and thus relieve the pain. The characteristic times at which the pain occurs are the periods when there is no food in the stomach to counteract the acid.

Therapy for an ulcer is directed towards neutralizing stomach acidity and relieving emotional tension. An antacid should be taken every hour while awake. (Since overdosage with this drug is not a problem, more rather than less should be administered if there is any question about the adequacy of dosage.) An antispasmodic which relieves distress from spasm of the muscles of the upper gastrointestinal tract should be taken four times daily.

A bland diet with large quantities of milk, cheese, puddings, and noncitrus fruit juices should be given in six meals scattered evenly over the waking hours. These foods tend to neutralize the stomach acids most effectively. Eating six meals a day tends to keep food in the stomach constantly and thus prolongs the acid neutralizing effect. Alcohol, coffee, tea, and spicy foods increase gastric acidity and should be strictly avoided.

A patient with an ulcer should avoid strenuous exertion and needs extra rest such as a midafternoon nap. However, he does not need to be confined to bed. A sedative or a tranquilizer may be given four times daily to provide sedation and relieve the emotional tensions which play a large role in causing ulcers. Patients who do not respond to therapy within ten to fourteen days should be evacuated to a physician's care as the danger of complications increases with time.

Indigestion

Indigestion is a vague, poorly defined disorder which is often not associated with any demonstrable abnormality of the upper gastrointestinal system. However, the symptoms of indigestion may be confused with those of an ulcer. Since an ulcer poses a threat of severe complications but indigestion does not, the conditions should be distinguished.

The symptoms of an ulcer and indigestion characteristically differ in several respects. Usually the symptoms of indigestion are associated with eating rather than coming on one to four hours afterwards. With indigestion a sense of fullness, excessive belching, or vomiting small amounts of food or sour stomach contents are more common than actual pain, although a burning sensation may be present beneath the breast bone (heartburn). Usually the symptoms of indigestion are related to only a single or an occasional meal, while ulcer symptoms are more consistent. The symptoms of indigestion may be relieved to some extent by antacids but are frequently aggravated by the ingestion of more food, contrary to ulcer symptoms. The symptoms of indigestion becomes less noticeable with time and the passage of food from the stomach, also the opposite of ulcer symptoms.

If indigestion becomes so severe that treatment is necessary, it can be treated with antacids and antispasmodics just as an ulcer. Eating smaller quantities of food with each meal may also be beneficial.

Gastrointestinal Hemorrhage

One of the more serious problems which can occur far from medical facilities is massive hemorrhage from the stomach or intestines. Even with the expert treatment available in large medical centers, a certain percentage of patients succumb to this condition. Since blood transfusions are usually necessary, every effort must be made to get the affected climber to a hospital. *Hemorrhage is very likely to recur. Any delay may prove fatal.*

Except for the rare individual who bleeds slightly after prolonged retching because small blood vessels in the esophagus or stomach are broken, essentially all gastrointestinal bleeding in otherwise healthy young adults is due to a peptic ulcer. On an expedition such bleeding should be assumed to be due to an ulcer since other conditions causing bleeding cannot be effectively treated in the field. Symptoms of an ulcer, although usually present prior to the hemorrhage, may be totally absent.

The signs and symptoms of serious gastrointestinal bleeding include:

1. Faintness or weakness, which is more prominent when erect than when lying down;
2. Vomiting obvious blood;
3. Vomiting "coffee ground" material (blood which has been partially digested in the stomach);
4. Rectal passage of obvious blood;
5. Rectal passage of liquid or solid "tarry black" material (stools containing digested blood);
6. Shock.

The treatment for an ulcer — antacids, antispasmodics, a bland diet in multiple feedings, and sedation — should be instituted as soon as vomiting ceases. The patient should be put to bed and forced to rest as much as possible. Treatment for shock should be instituted if signs of shock, particularly low blood pressure, are present.

A young person with a bleeding peptic ulcer usually stops hemorrhaging within twelve to twenty-four hours if he is kept quiet and given appropriate therapy. He should be treated in camp until the bleeding stops and for one to two days more prior to evacuation. Moving a patient with active gastrointestinal hemorrhage is likely to increase the severity of the bleeding.

The patient is usually very weak after such a bleeding episode and requires considerable rest and assistance during evacuation. He should by no means try to go on with his climb even though he feels quite well. *A small bleeding episode is often followed by a horrendous gush!*

DISEASES OF THE LIVER

Jaundice

Jaundice is produced by diseases of the liver. One of the numerous functions of the liver is to remove from the blood the pigment resulting from the normal destruction of old red blood cells. This pigment is excreted into the intestine through the bile ducts and, following further changes in the intestinal tract, imparts the normal brown color to the stool.

In diseases which severely damage the liver this pigment is not removed from the blood. As a result it accumulates in the body and imparts a yellow or bronze color to the whites of the eyes and later the skin. Since the pigment is excreted into the intestine in smaller amounts or not at all, the stool becomes pale or "clay-colored." The pigment is partially excreted by the kidneys, imparting a brown color to the urine and causing the foam produced by shaking to have a yellow color instead of the normal white appearance.

When jaundice is suspected, the patient should be examined in the sunlight. Flashlights and other artificial lights usually have a yellowish color which can be confusing — either masking or simulating true jaundice.

Hepatitis

Hepatitis is a virus infection which selectively involves the liver. The virus is spread principally by fecal contamination of water, but contaminated food, personal contact, and contaminated injection needles, syringes, and similar instruments are also important routes of infection. This disease is common, particularly where a large number of people are living in crowded conditions.

Hepatitis is the most important cause of painless jaundice likely to occur for the first time under mountaineering conditions. (Jaundice associated with pain is discussed in "Acute Abdominal Pain." Patients with previous attacks of jaundice should be evaluated by a physician and instructed in the treatment for their condition prior to undertaking an outing.) Untreated malaria and a few other conditions cause jaundice on rare occasions due to the excessive destruction of red blood cells. However, such disorders can usually be recognized from other findings.

The onset of hepatitis is usually rather insidious and follows an incubation period ranging from three weeks to six months. The earliest symptoms are loss of appetite, general malaise, and easy fatigability. Later a low fever and nausea and vomiting appear. Many patients have a peculiar loss of their taste for cigarettes. In patients with more severe infections the symptoms gradually increase in severity. Light colored stools and dark urine may precede the appearance of jaundice by several days. Vague upper abdominal discomfort and tenderness may be present, particularly in the right upper quadrant, but severe pain is absent. After the appearance of jaundice, some patients experience ill-defined joint or muscular pains. A highly variable skin rash may be present and some patients have generalized itching.

The severity of the disease runs a full range from cases so mild the patient does not realize he is ill — which probably are the most numerous — to the relatively rare fatalities. When jaundice does develop it usually lasts three to six weeks; malaise, easy fatigability, and loss of appetite may persist for several more months.

No specific treatment is available. A study of previously healthy young adults in the Army indicated that restriction of exercise had no effect on the course of the disease for that rather select group of patients. Most climbers would fall into the same group of previously healthy, relatively young adults. However, most patients do not feel capable of more than very mild exercise. A nourishing diet high in proteins and carbohydrates and supplemented with vitamins should be provided.

All drug therapy should be avoided if possible, including drugs to promote sleep. Most drugs are metabolized by the liver. When that organ's functions are impaired by hepatitis, such metabolism may be much slower than normal. If the drugs are not completely metabolized between doses, they can accumulate in the blood and may rapidly reach toxic concentrations.

Most hepatitis patients should be evacuated. Recovery usually takes so long that delaying evacuation until the patient is well is impossible. In addition, complications may develop which require a physician's care.

REFERENCES:
1. Grady, G. G., and Keusch, G. T.: Pathogenesis of Bacterial Diarrheas, New Eng. J. Med. *285*:831 and 891, 1971.
2. Gangrosa, E. J., and Barker, W. H.: Cholera: Implications for the United States, J.A.M.A. *227*:170, 1974.

CHAPTER 21

Acute Abdominal Pain

AN EPISODE of acute abdominal pain is often frightening because it is well known that conditions causing such pain often require immediate surgical treatment. However, the most common disorders producing abdominal pain do not require any specific therapy; many others can be effectively treated without surgery.

In mountaineering situations, the major problem in caring for a person with acute abdominal pain is deciding whether he requires surgical treatment. If there is any doubt, the most conservative course should be followed and the patient evacuated. Unattended abdominal emergencies have a mortality rate approaching 100 percent. Disrupting a carefully planned climb because a member has a belly ache requires mature judgment, but such decisions reflect mountaineering wisdom and leadership just as surely as turning back within view of a summit when avalanche conditions are encountered.

During evacuation the patient almost always must be carried. A supine position with the head and knees moderately elevated is usually most comfortable. Continuous antibiotic therapy, analgesics, intravenous fluids, and nasogastric intubation may all be required.

Signs and Symptoms

The key to proper treatment is an accurate diagnosis which, in turn, requires a detailed history and a careful physical examination.

The following outline should be followed in obtaining a history of the disorder:

Pain:
    Exact time of onset;
    Nature of onset – gradual or sudden;
    Location of pain, change in location, radiation;

Nature of pain — sharp, stabbing, gnawing, cramping, constant, or intermittent;

Progression of pain since onset;

Factors relieving or aggravating pain — coughing, deep breathing, voiding, position of body.

Other Symptoms:

Nausea and vomiting — time of onset of vomiting in relation to onset of pain — vomiting blood;

Diarrhea or constipation — time of last bowel movement;

Chills or fever;

Blood in the urine;

Presence of a hernia — reducibility;

Other members of the party with a similar disorder.

Past History:

History of having eaten food not eaten by other members of the group;

Previous episodes of similar pain — diagnosis and treatment at that time;

History of pain relieved by milk, food, or antacids;

History of indigestion or pain following ingestion of fried or fatty foods;

History of jaundice;

History of previous abdominal operations;

Time of last menstrual period — any abnormalities.

If possible the physical examination should be performed in a quiet secluded spot where the patient can be warm and comfortable. He should be lying on his back with his hands at his sides and the entire abdomen from the nipple line to the crotch bared for examination.

The abdomen should be examined by observation, auscultation, and palpation. Spasms of pain, aggravation of pain by breathing, and the presence of scars from previous operations should be noted. The examiner should place his ear or a stethescope against the patient's abdomen and listen for increased or absent bowel sounds. Increased bowel sounds can frequently be heard several feet from the patient. The absence of bowel sounds, which is indicative of intestinal paralysis (paralytic ileus), can only be diagnosed when no sounds are heard after listening for at least two or three minutes.

Palpation of the abdomen is a skill which requires years of practice and experience to perfect. However, valuable information can be gained from this examination by a beginner with a modicum of prior instruction and practice. The examiner must be gentle; his hands must be warm. He should place his hands on the patient's abdomen with the palms down and exert gentle pressure with the pads of the fingers. Jabbing with the finger tips causes the patient to contract his abdominal muscles so that no information can be gained from the examination.

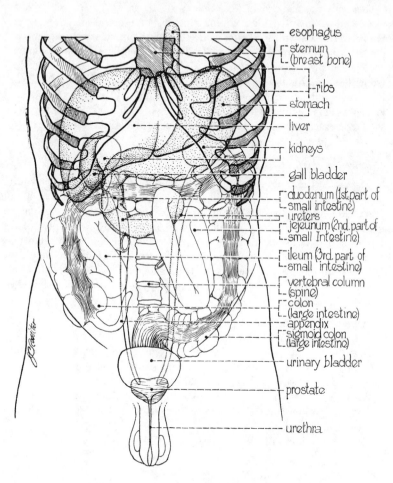

Figure 51. Organs of the abdominal cavity.

Areas of tenderness must be accurately located. Spasm in the abdominal muscles over tender areas should be identified. Rebound tenderness, which is a sudden sharp pain occurring when the pressure over a tender area is suddenly released, should be sought. Referred tenderness, pain in one portion of the abdomen elicited by pressure in another area (caused by the intestines shifting away from the site being depressed and irritating the diseased organ), must be recognized.

Generally speaking, pain associated with diarrhea or pain which is not associated with nausea and vomiting is not a sign of disease requiring operation. Severe pain which lasts for more than six hours or which prevents the patient from sleeping is usually indicative of a condition requiring surgery. Abdominal distension and paralytic ileus, rebound pain, exactly localized tenderness, and rigidity of the abdominal muscles are indicative of a serious intra-abdominal condition which is best treated by surgery. Jaundice is evidence of gallbladder or liver disease which is of such severity that the patient should be evacuated, since full recovery requires at least several weeks.

Reporting History and Physical Findings

Because decisions about a climber with abdominal pain must almost always include consideration of a major disruption of the outing and the expense of evacuating the casualty, consultation by radio or telephone should be obtained if possible. An appropriate decision can be made only if the report of the history and physical examination is given to the consultant physician in a systematic manner. The above check list concerning the history should be followed; all data should be recorded prior to the discussion. In addition, answers to the following questions about the physical examination should be recorded for discussion;

Temperature, pulse, and respiratory rate?
Does the patient look sick?
Does the patient appear to be complaining for an ulterior or perhaps subconscious motive? Does he appear to over-react to pain?
Is the abdomen rigid due to involuntary muscle spasm?
Where is the pain most severe (a) as the patient lies unexamined? (b) with gentle probing? and (c) after sudden release of the probing fingers (rebound pain)?
Is a hernia or intra-abdominal mass present?

CONDITIONS WHICH DO NOT REQUIRE EVACUATION

Gastroenteritis

The most common cause of abdominal pain is acute gastroenteritis which is discussed more thoroughly in "Gastrointestinal Disorders."

Gradually increasing, diffuse abdominal pain that culminates in waves of abdominal cramps and diarrhea is typical of acute gastroenteritis. During spasms of pain the patient frequently draws his knees up on his abdomen for relief, but the periods between spasms are relatively free from pain. Generalized abdominal tenderness is often present and may be slightly greater in the lower abdomen. Bowel sounds are louder than normal. Nausea and vomiting may be the most prominent symptoms; chills and fever may also be present.

Gastroenteritis must be distinguished principally from appendicitis. In appendicitis (1) no evidence of food contamination or of others suffering from the same disease is found; (2) pain is not diffuse and usually is not cramping; and (3) diarrhea is not prominent. The onset of appendicitis is usually gradual and the pain is relatively constant. Tenderness, if present, is localized in the right lower quadrant of the abdomen.

Mittelschmerz

Mittelschmerz, which is German for "middle pain," occurs in women midway between menstrual periods and is produced by minor bleeding accompanying ovulation. Women with this disorder usually have had previous episodes of such pain and can frequently identify the condition.

The pain comes on gradually, may be severe, and is usually localized in either the right or left lower abdominal quadrants, depending upon which ovary is involved. Vomiting or diarrhea usually does not occur. The abdomen is usually soft, but tenderness may be elicited by deep palpation in one of the lower quadrants.

Mittelschmerz may be difficult to differentiate from appendicitis if the right ovary is involved. The gynecologic condition should be suspected if the pain occurs half-way between menstrual periods.

No specific treatment is necessary. The pain can usually be controlled with aspirin and codeine and usually disappears within thirty-six to forty-eight hours. Symptoms persisting for a longer time should prompt reconsideration of the diagnosis.

Acute Salpingitis

Acute salpingitis is an infection of the fallopian tubes, the structures which conduct ova (eggs) from the ovary to the uterus. The infection is most often gonorrheal in origin, although many other organisms can also cause such infections.

The pain usually develops gradually, but can become quite severe. Both fallopian tubes are usually involved to some extent, causing pain in both the right and left lower quadrants of the abdomen. However, the pain commonly is much more severe on one side than the other. The pain may be accompanied by nausea and vomiting. Typically a high fever — 103°F or higher — is present. Tenderness, muscle spasm, and rebound pain may be present in either or both of the lower abdominal quadrants.

Acute salpingitis may be impossible to differentiate from appendicitis if the right tube is involved. The presence of a high fever is suggestive of salpingitis, but can also occur with appendicitis, particularly if the appendix has ruptured. A history of sexual contact followed by a vaginal discharge is suggestive of gonorrhea followed by salpingitis, but such patients can also develop appendicitis. Pain or tenderness in both sides of the abdomen is rather strong evidence of salpingitis.

If distinction from appendicitis is not possible, the patient should be treated as if she had appendicitis. If the disorder appears highly likely to be salpingitis, then the patient does not have to be evacuated. Surgery is not required for acute salpingitis. However, treatment for gonorrhea should be instituted (See "Genitourinary Diseases").

CONDITIONS THAT DO REQUIRE EVACUATION

Appendicitis

Appendicitis is the most common of the disorders producing acute abdominal pain which require surgical treatment. Individuals who are frequently in remote areas for prolonged periods should discuss with their physician the advisability of having a prophylactic appendectomy.

The onset of appendicitis is characterized by vague abdominal discomfort which becomes progressively worse. Cramps are usually absent. The earliest symptoms are frequently located in the mid-abdomen. One to three hours later the pain shifts to the right lower quadrant, during which time the patient usually becomes nauseated and vomits several times. One or two bowel movements may occur, but diarrhea is rare. Rarely has the patient had any previous similar attacks.

The area of maximum tenderness is in the right lower quadrant of the abdomen. Later referred tenderness, rebound tenderness, and muscle spasm appear in the same area. Usually a low fever of about 101° is present, but chills are rare.

If the appendix ruptures, pain may abruptly disappear. A few hours later the pain usually returns, but is more diffuse and is associated with signs of peritonitis. However, the infection can remain localized to the area around the appendix, forming an abscess. In the presence of this complication a low fever usually persists and the patient does not feel entirely well. However, there may be no other symptoms until the abscess ruptures at a later date, producing peritonitis which may be overwhelming.

Antibiotic therapy should be started at once. If the patient is not vomiting, tetracycline should be given orally every six hours. If oral therapy is not possible, ampicillin or gentamicin can be given intramuscularly every six hours. If the patient is in severe pain, morphine can be given intramuscularly every four hours. However, morphine masks the physical findings characteristic of appendicitis and should not be administered within four hours of the time the patient is to be examined by a physician.

Appendicitis is best treated by immediate surgery. Therefore, the patient should be evacuated as fast as possible. Intravenous fluids may be required to avoid dehydration if the patient is vomiting and evacuation requires more than thirty-six hours. If gastric distension and paralytic ileus appear, nasogastric suction should be instituted.

Some cases of appendicitis have been cured by antibiotic treatment alone. In a truly remote area such therapy can be tried. If the patient's fever and all abdominal pain *and* tenderness *completely* disappear, his appetite returns, and he feels completely well, he can probably resume climbing safely. However, only a physician can determine whether the disease has actually been cured or is merely quiescent. Therefore, the patient should be evacuated in less remote circumstances or if there is any question about his condition.

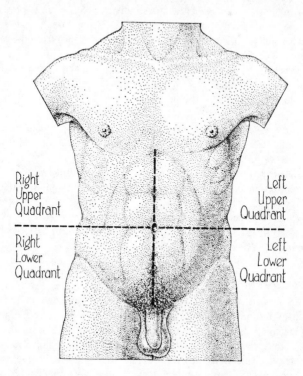

Figure 52. The four quadrants of the abdomen.

Intestinal Obstruction

Intestinal obstruction is produced by a number of conditions which block the passage of food and waste products through the stomach and intestines. The symptoms are similar regardless of the cause of the obstruction but do vary somewhat according to the location of the obstruction in the gastrointestinal tract. Bands of fibrous tissue from previous abdominal operations are a frequent cause of this disorder. Some patients have a history of repeated episodes of obstruction.

The onset of symptoms is gradual and is characterized by waves of cramping pain which increase rapidly in severity. The patient is frequently free of pain between spasms. Nausea and vomiting, which are almost invariably present, occur early in obstructions located in the upper portions of the intestine. If the obstruction is lower in the small intestine or in the large intestine, vomiting may not occur for several hours or even longer after the onset of pain.

The patient appears quite ill and usually has a rapid pulse. Sometimes other signs of shock are present. The abdomen is distended, particularly with obstructions in the lower part of the intestinal tract. Scars from previous abdominal operations are frequently present. Bowel sounds are much louder than normal, occasionally being audible a considerable distance from the patient.

Later in the course of the disease — twelve to twenty-four hours after onset — the intestines become so distended by fluid and air that contractions cease and the bowel sounds disappear. Signs of peritonitis — diffuse abdominal pain and tenderness and spasm of the abdominal muscles — are usually present at this stage.

In the early stages intestinal obstruction may simulate acute gastroenteritis. However, although one or two bowel movements may occur, diarrhea is rarely present with obstruction.

Immediate evacuation is imperative since surgery is almost always necessary. Nasogastric suction should be instituted if possible. Intravenous fluid therapy (and the replacement by Ringer's lactate of all fluids lost through vomiting or gastric suction) is necessary if evacuation requires more than thirty-six hours. Antibiotic treatment for peritonitis also should be instituted. No fluids or medication should be given orally.

Perforated Peptic Ulcer

Perforation is one of the complications which can occur with a peptic ulcer (see "Gastrointestinal Diseases"). The same processes which have digested the lining of the stomach or intestine to form the ulcer crater continue their action until the ulcer extends through the entire wall of the organ. The resulting perforation permits stomach acids, food, and other intestinal contents to enter the abdominal cavity. These substances cause an intense chemical irritation of the peritoneum and may initiate a severe infection.

The patient usually has a history of a peptic ulcer (upper abdominal pain coming on four to six hours after eating and relieved by food, milk, and antacids). However, approximately twenty percent of the patients with a perforated ulcer do not have such prior symptoms.

At the time of perforation the patient suffers the abrupt, almost instantaneous onset of severe upper abdominal pain which is sharp and continuous, and may spread over the entire abdomen. The pain is followed shortly by the vomiting of recently ingested food or bile. The patient appears quite sick and gets progressively worse for the next twelve to twenty-four hours.

The abdomen is diffusely tender, but pain is more marked in the upper quadrants. Spasm of the abdominal muscles is prominent, particularly in the upper abdomen. Bowel sounds disappear shortly after the perforation and distention of the abdomen soon follows due to intestinal paralysis.

A perforated ulcer is a severe emergency requiring immediate evacuation. Treatment for peritonitis should be administered during evacuation.

Incarcerated Hernia

A hernia (or "rupture") is a protrusion of the intestine from its proper location within the abdominal cavity. The most common site for such protrusions is in the groin, where they may extend into the scrotum. Usually such hernias are easily reduced (pushed back into the abdomen) and have existed for months or even years. The hernia itself does not constitute an emergency, but the involved intestine may be trapped in the abnormal position, resulting in intestinal obstruction.

The surgical repair of a hernia is a relatively minor operation and should be carried out whenever a hernia is detected, particularly before a mountaineering outing.

A patient with an incarcerated hernia usually has a history of a hernia which has always been easily reduced, but has become unreducible and very painful. The resulting intestinal obstruction causes vomiting, abdominal distension, and cessation of bowel movements. An obvious swollen, tender mass is usually present in the groin or scrotum. The abdomen may be distended and the patient may be vomiting (see "Intestinal Obstruction").

Treatment consists first of trying to reduce the hernia. The patient should be flat on his back, preferably with his head and chest lower than his abdomen so gravity can help return the intestine into the abdominal cavity. If the patient is tense and straining, morphine should be given to produce relaxation and thus help reduce the hernia. Moderate, steady pressure on the hernia for ten minutes or longer may ultimately make the mass of intestine pop back into the abdominal cavity through the narrow neck of the sac and temporarily relieve the emergency.

If the hernia cannot be reduced, the mass remains tender and inflamed, and the patient keeps vomiting and getting sicker. The bowel often becomes gan-

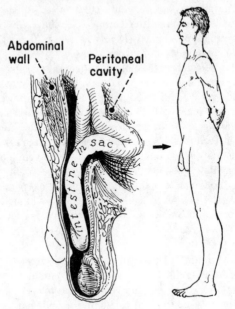

Figure 53. Anatomy of an inguinal hernia.

grenous. Immediate evacuation of the patient is mandatory. During evacuation the patient should be treated for intestinal obstruction. Intravenous fluids are required if evacuation takes more than thirty-six to forty-eight hours.

Occasionally the intestine is already gangrenous when the hernia is reduced. Therefore, anyone who develops an incarcerated hernia which is later reduced must be closely watched for at least twenty-four hours for signs of peritonitis, intestinal obstruction, or both. Symptoms should disappear rather promptly after reduction of the hernia. If relief does not occur, gangrene of the intestine should be suspected and the victim evacuated. On short outings the victim should be evacuated regardless of subsequent developments.

Acute Gallbladder Disease

The gallbladder is a sac-like organ on the undersurface of the liver in which bile is stored until it is secreted into the small intestine. For reasons that are poorly understood, the bile salts may be precipitated, forming gall stones. Subsequent contractions of the gallbladder to expel bile into the intestine are painful.

This condition, known as chronic cholecystitis or chronic gallbladder disease, is characterized by recurrent episodes of colicky pain and tenderness in the right upper quadrant of the abdomen. These attacks are rarely associated with jaundice. The ingestion of fried or fatty foods is usually associated with belching, indigestion, and abdominal pain.

A patient with acute gallbladder disease usually has a history of chronic cholecystitis. However, in an acute attack he typically suffers the rather sudden onset of a much more severe, sharp pain, located immediately below the ribs on the right. The pain may be intermittent or continuous, and may radiate through to the back or the shoulder blades. Vomiting is common; diarrhea is rare. The patient appears obviously ill and is frequently jaundiced. The urine is often dark and the stools may be light grey or clay-colored, particularly two to three days after the onset.

Right upper quadrant abdominal tenderness is present and may be very well localized. The points of maximum tenderness, rebound tenderness, and referred pain are all in the right upper quadrant. The temperature may be slightly elevated (99° - 101°F).

Treatment consists of rest with nothing being given by mouth until vomiting stops. Then only clear liquids should be ingested. All fried or fatty foods, including milk, must be avoided. Meperidine or morphine intramuscularly usually is required to control the pain. Meperidine is preferable. In an isolated area, ampicillin should be given intramuscularly every six hours as long as the pain continues.

The attack usually subsides spontaneously within one to two days. If the patient has had previous attacks, he may even be allowed to continue climbing after he has regained his strength. However, the safest course is for the patient to be evacuated, particularly if jaundice is present. Although most patients with acute gallbladder disease do not require emergency surgery, a few do need such therapy. Moving the patient to a physician is the safest and most conservative course. Occasionally gallbladder colic may be difficult to differentiate from appendicitis, pancreatitis, or a perforated ulcer.

Acute Pancreatitis

Acute pancreatitis is a severe inflammation of unknown cause involving the pancreas, an organ located in the upper portion of the abdomen behind the stomach. Some individuals suffer recurrent attacks of this disorder, which is one of the most painful diseases that afflicts man.

Pancreatitis typically develops after a heavy meal or the ingestion of large amounts of alcohol, but may appear at any time. The pain is located in the upper part of the abdomen in the midline or on the left side, but frequently radiates through to the back and to the shoulder blades. The onset is relatively rapid, building up to peak intensity over a few minutes to a few hours, but is not as abrupt as the onset of symptoms of a perforated ulcer. Loss of appetite is almost invariable; nauses and vomiting are usually present; diarrhea is rare.

In severe cases prostration and shock are prominent. The patient is frequently cyanotic and has a rapid pulse and a low blood pressure. Fever is usually present, particularly in severe cases, varies from 100° to 103°F, and persists as long as the disease is active.

Upper abdominal tenderness is almost always present. However, spasm of the abdominal muscles and rebound tenderness may be rather mild because the stomach is interposed between the pancreas and the abdominal wall.

Acute pancreatitis may be difficult to distinguish from acute inflammation of the gallbladder. In addition to a more rapid onset, the location of maximum pain and tenderness in the midline or on the left side of the upper abdomen rather than the right, and the presence of severe prostration and shock, pancreatitis is also characterized by the frequent failure of narcotics to completely relieve the pain. However, many patients with pancreatitis do have a history suggestive of previous gallbladder disease, incuding intolerance for fried or fatty foods.

Therapy for pancreatitis consists of rapid evacuation, efforts to relieve the pain, inactivation of the gastrointestinal system, and general care of the patient. Although the treatment of acute pancreatitis does not require surgery, it does require expert medical care. This disease causes an appreciable number of deaths, even with the best treatment currently available. Furthermore, complications which require a physician's attention are relatively common. Therefore, evacuation is essential.

Meperidine or morphine (preferably meperidine) should be administered intramuscularly every three to four hours for pain. Nitroglycerin tablets sublingually every two to three hours may provide some relief and should be given in conjunction with meperidine.

Nothing should be given by mouth and nasogastric suction should be instituted if possible. An antispasmodic given intramuscularly every four hours reduces stomach activity and diminishes the secretory activity of the pancreas. To maintain fluid balance the daily fluid needs as well as the replacement for losses due to vomiting or gastric suction should be given intravenously. Shock should be treated in the same manner as shock from other causes.

Peritonitis

A number of intra-abdominal catastrophies produce gross infection of the abdominal cavity (peritonitis). The appearance of patients with peritonitis is similar regardless of the underlying cause.

The patient lies very quietly, since motion is quite painful. He is pale, febrile — with a temperature usually over 101° F, and is obviously very sick. The appetite is entirely gone, the patient is usually nauseated, and he may be vomiting.

The abdomen may be somewhat distended and is diffusely tender and firm to palpation. No bowel sounds can be heard and the patient does not pass any flatus.

Signs and symptoms of the disease causing the infection are also present.

The patient must be evacuated — by stretcher — as rapidly as possible. During evacuation he should be made comfortable with morphine or meperidine, given nothing by mouth, and kept supine, warm, and quiet. Gentamicin and clindamycin should be administered intramuscularly or intravenously every six hours. Nasogastric suction should be instituted if gastric distention develops. Intravenous fluid administration is required if evacuation takes over thirty-six hours. All fluids lost by vomiting or nasogastric suction should be replaced with Ringer's lactate.

Kidney Stone

Occasionally minerals are precipitated from the urine and deposited in the kidney where they form a mass known as a kidney stone. This stone may be swept into the bladder by the urinary stream, causing excruciating pain as it passes through the duct (ureter) that connects the kidney with the bladder.

The symptoms produced by a kidney stone usually appear suddenly and are characterized by sharp, stabbing pain which may come and go in waves of increasing intensity. The pain usually begins in the back at the level of the lowest ribs, but frequently radiates around the side to the lower abdomen and into the groin or scrotum. The patient typically writhes in pain and is unable to lie still.

Bright red blood is often found in the urine but may be present in only small amounts (see "Genitourinary Tract Diseases"). Pain on urination and increased frequency of urination are common. Nausea, vomiting, and cold sweats are commonly present; chills and fever may be present but are not typical.

A kidney stone rarely requires emergency surgical care and is not associated with any danger of severe blood loss. The pain may last for twenty-four hours or more but usually subsides spontaneously in a shorter period of time as the stone is passed into the bladder.

Morphine or meperidine should be given intramuscularly every four hours to afford relief from the pain (complete masking of the pain may not be achieved). If the patient is not vomiting he should drink as much water as possible to help flush out the stone.

Following subsidence of the pain, the likelihood of a subsequent attack is slight. The victim can resume his usual activities as soon as he feels capable. However, if the stone is not passed and pain continues for forty-eight hours or more the patient should be evacuated. Serious renal damage can result if the stone remains impacted in the ureter, causing obstruction to the flow of urine.

CHAPTER 22

Genitourinary Diseases

ACUTE URINARY TRACT DISORDERS

THE URINARY tract is composed of the kidneys, ureters, urinary bladder, and urethra. The genital system includes the ovaries, fallopian tubes, uterus, vagina, and external genitalia in females, and the testes, epididymides, vas deferens, seminal vesicles, prostate gland, and external genitalia in males. The kidneys filter waste products from the blood and excrete them along with excess water. The urine is transported by the ureters from the kidneys to the urinary bladder where it is held until voided through the urethra. Approximately one cubic centimeter of urine is formed per minute. At this rate about sixty cc or two ounces per hour, and 1,500 cc or one and one-half quarts per day are excreted. Dehydration reduces urine volume; over-hydration increases urinary output.

The most common symptoms of acute urinary tract diseases are: back or flank pain, burning with urination, bloody urine, and changes in urine volume. The pain is characteristically located in the middle of the back or slightly to one side at the point where the lowest ribs join the vertebral column, but frequently radiates to the sides, just above the pelvis, and around to the groin. Such pain is usually a symptom of kidney disease.

The sensation of burning during voiding is unmistakable. Occasionally the patient may complain that he feels like he is passing gravel. Such symptoms are usually the result of disease of the urinary bladder, prostate, or urethra.

Bleeding may result in obviously bloody urine or may produce only cloudy or smoky urine. However, if the urine is allowed to stand so the sediment can settle out, a red sludge forms at the bottom of the container, confirming the presence of blood. Even small amounts of bleeding can be detected in this way.

Changes in urinary volume, except for very large deviations, usually go unnoticed unless the urinary output is measured. In mountaineering circumstances dehydration is by far the most common cause for a decreased urinary output. However, some renal diseases can result in almost total cessation of kidney function and almost no urine production.

254

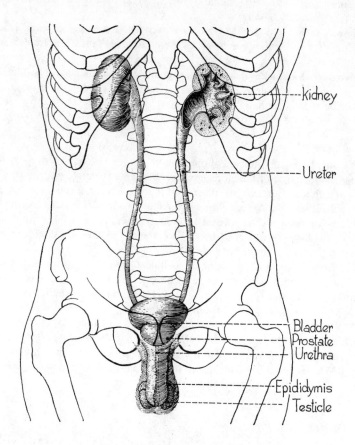

Figure 54. Anatomy of the urinary and male genital systems.

Cystitis

Cystitis is an inflammation of the urinary bladder which can occur with or without a concurrent infection. This disorder is rare in young males, but is not at all uncommon in females. When cystitis is associated with pyelonephritis, symptoms of the latter disease predominate.

The primary symptom of cystitis is burning or pain during voiding. The pain may increase somewhat as the bladder is emptied but disappears gradually after the flow is stopped. The frequency of voiding also is increased. Fever, a feeling of being ill, or any other symptoms are rare, although slight or moderate bleeding sometimes occurs, and rarely bleeding may be severe enough to make the urine obviously bloody.

Ampicillin or sulfisoxazole, which are excreted by the kidneys and reach rather high concentrations in the urine, should be given orally four times a day for at least one week or until the patient has been completely free of symptoms for two days, if that takes longer. The victim must also drink large quantities of fluids, considerably more than the usual requirements. Strenuous exertion should be avoided, although moderate exercise is tolerated reasonably well.

Pyelonephritis

Pyelonephritis, an infection of one or both kidneys, is characterized by the rather sudden onset of a high fever which is often associated with chills. The patient feels and appears quite ill. Pain of moderate severity is usually present just to the side of the spinal column in the midportion of the back. Pressing or gentle pounding with the fist just below the lower rib on either side of the vertebral column reveals tenderness. Symptoms of cystitis are often present, and slight to moderate bleeding may occur.

The patient should rest as much as possible. Copious quantities of fluids, at least twice the daily requirement, must be ingested. Fluid intake and urinary output must be measured and recorded. Evacuation from altitudes above 10,000 to 12,000 feet is desirable but not mandatory.

Antibacterial therapy is important. Ampicillin or sulfisoxazole should be given orally every six hours, and should be continued for five days after all signs of the disease have disappeared or for a minimum of ten days. Individuals with repeated episodes of pyelonephritis should consult their physician as irreversible kidney disease can result.

Acute Renal Failure

Renal failure, or the cessation of renal function, occasionally occurs following a severe injury, particularly if the victim is in shock for several hours or longer. (Certain poisons and allergic reactions to drugs can also cause acute renal failure.) If the patient can be kept alive through the period of nonfunction, which may last from a few days to several months, complete recovery is frequently possible.

The principle manifestation of renal failure is reduced urinary output. Dehydration may also cause a low urinary output. However, if a dehydrated subject is given fluids the urinary volume rises. The victim of acute renal failure cannot increase his urinary output, no matter how much fluid he is given. Any adequately hydrated subject with a urinary output less than 400 cc per day following a severe injury should be considered to be in renal failure.

Weakness, loss of appetite, nausea, vomiting, diarrhea, muscle twitching, confusion, convulsions, and eventually coma appear some time after the onset of renal failure. Usually the victim has no symptoms the first two or three days. However, weakness becomes apparent on about the third day and the other symptoms follow in short order.

Urinary retention due to spasm of the bladder muscles or rupture of the urinary bladder may simulate renal failure because there is no urinary output. However, urinary retention is usually accompanied by a strong urge to urinate as well as pain in the bladder or lower abdomen. If urethral catheterization discloses the bladder to be empty, urinary retention can be ruled out. Following bladder rupture evidence of an abdominal or pelvic injury as well as abdominal pain and tenderness are usually obvious (see "Abdominal Injuries"). However, acute renal failure can also be associated with an injury in which the bladder is ruptured.

Evacuation is urgent. Only a well-equipped medical center has the facilities to keep a victim of acute renal failure alive for more than a few days. Some form of dialysis equipment (artificial kidney) is usually essential. During evacuation fluid intake must be carefully controlled to prevent the patient from literally drowning in his own body liquids. To establish the diagnosis, the patient's previous state of hydration must be evaluated. If it appears that he probably was dehydrated, enough fluids must be given to at least partially correct that situation. If renal output does not return, subsequent fluid administration must be carried out very cautiously. Each day's fluid intake should be limited to one quart plus the total volume of fluids lost in the urine, by sweating, and through the lungs — if these losses are abnormally high — in the previous twenty-four hours. The patient should be encouraged to eat sweets such as hard candy or glucose tablets. However, fruit juices must be avoided as they contain potassium which is highly toxic for a subject with reduced renal function.

If the patient is not able to take fluids orally, intravenous therapy must be used. The quart of water, the previous day's urinary output, and the estimated losses through the lungs should be given as five or ten percent glucose solution. Fluids lost through vomiting and excessive sweating should be replaced with Ringer's lactate. To insure that replacement is given in exactly the amounts which have been lost, urinary output, loss from other sources, and oral or intravenous intake must be carefully measured.

Medications should be avoided if possible, since most drugs are excreted by the kidneys. In the absence of renal excretion the concentration of such drugs in the body can rapidly build up to toxic levels.

Acute Glomerulonephritis

Glomerulonephritis is a disease of the kidneys which usually follows a "strep throat" or some other streptococcal infection by a few days or a few weeks. This disorder appears to be caused — in a currently unknown manner — by an allergy to streptococcal bacteria. Since the advent of antibiotics, the incidence of glomerulonephritis has been reduced through treatment of the initial streptococcal infection with penicillin. This disorder is important because a small percentage of patients have severe, even fatal, renal disease.

In mild cases, which are more common, swelling or puffiness of the face, blood in the urine, and headache are the most common symptoms. More severe cases are also characterized by edema, visual disturbances, delirium, convulsions and coma. A low fever, loss of appetite, and nausea and vomiting may be present in mild or severe cases.

Puffiness or swelling of the face, which is the most common symptom, may be noticed by someone other than the victim. The swelling is more striking early in the morning when the victim first awakens and is particularly prominent about the eyes. High blood pressure is present in a fairly large number of cases and can be detected with a sphygmomanometer. Swelling of the feet and ankles may also be present.

Blood in the urine may be grossly visible, but is more frequently detectable only after the red blood cells have been permitted to settle to the bottom of the container. Protein is almost always present in the urine in acute glomerulonephritis. Boiling the urine causes the protein to form a thick, floculant coagulum which can be easily identified.

Few cases of nephritis manifest all these signs and symptoms. The presence of even one or two of them should serve as an indication to search for others and to restrict the activities of the patient.

Evacuation is desirable, but in a truly remote area may not be mandatory if the patient can maintain a urinary output of more than 500 cc per day. The patient should rest as much as possible. Salt, which tends to promote the formation of edema fluid, should be restricted.

Penicillin, four times a day, should be given for ten days in case a lingering streptococcal infection is present elsewhere in the body. Treatment for renal failure should be instituted if urine volume falls below 400 cc per twenty-four hours and no other cause can be found. Death is most commonly the result of heart failure. If edema, shortness of breath, or other evidence of heart disease appears, the patient must be evacuated.

OTHER URINARY TRACT DISORDERS

Renal Stones

Since the characteristic symptom of renal stones is severe pain, this disorder is discussed in "Acute Abdominal Pain." However, bloody urine and burning with voiding can also accompany the passage of a stone.

Hematuria

Hematuria, which means bloody urine, may be associated with traumatic injuries, tuberculosis, or tumors of the urinary tract, as well as the disorders already discussed. Traumatic urinary disorders are discussed in the chapter "Abdominal Injuries." Adequate treatment for tuberculosis or tumors is impossible in the field. Therefore, the appearance of obvious bloody urine, particularly in the absence of signs or symptoms of any other disorder, should prompt immediate medical consultation in order to determine the cause and institute appropriate therapy. Obvious hematuria is frequently a sign of a serious disorder. (The loss of blood itself is almost never of sufficient volume to be disabling.)

Hemoglobinuria

Severe injuries, burns, severe infections, and other disorders cause the destruction of red blood cells. As these cells are broken down the hemoglobin pigment they contain is released into the blood stream and is excreted by the kidneys. Urine containing this pigment is faint pink to deep red in color and resembles bloody urine. However, if the urine is permitted to stand, little or no blood settles to the bottom of the container.

Hemoglobinuria must be distinguished from hematuria which is caused by entirely different conditions. Renal failure sometimes follows disorders producing hemoglobinuria.

Occasionally strenuous exercise alone results in hemoglobinuria. This condition is usually benign and disappears with rest, although the subject must be sure to maintain a generous fluid intake. The pigment from some foods or dyes, particularly beets, occasionally imparts a reddish color to the urine. However, the patient can usually remember the ingestion of these substances, and the pigment disappears from the urine within a few hours or days.

FEMALE GENITAL PROBLEMS

Although gynecological problems are common and widely variable, few appear so rapidly they could create problems on a mountaineering outing. An examination by a physician beforehand should disclose any potential disorders and permit their correction before the outing is underway.

Two problems which could occur are dysmenorrhea and abnormal bleeding.

Dysmenorrhea

Dysmenorrhea means painful menstruation. The pain can be caused by many different abnormalities, including a wrongly positioned uterus and the passage of blood clots. Most women with dysmenorrhea have had it most of their postpubertal lives. Such pain encountered for the first time on a mountaineering outing must be most unusual. In fact, exercise is one of the remedies sometimes effective for dysmenorrhea.

The pain is typically a cramping pain associated with menstruation. The pain may be disabling, but usually is less severe. It may be worst the first day or two of the menstrual period and then ease off. Treatment with aspirin and codeine every four hours is usually sufficient. Diminished physical activity may also be of some benefit. Women bothered with this problem — and they are numerous — have usually learned to deal with it effectively long before it could create difficulties in a mountaineering situation.

Abnormal Bleeding

Abnormal uterine bleeding can take the form of excessive bleeding with menstrual periods or bleeding between periods, or both. Numerous disorders can cause such abnormal bleeding, but most commonly no clear-cut cause can be found. No specific treatment can be given under mountaineering situations. The bleeding is rarely severe enough to create a problem related to blood loss. Rest may be all that is needed to eliminate the problem. If a hemorrhage of massive proportions does occur, packing the vagina with tampons, gauze, or anything else available may help slow down the bleeding during evacuation, although complete control of bleeding by such means probably cannot be obtained. Such problems must be exceedingly rare; exercise seems to help control abnormal bleeding for many women.

PREGNANCY

Pregnancy does not necessarily require any curtailment of a woman's *customary* activities, but prudence does indicate some precautions should be observed in regard to mountaineering. During the first three months of pregnancy the risk of abortion is greatest. More than ten percent of all pregnancies result in spontaneous abortion, and abortion is occasionally associated with severe, even massive hemorrhage. Such hemorrhage usually cannot be successfully treated without hospital facilities. Therefore, a woman in this stage of pregnancy should probably not enter an area so remote that evacuation within twelve to twenty-four hours by stretcher could not be fairly readily accomplished.

During the last three months of pregnancy, the enlarged uterus and the baby it contains often cause problems with balance. Climbing that requires balance, such as a steep snow-covered ridge or face, may be unusually difficult. Falls, particularly if held by a rope tied with a conventional waist loop, may result in injury to the mother, baby, or both, even though such falls would not injure a woman who was not pregnant. Premature labor, whether caused by a fall or occurring spontaneously, could result in delivery in less than optimal circumstances, or the birth of a small immature baby who could not survive without the facilities available in a hospital.

Occasionally pregnancy creates or aggravates other medical problems such as diabetes, hypertension, or cardiac disease. The mother should consult her physician for any special care such problems would require on a mountaineering outing.

Contraceptives

One aspect of pregnancy, its prevention, does have direct implications for high altitude mountaineering. The oral contraceptives appear to cause an increased incidence of venous thromboses resulting in pulmonary embolism. High altitude mountaineering also predisposes climbers to the development of this frequently fatal disorder (see "Respiratory Diseases"). Women who are planning a mountaineering outing involving a prolonged stay at altitudes above 12,000 to 14,000 feet should discontinue oral contraceptives at least several weeks in advance of the outing. If some other form of contraception is needed and a mechanical intrauterine contraceptive device (IUD) is selected, it should be inserted long enough in advance of the outing to be sure it is well tolerated. Rarely these devices cause perforation, bleeding, or infection which could be difficult or impossible to control in mountaineering circumstances. However, many of these problems do show up during the first few months the devices are used.

MALE GENITAL PROBLEMS

Few male genital problems appear with sufficient speed or at such an age that they are likely to cause difficulties in a mountaineering situation. Two exceptions are acute epididymitis and torsion of the testis, two entirely different disorders which are discussed together since their features are similar and differentiation may be quite difficult, even for a physician.

Epididymitis and Testicular Torsion

Epididymitis is an inflammation of the epididymis, a part of the testicle in which sperm are collected before passing on through the vas deferens to the seminal vesicle where they are stored prior to ejaculation. Epididymitis sometimes is the result of gonorrheal infection, the organisms presumably passing backwards from the urethra through the vas deferens. Rarely are cultures taken from the inflamed tissues, and it appears likely that most cases of epididymitis have no relation to a venereal infection. Many cases may not be the result of infection at all.

Torsion of the testis refers to twisting of the testis within the scrotum. The twisting movement involves the spermatic cord which contains the vas deferens and the arteries and veins supplying the testis. As the spermatic cord is twisted the blood vessels, particularly the veins, are occluded. If the occlusion is not relieved, which usually requires surgery, the testis which has been deprived of its blood supply dies within about six hours. Most cases of testicular torsion involve only one testis and the individual suffers no diminution in fertility or male hormone levels. Also, most cases of testicular torsion involve an abnormality in the attachments of the testis to other structures within the scrotum. Without this abnormality, which is probably present at birth, torsion could not occur. Since the abnormality is present at birth, torsion usually occurs during childhood and not at an age at which it could produce problems on most mountaineering outings. At the time of surgery to remove a dead testis which has undergone torsion, some type of procedure to anchor the opposite testis within the scrotum and prevent it from twisting is usually carried out.

The presence of these disorders is quite obvious as they are both quite painful. The testis is usually swollen and quite tender. A firm nodular epididymis may be felt with epididymitis. The skin of the scrotum is often distended and may also be red and inflamed, particularly with epididymitis.

The patient should rest as much as possible. In urban surroundings many physicians keep their patients with epididymitis confined to bed. Such confinement is usually not difficult to impose because the disorder is so painful. Elevation of the scrotum and the application of ice packs are frequently helpful with epididymitis, but elevation of the scrotum usually does not help relieve the pain of testicular torsion, a point of difference between the two disorders which may be helpful in diagnosis. (With testicular torsion, the testis may appear to be higher in the scrotum.) If a fever is present, indicating the existence of an infection, tetracycline should be administered. If the patient has a history of gonorrhea or exposure to gonorrhea within the previous two months and he is not allergic to penicillin, that drug should be given instead of tetracycline. The dosage should be the same as that used to treat gonorrhea. If patients with testicular torsion cannot be evacuated right away, they should probably receive antibiotics also to prevent the establishment of an infection in the dead tissue of the twisted testis.

Most patients with either of these disorders should be evacuated. Patients with testicular torsion require surgery, even if they cannot reach a physician's care quickly enough to save the twisted testis. Patients with epididymitis require rest, antibiotics, and usually a considerable amount of time for the disorder to heal. Resumption of activity before all symptoms have completely cleared frequently re-activates the disease. Two to three weeks may be required for complete healing. However, epididymitis, although painful, poses little threat of spread of the infection to other areas, and patients with this disorder could probably be adequately treated in base camp if they were in a truly remote situation.

VENEREAL DISEASES

The venereal diseases are a group of infectious diseases spread by sexual contact – both homosexual and heterosexual. A number of disorders caused by viruses as well as bacteria are included in these diseases. Syphilis and gonorrhea are the most common of these infections and the only two for which completely satisfactory treatment is currently available. This discussion is limited to these two disorders.

All venereal diseases are spread by intimate personal contact. Infection from "toilet seats" or similar sources essentially does not occur because the organisms cannot survive well enough outside the body to produce infection by such means.

At the present time the only dependable way to prevent such infections is by avoiding sexual contact with infected individuals. Condoms are of only limited value in preventing infection. Prophylactic antibiotic therapy has many disadvantages as well as the significant hazard of allergic reactions to the drugs.

Syphilis

Syphilis is produced by infection with the spirochete *Treponema pallidum*. This disease has an intriguing history. It apparently originated in the western hemisphere, was transported to Europe by members of Columbus' crew, and in an amazingly short time was spread all over the world. The great variation in its clinical features, long duration, and potential for involving any of the body's organs and mimicking almost any other disease have held a great fascination for medical researchers. The discovery of penicillin therapy for this infection was a dramatic medical triumph. Some investigators feel that the treatment used before penicillin probably never cured a single case of syphilis. In contrast, not a single example of syphilis resistant to penicillin has been found.

Syphilitic infections follow three stages. The primary stage consists of the chancre, a one-quarter to one-half inch ulcer which appears generally at the site of infection. A characteristic and striking feature of this ulcer is that it is usually painless. Most chancres appear on the genitalia, but they are occasionally found on the mouth or lips, or the skin of other parts of the body. In women, chancres may be located within the vagina or on the uterine cervix and may not be visible to external examination. Sometimes primary chancres do not appear or go unnoticed, particularly when in a hidden location like the vagina.

The secondary stage of syphilis is characterized by the appearance of a skin rash about six weeks after the primary lesion. The apperance of this rash is highly variable, although it does not produce blisters, and it usually has a wide distribution including the palms and soles of the feet and the mucous membranes of the mouth. The rash does not itch and generally is symptomless. It usually lasts from a few days to a few weeks, but may not appear at all.

In its third or tertiary stage syphilis can affect any organ or tissue, and can produce fatal cardiac disease or disabling brain disease. However, tertiary syphilis takes years to develop — usually more than ten — and can be prevented by appropriate therapy.

A precise diagnosis of syphilis requires laboratory facilities not available even in most hospitals. Therefore treatment is generally based on a history of sexual contact and the presence of skin changes suggestive of a primary chancre or the secondary skin rash. The infection is most contagious during the primary and secondary stages.

The treatment of choice is the administration of penicillin. Benzathine penicillin G, a single injection of 1.2 million units (750 mg) in each buttock, is preferred in most urban settings because it insures that adequate treatment has been given regardless of whether the patient returns for further injections. Alternately, single daily intramuscular injections of 600,000 units (375 mg) of aqueous procaine penicillin G may be given for a period of ten days. Individuals allergic to penicillin can be treated with tetracycline, 0.5 gram four times a day for fifteen days. Follow-up care should be obtained from a physician after the mountaineering outing is over to be sure the infection has been totally eradicated.

Gonorrhea

Gonorrhea is an epidemic disease with an estimated three million cases in the United States and 150 million throughout the world in 1974. The infection in males is usually limited to the lower genital tract, principally the urethra. The urethral infection is associated with a small amount of purulent urethral discharge, but the characteristic symptom is pain with voiding which often is severe. The infection usually clears up after seven to ten days, but treatment should be administered regardless. Residual infection may persist, particularly in the prostate, or the infection may spread to other parts of the body.

In females, gonorrhea is a much more insidious infection. Seventy-five percent of infected women have no initial symptoms at all. The infection usually must be diagnosed by bacterial cultures from the vagina or uterine cervix. Treatment must be based on a history of sexual contact with a possibly infected individual in the absence of laboratory facilities for a definitive diagnosis. However, gonorrhea is a much more threatening disorder in females. Spread of the infection to other organs is much more common. Infection of the uterus and fallopian tubes can be very painful, causing symptoms highly suggestive of appendicitis (see Pelvic Inflammatory Disease in "Acute Abdominal Pain"), and can result in permanent sterility. Spread to other areas can produce destructive arthritis, disabling cardiac disease, or other serious damage.

The treatment of choice is penicillin. Procaine penicillin G 2.4 million units (1.5 gm), should be injected intramuscularly for two days or every other day for two doses. For individuals allergic to penicillin, tetracycline — 0.5 gm four times a day for at least four days — can be substituted. Follow-up care should be obtained from a physician after the mountaineering outing to insure no residual infection persists.

All patients with suspected or known venereal disease should consult a physician and receive appropriate therapy. The results of an untreated infection can be disastrous. The ease with which syphilis and gonorrhea can be successfully treated has caused a lack of concern about all venereal diseases. To encourage individuals to obtain the treatment they need, many states have recently changed their laws to permit physicians to treat minors with such infections without reporting the disease to the patient's parents or guardians.

CHAPTER 23

Diseases of the Nervous System

THE NERVOUS system is made up of the brain, the spinal cord, and the peripheral nerves. The brain and spinal cord are referred to as the central nervous system. Almost everything that happens in the body — voluntary and involuntary movements, respiration, blood circulation, even endocrine function — is controlled or regulated by the nervous system.

The diseases of this complex system are numerous and often disabling. However, most of these diseases are of a chronic nature and come on too slowly to create serious problems in mountaineering circumstances, even on expeditions lasting several months.

Signs and Symptoms

Diseases of the nervous system may cause altered intellectual function, impaired control of movements (motor disturbances), sensory disorders, loss of function of specific nerves, and a group of unrelated, less specific signs.

Alterations of intellectual function produce personality changes — most commonly increased irritability — and impairment in the patient's contact with his surroundings, such as confusion, hallucinations, delirium, or complete loss of consciousness (coma).

Motor disturbances may result in loss of coordination — causing the patient to stumble or fall repeatedly or to move clumsily — weakness, convulsions, or total paralysis.

Sensory disturbances which may occur include total anesthesis, tingling sensations and prickly feelings (commonly encountered when a limb "goes to sleep"), or loss of the sense of position in the fingers, toes, or even entire limbs. (Anesthesia involving an entire limb or portion of a limb in "stocking" fashion with a sharp margin of demarcation circling the limb is usually due to hysteria rather than organic disease. The distribution of the nerves is such that this pattern of anesthesia is produced only by emotional disorders.)

The loss of function of individual nerves originating in the brain can cause many varied symptoms. Disorders involving the nerves to the eye may cause blindness — occasionally limited to only a portion of the field of vision — double vision, or blurred vision. Impairment of the nerves to the eye muscles causes paralysis of eye movements. The pupils may fail to contract when exposed to light or may differ greatly in size. (Minor differences in pupillary size are normal in some individuals.)

Disorders of the nerves to the muscles of the face cause weakness or paralysis of facial movements and drooling on the affected side. Swallowing is impaired when the nerves to the muscles of the throat are affected, resulting in fluids being regurgitated through the nose or aspirated into the lungs. Involvement of the nerves to the ear can cause hearing loss, ringing or buzzing in the ears, or vertigo. Damage to other nerves may cause loss of smell, loss of taste, severe facial pain, weakness of the muscles of the neck, or impairment of respiration.

Damage to the nerves originating in the spinal cord causes paralysis or sensory disturbances in the portion of the body supplied by the injured nerve. Reflexes, such as the knee jerk, are often lost.

Other symptoms associated with nervous system diseases include nausea and vomiting, the latter often occurring without warning. Headache, which is discussed below, may accompany diseases of any organ; when associated with nervous system disease it is usually quite severe. Fever with central nervous system infections is often quite high; in other nervous system disorders the temperature is normal or only slightly elevated. Blood clots within the skull often cause a slower pulse rate and a wider separation of diastolic and systolic blood pressures than normal.

COMMON NERVOUS SYSTEM DISORDERS

The common nervous system disorders are usually not very serious and are frequently quite short in duration.

Headache

Headache is a very common ailment suffered by all but a very few fortunate individuals. Rarely can any specific cause for a headache be identified. Therefore, this disorder is frequently thought of as a disease in itself, although it is often only a symptom of another illness.

Headache after a rapid ascent to high altitude is quite common. Although most individuals have no symptoms other than headache, this is probably a mild form of the disorder that occasionally progresses to high altitude pulmonary edema or other less severe forms of acute mountain sickness.

The pain of a headache may be located in the back of the neck, behind the eyes, or all areas in between. Little significance can be attached to the location of the pain except for those cases in which it is limited to one side of the head. Unilateral headaches are frequently caused by a vascular disorder such as migraine.

A severe, persistent headache in an individual who usually does not suffer from headaches may be a sign of serious disease. Headache associated with confusion, forgetfulness, dizziness, nausea and vomiting, and occasionally convulsions or loss of consciousness, may be the result of an acute increase in blood pressure (hypertensive encephalopathy). This disorder usually occurs in persons with pre-existing hypertension, but requires prompt treatment to avoid brain damage which can be disastrous (see "Diseases of the Heart and Blood Vessels"). Headache associated with fever and a stiff neck are characteristic of meningitis. Following a head injury, headache of increasing severity may be indicative of the development of a blood clot within the skull (see "Injuries of the Head and Neck").

Aspirin every four hours relieves the pain of most headaches; aspirin and codeine every three or four hours is adequate for most of the remainder. Any underlying disease causing the headache must obviously receive appropriate treatment.

Individuals with frequent headaches should consult a physician. Headaches resulting from vascular disorders can often be treated very successfully. Some other causes of recurrent headaches, such as brain tumors or high blood pressure, are quite serious.

Fainting

Fainting is a common disorder which usually is not a sign of serious disease. It can follow strong emotion or pain and sometimes appears to occur almost spontaneously. Even when fainting is the result of disease, it is rarely a sign of a disease involving the nervous system. Fainting occurs following the dilatation of numerous peripheral blood vessels, particularly those in the muscles. As the blood fills these vessels, the blood supply to the brain is reduced, resulting in unconsciousness.

The episode of unconsciousness is usually preceded by a period of a few seconds to several minutes in which the person feels weak. This weakness is often accompanied by restlessness and occasionally by nausea. The victim frequently breaks out in a "cold sweat" in which his body is covered with perspiration but the skin feels cold and clammy. He appears quite pale and his pulse is rapid.

These signs and symptoms are similar to those of shock. However, in fainting the physiological derangements are not as severe as they are in shock and there is rarely any underlying illness which could be expected to produce shock.

If a person notices the onset of the symptoms which precede fainting he can usually avoid the period of unconsciousness. He must get off his feet — either by sitting or lying down — to avoid injury from falling. His head should be lower than the rest of his body so that gravity can help increase the flow of blood to the brain. The head can be placed between the knees, or preferably, the victim can lie down with the feet elevated. Help should be obtained if possible.

In taking care of someone who has fainted or is about to faint the same measures should be carried out. Maintaining an open airway is rarely a problem because unconsciousness is almost never very deep. No medications are necessary. Aromatic spirits of ammonia are of no real benefit and probably should not be used to avoid injuring the nasal mucosa. Any injuries resulting from falling should receive appropriate attention.

Unconsciousness rarely lasts more than a few minutes. (Persistent coma is a sign of a more serious disorder.) As soon as the victim feels well he can be on his way again, although he should sit up for a few minutes first and then stand up slowly and carefully. If the victim has not eaten for some time, he should try to obtain food or some beverage containing sugar, such as orange juice.

A single episode of fainting is rarely significant. Repeated episodes can be indicative of a serious underlying disease.

Convulsions

Convulsions often are a sign of disease of the nervous system and commonly occur during infections involving the brain or following brain injuries. However, convulsions also occur during the course of diseases which affect the brain only indirectly. Convulsions associated with renal failure are not at all uncommon. Occasionally a person suffers a single convulsion for which no cause can be determined and which never recurs.

Epilepsy is a condition in which a person suffers repeated convulsions over a long period of time. Sometimes a cause for these episodes can be found, but more commonly the etiology remains undetermined. However, epilepsy can usually be controlled regardless of whether the cause is known. Convulsions rarely recur as long as the person follows his prescribed treatment diligently.

A person with epilepsy need not refrain from mountaineering or similar activities provided his disorder is completely controlled and he is conscientious about keeping up with his medications. In fairness to his companions and the interest of his own well-being, his fellow climbers should be informed of his condition so they can learn in advance what measures to take should a convulsion occur. The stigma formerly attached to convulsions and particularly epilepsy are now generally recognized to be completely unwarranted.

The onset of a convulsion is usually sudden and may be marked by an outcry of some kind. The victim characteristically loses consciousness and falls to the ground, his body twisting and writhing and all four limbs twitching and jerking. The jaw may be involved also and the victim can badly injure his tongue by biting. He may salivate profusely resulting in drooling and frothing; he may defecate or void uncontrollably.

In any single convulsive episode all or none of these features may be present. Sometimes the victim exhibits only a slight twitching of the extremities. A person who is unconscious from a head injury may exhibit only a series of jerking movements which gradually increase in intensity and then subside. If one or more limbs has been paralyzed as a result of the injury, it is not involved in the movements.

The convulsion usually lasts only one or two minutes, but can persist for five minutes or even longer. A period of unconsciousness follows which lasts from a few minutes to several hours and may be a very deep coma in which the victim is almost completely unresponsive, even to painful stimuli.

Essentially nothing can be done to shorten or terminate the convulsive episode. However, the victim should be prevented from injuring himself. A folded handkerchief or similar padded object should be placed between his teeth to protect his tongue from being bitten. Clothing around his neck should be loosened to prevent strangulation. The arms and legs should be restrained only enough to prevent the victim from striking nearby objects and injuring himself as he flails about. No attempts should be made to hold the extremities perfectly still as muscular or tendonous injuries may result.

During the post-convulsive stage the victim requires the same care as any comatose person (see "Unconsciousness"). If possible he should be permitted to awaken from this coma without any stimulation and allowed to rest until he feels that his strength has returned and he has fully recovered. Thereafter, he must be closely attended for a period of at least twelve hours in case he should have a recurrence.

A barbiturate should be administered orally if the person is fully awake and able to swallow; otherwise it should be injected intramuscularly. Administration of phenobarbital should be repeated at six- to eight-hour intervals (four- to six-hour intervals for secobarbital) until the person can be placed in the care of a physician. A person who has received this amount of a barbiturate is usually drowsy and must not be left alone, particularly on a climb.

Any underlying disorders and any injuries received during the convulsion should be treated. Anyone suffering an unexplained convulsion should be thoroughly examined by a physician as soon as possible so that any underlying disease can be found and treated.

INFECTIONS

Meningitis and Encephalitis

Meningitis is an infection of the membranes surrounding the brain and spinal cord. Encephalitis is an infection of the brain itself. Meningitis is usually caused by a bacterial infection while encephalitis is usually of viral origin. However, the diagnostic facilities required for identifying the various infections cannot be found outside of a medical center. Since these diseases produce similar signs and symptoms, and in mountaineering circumstances the treatment by a nonphysician would be essentially the same for all, they are discussed in a single category. (Rabies, a form of encephalitis, is discussed under "Animal Bites.")

A variety of organisms can cause meningitis or encephalitis. Each organism has a certain amount of variation in the effects it produces. Thus, considering the entire group, there is a considerable spectrum of signs, symptoms, and severity which may be displayed.

These diseases are usually spread by human contact, or, in the case of some of the encephalitides, by insects. Meningitis may be the result of direct spread by bacteria from another area such as infected sinuses, a sore throat, tonsillitis, an ear infection, or open fracture of the skull.

Severe headache is usually the initial symptom, but is followed in a few hours by high fever and severe prostration. Confusion, delirium, or coma may ensue and are fairly common with encephalitis. Nausea, vomiting, and convulsions sometimes occur.

Paralysis is not usually produced by most of these infections. When paralysis occurs it more commonly involves only one or two nerves, usually those originating in the brain. (Polio, a striking exception, is discussed below.) Impairment of eye movements and double vision, ringing or buzzing in the ears, dizziness or vertigo, and difficulty in swallowing are the most common symptoms.

The most specific diagnostic signs in central nervous system infections are those which result from involvement of the fibrous membranes which cover the brain. These membranes are severely inflamed in meningitis and to some extent in cases of encephalitis. Any movement of these membranes such as bending the neck or back causes pain. In order to splint the back and neck and prevent such movement the muscles surrounding the vertebral column go into spasm. When asked to touch his chin to his chest — normally quite easy — the patient is unable to do so. If he is placed on his back and his leg lifted with the knees bent, straightening the leg causes pain in the back. This maneuver pulls nerves in the leg which in turn produces movement of the cord and its coverings, resulting in pain.

The treatment for meningitis and encephalitis consists of control of the infection and alleviation of some of its effects. Large amounts of antibiotics are necessary. These should be given intravenously if preparations suitable for intravenous administration are available because high blood concentrations of the antibiotic are required in order for therapeutic quantities to get out of the blood and into the brain and cerebrospinal fluid where the infection is located. Penicillin or ampicillin is the drug of choice for individuals who are not allergic to penicillin. Eight to twelve grams per day, depending on the patient's size, should be given in six equally divided doses. If the patient is allergic to penicillin, chloramphenicol should be substituted. Six to nine grams per day of this drug should be administered in four equal doses.

Fever in these infections can be very high and should be lowered if it goes above 104° F orally. Aspirin every four hours and cooling the arms and legs with wet cloths may be required.

The headache which accompanies these disorders is frequently very severe, but can usually be controlled with aspirin and codeine every four hours. Should convulsions occur, they must be controlled to avoid injuring the victim further. However, in the absence of convulsions, medications for sleep or medications for pain stronger than codeine should not be given as they may act with the infection to further depress the function of the brain.

Fluid balance must be maintained; intravenous fluids may be necessary. Coma requires the same care as unconsciousness from any cause. Evacuation to low altitudes or oxygen administration is desirable. The victim must be isolated with only one or two attendants to prevent spread of the disease. Evacuation to a hospital is always desirable, and may be essential.

Poliomyelitis

Poliomyelitis is a type of encephalitis which can be recognized by the presence of paralysis. The paralysis may come on rapidly or gradually and is usually accompanied or preceded by pain in the involved muscles. Swallowing and respiration may be impaired, requiring careful maintenance of an open airway.

Treatment is the same as for other diseases in this group except that particular care must be taken to avoid any exertion by the patient. Exercise of any type appears to definitely increase the severity of the paralysis and the ultimate disability resulting from the disease.

Poliomyelitis is essentially completely preventable by prior immunization; failure to obtain such preventive treatment appears inexcusable.

STROKE

"Stroke" is the term applied to a group of diseases in which the blood supply to the brain is disturbed. The most common of these disorders are hemorrhage, which may destroy much of the brain, and clotting of a blood vessel, which causes the death of tissue supplied by that vessel.

Strokes result from arteriosclerosis (hardening of the arteries), are often associated with high blood pressure, and occur predominately in elderly people. However, the dehydration and increase in red blood cells which occur at high altitude do tend to increase the likelihood for the occurrence of a stroke — at least theoretically.

Although many persons survive strokes, frequently with surprisingly little disability, the prognosis is still serious, particularly at high altitudes with the added stress resulting from cold and reduced atmospheric oxygen.

The onset is quite variable. Headache may or may not be present. Other symptoms, which may be transient, include weakness of an arm or leg or one-half of the body; vague, unusual sensations such as tingling, "pins and needles" sensations, or numbness; visual disturbances such as blurred vision or partial blindness (which may not be noticed by the patient); and difficulties with speech, both speaking and understanding the speech of others. Personality changes such as combativeness, indecisiveness, or irritability may occur.

With more severe strokes headache is more commonly present. Unconsciousness may follow fairly quickly and rapidly progress to a deep coma in which the victim does not respond to any stimuli. (These events may take place almost instantaneously.) Breathing is noisy and may be very irregular (Cheyne-Stokes respirations). Paralysis is usually present, most commonly affects one side of the body, and may include the face as well as the extremities. However, the paralysis can involve the entire body and is often difficult to evaluate in the presence of coma.

Regardless of the severity of symptoms, a patient with evidence of a stroke should be evacuated to lower altitude without delay. Oxygen should be administered at altitudes above 8,000 feet. Care for unconsciousness should be administered. If the patient has an elevated blood pressure, he should be given sedatives unless they interfere with his evacuation. After a lower elevation is reached, a conscious patient with hypertension may benefit from several days rest before continuing. However, a physician's care is essential. If the patient has only transient symptoms, further more disabling damage can often be prevented. For the patient with more severe disease, such recovery as will occur requires months.

CHAPTER 24

Diseases of the Eyes, Ears, Nose, and Throat

DISEASES of the eyes, ears, nose, and throat, which are the most common of all disorders, are rarely disabling, usually cause only a moderate inconvenience, and are of relatively short duration. However, all diseases of these organs, even the common cold, carry some threat of severe, possibly lethal, complications. Therefore, these disorders must be respected and treated in a careful manner, particularly under expedition circumstances.

DISEASES OF THE EYES

Conjunctivitis

Conjunctivitis is an inflammation of the delicate membrane which covers the surface of the eye and the under surface of the eyelids. The inflammation is most frequently caused by irritation from a foreign body, but is commonly the result of bacterial or viral infection. "Pink eye," a fairly common type of conjunctivitis which occasionally reaches almost epidemic proportions among school children, is produced by the bacteria which were the most common cause of pneumonia in pre-antibiotic days. Trachoma, a much more severe form of viral conjunctivitis, is the most frequent cause of blindness in those areas of the world where it is commonly found, particularly the Southeast Asian countries.

The patient with conjunctivitis characteristically feels as if he has something in his eye, even if the foreign body has been removed. Movement of the eye aggravates the irritation. The eye appears red and the blood vessels on its surface are engorged. The flow of tears is increased and exudate may be crusted on the margins of the eyelids and the eyelashes. This exudate may almost seal the lids together during a night's sleep.

If the conjunctivitis appears to be due to irritation from smog, campfire smoke, or a similar source, steroid free, antihistaminic, decongestant eye drops (such as Vasocon-A, Optihist, or Vernacel) can provide much symptomatic relief, including the relief of swelling of the eyelids and excessive tearing. If the presence of an exudate indicates an infection is present, an ophthalmic mixture of polymixin B, bacitracin, and neomycin in an ointment or solution (eye drops) should be placed beneath the lower lid every four hours until symptoms have disappeared. Such preparations should not be used except when genuinely indicated. Allergy to one of the components is fairly common, and the allergic reaction is often worse than the original infection. If symptoms persist for more than three days, and the conjunctivitis appears to be severe, penicillin should be administered orally every six hours. Dark glasses or blinders with only a pin hole to see through help reduce the discomfort. Since many forms of conjunctivitis are infective, contact between the patient and other members of the party should be limited.

If the disease shows no evidence of clearing after seven to ten days of therapy, the patient should be evacuated quickly. He may have a serious form of conjunctivitis which could cause blindness if not given medical attention.

Subconjunctival Hemorrhage

Occasionally following exertion or coughing (sometimes without any predisposing event) hemorrhages which range in size from a few millimeters to almost the entire visible area occur in the white portions of the eye. Although alarming, these hemorrhages are of no real significance and require no treatment. They disappear in ten to fifteen days, depending upon the size of the hemorrhage. Hot compresses applied to the eye at frequent intervals may speed resolution a little, but are not at all necessary.

Eyeglasses

All eyeglasses, whether prescription or merely tinted sunglasses, should be made of shatter-resistant (tempered) glass. A second pair should be carried in a secure place where they cannot be broken or lost. In an emergency, glasses can be constructed of cardboard or a similar material with a central pinhole for the person to see through. Such glasses provide fairly good vision for individuals with refractive errors as well as providing an effective sunscreen.

DISEASES OF THE NOSE

The Common Cold

A large number of viruses cause upper respiratory infections (colds), but the identity of many of these viruses remains unknown. In addition, secondary bacterial infection and allergy to the virus or bacteria cause many of the symptoms. Some generalized viral infections, particularly measles, often mimic a cold during their initial stages.

The virus is spread by personal contact. Chilling and exposure may play a role in contracting the infection, primarily by increasing the susceptibility to infection. However, in the absence of the causative viruses, chilling and exposure alone do not produce colds.

The symptoms of a cold are familiar to all. A sense of dryness, slight soreness, or tickling in the throat usually appears first, and is followed after a few hours by nasal stuffiness, sneezing, and a thin watery nasal discharge. After forty-eight hours, when the disease is full-blown, the eyes are often red and watery, the voice husky, and the nose obstructed. A fairly abundant nasal discharge is present, and taste and smell are diminished. A cough is commonly present which is dry at first, but later may be productive of a moderate amount of mucoid material. The patient characteristically is uncomfortable but not seriously ill. Fever is usually absent but may be as high as 102°F. The throat may be sore, but exudates are not present (see "Streptococcal Pharyngitis") and the lymph nodes around the neck and jaw are not enlarged.

The treatment for a cold consists of rest and measures to alleviate the symptoms; no treatment currently available is effective against the virus itself. The disease may last seven to ten days. The patient should avoid strenuous activity during the first few days when symptoms are most severe. He can partake in low altitude climbs of moderate severity and can do limited work at high altitudes for the additional three to six days required for complete recovery.

A decongestant nasal spray such as Neo-Synephrine may be used every four hours to reduce nasal congestion and obstruction. However, symptoms may be worse after the decongestant wears off than they were before it was used (rebound phenomenon). Therefore, it may be prudent to reserve use of the decongestant spray to the times when it is needed most, such as at night to permit restful sleep. When first administered, a decongestant usually relieves obstruction by reducing the swelling of the mucous membrane over the more prominent portions of the nasal passages. However, a second application ten minutes later is necessary to reach into the various recesses of the nasal cavity. The swelling in these areas should be relieved to promote drainage and lower the danger of sinusitis or a severe bacterial infection. A systemic antihistamine and decongestant such as Actifed may also be of some benefit when taken orally every four to six hours.

Antibiotics have no significant effect on the viruses that cause colds and should not be administered. The rare serious complications of colds may require antibiotic therapy, but such therapy should not be given until the conditions actually develop. Prophylactic antibiotic therapy should be avoided.

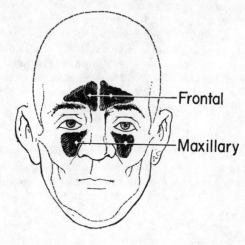

Figure 55. Location of the frontal and maxillary sinuses.

Sinusitis

Sinusitis is an infection of one of the sinuses of the skull. These sinuses are open spaces within the bone, lined by a thin mucous membrane similar to that of the nose, and connected with the nose by narrow canals. The sinuses serve no known function except to make the skull lighter in weight than it would be if these areas were occupied by solid bone.

Sinusitis is caused by obstruction of the canals which drain the sinuses, usually as a result of swelling of the mucous membrane around the opening due to a cold or allergy. Mucous collects within the sinus, becomes infected, and the infection spreads to the surrounding tissues.

Sinusitis, although sometimes painful, is rarely disabling by itself. However, complications may occur, particularly spread of the infection to the bones of the skull or to the brain itself, resulting in meningitis or a brain abscess. Both of these disorders are fatal about fifty percent of the time. However, such complications usually follow chronic sinusitis which should be treated by a physician before a climber leaves on a prolonged outing.

Acute sinusitis usually accompanies or follows a cold. The most prominent symptom is headache, which may be located in the front of the head, "behind the eyes," or occasionally in the back of the head. A purulent discharge frequently drains into the nose and back into the throat where it may be swallowed — the so-called "post-nasal drip."

Fever rarely gets higher than 102°F and may be entirely absent. Tenderness may be present over the involved sinus. Infection in the maxillary sinuses may produce pain or tenderness in the teeth of the upper jaw. If a small flashlight or penlight is placed in the victim's mouth with his lips closed over it, fluid in the maxillary sinuses can be detected by the failure of the sinus to be illuminated. (This examination must be carried out in total darkness and a normal individual should be examined at the same time for comparison. If both sinuses are involved, as often happens, the inexperienced examiner probably could not detect a difference between the two sides and thus would be unable to recognize any abnormality.) The frontal sinuses can be illuminated by pressing the flashlight into the upper inner corner of the socket of the eye, just below the eyebrows.

The treatment of sinusitis consists of drainage and antibiotic therapy. A decongestant nasal spray should be administered every four hours to reduce the swelling of the nasal mucosa and permit drainage through the canals which enter the sinuses. Spraying should be repeated ten minutes after the first administration to make sure the spray reaches the recesses where the openings of these canals are located. A systemic decongestant should also be given to reduce nasal congestion. In addition, penicillin should be given orally every six hours. Treatment should be continued until all signs of sinusitis have been absent for two days.

Acute sinusitis usually clears up within a few days. Symptoms persisting for more than seven to ten days may be indicative of the presence of some complication and should prompt serious consideration of evacuation of the patient. Swelling around the eyes or nose is a definite sign of spread of the infection. If the swelling is very marked the patient should be evacuated immediately.

Nose Bleed

Nose bleed is commonly a result of trauma, but most nose bleeds are spontaneous with no preceding injury. Regardless of the cause the treatment is similar. Care for this problem is discussed in the chapter "Injuries of the Head and Neck."

SORE THROAT

Sore throat is a common symptom which is produced by a number of different conditions.

Drying

Prolonged breathing through the mouth, particularly in hot, dry climates or at high altitudes where the air is low in moisture, causes drying of the mouth and throat resulting in a sore throat. An irritating, dry, hacking cough is also usually present. This condition can be diagnosed by recognizing the existence of conditions causing drying of the throat and excluding the presence of other diseases characterized by sore throat. Drying of the throat is not accompanied by chills or fever, or enlargment of the lymph nodes of the neck or under the jaw. The throat may be a little red and inflamed but exudates are not present.

Treatment of any kind is usually disappointing. Lozenges containing an anesthetic or antibiotics are available. However, hard candy or rock sugar melted in the mouth are probably just as effective, are much less expensive and easier to obtain, and do not carry the dangers associated with the indiscriminate use of antibiotics or anesthetics. Furthermore, candy can be kept in the mouth almost constantly, while lozenges should be taken only about once every four hours. Finally, the candy has nutritional value which is important at high altitudes where loss of appetite makes the ingestion of any food a problem.

Viral Pharyngitis

In conditions other than those which produce drying of the throat, viral infections are the most common cause of sore throats. Viral pharyngitis (viral sore throat) more commonly accompanies a cold, but frequently is not associated with any other disorder. The victim does not feel or appear seriously ill. Fever may be present, but is rarely higher than 101°F. The throat is inflamed, but exudates are not present and enlargement of lymph nodes is rare.

Before accepting a diagnosis of viral pharyngitis, the presence of streptococcal pharyngitis (see below) must be ruled out.

Viral sore throat usually clears up in four to six days — sometimes less — without any therapy. Lozenges may provide some relief but hard candies melted in the mouth are probably equally effective. Antibiotics are of no benefit and should be avoided unless streptococcal infection is seriously suspected. However, it may be impossible to distinguish between these two infections without laboratory facilities.

Streptococcal Pharyngitis

Streptococcal pharyngitis, or "strep throat" as it is more commonly called, is encountered less frequently than other causes of sore throat, but can be treated much more satisfactorily. This infection, which is caused by streptococcal bacteria, is potentially dangerous because it can lead to rheumatic fever, which often causes permanent damage to the heart, or glomerulonephritis, a serious kidney disease.

The victim of streptococcal pharyngitis typically feels and appears ill. Fever is usually present and may reach 103°F or higher. Chills often occur. The throat is beefy red and exudates, which are similar to the pus found in boils or infected wounds, appear as white or pale yellow points or patches scattered over the throat, particularly on the tonsils. The lymph nodes in the neck and under the jaw are enlarged and tender.

Fever, exudates, enlarged lymph nodes, and general malaise serve to differentiate "strep throat" from other forms of pharyngitis. However, malaise and fever may not be marked, lymph node enlargement may not be prominent, and fever may not be very high. Therefore, any case of sore throat should be regarded with suspicion. If a significant possibility of streptococcal infection appears to be present, appropriate antibiotic therapy should be instituted.

The therapy for streptococcal pharyngitis consists of the oral administration of penicillin every six hours for ten days. Symptoms and signs of disease usually disappear completely within twenty-four to forty-eight hours. Nonetheless, therapy *must* be continued for ten days to insure complete eradication of the infection and the prevention of complications, particularly rheumatic fever. Patients allergic to penicillin should be treated with erythromycin.

DISEASES OF THE MOUTH

Toothache

Toothache is almost invariably due to an infection. The infection initially produces a cavity; later it can spread to produce an abscess. Adequate dental care, including regular visits to a dentist, should almost completely prevent abscesses. However, such infections may occur among porters or similar members of an expedition for whom dental care is not available.

The diagnosis is based on pain and, sometimes, exquisite sensitivity of the involved tooth. Frequently a cavity is quite obvious. The presence of swelling in the gum and jaw indicates that the tooth has become abscessed. Fever and occasionally chills often accompany an abscess, but rarely occur with an uncomplicated cavity.

For a simple toothache a small wad of cotton soaked in oil of cloves and inserted in the cavity is usually quite effective in reducing the pain. Aspirin or aspirin and codeine every four hours also help to relieve discomfort.

The presence of an abscess is an indication that the tooth should be pulled. However, extraction should not be attempted in the field unless dental forceps are available and professional dental care is not available. The patient should be given morphine and ampicillin intramuscularly thirty minutes prior to the extraction. Chills and fever are common in the twenty-four hours after a tooth is pulled.

If the victim is to be evacuated to a dentist for the extraction, he should be given ampicillin every six hours until evacuation is completed.

Canker Sores

Canker sores are small painful ulcers which appear in the mouth without apparent cause. They first appear as small blisters which soon rupture, leaving small, white ulcers surrounded by an area of inflammation. Such sores may be caused by herpes simplex infection (see below).

No therapy is effective in curing these ulcers, which disappear in a few days with no treatment. A mouthwash consisting of a teaspoon of sodium bicarbonate (baking soda) in a glass of water is somewhat soothing; a mouthwash of half water and half three percent hydrogen peroxide solution helps prevent secondary infection.

Herpes Simplex

Herpes simplex (also known as "cold sores" or "fever blisters") is a viral infection which produces small, painful blisters on the lips and skin of the face and occasionally inside the mouth. Herpes sores often accompany diseases such as pneumonia or meningitis, and commonly result from sunburn of the lips or face. Very frequently herpes sores do not appear to be associated with any other disorder.

Initially a small, painful swelling appears, which rapidly develops into one or more small blisters containing a clear fluid and surrounded by a thin margin of inflamed skin. The blisters may rupture, particularly if they are traumatized, resulting in bleeding and crusting. Fever or other symptoms are rarely experienced.

The application of a local anesthetic ointment (Nupercainal) may provide some symptomatic relief, but no specific treatment is available. The blisters usually heal in five to ten days. Although uncomfortable and perhaps unsightly, they usually cause no significant disability. Preventing sunburn of the lips probably helps prevent the appearance of these sores.

EAR INFECTIONS

Ear infections are fairly common in infants and young children but are rare in older persons. The eustachian tube which drains the ear is easily blocked by swelling of the mucous membrane in the throat or enlargement of the adenoids in young people. However, this tube is so large in adults that these disorders rarely produce obstruction. In the absence of eustachian obstruction, ear infections are rare.

A cold, sinusitis, or hay fever usually precedes the ear infection. The principal symptom is pain in the ear. Fever or malaise may be present. Infrequently a purulent discharge from the ear can be found.

Therapy consists of the oral administration of penicillin every six hours until all signs of infection have been absent for two days. A systemic decongestant should be given to help reduce obstruction. A hot water bottle applied to the ear and aspirin or aspirin and codeine every four hours help reduce the pain. A warm (not hot), bland oil such as olive oil inserted in the ear also helps relieve the pain.

CHAPTER 25

Infections

AN INFECTION is the invasion of body tissues by protozoa, fungi, bacteria, rickettsia, or viruses, followed by multiplication of the organism and disturbances in function. All humans have living, growing organisms in many parts of the body, such as the skin, throat, and bowel. Such organisms do not interfere with normal functions, and their presence is termed colonization rather than infection. Most of these organisms are "nonpathogenic," meaning they are harmless and do not produce disease. "Pathogenic" organisms are capable of producing infection and disease. When conditions permit the entry of such organisms into tissues and they are not destroyed by the body's defense mechanisms — as they usually are — an infection is established.

Fortunately, many organisms including most bacteria are vulnerable to antibiotics. By identifying the organism and using the appropriate antibiotic, many infectious diseases can be effectively treated. Many viruses are not susceptible to antibiotics, but many viral and some bacterial diseases such as smallpox, polio, or whooping cough can be prevented by immunization. Some organisms, such as the diptheria and tetanus bacteria exert their harmful effects on the body by the liberation of powerful toxins. Immunization with the toxin or the administration of antitoxin is effective against such organisms.

Most infections, such as the common cold or tuberculosis, originate from other humans who have the infection or who may be carriers of the infectious agent. Many infectious agents are transmitted by animals (rabies), by insects (malaria), or by contaminated soil (fungal diseases).

A localized infection involves a discrete area or organ such as the lungs (pneumonia) or the liver (hepatitis), while a generalized infection such as Rocky Mountain spotted fever or malaria, involves essentially all of the body tissues. Localized infections may spread throughout the body by invasion of the blood stream (bacteremia or septicemia). Thus, pneumonia can be associated with meningitis or abscesses in other organs. For this reason, early diagnosis, prompt treatment with antibiotics, surgical intervention in some instances, and immobilization to prevent spread of the infection are important aspects of the management of infections.

Diagnosis

Localized infections involving skin, joints, or bone usually are accompanied by some or all of the following signs and symptoms: (1) swelling, (2) tenderness or pain, (3) redness of the overlying skin, (4) heat (an infected joint is warmer to touch than a normal joint), and (5) interference with motion (infected joints or tissues are stiff and painful to move).

Generalized infections, such as septicemia or influenza, may be accompanied by chills, sweating, fever, malaise (a generalized sense of feeling unwell), weakness, headache, loss of appetite, or nausea and vomiting. Chronic infections may be accompanied by weight loss.

The following discussion is limited to infections of the skin and superficial tissues and to selected generalized infections. Infections of specific organ systems are discussed in chapters dealing with those organs.

Antibiotics

A large number of antibiotics are available for the treatment of infectious disease. However, different infectious organisms vary greatly in their sensitivity to individual antibiotics. Therefore, the proper antibiotic must be used for each type of organism. The infecting organism can usually be suspected by the type of infection that is present. Boils and skin infections, for example, are commonly caused by staphylococci which are often sensitive to the penicillin group of antibiotics. Typhoid fever and dysentery are caused by bacteria which are not sensitive to penicillin. However, ampicillin and chloromycetin do kill these organisms and are used in treating infections they produce.

In order to eradicate an infection, antibiotics must be given in quantities large enough to produce concentrations in the blood that kill the infectious organisms. Hence dosage recommendations must be carefully followed. If nausea or vomiting are present or the antibiotic being given is not effective orally, it must be administered by intramuscular injection. Intravenous administration under field conditions is hazardous, but may be necessary if very high blood concentrations of antibiotics are required. Once therapy with an antibiotic has been started, it should be continued for a period of time sufficient to kill all the organisms and until all signs and symptoms of the infection have been absent for several days. The usual period of treatment varies from five to twenty days. Shortened courses of therapy may result in relapse of the infection.

Antibiotics should not be given prophylactically to prevent infections except under special circumstances. For example, an individual with a cold or a minor wound should not be given penicillin to prevent a subsequent pneumonia or wound infection. Available evidence indicates that use of an antibiotic under these circumstances does not prevent later infection. In addition, such treatment may allow organisms not sensitive to the antibiotic to multiply and produce an infection which may be very difficult to treat.

The most frequently used antibiotics are the penicillins. The potassium salt of phenoxymethyl penicillin is well absorbed from the intestines and is the usual form given orally for a wide variety of infections. If intramuscular injection of penicillin is necessary, procaine penicillin G is the usual preparation employed. Penicillinase-resistant penicillins are given for staphylococcus infections which are likely to be resistant to ordinary penicillin. Ampicillin is effective against organisms that produce typhoid fever, diarrhea, and dysentery.

Some individuals are allergic to penicillin and may have a severe — even fatal — reaction to either oral or intramuscular penicillin. Before giving penicillin to anyone, they must be carefully questioned about previous allergic reactions. If a patient does have a history even suggestive of penicillin allergy, another antibiotic effective against the infecting organism must be substituted.

BACTERIAL INFECTIONS

Bacterial infections of the respiratory tract and skin are undoubtedly the most common of all infections. Most of these disorders are relatively innocuous if treated in the proper manner. If mistreated, the results may be disastrous. Improper or neglected treatment could result in widespread infection throughout the body.

Abscesses

Abscesses, boils, carbuncles, and pimples are essentially identical localized infections which differ only in size. They are almost all caused by staphylococci, which are frequently resistant to antibiotics. These organisms release enzymes which cause clotting and obstruction of the blood vessels and lymphatics surrounding the site of infection. This vascular obstruction inhibits the spread of the bacteria so that the infection remains localized, but the obstruction also prevents antibiotics, antibodies, and other protective substances in the blood from reaching the infecting organisms. Other enzymes released by these bacteria destroy the tissues in the area of infection, producing a cavity which is filled with a mixture of bacteria, white blood cells, and liquified, dead tissue commonly known as "pus."

The treatment for such disorders consists primarily of drainage, and is similar to the treatment for infected wounds. However, pimples and small abscesses do not need to be surgically opened. They should be covered with a Band-Aid or a similar small dressing until they rupture and drain spontaneously. Squeezing should be avoided as this forces the bacteria out into the surrounding tissues and tends to spread the infection. A particularly dangerous area for such infections is the face around the nose and below the eyes. Squeezing a pimple in this region may force bacteria into veins and lymphatics which carry them directly to the brain.

Larger abscesses have to be incised to permit drainage. The abscess should be covered with hot, wet, sterile compresses until a white or pale area appears in the center, indicating the pus has extended beneath the skin. After the surrounding skin has been generously swabbed with aqueous Zephiran, alcohol, or clean water and soap, a small incision should be made through this area with a sterile scalpel or razor blade. (A local anesthetic may be necessary.) When the abscess has drained it should be gently probed with sterile forceps to make certain no pockets of infection remain. Then the skin should be cleansed again, a small piece of vaseline-impregnated gauze should be inserted into the opening of the abscess so it cannot seal off, and the whole area should be covered with sterile dressings.

Antibiotics are not only unnecessary, but are undesirable and usually ineffective in treating an abscess. However, if a high fever, chills, or other symptoms indicate the bacteria have invaded the blood stream or suggest a secondary infection at another location, a penicillinase-resistant penicillin should be given every six hours until all evidence of infection has been absent for two days. (Many staphylococci which cause skin infections are resistant to ordinary penicillin.) If prompt improvement does not take place, the patient must be evacuated immediately.

Similar antibiotic therapy should be instituted, even if signs of blood stream infection or secondary infection are not present, if the patient has multiple abscesses or if he is a diabetic, since such persons are more prone to develop severe infections.

Cellulitis

Cellulitis is a bacterial infection of the skin and underlying tissues which is produced by organisms which do not cause obstruction of blood vessels. Such infections do not tend to remain localized and the bacteria can spread to other areas more easily. The site of the infection is usually red, swollen, hot, and tender, and is usually not sharply demarcated from the surrounding tissues. Fever of varying severity is usually present.

Since the blood vessels remain open, these infections can be successfully treated with antibiotics. Penicillin should be administered every six hours until all signs of infection have been absent for two days. The area of the infection should be covered with a hot, wet cloth or towel which should be replaced at frequent intervals as it cools. The heat causes the blood vessels in the area to dilate and thus increases the quantity of antibiotics and similar substances to which the bacteria are exposed. Incision and drainage are of no benefit because the infection is not localized. The patient should rest quietly until the infection has cleared. Cellulitis is a more dangerous infection than an abscess and must be treated with proper respect for its potential complications.

Bacteremia and Septicemia

Bacteremia and septicemia are caused by bacteria invading the blood stream. If the organisms are destroyed while still in the bloodstream, the condition is referred to as bacteremia. In septicemia (also called "blood poisoning") the organisms multiply in the blood and produce other foci of infection throughout the body. Both conditions are usually preceded by a local infection such as an infected wound, an infected burn, or an abscess.

Bacterial bloodstream invasion is characterized by chills, irregular fever, sweating, and prostration. Septicemia may be impossible to distinguish from bacteremia. Signs suggestive of septicemia are an increase in severity of the chills and fever, persistence of the fever — particularly fever over 104°F — for more than four to six hours, and signs of involvement of other areas by the infection. Severe headache, stiffness of the neck, and nausea and vomiting may indicate involvement of the brain or meninges. Cough and pain with breathing are suggestive of pneumonia.

Prompt administration of antibiotics may be lifesaving. Nafcillin intramuscularly every six hours and gentamicin intramuscularly every eight hours is an optimal antibiotic combination. If only penicillin is available, five million units (3.2 grams) of potassium penicillin G should be given daily by a continuous intravenous drip. Patients who do not respond to treatment within three to four days should be evacuated, since complications may occur in spite of antibiotic therapy.

Patients with bacteremia or septicemia should be provided with rest, warmth, a soft or liquid diet, and an adequate fluid intake. Medications for pain and sleep are helpful; aspirin may be given to reduce fever. A temperature record must be kept, and should include the times aspirin is administered.

OTHER INFECTIONS

Influenza

Influenza, a viral infection, is an acute, self-limited disease of five to six days duration. Although the infection is limited to the respiratory tract, the symptoms may suggest a generalized disease. Many different viruses produce this disorder (Influenza A is most common), but the disease produced by each type is identical. Spread occurs by sneezing, coughing, or close contact with an infected person. Epidemics are common.

The incubation period is short, one or two days. The onset is heralded by chilliness, fever, weakness, lassitude, headache, loss of appetite, and aching muscular pains. Respiratory tract symptoms, such as a dry, hacking cough, sneezing, sore throat, nasal irritation, and hoarseness are often present but are usually not severe. Fever is oscillating, usually lasts two to three days, and occasionally reaches 104°F. The pulse rate may be quite rapid. The throat is sometimes inflamed, and the nasal mucosa is often red and swollen, causing noisy breathing as a result of obstruction.

The signs and symptoms of upper respiratory tract involvement usually differentiate influenza from other systemic infections. A history of contact with other persons with influenza is helpful in making a diagnosis. Gastrointestinal symptoms are usually absent, but diarrhea may occur.

No specific treatment is available. Symptoms are partially relieved by rest, warmth, a light diet with an abundance of juices and other liquids, and medication to relieve discomfort. Nasal stuffiness may be relieved by a decongestant spray. Aspirin every four hours relieves discomfort from the fever. Medication to promote sleep is helpful.

Antibiotics are not part of the treatment of influenza. However, if fever returning after several days and a cough productive of purulent sputum appear, a staphylococcal pneumonia, which is the most serious complication of influenza, should be suspected. A pneumonia of this type should be treated with a penicillinase-resistant penicillin intravenously or by intramuscular injection.

Infectious Mononucleosis

Infectious mononucleosis is a common viral infection of young adults which appears to be contracted through close personal contact. This disease is rarely severe, although sometimes it is incapacitating, but complications do occur and can be fatal.

The most common symptom is a persistent sore throat which is present in eighty-five percent of all patients. The other complaints are not specific — most commonly a feeling of tiredness, loss of energy, or easy fatigability. Lymph nodes in various portions of the body are usually enlarged. The nodes in the sides and back of the neck are most often involved. Fever is also present, but is not very high and varies widely from case to case.

The triad of sore throat, lymph node enlargement, and fever is characteristic of infectious mononucleosis, but this disease is notorious for its great variability. A skin rash, headache, weakness, loss of appetite, and generalized aching may also be present. Jaundice sometimes occurs (six percent of all cases) and is indicative of a severe infection which has involved the liver.

No specific treatment is available; antibiotics are of no avail. Rest is important; activity by the patient should be limited while any signs of disease persist. In particular, all climbing should be avoided. Minor abdominal trauma, such as that produced by the rope in a short fall, could easily rupture the spleen, which is unusually susceptible to trauma in infectious mononucleosis. Recovery in most cases takes place in two to four weeks.

If jaundice is present, the patient should be treated as if he had hepatitis. Evacuation should be carried out since recovery requires four to six weeks in cases of such severity.

Rocky Mountain Spotted Fever

Rocky Mountain spotted fever is caused by a bacteria-like organism, Rickettsia rickettsii, which is transmitted to man by the bite of a tick (principally *Dermacentor andersoni* and *D. variabilis*).

Some three to fourteen days after the bite, mild chilliness, loss of appetite, and a general run-down feeling usually appear. These symptoms are followed by the onset of chills, fever, headache, pain in the bones and muscles, sensitivity of the eyes to light, and confusion. Between two and six days after onset of the disease a red rash appears on the wrists and ankles and spreads over the entire body. The rash may be present on the palms of the hands and the soles of the feet and consists of small red spots. These spots are actually hemorrhages into the skin and in severe cases large blotchy red areas may appear all over the body. The fever lasts about two weeks. The patient has the appearance of being seriously ill without obvious cause.

Diagnosis is aided by a history of a tick bite in an endemic area. Important endemic areas are North Carolina, Virginia, and Maryland, with fewer cases being seen in Rocky Mountain states such as Utah, Idaho, Wyoming, and Colorado. Cases have occurred in Washington.

Tetracycline should be given four times daily until the temperature has been normal for two to three days. Prednisone four times a day for three days may provide prompt relief of symptoms, but should be administered only in severe cases. In treating this disorder general measures such as bed rest, fluid replacement, aspirin every four hours, and medication for sleep are also important.

Rocky Mountain spotted fever can be prevented by careful daily inspection for ticks when in an endemic area. The ticks should be touched with a cotton pledget soaked in gasoline or kerosene to make them detach, and then extracted with tweezers, using care that the ticks are not crushed during extraction. The wound should be washed carefully with soap and water and then rinsed with Zephiran. When moving about in brush in an endemic area, sleeves should be rolled down and the cuffs buttoned. Collars should be buttoned, heads covered, and long trousers rolled down or tucked into boot tops.

Vaccines are available and are of value to individuals who are repeatedly exposed to ticks, especially in areas where the disease is common.

Colorado Tick Fever

Colorado tick fever is a viral disease which is transmitted by the wood tick, occurs in all of the Western states, and is far more common than Rocky Mountain spotted fever. Infections usually occur in spring and early summer when ticks are active. Four to six days after exposure, chills and fever appear along with headache and generalized aching. Photophobia (sensitivity of the eyes to sunlight) may be present. The attack lasts about two days, is followed by a disappearance of fever and symptoms, and then by recurrent attacks with similar symptoms. The outlook for complete recovery is good, even though no specific treatment is available. Bed rest, fluids, and aspirin are helpful. A physician should evaluate the patient to be sure that Rocky Mountain spotted fever is not present, since that is a more serious disease, but one which can be effectively treated with antibiotics. Precautions against tick bites in Western states help prevent infection.

Relapsing Fever (Tick Fever)

Tick fever occurs in Western and West-Central states. It is a blood stream infection by a spirochete transmitted to man by a tick bite or, in some areas, by the body louse. About two to fifteen days after the bite, chills, fever, headache, muscle aches and pains, cough, and often nausea and vomiting appear. A red rash may appear on the body and limbs. The initial attack lasts two to eight days and may be followed by a remission lasting three to ten days. During the remission, fever is absent and the patient may feel well. A relapse usually occurs in untreated cases with return of the fever and all previous symptoms. Hospitalization for identification of the organism in the blood is desirable. Chlortetracycline should be given, one-half gram every six hours for five days, and then one gram twice daily for another five days.

Yellow Fever

Yellow fever is an infection of man and monkeys caused by a virus transmitted by the *Aedes* mosquito. Following an incubation period of three to six days, the illness begins with chills, headache, and backache. The fever often falls temporarily after three days, at which time the patient is flushed, nauseated, often vomiting, and may appear seriously ill. The eyes may be blood-shot and the tongue appears red. Bleeding from the gums and under the skin may occur; black vomitus or stools is evidence of bleeding in the stomach or intestines. Slight jaundice or yellowness of the whites of the eyes and skin may be present. The heart rate may be slow in relation to the severity of the fever. Mild cases may resemble influenza or malaria. Jaundice, however, does not occur in influenza and only rarely in malaria. When present, it is an important sign of yellow fever.

The treatment of yellow fever consists of rest in bed and a liquid or soft diet high in carbohydrates. Fluid and salt replacement may be necessary for vomiting, diarrhea, or high fever. Aspirin every four hours for discomfort and bedtime medications for sleep are helpful. No specific treatment is available. If travel into a yellow fever area is planned, vaccination must be obtained.

Malaria

Malaria is caused by protozoa of the genus *Plasmodium*, and is transmitted by the bite of infected mosquitoes. When considered on a world-wide basis, malaria is the most common of all diseases.

Malarial parasites are ingested along with the blood of an infected person or animal at the time of biting by female *Anopheles* mosquitoes. The parasites undergo fertilization and produce sporozoites in the gut of the mosquito. The sporozoites are then transmitted to humans as the mosquito injects saliva into the skin during a subsequent bite. Sporozoites invade red blood cells and multiply, producing daughter parasites. These daughter parasites are released, destroying the red blood cells in the process, and invade other red blood cells where the process is repeated. The periodic release of parasites produces fever; the destruction of red blood cells can, over a fairly long period of time, result in anemia.

The initial symptoms of malaria are muscular soreness and a low fever (without chills) which appear about six to ten days after the bite of an infected mosquito. Some four to eight days later the typical chills and fever appear. The chills are characterized by shivering, chattering teeth, blue and cold skin, and a feeling of chilliness which is not relieved by heat pads or blankets. An hour later the febrile stage begins with a flushed face, a feeling of intense heat, headache, often delirium, and temperatures as high as 107°F. This stage lasts about two hours, and is followed by intense sweating and a fall in temperature. Headache, backache, and muscular aches may be unusually severe.

The repeated occurrence of febrile episodes at regular intervals such as every day, every other day, every three days, or occasionally at irregular intervals, is characteristic of malaria. In severe cases vomiting, diarrhea, severe anemia, dark urine containing the breakdown products of destroyed red blood cells, shock, and coma may occur. Enlargement of the liver may be present.

Treatment should consist of general supportive measures and specific drug therapy. Rest in bed and maintenance of body warmth during the chill is highly desirable. Since water loss due to sweating may be severe, a high fluid intake should be encouraged. Fluids and salt lost by vomiting or diarrhea must also be replaced. A careful record of temperature and pulse should be kept. If possible, blood smears should be made a few hours after the chill for later identification.

During an acute episode of malaria, the subsequent period of therapy, and for two weeks following recovery, strenuous exercise should be avoided to prevent rupture of the spleen.

Specific treatment of malaria should be given by a physician. The most effective general regimen consists of chloroquin and primaquine. Chloroquin should be given as an initial dose of one gram followed by a single dose of one-half gram in six hours and one-half gram on the second and third days. Primaquine should be given in a dose of fifteen milligrams each day for fourteen days.

Plasmodium falciparium malaria is the most dangerous form, and several strains have been found in South America and Southeast Asia which are resistant to most antimalarial drugs. Expeditions into such areas should carry quinine, pyrimethamine, and sulfonamides which are necessary for the treatment of these forms of malaria. However, a physician's advice should be obtained regarding the use of these drugs.

Chloroquin prophylaxis is an effective means for preventing malaria caused by strains which are not resistant to antimalarial drugs. One-half gram of chloroquin should be taken on the same day each week. Prophylaxis should begin two weeks before entering the area in which malaria is endemic, and must be continued for five weeks after leaving the area. If the possibility of contact with malaria-bearing mosquitoes is high, a physician should be consulted concerning the advisability of treatment with primaquine for fourteen days after the chloroquin is discontinued. In addition, any illness occurring within five weeks after leaving a malarial area should be reported to a physician since malaria may occur long after exposure.

Advance information regarding the presence of malaria in areas that are to be visited should be obtained. In cities and towns which are frequently visited by tourists malaria is rare, and malaria-carrying mosquitoes are rarely found at elevations above 3,000 feet. In malarial areas contact with mosquitoes should be minimized by the use of screens or mosquito netting, protective clothing, and insect repellents. The best available repellent at present is N,N-dethyltoluamide, which remains effective for up to eighteen hours, a considerable advantage over the odor repellents which are effective for only two to four hours. It may be easier to avoid malarial areas than to take chloroquin for five weeks, as this drug does occasionally cause itching and gastrointestinal complaints.

Trichinosis

Trichinosis is caused by eating raw, improperly cooked, or improperly treated pork containing larvae of the roundworm *Trichinella spiralis*. After the larvae are ingested they attach themselves to the wall of the small bowel, mature, and produce eggs. The larvae released when these eggs hatch are spread throughout the body by the circulation and localize in the muscles.

The severity of the symptoms depends upon the number of organisms in the ingested pork. If infection is heavy, penetration of the intestinal wall by the larvae one to four days after infection produces nausea, vomiting, abdominal cramps, and diarrhea resembling food poisoning. The migration of the larvae to the muscles seven days after ingestion produces fever, chills, muscular weakness, a skin rash, and swelling of the face and tissues around the eyes. Headache may be severe.

The diagnosis is based upon the onset of symptoms following the ingestion of raw or uncooked pork or improperly prepared pork products such as salami. Swelling of the face and muscle soreness are also important diagnostic findings. A differential white blood count may reveal the presence of a large number of eosinophils. A skin test is also available.

No specific treatment for trichinosis has been of proven value except thiabendazole, which should be given by a physician. Symptomatic treatment consists of rest, aspirin and codeine, and sedatives to promote restful sleep. Prednisone may be beneficial in the early stages of the disease.

Since trichinae are present in essentially all pork products, prevention of infection is imperative. All pork must be thoroughly cooked. In addition, refrigeration at 0°F for twenty-four hours or 5°F for twenty days usually kills all trichinae.

CHAPTER 26

Allergies

WHEN foreign materials gain entrance to the tissues, the body reacts by forming antibodies which combine with the foreign compounds and facilitate their elimination by the body's defense mechanisms. This response is evoked by substances in bacteria and viruses and plays a large role in the prevention and eradication of infection. Once a person has contacted some foreign substances, a certain amount of antibody persists in his blood for years. These persistent antibodies provide permanent immunity following infections such as measles or mumps. Antibodies against specific organisms are also produced by vaccinations or immunizations. However, many vaccines do not elicit the degree of antibody response an actual infection does and must be repeated every few years.

Occasionally a person reacts to a foreign substance by forming an excessive amount of antibody, resulting in the condition of hypersensitivity or allergy. Further contact with the allergenic substance elicits an excessive antibody response and the concomitant release of several substances, including histamine, which produce the allergic reaction.

The periodic injection of gradually increasing amounts of an allergen can frequently overwhelm the excessive antibody response. This process, known as desensitization, eliminates or greatly reduces the allergic reaction. If desensitization is stopped, the original allergic condition usually returns. Nonetheless, desensitization can be quite useful in helping to control allergic reactions.

The substances to which an individual may become allergic are legion. Certain foods, pollens, animal dander, and dust are the most frequent offenders. Reactions to therapeutic agents are also common. Insect stings and penicillin reactions are notorious for causing anaphylactic shock, which is often explosive in onset and may be rapidly fatal.

Hay Fever

Hay fever, or acute nasal allergy, is usually caused by pollens, dust, or other allergy inducing particles in the air. Hay fever is rare in an ice and snow world, but is a common, and occasionally a severe problem, at lower altitudes. The nasal membranes are red and swollen, causing nasal stuffiness and nasal discharge. The eyes are often red and watering of the eyes is common.

An individual with recurrent hay fever which handicaps his activities should consider desensitization with his physician. He should also receive from his physician the medications which are most effective for him personally. The most effective treatment for hay fever usually combines the administration of an antihistamine with a decongestant. However, some drugs and drug combinations are more effective for certain individuals than others. Actifed combines an antihistamine with a decongestant and is commonly used for the treatment of hay fever.

Hives

Hives are often caused by a food allergy — chocolate, sea food, and fresh fruit being the most common offenders — but can also occur as an allergic reaction to many substances, including thorns, insect bites and stings, or drugs, occasionally even to drugs as commonly used as aspirin. The hives appear quickly following contact with the allergen, are usually widely scattered, and consist of red or white, raised wheals or "bumps." The appearance of the hives is accompanied by rather intense itching. Hives may rapidly appear and disappear several times from a single exposure. Repeated exposures to the same substance usually reproduce the attacks indefinitely. However, the condition is more miserable than serious.

Treatment consists of administering an antihistamine. Those used for motion sickness are usually effective. Cornstarch packs or baths, or Calamine lotion applied to the affected area of the skin helps reduce itching. Spontaneous recovery occurs without treatment if further exposure to the offending substance is avoided.

Contact Dermatitis

A rash occasionally develops due to contact with a specific material such as ear rings or the case of a wrist watch. Very often the cause cannot be determined. Rarely is the rash very severe — it is usually more annoying than disabling. Severe cases should be treated like poison ivy dermatitis.

Poison Ivy Dermatitis

Poison ivy, poison oak, and poison sumac dermatitis are caused by a cutaneous allergic reaction to urushiol, a component of the sap of these three plants. As the result of exposure to this allergen the victim develops an acute contact dermatitis. The sites at which the rash appears are generally those of contact, but may be far removed from any point touched by these plants. The rash frequently appears a few days after contact on the skin of the hands and face, but may appear elsewhere as much as a week after contact. The rash generally disappears in the same order it appeared after four to seven days.

The rash first consists of streaks or patches of red discoloration of the skin associated with itching. Later blisters develop which break down, resulting in oozing and crusting from the surface. Usually swelling of the tissues, burning, and itching are present. Scratching should be avoided because it can introduce infection or cause scarring. Scratching does not spread the rash. The blisters are filled with serum, not the urushiol which causes the dermatitis.

Treatment depends on the extent of the rash. If the area covered is small, no therapy at all may be necessary. For larger areas, itching may be relieved by cool salt water compresses (two teaspoons of salt per quart of water) applied for ten minutes four times a day. Calamine lotion is often effective for relief of itching. A steroid ointment – 0.025 percent triamcinolone acetonide (Kenalog or Aristocort) or 0.01 percent fluocinolone acetonide (Synalar) – can be applied after the compresses.

Patients with extensive, disabling poison ivy dermatitis require systemic steroid therapy. (In urban surroundings such patients have been defined as those sick enough to seek a physician's care.) One easily remembered technique for giving such therapy is to provide the patient with thirty-four 5 mg tablets of prednisone. He is instructed to take two tablets three times a day for three days (eighteen tablets) and two tablets twice a day for four days (sixteen tablets). Six tablets should be taken the first day, even if they all have to be taken at once. When all of the tablets have been consumed, therapy is terminated.

Desensitization for poison ivy allergy is available. Avoiding the weed is probably easier. Efforts to develop an oral desensitizing agent are under way, but at the present time the side effects from these preparations may be worse than the disease.

Many over-the-counter preparations sold for the treatment of poison ivy dermatitis contain antihistamines, analgesics, or even antibiotics, and can produce a secondary allergic reaction to these agents. The result is often worse than the original problem.

Insect Stings and Anaphylactic Shock

Anaphylactic shock is an acute, severe, allergic reaction which involves essentially the entire body. Fortunately it is uncommon, for death can occur in five minutes or less if appropriate treatment is not given without delay. However, anaphylactic reactions have undoubtedly gone unrecognized in the past, and may well occur more frequently than appreciated.

Insect stings are known to be one of the more common causes of anaphylactic shock. It appears clear that deaths due to insect stings far outnumber those caused by all other venomous animals, including poisonous snakes, spiders, and scorpions. An individual allergic to insect stings has usually experienced milder allergic reactions following prior stings, and should take precautionary steps, particularly desensitization, to avoid an anaphylactic reaction or to be prepared if one occurs. Kits which contain the necessary medications for treating anaphylactic reactions to insect stings and the syringes and needles required for their administration are now readily available within the United States.

Medications constitute another prominent group of causes for anaphylactic shock. The most common offenders of this type are penicillin and foreign serum such as horse serum. The danger of anaphylactic shock dictates that these medications must never be given to patients who are allergic to them.

Anaphylactic reactions are most common after the administration of drugs or other substances by injection. However, fatal anaphylactic reactions have been caused by orally administered medications. Very rarely, anaphylactic reactions have been caused by food to which the individual was allergic.

The symptoms of anaphylactic shock usually appear within five to twenty minutes after exposure to the allergen. Occasionally an hour may pass before symptoms appear, and very rarely up to twenty-four hours have elapsed, particularly after the oral ingestion of the offending substance.

The most prominent symptom of anaphylactic shock is respiratory distress which is similar to the respiratory difficulty which occurs with asthma. The cause, spasm of the muscles in the smaller bronchi resulting in severe constriction of the air passages, is also similar. However, in anaphylaxis the onset is quite abrupt, usually occurring within a few minutes, and may be much more severe than is common with asthma.

Laryngeal edema may also appear as part of the allergic reaction. This disorder is characterized by swelling of the tissues of the upper air passages, particularly the larynx where the vocal cords are located. This swelling produces severe narrowing of the air passages. If untreated, the resulting respiratory obstruction is frequently fatal.

The other common symptoms of anaphylaxis resemble a sudden, extremely severe attack of hay fever. The eyes are swollen and red and the flow of tears is greatly increased. The nose is plugged by a red, swollen mucosa and mucoid discharge. Hives or other signs of cutaneous allergic reaction may be present. Nausea, vomiting, abdominal pain, and diarrhea may reflect involvement of the gastrointestinal system in the allergic reaction. Rarely, involvement of the cardiovascular system can result in shock or a cardiac arrhythmia which also can be fatal.

Treatment must be instituted without delay. Anaphylactic shock is a true medical emergency in which seconds may make a difference between therapeutic success and failure.

Treatment consists of the injection of epinephrine (adrenalin). Using a 1:1,000 aqueous solution, 0.3 to 0.5 cc should be injected, depending on the patient's size. The route of administration is determined by the patient's condition. If the reaction seems rather mild and only moderate respiratory distress is present, the adrenalin should be injected subcutaneously. If the patient is in severe respiratory difficulty, the epinephrine should be injected intramuscularly where it is absorbed more rapidly.

For the rare occasions where shock is so severe that the pulse cannot be felt, intravenous injection is necessary. Intravenous administration of epinephrine carries a considerable risk of inducing a fatal cardiac arrhythmia and should be reserved for desperate situations. The medication should be administered very slowly while monitoring the patient's pulse. If a strong pulse is restored, the remainder of the dose should be injected intramuscularly.

Injections of epinephrine can be repeated every twenty minutes. In fact, the patient must be closely observed, because some individuals have a tendency to relapse in fifteen to twenty minutes as the epinephrine wears off.

Respiratory obstruction due to laryngeal edema may require tracheostomy.

Other steps can also be taken in treating patients with anaphylaxis, but none can substitute for the injection of epinephrine. If the allergen has been injected, placing tourniquets above the injection site and injecting the epinephrine around the injection site can help slow absorption. Oxygen should be administered during the period of respiratory difficulty regardless of altitude. Other forms of treatment for shock should be instituted; appropriate care should be given if the patient is unconscious. Antihistamines may help control the itching of hives and other symptoms, but should be administered only after anaphylaxis has been controlled.

Prevention of anaphylactic shock by avoiding the allergen or by desensitization is far safer than treatment. However, desensitization for insect sting allergy with whole-insect extracts is not always effective. Insect venoms have been successfully used for desensitization on an experimental basis but are not yet (1975) available for general distribution. Therefore, even after desensitization, individuals subject to anaphylactic shock from insect stings or similar uncontrollable sources should always carry an "insect sting kit" so that the necessary medications for treatment are available. Injectable drugs may not be suitable for use by an individual who happens to get stung while in the center of a sheer rock face. Rock climbers allergic to insect stings should equip themselves with an epinephrine inhaler for use in such an emergency. Administration of epinephrine by this route is as effective as by injection.

REFERENCE:

1. Kelly, J. F., and Patterson, R.: Anaphylaxis: Course, Mechanisms and Treatment, J.A.M.A. *227*:1431, 1974.

APPENDIX A

Medications

THE DOSAGES for most of the medications recommended in this text are provided only in this appendix. By this means, anyone administering these agents can be informed of the precautions which must be observed without undue repetition in the text.

The major side effects of the various medications have been described, but many minor aberrations, such as nausea, vomiting, indigestion, or similar symptoms, which may occur with almost any medication, have not been included.

The dosages which are listed are those which can be safely administered to a young or middle-aged adult in basically good health. The dosage for children or elderly individuals is often quite different. Administration of the stated doses of these drugs to such persons could lead to disaster. For some medications a range of doses has been given, indicating the dose must be adjusted for the patient's weight and the severity of his disease.

Most medications have been listed by their generic or pharmacological names with the manufacturer's trade names listed in parentheses. Generic names may not be as familiar to the nonprofessional audience for which this book is intended, but are familiar to physicians through whom most of these drugs must be obtained. To a large extent (although not completely) the same generic names are used outside of the United States, but the manufacturer's names vary so widely that names commonly used by American manufacturers may be totally unrecognizable, even in other English-speaking nations such as Great Britain. Reference to a drug by its trade name is not intended to imply a preference for the product of any single manufacturer if identical preparations are available from other firms.

298

MEDICATIONS FOR THE RELIEF OF PAIN

The only drugs effective for the relief of severe pain suffer the common disadvantage of being addicting. The sale and distribution of these agents is closely controlled by narcotics laws and governmental agencies. Therefore, these drugs may be difficult for a nonphysician to obtain.

To avoid difficulties with the regulatory agencies precise records must be maintained. The records must indicate the total amount of all narcotics on hand, the place where they are stored between outings, the persons responsible for the drugs whenever they are removed from storage, the person to whom such drugs are administered, and the time, place, quantity, and reason for which they are administered.

Addiction in individuals receiving narcotics for bona fide reasons is rare. However, to minimize the danger of addiction, the following precautions should be observed:

1. Narcotics should never be administered for any purpose except the treatment of pain for which such drugs are required for relief.
2. A less potent analgesic should be substituted for morphine or meperidine (Demerol) as soon as possible. (Severe pain following a traumatic accident rarely persists for more than three or four days.)
3. If therapy with meperidine or morphine must be continued for more than seven days, a switch from one to the other at that time may be of some help in preventing addiction.
4. Narcotic administration should not be continued for more than twelve to fourteen days except under extraordinary circumstances.

On the other hand, persons using these agents must not be pusillanimous. If a potent analgesic is needed, it should be administered, and in amounts adequate to relieve the pain. A person with severe pain desperately needs the rest and relief which these drugs alone can provide. Half-way measures such as inadequate doses or inadequate drugs do not suffice. Narcotic addiction, although deserving its dreadful reputation, is not as hopeless as death resulting from exhaustion brought on by prolonged unrelieved pain.

Aspirin

Aspirin is a highly effective agent for the relief of minor pain. Since it can be so easily obtained and is used so widely, it often is not highly regarded as an analgesic. However, no other medication currently available is as effective as aspirin for analgesia except acetaminophen and the narcotics.

Aspirin is aspirin, and all brands are identical in quality and effectiveness even though the prices may differ as much as 1,000 percent. The addition of buffering agents or antacids does not increase the analgesic potency of the drug, but may reduce some of the gastric irritation that occasionally is produced by aspirin. Combination with other compounds offers no significant benefits to anyone other than the manufacturers and their advertising agencies.

Aspirin effectively relieves the pain of most headaches, toothaches, muscle pains resulting from exercise, and painful menstruation. It also provides some symptomatic relief for colds and respiratory infections.

An apparently unrelated action of aspirin is its ability to reduce fever. Therefore, this medication is also used in the treatment of high fevers when reduction of the body temperature is mandatory.

PRECAUTIONS

Aspirin is poisonous when taken in large quantities. It is by far the most common cause of poisoning in children. Like all medications, aspirin must be kept in a location where it is not accessible to children.

Aspirin does cause stomach irritation. It should not be used by persons with peptic ulcers, and probably should not be used by individuals with severe indigestion.

Aspirin should not be used in circumstances in which it might mask a fever which could be the first indication of an infection.

Aspirin prolongs the clotting time for blood a modest amount, and also causes a mild tendency for more severe bleeding from minor wounds. This side effect is not of sufficient severity to require consideration by anyone in good enough health to be taking part in a mountaineering outing and may be of some benefit in caring for patients with thrombophlebitis or pulmonary embolism.

Rare individuals are allergic or have some other hypersensitivity to aspirin and should not receive this medication.

DOSAGE

0.6 gm (10 grains) orally every four hours.

Acetaminophen

Acetaminophen (Tylenol and others) is just as effective as aspirin for relieving minor pain and for reducing fever. It has an advantage over aspirin in that it has less tendency to cause stomach irritation. Its major disadvantage is its greater cost.

Acetaminophen is a safe substitute for persons who are allergic to aspirin.

DOSAGE

One or two tablets (325 to 650 mg) three to four times a day.

Codeine

Codeine is an opium derivative used to provide analgesia for pain which is not relieved by aspirin alone but which does not require a stronger drug such as morphine or meperidine. Codeine is also used instead of aspirin for minor pain relief when the antifebrile action of aspirin could obscure a fever and delay recognition of the presence of an infection.

The analgesic effect of codeine alone is no stronger than aspirin. However, the effects of aspirin and codeine together are additive, and the resulting analgesia is almost twice that produced by either agent alone. Therefore, aspirin should be administered along with codeine except in those circumstances where codeine is being substituted for aspirin.

Codeine is legally classified as a narcotic in the United States. In Great Britain and many other countries it is not considered a narcotic and can be purchased as freely as aspirin. Since codeine has very little of the euphoric effects of other narcotics (it actually gives more recipients heartburn or an upset stomach), true physical addiction of the kind which develops to morphine or other narcotics is quite rare.

PRECAUTIONS

In therapeutic doses codeine has few toxic effects. Symptoms of heartburn, indigestion, or nausea do occur fairly frequently. Constipation commonly follows codeine administration.

Codeine, as do all of the opium derivatives, causes spasm of the biliary system and should be used sparingly for patients with liver disease, gallstones, or acute cholecystitis or acute pancreatitis.

Codeine has some addicting effects, even though they are minimal. Therefore, this drug should be administered only when it is definitely needed and should not be used if aspirin can serve as an adequate substitute.

DOSAGE

32 to 64 mg (0.5 to 1.0 grain) orally or, if necessary, intramuscularly, every three to four hours.

Morphine

Morphine, an opium derivative, is a powerful analgesic that is so widely used and so effective for the relief of severe pain that it has been called "God's own medicine." It is one of the oldest and most valuable agents in the armamentarium of a physician.

In addition to its analgesic properties, morphine also has a strong sedative effect which is highly useful in preventing an injured patient from thrashing about and perhaps aggravating his wounds or hindering evacuation. This sedative action and the euphoria produced by the drug are also important for the relief of anxiety an injured person may suffer following an accident.

PRECAUTIONS

The sedative effects of morphine depress function of the brain. This drug must never be given to patients with severe central nervous system injuries or diseases. As a result of its depressive effect on the brain, morphine also depresses respiratory function. Therefore morphine must not be given to patients with chest injuries or serious pulmonary diseases.

Morphine is addicting. It should be used only when specifically needed (for the relief of severe pain) and must never be administered for its euphoric effects or the "thrill" it might produce. Furthermore, morphine should be discontinued when less powerful analgesics, such as aspirin and codeine, can produce adequate pain relief. However, morphine addiction rarely occurs after less than seven to ten days of continuous administration, particularly when being administered for severe pain. In contrast, addiction to heroin — which really constitutes almost all of the narcotic addiction problem — can occur after a single dose, and usually results after much shorter periods of administration than morphine.

Morphine inhibits the activity of the lower intestinal tract, resulting in constipation and occasionally fecal impaction if adequate precautions are not observed. The upper portion of the gastro-intestinal system may be affected in an opposite manner, resulting in nausea and vomiting.

Morphine may cause spasm of the muscles closing the urethral outflow tract of the urinary bladder resulting in urinary retention, particularly in patients with abdominal injuries.

Like codeine, morphine causes spasm of the biliary system and should be used with caution for patients with liver disease, gallstones, or acute cholecystitis or acute pancreatitis.

DOSAGE

16 mg (¼ grain) intramuscularly, or 20 mg (⅓ grain) orally every four hours for individuals weighing more than 150 pounds; 12 mg (3/16 grain) intramuscularly, or 15 mg (¼ grain) orally for individuals weighing less than 150 pounds. (Oral administration in the amounts specified is just as effective as intramuscular administration, but thirty to sixty minutes are required for the drug to take effect whereas a delay of only ten to fifteen minutes follows intramuscular injection.)

Meperidine

Meperidine, or Demerol as it is more commonly known in the United States, is a synthetic analgesic first introduced in 1938. It is not an opium derivative, as are codeine and morphine, but has an analgesic effect fully equal to that of morphine. Demerol may not have as much sedative and euphoric action as morphine and may not provide relief from severe pain which is as satisfactory as that obtainable with morphine.

Demerol has replaced morphine as an analgesic agent to a large extent because it has been thought to be somewhat safer. Demerol is definitely an addicting drug, but addiction usually takes longer to develop and, since Demerol has less euphoric action, occurs less frequently. In addition, depression of central nervous system and respiratory function, constipation, nausea and vomiting, and spasm of the urethral muscles may occur less frequently and be less severe following Demerol administration. Demerol may not produce spasm of the biliary system as often as do the opiates. Finally, the difference between a therapeutic dose and a toxic dose appears to be somewhat greater with Demerol than it does with morphine.

However, some recent reports have questioned whether any of these advantages of Demerol, which are quite difficult to measure in an objective manner, really exist.

PRECAUTIONS

Like morphine, Demerol must not be administered to patients with severe head injuries, central nervous system diseases, chest injuries, or respiratory diseases.

Although Demerol may be less addicting than most of the opiates, Demerol addiction does occur. Therefore, precautions to avoid this complication must be observed.

DOSAGE

100 mg orally or intramuscularly every three to four hours as needed. (The oral route of administration is just as effective as the intramuscular but the onset of action of the drug is delayed.)

Dibucaine Ointment

Dibucaine is a local anesthetic which is neither a narcotic nor related to procaine or cocaine and can be used by individuals allergic to those agents. The ointment (Nupercainal) can be used to provide temporary relief from the pain and discomfort of many minor disorders such as hemorrhoids or other rectal problems, insect stings, poison ivy (if not very extensive), small abrasions, and similar problems.

PRECAUTIONS

Few precautions are necessary, although no more than one ounce of the one percent ointment should be used in a single twenty-four hour period.

Allergy to this agent may develop and usually produces a rash covering the area to which the ointment has been applied.

Lidocaine

Lidocaine (Xylocaine) is an injectable local anesthetic which is widely used for dental procedures and for minor surgery. It is frequently used to produce local anesthesia for suturing minor lacerations.

Epinephrine is frequently added to the lidocaine solution to cause constriction of the blood vessels at the site of injection. Such vascular constriction reduces the speed of absorption and prolongs the local anesthesia. However, in mountaineering circumstances such prolongation is rarely desirable and solutions containing epinephrine should not be used.

Solutions are available which range from five-tenths to two percent in concentration. A one percent solution appears to provide the best combination of small volume without excessive dose.

PRECAUTIONS

A few individuals are allergic to lidocaine and should not receive this drug. Adverse reactions include anaphylactic reactions, but a few patients have developed convulsive seizures.

During injection, repeated aspirations should be made with the syringe to ensure the drug is not being injected into a blood vessel.

DOSAGE

The usual dose consists of 5 to 10 cc of a one percent solution, although more is needed occasionally. The solution should first be injected into and just beneath the skin, and then into deeper tissues. Before each injection the syringe should be pulled back to make certain the needle is not in a blood vessel. The onset of anesthesia is almost immediate and persists for thirty to forty-five minutes. The anesthesia can be tested by pricking the anesthetized area with the tip of the needle used for the injection.

MEDICATIONS FOR SLEEP OR SEDATION

Barbiturates

Barbiturates are the most commonly used drugs for inducing sleep, sedating anxious, hyperexcited, or hysterical individuals, and for controlling convulsions. Pentobarbital (Nembutal) and secobarbital (Seconal) are short acting barbiturates, usually taking effect fifteen to thirty minutes after administration.

These preparations are useful for inducing sleep because they do take effect so rapidly. However, their effectiveness lasts only two to four hours. Amobarbital is an intermediate speed barbiturate, taking somewhat longer to take effect, but lasting for four to six hours. A combination of secobarbital and amobarbital (Tuinal) is used for sleep to obtain the fast onset of the short acting barbiturate and the longer duration of the other. Phenobarbital is a long acting barbiturate. It takes effect in thirty to sixty minutes and persists for six to eight hours or occasionally considerably longer. Phenobarbital is used for controlling convulsions, but because of its long duration and side effects is not as useful for inducing sleep. All of the barbiturates are approximately equally effective for sedation. A choice should be based on the duration of sedation desired and, in a mountaineering situation, the drugs available.

PRECAUTIONS

All of the barbiturates can cause a "drug hangover" consisting of lassitude and somnolence. This side effect can cause considerable difficulty when trying for an early morning start on a climb or any other activity. For this reason, phenobarbital is rarely used for inducing sleep because it has the greatest tendency to cause hangovers. The shorter acting barbiturates may cause hangovers also, but the hangover often has disappeared by the time the individual awakens if he sleeps a full eight hours. Individuals vary widely in their sensitivity to the barbiturates — some being so resistant that barbiturates are useless as sleep inducing medications — and in their tendency to develop hangovers. Therefore, these medications should be given only to individuals with whom the desired effects can be achieved.

Barbiturates must not be given to individuals with head injuries or any other form of central nervous system disease since fatal depression of brain function can be produced. However, individuals with recurring convulsions following a brain disorder should receive enough phenobarbital to control their convulsions.

The barbiturates and alcohol both have a depressive effect upon the brain. When the two are combined, the results are greater than would be expected from just the summation of their individual effects. A number of apparently accidental deaths (including some very prominent entertainers) have occurred as the result of taking barbiturates to induce sleep after an evening of social drinking. Because the effects can not be accurately determined in advance, barbiturates should never be taken in combination with alcohol.

Individuals with hepatitis, heart failure, diabetes, or fever may be unusually sensitive to the effects of barbiturates. Such patients must be closely observed for unusual lassitude or somnolence and the medication stopped or reduced in quantity if such signs appear.

Some individuals have an idiosyncrasy for barbiturates and react to it in unusual manners, the most common of which is a state of hyperexcitability instead of sedation. Such reactions are most common in the elderly or in individuals with uncontrolled pain from an injury.

Large doses of barbiturates are poisonous. These drugs are probably the most commonly used for committing suicide. The signs of overdosage are somnolence which progresses to coma and reduced respiratory function.

Barbiturates tend to be rather severely habit forming, although they are not addicting in the manner of narcotics. They should not be used unless conditions require their administration.

Individuals who have been given phenobarbital to control convulsions are usually drowsy and must be closely attended while climbing or in a perilous situation.

DOSAGE

To induce sleep: 100 mg orally fifteen to thirty minutes before going to bed. A second dose may be given one to two hours later if needed.

For sedation: 50 to 100 mg orally every four to eight hours depending upon the circumstances and the barbiturate being used.

To control convulsions: 200 mg orally or intramuscularly for individuals weighing more than 150 pounds; 150 mg for smaller adults. An additional 100 mg should be administered if convulsions recur.

Benzodiazepines

The benzodiazepines are a group of drugs most commonly used as tranquilizers. Included in this group are flurazepam (Dalmane), chlordiazepoxide (Librium), and diazepam (Valium). Flurazepam has been most widely promoted for inducing sleep, but there are no qualitative differences in the pharmacological effects of any of these medications.

Controlled studies have shown that flurazepam is as effective as the barbiturates and other commonly used drugs for inducing sleep. A number of physicians have found these drugs to be more effective at high altitude, but no controlled studies of such benefits have been done.

The benzodiazepines are definitely safer than the barbiturates. Overdosage is seldom, if ever, lethal in healthy patients who have not taken other drugs.

PRECAUTIONS

The benzodiazepines can produce "hangover" just like the barbiturates. However, many individuals who develop barbiturate hangovers do not have similar results with benzodiazepines and vice versa. Therefore the drug selected for the induction of sleep must be matched to the patient.

Like the barbiturates, benzodiazepines can cause depression of brain function and should not be given to individuals with head injuries or central nervous system diseases.

Like barbiturates, the benzodiazepines can potentiate the depressive effects of alcohol.

DOSAGE

To induce sleep: 30 mg at bedtime.

Others

A number of additional medications are used for inducing sleep. For a few individuals they may be more effective than the barbiturates or benzodiazepines, but for most this is not true. The most widely used in clinical medicine is chloral hydrate. Others include glutethimide (Doriden) and methaqualone (Sopor and others). The precautions which must be observed are similar to the barbiturates. Dosage information should be obtained from a physician or similar source at the time the drug is obtained.

Diphenhydramine hydrochloride (Benadryl) is a fairly widely used antihistamine. All of the antihistamines tend to cause drowsiness, but Benadryl has such sedative properties that for some persons it is an effective sleep inducing medication. It may not produce hangover in some individuals who do get that result from other drugs. The precautions which must be observed are those for both the sleep inducing drugs and the antihistamines. The usual dose is 50 mg shortly before bedtime.

ANTIMICROBIAL MEDICATIONS

Bacteria are classified according to their shape or form, their staining characteristics with the Gram stain, and their ability to grow in the presence of oxygen. The cocci are small spherical organisms; bacilli are rod-shaped bacteria. A few bacteria, such as the organism which causes syphilis have spiral forms; also a few, such as the organism which causes cholera, have a comma shape. Some bacteria are stained by the Gram stain and are termed Grampositive; others are not stained and are called Gram-negative. Organisms which can grow in the presence of oxygen are called aerobic; those which cannot are anaerobic.

The Gram-positive cocci include streptococci, pneumococci, staphylococci, enterococci, and other less common organisms. Streptococci are the infectious agents which cause strep throats, some forms of impetigo, and some cases of cellulitis. Staphylococci cause boils and abscesses, and are the most common organisms producing infection in wounds. Pneumococci can cause pneumonia, but this type of pneumonia has become much less common since the introduction of antibiotics. The enterococci are normal inhabitants of the intestines but can cause intra-abdominal infections, some wound infections, and kidney infections.

The Gram-negative cocci include the Neisseria, the organisms which cause meningococcal meningitis and gonorrhea.

Most of the significant Gram-positive and Gram-negative cocci are aerobic.

The Gram-positive bacilli include a wide variety of organisms. The Clostridia include the organisms which cause botulism, tetanus, and some cases of gas gangrene. These organisms are anaerobic. The Gram-negative bacilli are more common, since most of the organisms in the intestines are Gram-negative bacilli, both aerobic and anaerobic. The anaerobic Gram-negative bacillus *Bacterioides fragilis* is a common agent in peritonitis. Gram-negative bacilli are commonly the cause of urinary tract infections, infections in wounds which involve the intestines, and infections in contaminated wounds elsewhere in the body.

Specific antibiotics tend to be effective against organisms which fall into specific classifications such as the Gram-positive cocci or the Gram-negative bacilli.

The Penicillins

Penicillin was the first antibiotic to be discovered and is still the "king." It is the most widely used and most effective of all antibiotics (against susceptible organisms.) Penicillin is effective against streptococci, pneumococci, some staphylococci, anaerobic streptococci, Clostridia, Neisseria, and a number of other Gram-positive cocci and bacilli. Penicillin has little effect against Gram-negative bacilli.

A number of penicillin preparations are available. Aqueous crystalline penicillin G is usually used for intravenous administration. Procaine penicillin G is used for intramuscular administration because it is less painful and lasts longer. Benzathine penicillin G is given intramuscularly and is slowly released over a period of three to four weeks. Its usefulness in a mountaineering situation would be limited because the concentration of the drug in the blood is limited by the slow release and does not reach high enough levels to be effective against many acute infections. Phenoxymethyl penicillin is usually used for oral administration because it is resistant to destruction by acid in the stomach.

Ampicillin is a chemical variant of penicillin which is effective against the same organisms, but in addition is effective against many Gram-negative bacilli including most of the organisms which have been implicated in traveler's diarrhea. Ampicillin can be used instead of penicillin for any infection, but is more expensive.

Some of the staphylococci produce an enzyme called penicillinase which destroys penicillin and renders that drug ineffective against such organisms. Several semi-synthetic penicillins have been developed which are penicillinase-resistant and are effective against such organisms. The orally effective penicillinase-resistant penicillins include cloxacillin and dicloxacillin. Nafcillin and methicillin are also penicillinase-resistant penicillins, but are usually administered intramuscularly and intravenously.

PRECAUTIONS

The penicillins are essentially nontoxic, but have been used so widely and indiscriminantly that allergic reactions occur in about ten percent of the patients receiving these drugs. Most of these reactions consist of skin rashes of varying kinds, a low fever, or other minor symptoms. However, a few individuals develop severe anaphylactic reactions which may be lethal within minutes. If signs of allergy occur in a patient receiving a penicillin, the drug should be discontinued immediately. The patient should be warned of his allergy to penicillin and must transmit that information to his physician or anyone subsequently caring for him in an emergency. He should wear a bracelet or similar tag containing this information. A climber with such allergy should inform the other members of the party, and must make preparations in advance to have other antibiotic preparations available in case he needs them. Anyone who has suffered an allergic reaction to any type of penicillin should not be treated with that or any other form of the drug again. Not only is there a danger of a more severe reaction, but the allergic reaction may inactivate the drug so that it would be ineffective against an infection.

DOSAGE

Aqueous crystalline penicillin G: 0.6 to 20 million units (375 mg to 12.5 gm) per day in equally divided doses every two to six hours intravenously.

Procaine penicillin G: 600,000 to 4.8 million units (375 mg to 3 gm) per day in equally divided doses every six to twelve hours intramuscularly.

Benzathine penicillin G: 600,000 to 2.4 million units (375 mg to 1.5 gm) every four weeks intramuscularly.

Phenoxymethyl penicillin: 500 mg to 1.0 gm every six hours orally.

Ampicillin: 500 mg to 1.0 gm every six hours orally; 1 to 4 gm every six hours intravenously or intramuscularly.

Cloxacillin: 500 mg to 1.0 gm every six hours orally.

Dicloxacillin: 250 mg to 500 mg every six hours orally.

Nafcillin: 1.0 to 4.0 gm every two to six hours intravenously or intramuscularly.

The Cephalosporins

The cephalosporins are a group of antibiotics which have antibacterial actions generally similar to those of penicillin. Their principal value in a mountaineering situation would be for climbers allergic to penicillin. Cephalexin (Keflex) is the only one of the cephalosporins which is effective orally. The other cephalosporins usually must be given intravenously because intramuscular administration is quite painful. However, intravenous administration is associated with a tendency for the development of thrombophlebitis. In view of the tendency for thrombophlebitis that is an inherent risk of high altitude mountaineering, these drugs should probably not be used in such circumstances.

PRECAUTIONS

Some patients allergic to penicillin are also allergic to the cephalosporins. Patients who have had an anaphylactic or a very severe reaction to penicillin should not be treated with a cephalosporin.

The cephalosporins enter the cerebrospinal fluid poorly and should not be used for treating meningitis.

DOAGE

Cephalexin (Keflex): 500 mg to 1.0 gm every six hours orally.

Erythromycin

Erythromycin is effective against pneumococci, streptococci, and some staphylococci. Its primary use is as a substitute for penicillin in individuals who are allergic to that drug. However, erythromycin is a bacteriostatic agent, meaning it prevents the bacteria from multiplying but does not actually kill them as a bacteriocidal drug such as penicillin does. Therefore erythromycin is not as effective as penicillin. Even as a substitute it probably should not be used for severe staphylococcal infections.

PRECAUTIONS

Very few toxic reactions to erythromycin occur and they are rather mild. However, erythromycin is not as effective as penicillin and some other antibiotics.

DOSAGE

500 mg to 1.0 gm every six hours orally.

Clindamycin

Clindamycin is another antibiotic with antibacterial effects similar to penicillin which is a suitable substitute for penicillin for individuals allergic to that drug. In addition, clindamycin is effective against a number of anaerobic organisms. Therefore clindamycin is helpful in the treatment of peritonitis, which is usually caused by a variety of organisms, many of which are anaerobic. Clindamycin is particulary effective against *Bacteroides fragilis* which is the most common of the anaerobic organisms that cause peritonitis.

PRECAUTIONS

Approximately twenty to thirty percent of patients being treated with clindamycin develop diarrhea. Usually the diarrhea is rather mild and does not require cessation of treatment with this antibiotic. However, some patients — estimates range between one in ten thousand to one in ten — develop a very severe, life-threatening colitis. This disorder is associated with copious fluid and electrolyte loss in the stools along with the passage of large amounts of blood and mucous. Therapy with clindamycin should be stopped at once for patients that develop this complication. Failure to do so could be disastrous.

DOSAGE

Oral: 100 to 300 mg every six hours.
Intramuscular or intravenous: 200 mg to 1.5 gm every eight hours.

The Aminoglycosides

The aminoglycosides are a group of antibiotics that include streptomycin, neomycin, kanamycin, and gentamicin. Streptomycin is no longer used except for tuberculous infections because less toxic drugs are available. Neomycin is also highly toxic and is used principally in situations where it cannot be absorbed such as in Neosporin Ophthalmic Ointment. Kanamycin and gentamicin are effective against a large number of Gram-negative bacilli and are used for severe infections caused by these organisms such as peritonitis. Due to their toxicity these antibiotics should not be used for relatively minor infections. They are ineffective against anaerobic bacteria.

PRECAUTIONS

The aminoglycosides can cause kidney damage. In addition, these drugs are excreted by the kidneys. Patients with renal disease should not receive these drugs, or should receive them in much smaller doses.

The aminoglycosides can cause damage to the inner ear and the auditory and vestibular nerves resulting in deafness, ringing or buzzing in the ears, loss of balance — particularly with the eyes closed — or vertigo.

The aminoglycosides should not be injected directly into a body cavity or be given rapidly by vein. A form of neural block can occur resulting in the cessation of respirations.

DOSAGE

Gentamicin: 100 mg (1.7 mg per kg) intramuscularly every eight hours.
Kanamycin: 300 mg (5 mg per kg) intramuscularly every eight hours.

Chloramphenicol

Chloramphenicol is a potent antibiotic with a wide spectrum of antibacterial activity. This medication could be one of the most valuable of all antibiotics but for one fatal flaw. In about one of every 25,000 to 50,000 patients receiving this drug, it causes a lethal bone marrow suppression. This reaction is a type of idiosyncratic reaction which cannot be predicted before the drug is administered. Some investigators have claimed that the death rate due to adverse reactions to chloramphenicol is no higher than the death rate caused by adverse reactions to penicillin. Nonetheless use of chloramphenicol is usually limited to a few specific conditions which include (1) severe bacterial meningitis in patients allergic to penicillin, (2) severe anaerobic infections for which clindamycin is not effective, (3) infections by Gram-negative bacilli which do not respond to other antibiotics, and (4) severe rickettsial infections for which tetracycline is not effective.

PRECAUTIONS

In view of the severe bone marrow depression that can result for chloramphenicol therapy, this drug must only be used in those conditions for which it is specifically indicated.

DOSAGE

250 mg to 1.0 gm orally or intravenously every six hours.

Tetracycline

The tetracyclines have a very broad spectrum of activity which includes rickettsia and some virus-like organisms as well as a large number of Gram-positive and Gram-negative bacteria. However, the tetracyclines are bacteriostatic drugs rather than bacteriocidal and a number of more effective drugs have replaced them in the treatment of many infections. Currently the disorders in which tetracycline is the antibiotic of choice are (1) the treatment of certain viral and rickettsial infections, (2) treatment of gonorrhea and syphilis and occasionally other infections in patients allergic to penicillin, (3) and the treatment of certain urinary tract infections caused by Gram-negative organisms. Tetracycline is also useful in treating cholera and is frequently effective for traveler's diarrhea, for which it should be administered for patients allergic to penicillin.

PRECAUTIONS

Tetracycline therapy may be associated with a mild diarrhea due to the suppression of the bacteria which normally predominate in the intestines and their replacement by other organisms. The diarrhea is rarely severe, and usually stops after administration of the drug has been terminated.

Nausea and vomiting commonly occur in patients receiving tetracycline therapy.

To avoid permanent staining of the dental enamel, young children should not receive tetracyclines.

Tetracycline and penicillin tend to be antagonistic and the two drugs should not be administered together.

DOSAGE

250 to 500 mg every six hours orally.

Sulfisoxazole

The sulfonamides are somewhat effective in the treatment of a large number of infections. However, more effective antibiotics have replaced most of these drugs in contemporary therapy. For treating certain infections of the gastro-intestinal and urinary tracts sulfonamides are still useful because their mode of absorption and excretion can produce high concentrations in those areas. Sulfisoxazole (Gantrisin) is a sulfonamide which attains high concentrations in the urine and is useful for treating uncomplicated, acute urinary tract infections.

PRECAUTIONS

Sulfonamides in general are not very soluble in water and tend to precipitate in the urine, in effect forming small kidney stones which can cause significant damage. Although sulfisoxazole is more soluble than many sulfonamides, the patient still must be given enough fluids to maintain a fairly high urinary output (at least one quart of urine a day — preferably more) and keep the drug dissolved in the urine.

Some individuals are allergic to the sulfonamides and should not be treated with them.

DOSAGE

1.0 gm orally every six hours. The initial dose should be 4.0 gm in order to achieve a high concentration of the drug in the blood and urine as rapidly as possible.

Polymyxin B, Bacitracin, and Neomycin Mixture

This antibiotic mixture, known as Neosporin, is prepared as an ophthalmic ointment and as ophthalmic drops. It is used to treat conjunctivitis caused by a wide variety of organisms.

PRECAUTIONS

Some individuals are allergic to one or more of the components of these preparations and should not be treated with them.

A similar ointment is produced for use in other parts of the body and is called simply Neosporin Ointment. This preparation must not be confused with the ophthalmic ointment because it is not prepared to the same standards and may contain minor impurities which could be irritating or injurious to the eye even though they could not harm less sensitive tissues.

The antibiotics used in this preparation are valuable for the treatment of infections in locations where the antibiotics are not absorbed. However, these antibiotics produce serious side effects which prevent their use for infections in locations other than the body surface. They must never be taken orally.

DOSAGE

A small amount of the ointment or one or two drops of the solution should be installed behind the lower lid every three to four hours.

Chloroquin

Chloroquin is used primarily in the treatment of parasitic infections, principally malaria. This drug is highly effective for both preventing malaria and treating the disease after infection has occurred except for cases of chloroquin resistant *falciparum* malaria. This drug is also effective to some extent in the treatment of amebiasis.

PRECAUTIONS

In the dosage used for prevention or therapy, chloroquin has almost no serious side effects. Therapeutic dosages may cause minor gastro-intestinal disturbances. Skin rashes or itching occasionally occur. However, these symptoms do not require interruption of therapy and rapidly disappear after treatment is completed.

DOSAGE

For prevention of malaria: 0.5 gm orally as a single dose administered once weekly on the same day of the week.

For treatment of malaria: 1.0 gm orally followed in six to eight hours by 0.5 gm. A single dose of 0.5 gm is then administered on each of the next three days. (Total dose: 3.0 gm over a period of four days.)

Benzalkonium Chloride

Benzalkonium chloride (Zephiran) is a cationic quaternary ammonium surface acting agent which is a highly effective antiseptic. Zephiran is the only currently available agent capable of killing bacteria in the depths of a wound without killing or seriously damaging the tissues.

PRECAUTIONS

When used as intended benzalkonium chloride has very little toxic effects. However, serious results including collapse, coma, and death can result if the solution is ingested.

DOSAGE

Zephiran is supplied as a 1:750 solution. For sterilizing intact skin prior to needle puncture or for cleaning minor wounds this solution can be used without dilution. For washing out deep infected wounds the original solution should be diluted with the cleanest water available to about 1:3,000. Copious quantities of the solution should be used to thoroughly rinse all wounds, particularly those inflicted by an animal suspected to be rabid.

MEDICATIONS AFFECTING THE HEART AND RESPIRATORY SYSTEM

Nitroglycerin

Nitroglycerin relaxes the walls of small blood vessels, permitting them to dilate and increase the flow of blood to the organs which they supply. This compound (which is identical to the explosive) is used to treat angina pectoris, a condition characterized by severe chest pain due to inadequacy of the blood supply to the heart. Throbbing headaches frequently follow the use of nitroglycerin due to dilatation of the blood vessels around the brain.

PRECAUTIONS

The most serious side effect of nitroglycerin therapy is a drop in blood pressure due to the dilatation of blood vessels. Fainting or − even worse − aggravation of the cardiac damage could result. Therefore, a patient receiving this drug should be closely attended. He should lie down with his head lowered if symptoms of faintness or dizziness appear.

The tablets should be kept in their original brown bottle, and should not be kept longer than six months after purchase as they begin to lose their potency after this period. Cotton wads should not be kept in the bottle, which must be kept tightly stoppered.

DOSAGE

One or two 0.6 mg (1/100 grain) tablets held under the tongue at the onset of an attack. If the pain persists, additional tablets may be taken at fifteen or thirty minute intervals for a total of four tablets during one hour. The tablets may be chewed but must not be swallowed. About three minutes is required for the medication to take effect.

Digoxin

Digoxin is one of the digitalis preparations which are among the most valuable drugs available for the treatment of a variety of heart disorders. Digitalis strengthens the contraction of the heart muscle, permitting more effective cardiac function for patients in heart failure. (These drugs are not beneficial for persons with normal hearts, and may be quite harmful.) Digitalis preparations also help restore abnormal cardiac rhythms to normal.

PRECAUTIONS

Loss of appetite, nausea, or vomiting, or slowing of the heart rate to less than sixty per minute, are indications of digoxin toxicity. If such signs appear in a patient receiving this drug, the dosage must be reduced.

Digoxin must be given with great care to anyone who has taken any digitalis preparation within the previous week. These drugs are excreted slowly over a period of several days or longer. Overdosage could result if treatment was restarted shortly after it had been discontinued without appropriate reduction in the quantity of the drug administered.

Digoxin should not be confused with digitoxin, another digitalis preparation with similar effects for which the therapeutic dosage is quite different.

DOSAGE

Initially: one 0.25 mg tablet every two hours for a total of six tablets (1.5 mg).
Maintenance: one 0.25 mg tablet at the same time every twenty-four hours.

Epinephrine (Adrenalin)

Epinephrine is a hormone secreted by the medulla of the adrenal gland. It is used to treat spasm of the bronchi due to severe asthma or anaphylactic shock, or to relieve the spasm and respiratory obstruction of laryngeal edema. Adrenalin is effective when injected subcutaneously or when applied directly to the involved tissues. It is destroyed by the acid and digestive enzymes in the stomach and is ineffective when administered orally.

PRECAUTIONS

Epinephrine should not be administered to elderly individuals or to persons with heart disease of any kind, high blood pressure, thyroid disease, or diabetes. It also should not be given to persons in shock. Adrenalin is a very powerful cardiac stimulant. Its effect on individuals with these disorders would often be fatal.

The dose of adrenalin must not be repeated until all effects of a previous dose have worn off. Overdosage with this drug can cause death in persons with normal hearts.

The epinephrine preparation should not be used if it has turned brown or contains a precipitate.

The solutions of epinephrine for injection (1:1,000) and for inhalation (1:100) must be clearly and carefully marked. Confusion would probably prove fatal if the solution for inhalation was injected.

Following use of the nebulizer, the patient should wash his mouth out carefully to avoid swallowing the adrenalin, which can cause fairly severe stomach distress.

DOSAGE

Subcutaneously: 0.3 to 0.5 cc (depending upon the patient's size) of a 1:1,000 solution every fifteen to thirty minutes.

Inhalation: Prepared aerosols have varying dose schedules. The Medihaler-Epi dosage is one inhalation every two minutes until relief is obtained. If such prepackaged preparations are used — and they are much more convenient and reliable — the directions accompanying the kit should be followed. If a prepared aerosol is not available, one can be made up by placing 0.5 cc of a one percent (1:100) solution of epinephrine in a nebulizer. Four to six inhalations should provide relief within one to three minutes. Care must be taken to avoid overdosage.

Aminophyllin

Aminophyllin is closely related to caffeine chemically and pharmacologically but does not have as much stimulating effect on the central nervous system. This drug is used in the treatment of asthma because it relaxes the bronchial walls and permits the bronchi to dilate, thus relieving respiratory difficulty. At high altitudes aminophyllin may be beneficial in preventing the interruption of sleep by Cheyne-Stokes respirations.

PRECAUTIONS

Aminophyllin in therapeutic doses has few toxic effects.

DOSAGE

One 500 mg (0.5 gm) suppository inserted well up into the rectum.

Isoproterenol

Isoproterenol (Isuprel) is a compound similar to adrenalin, and is used to provide relief for bronchial spasm and obstruction in asthma. When used as an aerosol it has a somewhat wider margin of safety than adrenalin. It is also effective sublingually or orally.

PRECAUTIONS

Isuprel must not be administered with adrenalin. Their combined action on the heart could be disastrous. Isuprel also should not be administered to a patient known to have serious cardiac disease.

DOSAGE

Oral: one or two tablespoons of the elixir (which also contains phenobarbital, ephedrine — a compound similar to epinephrine, theophylline — a compound almost identical to aminophyllin, potassium iodide, and nineteen percent alchohol) three or four times daily. The dosage should be adjusted to the severity of the asthma. Individuals allergic to iodides should not use this preparation.

Sublingual: one or two 10 mg or one 15 mg glosset every four to six hours. A total of 60 mg should not be exceeded in any twenty-four hour period. The glossets should be held under the tongue until they disintegrate. The patient should not swallow saliva until absorption is complete.

Inhalation: dosage depends upon the type of nebulizer used. The Mistometer is a prepackaged unit from which a single inhalation of a 1:400 solution is usually adequate. A full minute should elapse before repeating the inhalation. With other less efficient nebulizers three to seven inhalations of a 1:100 solution are usually required.

Phenylephrine

Phenylephrine hydrochloride is a decongestant well known in the United States as Neo-Synephrine, but which is also present in many other equally well known preparations. Phenylephrine is a decongestant that exerts its effects by causing the blood vessels in the mucosa to contract. In the nose this reduces the volume of the mucosa by decreasing the volume of blood within the blood vessels and by reducing the fluid collected outside of the blood vessels (edema) in the mucosa.

As a nasal spray, phenylephrine is used to shrink the swollen mucosa of the nose for patients with colds or hay fever. Such shrinkage relieves obstruction to the passage of air through the nose, but also relieves obstruction and promotes drainage from the small canals draining the paranasal sinuses.

The nasal spray can also be used as an inhalant in the treatment of asthma if epinephrine or isoproterenol are not available. Although not as effective as these agents, phenylephrine has a definite beneficial action in asthma and produces no significant side effects.

PRECAUTIONS

Administration of the nasal spray should be repeated ten minutes after the first application. Initially contact is made only with the mucosa over the more prominent portions of the nasal cavity. A subsequent application is required to reach into the recesses where the small canals draining the sinuses open.

After the effects of the nasal spray have worn off, the swelling of the nasal mucosa and airway obstruction recur. With this type of "rebound," symptoms may be worse than before the spray was administered. In addition, the period of time during which the spray is effective rapidly gets shorter and shorter. For this reason, it may be practical to reserve use of the nasal spray for the hours when effective decongestant action is desirable to promote restful sleep. An oral decongestant also should be used in conjunction with the spray to obtain better and longer lasting results.

DOSAGE

A 0.25 to 0.50 percent solution sprayed into both nostrils and repeated after a ten minute interval. Administration may be repeated every three to four hours as necessary.

Pseudoephedrine

Pseudoephedrine (Sudafed and others) is a systemic decongestant. The tablets are taken orally, absorbed in the intestines, and spread through the blood stream. The drug acts on the nerves supplying the blood vessels in the mucosa of the upper respiratory tract, causing them to contract. As a result, the excess fluid in the mucosa (edema fluid) is reduced and the mucosa shrinks down to a more normal thickness. As a result, obstruction to the passage of air is relieved. This drug also shrinks the mucosa in the eustachean tubes to the middle ears and the narrow canals that drain the paranasal sinuses, allowing air or fluid to flow into or out of those anatomical structures, and preventing aerotitis media, aerosinusitis, or infectious sinusitis.

PRECAUTIONS

Pseudoephedrine should not be given to individuals with high blood pressure, heart disesase, thyroid disease, or diabetes.

Pseudoephedrine acts as a mild stimulant in some people and tends to make them nervous and jumpy. In a mountaineering situation this type of reaction could make restful sleep even more difficult to obtain. Reducing the dosage of the drug by breaking up the tablets and only taking part of one usually relieves these side effects.

DOSAGE

60 mg every six to eight hours. (Sudafed is available in 30 mg and 60 mg tablets.)

Pseudoephedrine with Triprolidine

This combination of an antihistamine with a systemic decongestant (Actifed) is one of the most effective for controlling the symptoms of allergic reactions such as hay fever or for colds.

PRECAUTIONS

The precautions which must be observed are those for both the antihistamines and pseudoephedrine.

DOSAGE

One tablet every eight hours.

DIURETICS

A number of articles about the use of diuretics for treating acute mountain sickness and high altitude pulmonary edema have appeared in the medical literature in recent years. In a carefully controlled study acetazolamide was found to be mildly beneficial for relieving the symptoms of acute mountain sickness. The authors of the study emphatically recommend that this drug not be taken prophylactically or therapeutically. If ascent and acclimatization are carried out slowly, no drugs are needed. After rapid ascent, the effects of acetazolomide are so minor that climbers would be handicapped in spite of the drug.

Furosemide has been used for treating high altitude pulmonary edema. However, it has always been used in conjunction with oxygen therapy or evacuation to lower altitudes. Furosemide alone is not adequate for high altitude pulmonary edema. If oxygen is given or evacuation carried out, furosemide is not necessary. No studies to evaluate the administration of this drug to prevent high altitude pulmonary edema have been done. Anecdotal accounts of the use of furosemide for such prophylaxis have appeared, but cannot be considered reliable guidelines for general application. Failure of such uncontrolled therapy is generally not reported. The medical scientists in this country who are most familiar with high altitude pulmonary edema have uniformly denounced the use of diuretics in attempts to prevent the development of this disorder.

The following discussion is included only so that those individuals who persist in medicating themselves or others in spite of the opinions of physicians most knowledgable about high altitude disorders can at least administer these drugs in proper dosages.

Acetazolamide

Acetazolamide (Diamox) inhibits the enzyme carbonic anhydrase, which catalyses the reversible combination of carbon dioxide with water to form carbonic acid. It tends to reverse the changes in blood carbon dioxide content and pH resulting from the increased carbon dioxide loss associated with faster and deeper breathing which typically occur at high altitudes.

PRECAUTIONS

Acetazolamide is a sulfonamide, although it does not have any antibacterial actions. Persons allergic to sulfonamides are allergic to this drug.

Patients with liver or kidney disease should not be treated with acetazolamide.

Some patients develop tingling sensations in the lips and finger tips, blurring of vision, and alterations of taste when taking this drug.

DOSAGE

250 mg every twelve hours starting one to two days before ascent and continuing for three to five days. (Such therapy should be provided by a physician, and is recommended for use only in exceptional circumstances.)

Furosemide

Furosemide, which goes under the generic name "frusemide" in the United Kingdom or the trade name Lasix, is a potent medication. The U.S. Food and Drug Administration requires the following warning to be printed preceding the manufacturer's information about this drug: "Warning — Lasix (furosemide) is a potent diuretic which if given in excessive amounts can lead to a profound diuresis with water and electrolyte depletion. Therefore, careful medical supervision is required, and dose and dose schedule have to be adjusted to the individual patient's needs."

This drug acts by inhibiting sodium reabsorption in the tubules of the kidney. The resulting loss of fluid and electrolytes can be devastating. At least one climber has required evacuation by stretcher due to the effects of furosemide after he had walked down to a lower elevation under his own power and had recovered from the high altitude pulmonary edema for which the drug was given.

PRECAUTIONS

Excessive diuresis may cause dehydration and reduction in blood volume, resulting in circulatory collapse (shock) and increasing the possibility of venous thromboses and pulmonary embolism.

Patients with liver or renal disease should not receive this drug.

Persons allergic to sulfonamides may be allergic to furosemide.

Some cases of irreversible hearing loss resulting from high doses of furosemide have been reported.

Furosemide and cephaloridine should not be given together as renal damage may result.

DOSAGE

20 to 40 mg orally; a second dose may be given twelve to twenty-four hours later in treating high altitude pulmonary edema. This drug should not be used prophylactically for high altitude disorders.

ANTIHISTAMINES

Antihistamines are a group of drugs which block the effects of histamine, a substance released from certain cells during allergic and inflammatory reactions. This substance is thought to be responsible for many of the symptoms produced by allergies, but the mechanism by which the symptoms are produced is unknown. In addition to blocking the effects of histamine, the antihistamines have many additional effects which have become the primary reason for administering many of these drugs.

Chlorpheniramine and Triprolidine

Chlorpheniramine and triprolidine are two antihistamines which are used principally for their antihistaminic action. They tend to block the effects of allergic reactions and so relieve the symptoms of hay fever and similar allergies. They may also provide some relief with colds and similar upper respiratory infections, although the role of allergy in producing symptoms in these disorders is unclear. Chlorpheniramine is a widely used antihistamine present in Alka-Seltzer Plus Cold Tablets, Allerest, Chlor-Trimeton, Coricidin, Co-Tylenol, Novahistine, Sinarest, Teldrin, Tuss-Ornade, and many others. Some of these products are available in delayed release forms which result in effective drug action for twelve hours after a single administration. Such long acting preparations reduce the quantity of the drug which must be carried and may also prevent disturbance of sleep in order to take another dose of a short acting preparation. Triprolidine is present only in Actidil, which is not as widely used as other antihistamines. However, triprolidine is combined with pseudoephedrine in Actifed, one of the most widely used combinations of an antihistamine with a decongestant.

Cyclizine and Dimenhydrinate

Cyclizine (Marezine) and dimenhydrinate (Dramamine) are two examples of antihistamines that are used primarily for a beneficial side effect. These two drugs are effective in the control of nausea and vomiting. They are approximately equally effective for the control of motion sickness, but cyclizine may be slightly better for the control of nausea and vomiting due to other causes. Both are also fairly effective against allergies.

Diphenhydramine

Diphenhydramine (Benadryl) is an antihistamine which is highly effective for the treatment of allergic reactions. All antihistamines have some tendency to make the recipient somewhat drowsy. This side effect is so pronounced with Benadryl that it is effectively used as a medication to induce sleep.

PRECAUTIONS

All antihistamines have a tendency to cause drowsiness, although most do not produce as much sleepiness as diphenhydramine. In addition, the susceptibility to this side effect varies widely. Some individuals become quite drowsy after almost any antihistamine, while many others do not become drowsy at all. Anyone taking an antihistamine must be very careful about engaging in activities — such as driving a car — in which drowsiness could be a hazard.

DOSAGE

Chlorpheniramine: dosage depends upon the preparation being used.
Triprolidine: Actifed or Actidil — one tablet every eight hours.
Cyclizine: One tablet or suppository every four to six hours but no more than four in any twenty-four hour period.
Dimenhydrinate: One or two tables or suppositories every four hours.
Diphenhydramine: One 50 mg tablet at bedtime for sleep; one 50 mg tablet every six to eight hours for allergies.

MEDICATIONS FOR GASTROINTESTINAL DISORDERS

Paregoric

Paregoric is a mixture of several compounds, the most important of which is a four percent tincture of opium (in effect, 0.04 percent morphine). This mixture is used to control diarrhea through the paralytic action of opium derivatives on the lower gastrointestinal tract.

PRECAUTIONS

The most important complication resulting from the administration of paregoric results from the drug's effectiveness in controlling a hyperactive colon. The large intestine may be immobilized while still containing a large volume of liquid stool. The water and salt in this stool are effectively lost from the body because the disorder which causes the diarrhea prevents their absorption in the colon. However, the loss of these substances may go unrecognized and they may not be replaced, resulting in aggravation of the fluid and salt imbalance which frequently results from severe diarrhea. The retention of fluid within the colon may also increase the toxic effects of the bacteria which inhabit the colon and may have caused the diarrhea.

The usual dose of paregoric contains ten percent of the therapeutic dose of morphine for an adult. Although rare, addiction to paregoric does occur. Therefore this medication must not be used promiscuously. Paregoric is controlled by the laws governing the control of other narcotics. Transporting this drug into other countries may prove quite difficult or impossible.

DOSAGE

5 cc (1 teaspoonful) orally every two hours or after each bowel movement as indicated by the nature of the disorder.

Diphenoxylate with Atropine

This preparation (Lomotil) is a combination of two compounds which is used to control diarrhea through the slowing of intestinal motility by diphenoxylate. (The atropine serves principally to discourage abuse of this preparation.)

PRECAUTIONS

The most important complication resulting from the administration of Lomotil is the unrecognized retention of fluid and electrolytes just as can result from administration of paregoric.

Diphenoxylate is very similar chemically to meperidine, although it lacks its analgesic and euphoric properties. Addiction is at least theoretically possible and this drug is controlled by federal narcotics laws in the United States.

DOSAGE

Two tablets four times a day is the maximum recommended dosage. Smaller amounts should be used if they are found to be effective, particularly in the later stages of a diarrheal disorder.

Antacids

Antacids are a group of preparations which use various combinations of compounds such as aluminum hydroxide, calcium carbonate, magnesium carbonate, magnesium hydroxide, and magnesium trisilicate to neutralize the acids in the stomach in the treatment of peptic ulcer and indigestion. Some of the preparations are flavored. Among the better known antacids are Alka-Seltzer, Alka-2, Aldurox, Amphojel, Ducon, Gelusil, Maalox, Trisogel, and WinGel.

PRECAUTIONS

Antacids sometimes produce a mild diarrhea, but this side effect rarely requires treatment or interruption of therapy. These drugs are not absorbed from the gastro-intestinal tract and therefore cannot produce any effects on the rest of the body.

DOSAGE

Dosage varies with the preparation being used, but usually consists of one or two tablets as often as required by the pain or distress of an ulcer or indigestion.

Antispasmodics

Antispasmodics reduce the amount of acid in the stomach secretions and diminish the total volume of these secretions. They also reduce the muscle tone and peristaltic activity of the stomach, both of which are highly desirable in the treatment of indigestion, peptic ulcer, or acute pancreatitis, the conditions for which these drugs are recommended.

Some of the better known antispasmodics are Donnatal, Pamine, Pro-Banthine, and tincture of belladonna. Many others of equal effectiveness are produced.

PRECAUTIONS

Antispasmodics produce dryness of the mouth and blurring of vision as their most common side effects. Following ingestion of one of these drugs the patient might not be capable of partaking in activities — such as driving a car — which require visual acuity.

Blurring of vision results from dilatation of the pupil and paralysis of the muscles which focus the eyes. The former effect can seriously aggravate glaucoma, a condition characterized by increased pressure of the fluid within the eyes. Persons with a history of glaucoma should not be treated with these drugs.

Some antispasmodics have a significant constipating effect and should not be used alone. Combination with antacids which have a laxative action, as most do, effectively counteracts this tendency.

These drugs also have a tendency to produce paralysis of the urinary bladder resulting in urinary retention. Although this complication would be rare in climbers, therapy may have to be discontinued for several days and then resumed at a lower dosage if it occurs.

DOSAGE

Dosage depends upon the preparation being used. The drugs are typically given one-half hour before meals and at bedtime. A dose twice as large as usual may be given at bedtime if the patient tends to be awakened at night by ulcer pain.

Intramuscular preparations are available for treatment of patients with acute pancreatitis for whom oral treatment is impossible.

DRUG ABUSE AND OVERDOSAGE

The ingestion of drugs which have widely varying actions on the central nervous system is an established behavior pattern in contemporary society. Many individuals who totally disdain the "drug culture" can hardly get through the morning without the stimulant effect of the caffeine in their coffee, or require the depressant effect of alcohol in a before-dinner cocktail in order to relax after the day's irritations and anxieties. Tranquilizers have become an almost equally widespread habit.

Drug abuse should be considered the administration of such quantities of pharmacologically active substances for reasons not related to physical health that the individual's ability to function effectively in his environment is significantly impaired. Drug abuse is widespread, and the most commonly abused substance is ethyl alcohol. The number of individuals incapacitated by abuse of all other drugs is not equal to the number of alcoholics.

Patterns of drug abuse are constantly changing, except for the constant preponderance of alcoholism, which may be related to its availability. Ten years ago LSD was one of the most widely abused drugs. At the present time use of LSD has diminished to the point that it is a relatively minor problem.

Consistent drug abuse is probably incompatable with serious mountaineering. Nonetheless, climbers are quite likely to encounter individuals incapacitated by drugs in the approach areas to many climbs. In addition, alcohol and possibly other drugs have been associated with several recent climbing fatalities. For his own protection, no climber should undertake any mountaineering activity with an individual known to be under the effect of "mind altering" drugs.

Treatment of Drug Overdosage

The signs and symptoms of drug overdosage depend upon the agent that has been taken. Drugs taken for valid medical reasons produce widely varying disorders, although nausea and vomiting are the most common. In any case, the drugs which have caused the overdose in such situations are known, and appropriate steps to remedy the problem can usually be carried out.

In contrast, drugs which are abused usually fall into two groups — stimulants and depressants.

Stimulants: amphetamines ("speed" or "pep pills")
             cocaine
             lysergic acid diethylamide (LSD)
Depressants: alcohol
             narcotics (heroin, methadone, propoxyphene
                (Darvon) most commonly)
             barbiturates
             tranquilizers

Upon encountering a person suffering from drug overdose, an effort should be made at once to determine (1) all the drugs available to the individual, including alcohol (more than one is very commonly taken, particularly if one of the drugs is alcohol), (2) the duration of unconsciousness or the time since the drugs were taken, and (3) whether the patient has vomited. He should be examined to determine (1) his state of consciousness or depth of coma, (2) respiratory status including the adequacy of his airway, and (3) whether he is in shock.

Regardless of whether the drug is a depressant or a stimulant, the victim usually is unconscious. The usual measures for caring for an unconscious individual must be instituted, particularly the maintenance of an open airway. With severe drug overdose artificial respiration (mouth-to-mouth) may have to be continued until the victim is delivered to a hospital. (Patients with barbiturate overdosage have required artificial respiration for as long as five to seven days and still have recovered completely.) If the patient has vomited, measures to remove aspirated vomitus from the mouth, throat, and airway may be necessary.

It probably does no good to try to make a drug overdose victim walk around or to use stringent measures such as cold water or pain to try to keep him awake. If he has taken a large quantity of a drug, such measures cannot keep him from lapsing into unconsciousness. If he has taken such a small amount that these measures can keep him awake, he is not in serious danger.

After an airway is established the victim should be treated for shock. If possible, intravenous fluids should be started using Ringer's lactate solution. If a nasogastric tube is available, the drug has been taken orally, and less than four hours have elapsed since the drug was ingested, the tube should be inserted into the stomach and the stomach washed out with Ringer's lactate or just plain water. Any fragments of pills or similar material that are recovered, and any vomitus, should be saved for chemical analysis.

No drugs to counteract the effects of depressant agents should be given. However, some medications may be helpful for victims of stimulants to control seizures or make the patients more manageable. LSD victims are often calmed by the benzodiazepines such as flurazepam (Dalmane) or diazepam (Valium). Individuals who have taken amphetamines may benefit from chlorpromazine (Thorazine), although this drug would rarely be available in an injectable form on a mountaineering outing. Individuals with an overdose of cocaine may benefit from small amounts of the short acting barbiturates to control convulsions.

Persons incapacitated by an overdose of alcohol can usually be cared for most easily by waiting a few hours for the effects of the drug to diminish, and then allowing them to walk to a place where they can get any further help they need. Individuals incapacitated by other drugs usually require much longer to recover, and may have to be evacuated while still unconscious. A few patients require artificial respiration during evacuation. Such patients can probably be best cared for by bringing portable respirators and other equipment to the patient while waiting for a helicopter or similar mechanical evacuation.

Table 5. English and Metric Measures

Linear Measures

10 millimeters (mm)	= 1 centimeter (cm)
100 centimeters (cm)	= 1 meter (m)
1/16 inch	= 1.59 millimeters
1 centimeter	= 0.39 inches
1 inch	= 2.54 centimeters
1 foot	= 30.48 centimeters
1 meter	= 39.37 inches

Area Measures

1 square centimeter	= 0.155 square inches
1 square inch	= 6.45 square centimeters

Volume Measures

1,000 cubic centimeters (cc)	= 1 liter (l)
1 liquid ounce	= 29.57 cubic centimeters
1 liquid quart	= 946.33 cubic centimeters
1 liter	= 1.057 quarts

Weight Measures

1,000 milligrams (mg)	= 1 gram (gm)
1,000 grams	= 1 kilogram (kgm)
1 grain	= 64.80 milligrams
1 ounce	= 28.35 grams
1 pound	= 453.59 grams
1 kilogram	= 2.20 pounds

APPENDIX B

Therapeutic Procedures

ADMINISTERING MEDICATIONS

Oral Medications

The oral route is the easiest and most convenient method for administering medications. The major disadvantages of this route are the time required for the drugs to be absorbed, which delays the onset of the medication's effects, and the variability of absorption. The acid and digestive enzymes of the stomach and small intestine completely inactivate some therapeutic agents which must be administered by another route.

Patients who are not fully conscious may aspirate medications given orally, resulting in pneumonia or even respiratory obstruction. Unconscious or stuperous patients must never be given any medications, food or fluids orally.

Oral therapy is futile for patients who are vomiting, because the drugs are expelled before they can be absorbed. Furthermore, if the patient is nauseated, emptying of the stomach is greatly retarded, resulting in a further delay in onset of orally administered medications, which are usually absorbed only in the small intestine.

With the exceptions of drugs which are irritating to the stomach (such as aspirin or codeine), medications should be taken one-half to one hour before meals. The stomach empties more slowly and irregularly when it is filled with food, and the absorption of a drug taken during or shortly after a meal is delayed and erratic.

Intramuscular Medications

The intramuscular route for administration of drugs is more reliable than the oral since the vagaries of intestinal absorption are avoided. However, intramuscular injections are associated with several hazards. The most serious is the risk of overdosage. An excessive dose of a drug or the wrong drug given orally can be partially recovered by making the patient vomit. No similar "safety valve" is available for medications which have been injected. In addition, with intramuscular injections there is a slight risk of injecting the drug directly into a blood vessel inside the muscle, producing much higher and more toxic concentrations of the agent in the blood than the slower absorption from a true intramuscular site.

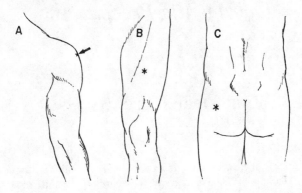

Figure 56. Sites for the administration of intramuscular injections. (A-shoulder; B-thigh; C-buttock.)

Intramuscular injections are usually not absorbed well by patients in shock. If several injections of a drug are given, the medication may not be absorbed until the patient recovers from shock, at which time all of the injections are absorbed at once, leading to over-dosage and possible serious toxic effects.

The needle used for an intramuscular injection may injure nerves, blood vessels, or other structures if the site for the injection is not carefully chosen.

The most common complication of intramuscular injections is the production of an abscess by bacteria which are introduced with the needle. Although the needle may be free of bacteria, the skin through which it must pass cannot be completely sterilized. Bacteria from this site are essentially always carried deeper into the tissues by the needle. However, thorough cleansing of the skin before the injection and care to avoid contamination of the needle usually reduce the quantity of bacteria which are introduced to a number which the body's defenses can destroy without such complications.

The following steps should be followed in administering any therapeutic agent intramuscularly:

1. The skin over the injection site should be scrubbed with soap and water, and then swabbed with alcohol or Zephiran and permitted to dry.
2. The label on the drug container should be examined carefully to ensure the proper medication in the correct dosage is being administered.

3. A syringe of appropriate size should be fitted with a twenty-three gauge needle.
4. The top of the bottle through which the needle is to be inserted should be swabbed with alcohol or Zephiran.
5. The drug should be extracted from the bottle by inserting the needle through the rubber top, injecting a volume of air equal to the volume of fluid to be removed, and then withdrawing the medication.
6. The needle should be pointed upward and any air bubbles or excess drug expressed from the syringe.
7. The label on the bottle must be examined again to make sure no mistakes have occurred. Such errors are far easier to prevent than they are to correct.
8. Without touching the injection site, a mound of skin and muscle should be pinched up so that the needle does not strike the underlying bone, and the needle should be inserted with a quick, jabbing motion.
9. *Before* injecting the medication, the plunger of the syringe must be pulled back to make certain the needle is not in a blood vessel. If blood is pulled back into the syringe, the needle must be removed and inserted in a different spot.
10. The contents of the syringe should be injected fairly slowly to minimize discomfort.
11. The needle should be withdrawn quickly.

Subcutaneous Injections

Subcutaneous injections are desirable for a few drugs — principally epinephrine — to provide somewhat slower absorption than intramuscular injections. The technique for subcutaneous injections is the same as for intramuscular injections, but the needle should be inserted at an angle so that it stays in the subcutaneous fatty tissue and does not enter the muscle. Injections can be made any place where there is a significant amount of fat beneath the skin.

Intravenous Medications

Intravenous drug administration is required in a few medical emergencies and for some infections in order to get medication into the blood faster or in higher concentrations than can be attained with other routes of administration. However, intravenous injections are more hazardous than intramuscular because the drugs reach high concentrations in the blood quite rapidly. If a medication is injected too quickly, the resulting overdosage can produce severe complications — even death. Furthermore, once the drug is injected, it cannot be recovered. If the patient has an allergic reaction to the drug, little can be done to reverse the process. Such injections must be given only when necessary; specified rates of injection and other precautions must be closely observed.

The technique for administering intravenous medications is the same as that for intravenous fluid administration if the drug is to be given over a long period of time. Intravenous antibiotics are usually administered by injecting the antibiotic directly into a bottle of intravenous fluids. Care must be taken to ensure the fluids and the antibiotic are not incompatible. If the injection is only for an emergency — such as an injection of epinephrine for the treatment of anaphylactic shock — the large veins located in the fold of the arm at the elbow can be used, and the needle does not have to be threaded into the vein or taped in place for a prolonged period. These veins should not be used for intravenous fluid therapy if other veins can be found because flexing the arm usually causes the needle to penetrate the vein, allowing the fluids to infiltrate under the skin.

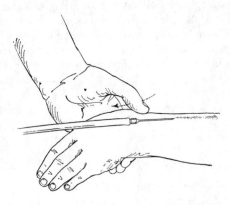

Figure 57. Technique for inserting a needle for intravenous fluid therapy.

INTRAVENOUS FLUID THERAPY

Intravenous fluid therapy is required to replace normal and abnormal fluid losses for patients who are not able to take fluids orally, to administer blood or plasma following a severe hemorrhage, and for the intravenous administration of some medications. The technique for administering fluids intravenously is basically simple and easy, although it may appear difficult. Climbers planning outings to areas where intravenous fluids might be required should learn the technique under the guidance of a nurse or physician.

Although details in the method for administering intravenous fluids vary between individuals, the basic technique is as follows:

1. The patient should be placed in a supine position and a tourniquet which blocks the flow of venous blood but does not obstruct the artery should

be placed around the upper arm. (The pulse must be present at the wrist.)

2. The patient should open and close his fist several times to engorge the superficial veins with blood. Letting the arm hang down or covering it with a warm, moist towel also helps to make the veins more prominent.

3. A large prominent vein on the inner, flat surface of the arm should be selected and the overlying skin cleaned with soap and water and then swabbed with Zephiran or alcohol.

4. The protective cap should be removed from the bottle of fluids to be administered, and the dispensing apparatus inserted into the proper opening. The air intake for the bottle should be opened and the dispensing tubing filled with fluid. To avoid forcing air bubbles into the patient's vein, the drip chamber just below the bottle should be filled to an appropriate depth by lowering the bottle and letting the fluid in the tube run back into the chamber. Then the tube should be refilled, clamped, and a sharp, eighteen or nineteen gauge needle which is not plugged attached to the end.

5. The attendant should hold the patient's arm in one hand and stretch the skin tight over the vein into which the needle is to be inserted with his thumb.

6. The needle should be held parallel to the vein with the bevel upward. It should be inserted quickly through the skin and more slowly into the vein. A slight amount of "give" may be felt as the vein is entered. To prevent its being dislodged, the needle should be threaded upward inside the vein for a short distance. This step usually causes the most trouble because the needle is thrust through the opposite side of the vein. If the tip of the needle is lifted slightly to pull the bevel toward the upper vein wall with the point in the center of the lumen, the danger of penetrating the opposite wall is reduced.

7. If the needle has been properly inserted, blood may be seen in the tubing. Squeezing the tubing or lowering the bottle of fluids below the level of the patient and opening the clamp does cause blood to flow back into the tubing if the needle is correctly located within the vein, and indicates that administration of fluids can be started.

8. The bottle of fluids should be suspended two to five feet above the patient's body, the clamp on the tubing released, and the tourniquet removed from the patient's arm.

9. Once the fluids are flowing satisfactorily, the needle should be anchored with adhesive tape. Gauze pads may be helpful in securing the hub of the needle. The last eight to ten inches of tubing should be formed into a loop and taped to the patient's arm to prevent dislodging the needle by any accidental pulls on the apparatus. If the victim is not fully conscious or is thrashing about, his arm should be anchored in some manner while

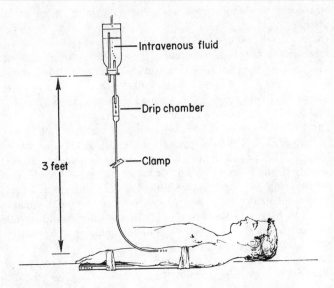

Figure 58. Apparatus for the administration of intravenous fluids.

fluids are being given. During all manipulations with the needle or dispensing apparatus caution must be exercised to prevent penetrating the wall of the vein with the needle.

10. Usually the clamp on the tubing should be partially closed so that the fluid is flowing at approximately 125 drops per minute (500 cc per hour). However, the administration of plasma following a severe hemorrhage or the replacement of fluids for disorders such as cholera may have to be made at much faster rates in order for the patient to receive adequate quantities in an appropriate time. Rarely fluids must be given at more than one site in order to achieve the desired speed of administration.

11. Swelling at the site of the needle tip indicates the needle has punctured the vein, fluids are being infiltrated into the tissue, and the needle must be withdrawn and inserted at another site. The swelling disappears after a few hours without treatment and usually produces little or no discomfort. (See below.)

12. If the fluid fails to flow when the tubing is unclamped, the needle may be obstructed. Changing its position slightly may move the bevel away from the wall of the vein and permit flow to restart. Squeezing the tubing may force out small clots or plugs of tissue stopping up the needle. If the tourniquet on the upper arm is not removed the fluid cannot flow. Occasionally such measures are not successful in starting (or restarting)

the flow and the needle must be withdrawn, a new needle attached to the tubing, and the fluids administered at another site.

13. When more than one bottle of fluid is to be given, as is usually the case, a dispensing apparatus often can be inserted into the second bottle, the tubing filled as described, and the tip of the tubing inserted into the air intake of the first bottle. This measure eliminates having to clamp the tubing to the patient just as the last fluid runs out of the bottle but before the drip chamber empties, and then trying to insert the dispensor into the second bottle before blood clots in the needle and obstructs it.

14. If the vein is traversed during insertion of the needle or subsequently, the needle must be removed and inserted at another site. No effort should be made to re-insert the needle in the original vein until all swelling has disappeared. Usually the site is not suitable for further intravenous therapy for at least twenty-four hours.

15. The veins used for intravenous fluid therapy frequently become clotted after the needle is withdrawn and are not suitable for subsequent use. In situations where intravenous fluid therapy for several days or more is anticipated the attendants should place the first infusions near the patient's wrists and work up the arm as the veins become obstructed. The veins on the back of the hands should not be used for intravenous therapy if other sites are available as this area is quite sensitive and needles inserted into these veins tend to be easily dislodged. The veins in the fold of the arm at the elbow where blood for laboratory analysis is usually withdrawn are also less suitable for fluid administration because very slight flexing of the arm tends to dislodge the needle.

16. Occasionally veins for intravenous therapy are impossible to find, particularly in fat people or patients in shock or severely dehydrated. In such circumstances, intravenous fluids can be administered by inserting the needle beneath the skin of the back, abdomen, or upper thighs and letting the fluid infiltrate the subcutaneous space. The fluid is absorbed from this site, but absorption is somewhat erratic, and administration may produce some discomfort. Therefore, this route should be used to give fluids only as a last resort, and should never be used for medications.

NASOGASTRIC INTUBATION

Nasogastric intubation is highly desirable for the care of patients with intestinal paralysis. All of the serious diseases associated with severe abdominal pain produce such paralysis, but the results are most severe in disorders causing peritonitis or intestinal obstruction.

Everyone swallows large quantities of air with meals and between meals. This air is the source of most of the gas always present in the gastro-intestinal tract. If the stomach is paralyzed so that its contents cannot be expelled into the intestine, it quickly becomes ballooned with air. The distended stomach impinges on the diaphragm, interfering with respiration; it also presses on the veins in the abdomen, impeding the return of blood from the lower half of the body to the heart. In addition, large quantities of digestive juices, partially digested food, and other fluids are pooled in the stomach. The fluid accumulation and distension eventually lead to vomiting and the associated danger of pneumonia or respiratory obstruction if the vomitus is aspirated.

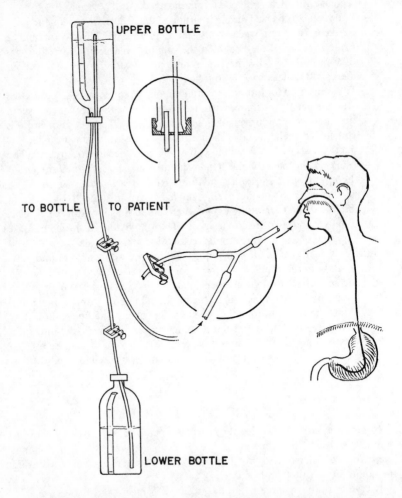

Figure 59. Apparatus for applying gentle suction to a nasogastric tube.

A tube inserted through the nose and esophagus into the stomach permits the air which is swallowed to escape and prevents most of these complications. This tube may be uncomfortable because it gives the patient a sore throat, but it does not cause as much gagging or similar symptoms as might be expected.

The use of nasogastric suction is not without hazard since fluids are removed from the stomach as well as air. If these fluids are not replaced intravenously with Ringer's lactate, serious salt and water depletion inevitably results. If fluids for intravenous therapy are not available, the nasogastric tube should only be used to remove the air which has collected. The tube must then be clamped and only re-opened when significant quantities of air have collected again.

The technique for nasogastric intubation is as follows:

1. The tube, at least a size 18 French, should be chilled with ice or snow and the tip lubricated with a bland lubricating jelly, mineral oil, or at least water before it is inserted.

2. The patient should be sitting up and should have a container of cold water and a straw, a few pieces of crushed ice, or a handful of snow to swallow.

3. The tube should be inserted through one nostril, along the floor of the nasal cavity, to the back of the throat. Then the patient should be told to swallow. As he swallows the tube should be thrust further in so the tongue and muscles of the throat can guide it into the esophagus. Several attempts are often necessary before the tube passes into the esophagus. When the tube does start down the esophagus, the patient is told to keep swallowing. With each swallow the tube should be rapidly thrust further down until a length equal to the distance from the patient's nose to his stomach has been inserted.

4. After the tube is in place, a small amount of air should be injected through the tube. If the tube is in the stomach, bubbling sounds made by the injected air can be clearly heard. However, the tube sometimes becomes coiled in the back of the patient's throat or gets turned on itself in his esophagus and does not enter the stomach. In such cases the tube must be partially withdrawn and reinserted.

5. Rarely the tube may enter the patient's trachea, causing him to cough and sometimes be unable to talk. If the tube is withdrawn promptly no harm will be done, although the patient may be understandably reluctant to undergo further attempts at intubation.

6. After the tube is in place it should be taped to the patient's nose or forehead to prevent its being expelled or swallowed entirely. Air and fluid in the stomach can be withdrawn with a syringe and an attachment to fit the tubing. After the stomach is emptied, the tube should be attached to a suction apparatus constructed by suspending a jar filled with water several feet above the patient's body as shown in the accompanying diagram.

7. Nasogastric tubes have a tendency to become obstructed by mucous or particles of food. Therefore, the tube should be flushed with a small amount of saline or Ringer's lactate every two hours. Water should not be used for flushing if one of these two fluids is available. The fluid used to irrigate the tube must be subtracted from the total volume lost through the tube when calculating the patient's fluid requirements.

8. The total volume of fluid lost through the nasogastric tube must be carefully measured and exactly recorded. All of the fluid lost in this manner must be replaced intravenously with Ringer's lactate.

URETHRAL CATHETERIZATION

Following prolonged periods of unconsciousness or severe injuries, particularly injuries in which the lower portion of the body is paralyzed, the urinary bladder may become severely distended. Due to stretching of the bladder muscles and pressure against the opening of the bladder the patient may be unable to void. To relieve the distension, a small tube (urethral catheter) must be inserted into the bladder through the urethra. The discomfort from this procedure is surprisingly small, often much less than the pain from the distended bladder. Catheterization is rarely required for females. The absence of a prostate gland and the much shorter urethra offer much less resistance to voiding, particularly for young women who might be partaking in a mountaineering outing.

Rarely an individual with a distended bladder repeatedly voids a small amount, but does not completely empty his bladder. For such individuals severe distension requires much longer to develop and is less obvious. Since the individual is voiding, the primary symptom is the severe discomfort from the overdistended bladder.

About eight to ten hours are required for the bladder to become distended. Urethral catheterization can often be avoided if the patient can be induced to void before that much time has elapsed. Having him stand up and walk around for a few minutes or placing his hand in a pan of warm water are measures which are frequently helpful in achieving this goal.

The greatest hazard from urethral catheterization is the danger of introducing infection. Meticulous care in avoiding contamination of the catheter greatly reduces the incidence of such infections.

The technique for urethral catheterization is as follows:

1. The patient should be placed in a supine position.
2. The attendant must assemble everything he needs before initiating the procedure. Any break to obtain some other items invites contamination and infection. The equipment required consists of a sterile urinary catheter (size sixteen or eighteen French), sterile rubber gloves or sterile

instruments to handle the catheter, sterile lubricating ointment, and alcohol sponges. A sterile towel on which to place the items is a great convenience and helps avoid contamination. A receptacle to collect the urine should also be on hand, particularly if the volume of urine must be measured.

3. The glans penis must be cleaned with alcohol, Zephiran, or soap and water, and the catheter must be removed from its container without being contaminated. The circumstances and assistance available should determine which is done first, but the glans should not touch any nonsterile objects after it has been cleaned, and the catheter must not be contaminated.

4. After a small amount of sterile lubricating jelly has been applied to the tip, the catheter should be inserted into the urethra and gently threaded upward until urine begins to flow from the open end. This maneuver is facilitated if the penis is pulled upward to straighten the urethra and eliminate any folds in the mucosa lining this passage.

5. After the urine has ceased to flow the catheter should be gently withdrawn.

6. Most patients require only a single catheterization and are subsequently able to void without difficulty. However, patients with paralysis of the lower portion of their bodies usually have to be catheterized every eight hours to prevent overdistension of the bladder and possible renal damage. In such patients an indwelling catheter (Foley catheter) should be inserted. This type of catheter has a small balloon just above the tip. After the catheter has been inserted this balloon should be inflated by injecting fluid with a syringe and needle into the nipple provided for this purpose on the external end of the catheter. The balloon must be deflated by clipping off the end of this nipple before the catheter is withdrawn. However, a catheter of this kind can usually be left in place for three to five days. To reduce the risk of infection the patient may be treated with sulfisoxazole.

TUBE THORACOTOMY

Tube thoracotomy is a severely hazardous procedure. The possible complications include infection, puncture of the heart or a major blood vessel, laceration of the lung, or even penetration of the diaphragm and laceration of the liver or spleen, all of which would probably be disastrous.

This procedure must only be attempted when all of the following conditions can be met:

1. The patient is dying as the result of impaired respiratory function due to air or fluid in the chest (which would almost always be the result of traumatic injury).

2. All of the necessary equipment is available: flutter valve, trochar or means for inserting the tube, and the necessary tubing. A local anesthetic and means for preventing infection are also desirable.

3. The person performing the procedure has received prior instruction from a physician.

In spite of the hazards it presents, this procedure may be life-saving if performed properly for patients with a severe pneumothorax, particularly at high altitudes.

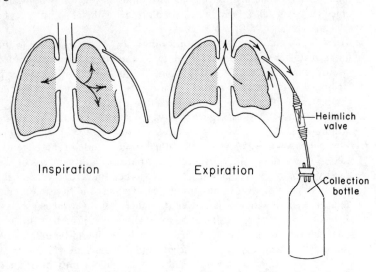

Inspiration   Expiration   Heimlich valve

Collection bottle

Figure 60. Pulmonary function with a pneumothorax treated by tube thoracotomy. (Adapted from *Surgery of the Chest,* 3rd ed. See note, Fig. 26.)

Tube thoracotomy should be performed as follows:

1. If possible the patient should be sitting up with his arms forward. He may be propped up in this position if necessary. If he cannot sit up, he should have his head and chest higher than the rest of his body, and the side of the chest in which the tube is to be inserted should be uppermost.

2. If the patient's condition allows time, the attendant should scrub his hands and arms with soap (preferably one containing hexachlorophene) and a brush for ten minutes *by the clock.*

3. A wide area of the patient's chest wall above the nipple on the injured side should be similarly scrubbed. This area next should be swabbed with iodine followed by alcohol, Zephiran, or just alcohol if nothing else is available.

4. If sterile rubber gloves are available, they should be put on after the attendant's hands have been scrubbed and the patient's chest has been scrubbed and swabbed with the antiseptic.

5. The rib at the same level or at the upper margin of the nipple should be identified. A point just lateral to the nipple, or just beyond the edge of the breast for females, and at the upper margin of the rib should be selected for the thoracotomy.

6. The point selected should be anesthetized by infiltration with a local anesthetic (lidocaine). The infiltration should extend down to the rib and over its upper border.

7. A flutter valve (Heimlich valve) should be prepared for attachment to one end of the chest tubing before the thoracotomy is begun. The valve must be checked to be certain it is not attached backwards.

8a. If a trochar is available, a small nick about one-quarter inch in length should be made in the skin with a sterile scalpel blade to facilitate insertion of the trochar. The trochar should be pushed firmly through the chest wall until it stops against the rib. Then the tip should be moved upward slightly until it passes over the top of the rib, thus avoiding the blood vessels which course along the bottom of every rib. The chest wall is one and one-half to two and one-half inches thick depending upon the individual's muscularity and the amount of fat present.

9a. After the trochar passes over the top of the rib, it should be pushed into the chest cavity. A gush of air or fluid should be encountered as the pleura is entered. The tubing should be passed through the trochar so that two to three inches of tubing extends beyond the trochar into the chest. While holding the tubing to make sure it is not pulled out, the trochar should be withdrawn and the valve quickly attached. The muscles and other tissues of the chest wall close around the tube and seal it off.

8b. If a trochar is not available, a one inch long incision should be made with a sterile scalpel and carried down to the rib. The bleeding that accompanies this incision can safely be ignored. The rib should be palpated with a sterile finger to ensure its upper margin is located.

9b. With a pair of forceps or with a scalpel — carefully — the muscles between the ribs and the underlying pleura should be punctured. A gush of air or blood should be encountered. Puncturing the pleura is usually painful in spite of the local anesthetic and the patient may require reassurance. A sterile finger can briefly palpate the inner surface of the pleura to ensure the chest has been entered. Then the tubing should be inserted, using the finger in the incision to guide it into position with about two inches extending into the pleural cavity.

10. The tube should be anchored to the chest wall with tape so that it cannot be pulled out or forced farther into the chest. A sterile bandage should be placed around the opening in the chest wall.

11. After the tube is in place, air and perhaps a little blood can be seen to pass through the valve whenever the patient coughs. With severe injuries such emissions can be seen with quiet respirations. The valve should collapse during inspiration and prevent air from being sucked back into the chest.

12. If a large amount of fluid or blood is being lost through the tube, a sterile receptacle of some type should be attached to the end of the valve away from the patient, preferably with a second length of tubing, in order to measure the volume of the loss and prevent soiling the patient's clothing, sleeping bag, or similar items.

STERILIZATION

Syringes, needles, and other instruments must be sterilized before being used. At sea level, boiling for fifteen minutes in water usually provides adequate sterilization (but equipment must be available for removing the items from the water without contaminating them). At altitudes above 3,000 to 4,000 feet, the boiling temperature of water is so low that boiling must be continued for an hour to obtain adequate sterilization. However, boiling in a pressure cooker for fifteen minutes under fifteen pounds of pressure should be adequate at almost any altitude. Regardless of the manner in which they are sterilized, needles and syringes used for one individual must never be used to administer injections to another. The methods of sterilization in the field are too uncertain and the danger of transmitting hepatitis is too great to risk such a dangerous infection in this manner.

The ideal solution for the problem of sterilization is now available in the form of needles and syringes designed to be used only once and then discarded. These items come in a variety of sizes, are lightweight and individually packaged, and are less expensive than the cost of purchasing and repeatedly sterilizing nondisposable equipment. Such items have become standard equipment in most hospitals and should be used on mountaineering outings. Other items, such as forceps and scalpels, are also being produced in sterile disposable kits which are equally convenient and relatively inexpensive.

Scalpels, forceps, scissors, and similar metal instruments can be sterilized by washing them thoroughly, dipping them in alcohol, and lighting the alcohol. (The instruments obviously must be permitted to cool before they are used. However, blowing on the items to cool them causes contamination with bacteria from the nose and mouth.)

Dressings and instruments should be placed in paper wrappers and autoclaved before starting on a trip. Such items remain sterile for several months if undisturbed. However, if they are wet, the water carries bacteria through the paper wrappers and sterility is lost.

APPENDIX C

Medical Supplies

THE ONLY way a climbing party could be completely prepared for any and all accidents and illnesses would be to have a fully equipped and staffed field hospital available at all times. Since this is obviously out of the question, a compromise is necessary. The materials needed for care of the more common medical problems must be carried by any mountaineering outing. However, additional supplies should be selected on the basis of the size of the party, the nature or location of the outing or expedition, the transportation facilities available, and the group's financial resources.

The following lists contain the materials necessary for treating the medical disorders likely to be encountered in most circumstances. Medications for pre-existing disorders, such as diabetes or asthma, must also be included by individuals with such conditions.

Personal Medical Supplies

Aspirin — 300 mg tablets .... 20 or more
Meperidine — 50 mg tablets .... 10 or more
Personal medications
A wound antiseptic such as benzalkonium chloride, an appropriate soap, or seventy percent ethyl alcohol or isopropyl alcohol.
Sunburn preventative containing para-aminobenzoic acid
Moleskin or similar material .... 4 to 6 four-inch squares
Band-Aids — large size .... 10 or more
Sterile gauze pads — four inch square .... 6 or more
Adhesive tape .... 1 two-inch roll

Elastic bandage   .... 1 or 2 three inches wide
Triangular bandage   .... 2 or 3
Tweezers
Snake bite kit   .... 1 per party
Manual of medical care   .... 1 per party

If each person in a climbing party carries these items, the party would be prepared for most medical emergencies provided (1) other material is available to bind splints for broken extremities, and (2) additional medical supplies such as the "Outing Medical Kit" or a physician's attention can be obtained within eight to twelve hours.

Parties traveling in areas so remote that several days would be required to obtain additional medical supplies or a physician's assistance should carry larger quantities of these materials as well as antibacterial agents, drugs for treating gastrointestinal disorders, and possibly other medications or materials listed in the "Outing Medical Kit." Such parties should also consider carrying a lightweight, two-way radio to obtain help more rapidly if it is needed.

Outing Medical Kit

Medications (oral unless specified otherwise)

Analgesics
Aspirin or acetaminophen
Codeine
Morphine or meperidine (oral and injectable)
Dibucaine ointment

Sleeping medications
Short or intermediate acting barbiturate
A benzodiazepine

Antimicrobial preparations
One or more penicillins — preferably a penicillinase-resistant penicillin and ampicillin if traveler's diarrhea is anticipated
Clindamycin and gentamicin or a similar aminoglycoside for treating peritonitis
Tetracycline
Neosporin Ophthalmic Drops
Appropriate substitute antibiotics for individuals allergic to penicillin
Gantrisin
Chloroquin
A wound antiseptic such as benzalkonium chloride, an appropriate soap, or seventy percent ethyl alcohol or isopropyl alcohol

Cardiac and respiratory drugs
   Nitroglycerine
   Digoxin
   Epinephrine
   A systemic decongestant
   A local decongestant spray

Gastrointestinal medications
   One or more laxatives
   Antidiarrheal agents (paregoric, diphenoxylate)
   One or more antacids
   One or more antispasmodics
   One or more antinauseants

Other preparations
   One or more antihistamines
   Sunburn ointment containing para-aminobenzoic acid
   Sunscreen
   Poison ivy medication

Bandages and dressings
   Sterile gauze pads
   Vaseline gauze
   Band-Aids
   Sterile absorbent cotton
   Eye pads
   Triangular bandages
   Adhesive tape (two-inch can be torn into one-inch strips)
   Elastic bandages
   Moleskin

Equipment
   Surgical forceps and tweezers
   Scissors
   Scalpel with blades
   Syringes and needles
   Stethoscope
   Sphygmomanometer
   Plastic oral airway
   Tracheostomy needle
   Tongue blades
   Inflatable splints
   Snake bite kit with antivenin
   Hot water bottle

These supplies should be adequate for treating most medical disorders occurring at a·base camp or a location from which disease or accident victims could be evacuated within thirty-six hours.

Air Drop Medical Kit

The easiest and most reliable method of providing emergency medical supplies for a climbing party in a remote area is by airplane or helicopter. These supplies can be dropped, with or without a parachute, in the immediate vicinity of the party within a few hours after a rescue organization is informed of the group's distress.

Mountain rescue organizations should maintain such kits in a continuous state of readiness. Arrangements should be made with a nearby hospital or blood bank to obtain plasma at the time it is needed, since most organizations cannot store the plasma themselves. Containers, padding, parachutes, and similar materials must be on hand and flying arrangements must be made in advance if undue delay is to be avoided.

The nature and quantity of the items which are actually dropped should be determined by the nature of the party's medical problems, the number of persons involved, and the time required to evacuate the victims. The kits must be flexible so that only the needed materials are provided. Most groups would not be able to carry out any extra supplies, and the equipment lost in this way would greatly increase the cost of rescue operations.

The kits should include some or all of the following:

Items in the "Outing Medical Kit;"
Intravenous fluids including blood plasma, Ringer's lactate and five or ten percent glucose (in plastic containers if possible);
Tubing and needles for intravenous fluid therapy;
Intravenous antibiotics;
Oxygen bottles, masks, valves, and tubing;
Trochar, tubing, valves, and lidocaine for thoracotomy;
Tubes, bottles, and syringes for nasogastric intubation;
Catheters and sterile jelly for urethral catheterization;
Sterile gloves;
Inflatable leg and arm splints;
Collapsible basket stretchers;
Food and drinking water;
Sleeping bags, clothing, tents, ropes, ice axes, and similar equipment.

In addition the kit should contain a two-way portable radio which can survive the drop. By this means the members of the party could communicate with a physician in the plane or at a nearby ground station. Alternately, the

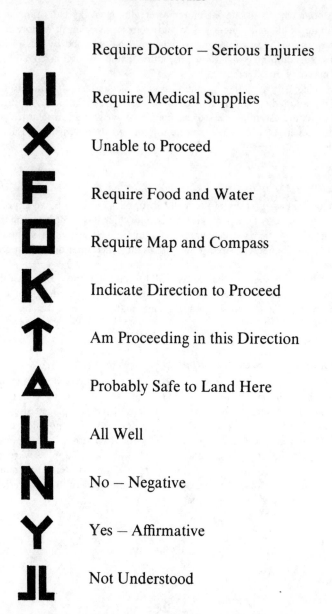

I — Require Doctor – Serious Injuries

II — Require Medical Supplies

X — Unable to Proceed

F — Require Food and Water

□ — Require Map and Compass

K — Indicate Direction to Proceed

↑ — Am Proceeding in this Direction

▲ — Probably Safe to Land Here

LL — All Well

N — No – Negative

Y — Yes – Affirmative

JL — Not Understood

Figure 61. Standard symbols for ground-to-air communication.

plane's pilot, who would have a more powerful radio and greater range due to his altitude, could relay messages to and from a physician at a more distant location. The value of the advice which could be obtained by this means is obvious. In addition, evacuation procedures could be organized and other problems could be solved.

The most easily available oxygen flasks are E cylinders which are found in hospitals and medical supply stores. A regulator valve, flow meter, tubing, and a face mask are essential accessories. Each flask weighing fourteen to sixteen pounds delivers two liters per minute for four to six hours if filled at 2,000 pounds per square inch.

Expedition Medical Supplies

The nature and quantity of the medical supplies required by an expedition depends on the size of the party and the area in which it is climbing. Himalayan expeditions often carry considerable amounts of extra medical supplies in order to provide medical care for the natives they encounter on their approach marches.

In addition to the supplies described for the "Outing" and "Air Drop Medical Kits," the members of an expedition should include oil of cloves, dental forceps, and possibly additional materials to care for dental emergencies.

Maintenance of Medical Supplies

The maintenance of a supply of medications and medical equipment for climbers is expensive. The initial cost of the items is high; drugs deteriorate and must be replaced; and sterile items must be resterilized or replaced after one or two years. Furthermore, the experience of most climbing groups indicates that the need for such supplies arises rather infrequently. Perhaps the expense for individual climbers could be reduced considerably if the supplies were maintained in a central location by a climbing organization and rented to members for each outing. However, no one can deny that the value of these materials far exceeds their cost when they are needed.

APPENDIX D

Legal Considerations

No CLIMBER would question his obligation to provide medical or evacuation assistance to another climber; none of the following comments should raise any doubts about this responsibility. However, for the sake of completeness, some discussion of the legal rights and obligations of persons rendering medical aid to others appears appropriate. These comments provide only a general outline of the laws applicable in the U.S. and Canada. Each state, province, and nation makes its own rules concerning many problems and the variation from place to place is often considerable.

Personal Liability

Almost no country has laws which require anyone to help a stranger in distress. A climber can decline to render first aid or assistance to a stranger found injured in the mountains with legal impunity. An obligation does exist in such circumstances, but the obligation is ethical, not legal.

A legal obligation to render first aid and assistance does exist when one has negligently caused injury to another. This obligation would probably exist when the injured person is a member of the same climbing party, even though the injury was caused by someone else or simply by chance.

Even though no one is required by law to render aid, if assistance is undertaken, it must be performed in a reasonably careful manner. That is, one must exercise that care which an ordinarily prudent person would exercise under similar circumstances. Thus anyone rendering first aid is liable for harm to the injured man when the harm could have been avoided by the exercise of reasonable care. A physician is held to a higher standard. He must conduct himself as an ordinarily prudent doctor, not as a layman. The need for knowledge of first aid by climbers is well recognized, and many of them have such knowledge. A climber could be held liable for injuries resulting from his failure to be familiar with first aid techniques generally known to climbers if he had indicated in some manner beforehand that he did have such knowledge.

The circumstances in which assistance is rendered are also important. The care legally required is that which is reasonable under the circumstances. More severe disorders require closer attention and more extensive and sophisticated medical assistance. Yet the law also takes into account such factors as the location of the victim, any danger for the person rendering aid, the equipment available, and the physical condition of the parties.

Although a legal basis for claims does exist, lawsuits arising from voluntary medical assistance are very rare. In mountaineering circles they are essentially non-existent.

Establishing Death

The problem of establishing the fact that a person is dead is primarily medical – not legal. A doctor's certificate is the customary method for establishing death. If a doctor is not available, a statement by persons who have actually seen the body and checked it for life usually suffices. Following a fall or an avalanche in which the body cannot be recovered, and possibly cannot even be found, the statements of those who witnessed the accident is ordinarily adequate. If no one saw the accident, death may still be established satisfactorily by circumstancial evidence, such as abandoned equipment, a deserted automobile or campsite, or the last statements of the deceased.

However, if such evidence cannot be found, and only the disappearance of the missing person into the mountains can be demonstrated, it might be impossible to establish death and enough time must pass to allow a legal "presumption" of death, usually a period of seven years.

Disposal of the Body

The next of kin and the local law enforcement agencies both have a legal interest in the body. The next of kin usually have the right to determine whether the body shall be cremated or buried, where this shall be done, what religious ceremony shall be performed, and what other customs are to be followed. The law enforcement agencies must determine the cause of death, ensuring no crimes have been committed and no threat of an epidemic or similar public health hazard exists, and make certain the body is disposed of promptly without offending public sensibilities. Ordinarily cremation or burial must be performed within a few days and the remains placed in a cemetery.

If the body is in a remote, inaccessible location, the next of kin and the law enforcement officials may decide to leave the body where it is. Following a mountaineering death, the members of a climbing party are not legally obligated to retrieve the body or even find it if such efforts would expose them to a significant danger of serious, possibly fatal injury.

Estate and Life Insurance

Death occurring in the mountains, even if the body is not recoverable, does not pose insurmountable problems in the administration of the estate or in the settlement of life insurance claims. For administration of the estate death must be proven, but the testimony of persons who actually saw the body is sufficient to establish the fact of death. (See above.)

If the deceased had life insurance, proof of death is a necessary condition for the payment of benefits from such insurance. In general, proof of death which is adequate for administration of the estate is sufficient for life insurance.

A different problem is raised by insurance that has a "double indemnity" provision. Such clauses provide a payment which is double the face amount of insurance if death is accidental. Therefore, the exact cause of death must be ascertained as far as is possible. After a fall, for example, the question of whether death occurred from a heart attack which then precipitated the fall might be raised. If the cause of the fall was a heart attack, then death would not have been accidental, and the double indemnity provision would not apply. The best means for answering such questions is by carefully examining the accident site and the victims, thoroughly questioning all witnesses of the accident, and recording all details of the findings, all of which should be completed as soon as possible after the accident has occurred. If practical, the body should be evacuated and an autopsy performed.

APPENDIX E

Glossary

ACUTE — 1. Appearing after or persisting for a relatively brief period of time. (This term does not indicate a specific time period, but refers to a short interval of time relative to the condition for which it is used. An acute onset would mean minutes for some diseases, weeks for others.) 2. Requiring immediate or urgent attention.

AIRWAY — The passages through which air enters and leaves the lungs.

ANALGESIA — The relief of pain. (Analgesic — a medication which relieves pain.)

ANEMIA — A condition in which the number of red blood cells in the blood is abnormally low.

ARRHYTHMIA — An abnormal rhythm, usually referring to the heart.

ASPIRATE — To breathe in (as air is aspirated into the lungs); to draw in by means of suction (as fluid is aspirated into a syringe).

AVULSION — A pulling off or tearing away; a forcible separation.

BLEB — A large blister.

CARRIER — A person who is immune to an infection but transmits it to others as a result of carrying the bacteria in his body.

CATHETER — A slender, tubular instrument introduced through anatomical passages into internal organs. (Urethral or urinary catheter — a catheter passed into the urinary bladder through the urethra.)

CENTRAL NERVOUS SYSTEM — The brain and spinal cord.

CERVICAL — Pertaining to the neck.

CHRONIC — Appearing after or persisting for a relatively long time (see "acute").

COMA — A state of total unconsciousness. (Comatose — totally unconscious.)

CYANOSIS — A purple or bluish discoloration observed in the lips and nails and sometimes in the skin resulting from reduced amounts of oxygen in the blood or diminished flow of blood to the affected area.

DIAGNOSIS — Distinguishing one disease or injury from another; identifying an illness or injury.

DYSPNEA — Abnormal breathing; shortness of breath.

EDEMA — An abnormal collection of fluid in some part of the body. (Pulmonary edema — an abnormal collection of fluid in the lungs.)

EMBOLUS — A clot or other plug brought by the blood stream from a distant vessel and forced into a smaller one, obstructing the circulation. (Embolism — the sudden obstruction of a blood vessel by an embolus.)

ENDEMIC — Peculiar to or prevailing in or among some (specified) country or people.

ETIOLOGY — The cause or reason for a disorder.

EXUDATE — Any substance which filters through the walls of living cellular tissue and is available for removal or extraction.

FASCIA — A sheet or membrane of fibrous tissue investing muscles or various other structures of the body.

FLACCID — Completely relaxed.

FLATUS — Gas or air in the intestines.

GANGRENE — The death of a part of the body such as an arm or a leg. (Gas gangrene — gangrene resulting from infection with bacteria which produce gas within the infected tissues.)

GENERALIZED — Spread throughout the entire body; involving the entire body.

HALLUCINATION — A sound, sight, or other sensation perceived by a person as a reality in the absence of a corresponding external object or source.

INCUBATION PERIOD — The period of time between infection by bacteria or viruses and the onset of detectable signs or symptoms of the disease.

JAUNDICE — An abnormal condition caused by bile pigments in the blood, usually resulting from liver disease, and characterized by yellow discoloration of the skin and eyes.

MACERATE — To reduce to a soft mass by soaking; to digest.

MALAISE — A feeling of generalized discomfort or indisposition; feeling ill.

MENINGITIS — Inflammation of the thin membranes which surround the brain and spinal cord, usually the result of infection.

METABOLISM — The processes taking place in living organisms which use energy to build substances from assimilated materials or break them down to release energy.

NEUROLOGICAL — Of or pertaining to the nervous system.

OSMOSIS — The diffusion of a solution through a semipermeable membrane. (Osmotic pressure — the hydrostatic pressure created by diffusion through a semipermeable membrane.)

PALPATE — To feel or examine by touch. (Palpation — the process of examining the body by touch.)

PALPITATION — A rapid or irregular action by the heart of which the patient is aware.

PARALYTIC ILEUS — Paralysis of the instestine producing obstruction, most often caused by peritonitis.

PATHOGENIC — Producing disease.

PERITONITIS — Inflammation of the thin membrane lining the abdominal cavity, usually resulting from infection.

PROGNOSIS — A prediction or conclusion regarding the course and termination of a disease or injury.

PRONE — Lying flat on the stomach with the face down.

PROPHYLAXIS — Preventive treatment for disease.

PULMONARY — Of or pertaining to the lungs.

PURULENT — Consisting of or containing pus; associated with the formation of or caused by pus.

RADIATION OF PAIN — The sensation of pain experienced in an area other than the anatomical site of the injury or disease producing the pain.

RENAL — Of or pertaining to the kidneys.

RESORB — To reabsorb.

SOFT TISSUE — The nonosseous tissues of the body. (The joint ligaments and internal organs are not included in the most common usage of this term.)

SOMNOLENCE — Oppressive drowsiness or sleepiness.

SPASM — An involuntary muscular contraction.

SPINAL CANAL — The canal within the vertebral column which contains the spinal cord.

SPRAIN — An injury characterized by incomplete rupture of the supporting ligaments around a joint.

STRAIN — An injury characterized by stretching, with or without mild tearing, of a muscle or tendon.

SUBACUTE – Appearing after or persisting for a period of time which is intermediate between acute and chronic in duration (see "acute").

SUBCUTANEOUS – Beneath the skin.

SUPINE – Lying flat on the back with the face up.

SUTURE – To unite parts by stitching; to sew together the cut edges of injured tissues.

SYNDROME – A group of signs and symptoms which occur together and comprise a disease entity.

TOXIN – A noxious or poisonous substance. (Toxic – having a poisonous or noxious effect.)

TRAUMA – An injury to the body caused by a physical force. (Traumatic – of or pertaining to trauma.)

VASCULAR – Of or pertaining to the blood vessels.

INDEX